Enriching Your Math Curriculum

A Month-to-Month Resource

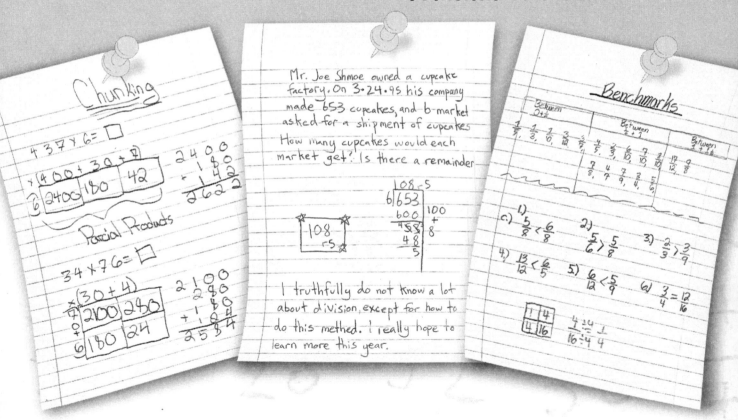

Lainie Schuster

Math Solutions
Sausalito, California, USA

Math Solutions
150 Gate 5 Road
Sausalito, CA 94965
www.mathsolutions.com

The publisher would like to thank those who gave permission to reprint borrowed material:

Massachusetts Comprehensive Assessment System (MCAS) 2009 Released Test Questions, Mathematics, Grade 5, Items no. 13 and 15: Reprinted with permission from the Massachusetts Department of Elementary and Secondary Education.

Fair Game 2, The Horse Problem, Things That Come in Groups, Where Does 100 Land?, Leftovers, Fraction Kit investigations, Cover Up, Uncover Versions 1 and 2, Put in Order, and The Factor Game: Adapted from *About Teaching Mathematics: A K–8 Resource,* Third Edition, by Marilyn Burns (Math Solutions Publications, 2007).

Continued on page 442, which is an extension of the copyright page.

Library of Congress Cataloging-in-Publication Data
Schuster, Lainie.
  Enriching your math curriculum : grade 5 / Lainie Schuster.
     p. cm.
Includes bibliographical references and index.
Summary: "Presents practices and routines designed to support and nourish teachers as they prepare and present a meaningful year of mathematics instruction for fifth-grade mathematicians. Offers activities, lessons, and narration that can be easily adapted or adjusted to fit the particular needs of the students or the requirements of a prescribed curriculum"—Provided by publisher.
  ISBN 978-1-935099-02-4 (alk. paper)
  1. Mathematics—Study and teaching (Elementary). 2. Education, Primary—Activity programs. 3. Mathematics—Problems, exercises, etc. I. Title.
  QA135.6.S434 2010
  372.7049—dc22
                              2010026175

Editor: Jamie Ann Cross
Production: Melissa L. Inglis-Elliott
Cover and Interior design: Catherine Hawkes/Cat and Mouse; Susan Barclay/Barclay Design
Composition: Aptara

Printed in the United States of America on acid-free paper
14 13 12 11 10   AA   1 2 3 4 5

A Message from Math Solutions

We at Math Solutions believe that teaching math well calls for increasing our understanding of the math we teach, seeking deeper insights into how students learn mathematics, and refining our lessons to best promote students' learning.

Math Solutions shares classroom-tested lessons and teaching expertise from our faculty of professional development consultants as well as from other respected math educators. Our publications are part of the nationwide effort we've made since 1984 that now includes

- more than five hundred face-to-face professional development programs each year for teachers and administrators in districts across the country;
- professional development books that span all math topics taught in kindergarten through high school;
- videos for teachers and for parents that show math lessons taught in actual classrooms;
- on-site visits to schools to help refine teaching strategies and assess student learning; and
- free online support, including grade-level lessons, book reviews, inservice information, and district feedback, all in our *Math Solutions Online Newsletter*.

For information about all of the products and services we have available, please visit our website at *www.mathsolutions.com*. You can also contact us to discuss math professional development needs by calling (800) 868-9092 or by sending an email to *info@mathsolutions.com*.

We're always eager for your feedback and interested in learning about your particular needs. We look forward to hearing from you.

Math Solutions.
FOUNDED BY MARILYN BURNS

To my father, Robert P. Demyan, who tried to teach me that
Algebra I was not the enemy and that numbers could tell stories
as fascinating as could words.
I get it now . . .

Contents

Contents

For those who prefer to use months.

 Reproducibles
All reproducibles are located on the accompanying CD.

The reproducibles are referenced and used throughout the book. Text page reference follows the title.

Foreword

One of the challenges of teaching mathematics is planning a coherent year of instruction. Not only must we address the important mathematics children need to learn but we also need to help children learn to think, reason, and become proficient problem solvers. And we also want to inspire children to enjoy mathematics and see it as useful to their lives. Accomplishing this is a tall order that calls for understanding the full scope of the mathematics curriculum, having a rich repertoire of instructional options, being skilled at managing instruction in the classroom, and understanding the needs of the individual students in your class.

This book is a month-by-month resource for planning a year of math instruction. It is one of a five-book series, each written by a master teacher to address teaching mathematics in grades 1, 2, 3, and 4, and 5. The author of each book acknowledges that her suggestions do not comprise the only approach to accomplish planning, or necessarily the best approach for others to follow. Rather, each suggests a thoughtful, practical, and very personal approach to planning that has grown out of her years of experience in the classroom.

The authors of this series are truly master teachers—experienced, caring, hardworking, and incredibly accomplished. They bring their wisdom and experience to their books in unique ways, but as teachers they share common experiences and outlooks. Each has offered many professional development classes and workshops for teachers while also choosing to make classroom teaching the main focus of her career. For all of them, mathematics was not their initial love or strength. However, they each came to study and learn to appreciate mathematics because of their need to serve their students. They are committed to excellence in math instruction, they understand children, they know how to manage classrooms, and they are passionate about teaching. It is a great pleasure to present these books to you.

—Marilyn Burns

Acknowledgments

We teach in an era of wonderful resources and standards-based curricula. I would like to acknowledge two curricula in particular: Connected Mathematics (Pearson Prentice Hall 2006) and Investigations in Number, Data, and Space (Pearson Education 2008). Although no curriculum can meet every need and demand, these two present the very best of instructional frameworks. A special thanks to Suzanne Chapin, whose Project Challenge curriculum offered the grounding for much that I have used and developed for my fifth-grade class.

I would like to give special thanks to Joan Carlson, my reader, and Jamie Cross, my editor. Our mutual love of mathematics and writing and endless email discussions have made me such a better thinker, teacher, and writer. Thank you.

I cannot think of any one person who has so influenced how I think about mathematics as Marilyn Burns. She is as passionate and masterful a teacher as I have ever known. To have been able to work for her and with her has been a gift.

It is my fifth-grade students, however, for whom this book is written. You have amazed, delighted, entertained, and exhausted me with your thinking about mathematics. I truly hope I have exposed the wonders of mathematics to you as much as you have exposed the wonders of your worlds to me!

Introduction

"I'm not very good at problems," admitted Milo.

"What a shame," sighed the Dodecahedron. "They're so very useful. Why, did you know that if a beaver two feet long with a tail a foot and a half long can build a dam twelve feet high and six feet wide in two days, all you would need to build Bolder Dam is a beaver sixty-eight feet long with a fifty-one-foot tail?"

"Where would you find a beaver that big?" grumbled the Humbug as his pencil point snapped.

"I'm sure I don't know," he replied, "but if you did, you'd certainly know what to do with him."

"That's absurd," objected Milo, whose head was spinning from all the numbers and questions.

"That may be true," he acknowledged, "but it's completely accurate, and as long as the answer is right, who cares if the question is wrong? If you want sense, you'll have to make it yourself."

The Phantom Tollbooth
Juster 1961, 174–75

I had two epiphanies in 1965 while I was greatly enjoying my own fifth-grade year in school. One was that I wanted to be a fifth-grade teacher. The other was that I, like Milo, realized that I had no use for math problems. Long division was hard enough in the fifth grade, but fractions were even worse. I could write well, my spelling was coming along, and I

xix

really enjoyed American history. So what if I couldn't simplify a fraction or find a greatest common factor? The way I saw it back in 1965 was that there was little sense to be made of mathematics. Milo and I viewed the world of mathematics in very much the same way!

Something happened on my way to becoming that fifth-grade teacher—yet another epiphany of sorts. I began to find the world of mathematics somewhat intriguing—much to my surprise! It did not happen all at once, mind you, but bit by bit (in much the same way as *The Velveteen Rabbit* became real). My interest in how children learn began to carry over and seep into my own mathematical thinking, experiences, and teaching. If I was asking my children to make sense of the mathematics, then I had better be able to do the same! And so began this wonderful journey of thinking and working through a year of fifth-grade mathematics.

While I spend hours in my garden each August tending to my perennials, my mind often drifts to the upcoming school year. I have come to realize that I do some of my very best thinking and planning in the garden. I find myself thinking about how to best implement those new materials that I ordered back in June and that first unit of the year on factors and multiples. I find myself thinking about meaningful mathematical writing tasks and good questions that will need to be asked. I find myself thinking about Ava and how best to challenge her and about Bobby and how best to support him. As I weed and transplant, I find myself slowly warming up to the idea of returning to the frenetic pace of the fifth grade. Even after thirty-something years of teaching, I catch myself smiling as I anticipate the start of a new school year.

Developing a yearlong mathematics curriculum can be a daunting task at any grade level. Teaching fifth-grade mathematics presents its own unique challenges. Our fifth graders can articulate the relationship between the number of factors and the number of arrays of a given number. They can identify the difference between doubling the volume of a prism and doubling its dimensions. They can discover how $23\frac{3}{5}$ could be another interpretation of 23r3. They can be brilliant. Our fifth graders can also dissolve into giggles when Paul asks how to "equivalate" fractions. Or dissolve into tears when they are convinced that $5^2 = 10$. They can be fragile. They walk that fine line between thinking concretely and thinking abstractly. They are the "tweeners." As we develop a year of mathematics instruction, we need to be mindful of the children we teach and love. Chip Wood, author of *Yardsticks: Children in the Classroom* (1997), writes of ten-year-olds and their "golden" age as relaxing in their childhood, gathering strength for the impending storm of adolescence, and consolidating their gains from early childhood (106). I could not agree more.

Enriching Your Math Curriculum, Grade 5 presents a sampling of practices and routines designed to support and nourish as you prepare and present a meaningful year of mathematics instruction for our fifth-grade mathematicians. This book offers activities, lessons, and narration that can easily be adapted or adjusted to fit the particular needs of your students or the requirements of your prescribed curriculum. Developing powerful mathematical thinkers requires the patience, persistence, and practice of all those involved: teachers, students, parents, and administrators. Teaching mathematics well, or perhaps better phrased, teaching good mathematics, is just plain hard work. Planning and implementing a meaningful mathematics program takes mindful and comprehensive planning and selective resourcing. I hope that this book will help you with both.

Perhaps we have once been a Milo, or taught a Milo, or know a Milo when we see one.

> "It seems to me that almost everything is a waste of time," he [Milo] remarked one day as he walked dejectedly home from school. "I can't see the point in learning to solve useless problems, or subtracting turnips from turnips, or knowing where Ethiopia is or how to spell February." And, since no one bothered to explain otherwise, he regarded the process of seeking knowledge as the greatest waste of time of all. (Juster 1961, 9)

Obviously, Milo had never experienced the world of fifth-grade mathematics. If he had, he could never have been bored or ever wondered why he bothered.

Connections to the Common Core State Standards Initiative

About the Common Core State Standards

> For over a decade, research studies of mathematics education . . . have pointed to the conclusion that the mathematics curriculum in the United States must become substantially more focused and coherent in order to improve mathematics achievement in this country. (National Governors Association Center for Best Practices and Council of Chief State School Officers 2010, 3)

The Common Core State Standards offer a set of focused standards that aim for clarity, coherence, and specificity. The Core Standards for Mathematics define what students should understand and be able to do in their study of mathematics. The activities in this resource are aligned to the Standards that follow.

Please note that some activities are more clearly aligned with Grade 4 or Grade 6 Standards. Mastery of these concepts and procedures comes over time and with a curriculum and instruction that continues to address these important skills throughout subsequent units and years of mathematics instruction. Offering activities and lessons that mathematically support children as well as bridge their instruction as they move from one year of study to the next becomes increasingly important as we continually refine and articulate what children should know and be able to do in mathematics.

Page	Month	Domain	Standard	Focus	Activity
33	September/ October	Measurement and Data	5.MD.2	Collect, analyze, and interpret data in a literature context.	*Chrysanthemum* by Kevin Henkes
40	September/ October	Operations and Algebraic Thinking	4.OA.4	Find factors of the numbers 1 to 30; explore the relationship among factors, divisors, and multiples.	*The Factor Game*
44	September/ October	Operations and Algebraic Thinking	4.OA.4	Identify an array's dimensions as the factors of that product; recognize that factors come in pairs.	Factor Pairs and Arrays
56	September/ October	Operations and Algebraic Thinking	4.OA.4	Investigate odd and even sums and products based upon their respective addends and factors.	*Fair Game 2*

(Continued)

Page	Month	Domain	Standard	Focus	Activity
63	September/ October	Operations and Algebraic Thinking The Number System	4.OA.4 6.NS.4	Explore and identify prime and composite numbers.	*The Sieve of Eratosthenes*
69	September/ October	Operations and Algebraic Thinking	4.OA.4	Multiplication fact practice in a game context.	*Rio*
71	September/ October	Operations and Algebraic Thinking The Number System	4.OA.4 6.NS.4	Multiplication and division fact practice in a game context.	*Multiplication Tic-Tac-Toe (The Product Game)*
71	September/ October	Operations and Algebraic Thinking	5.OA.6	Investigate the rules of divisibility and why they make sense.	Exploration of Divisibility Rules
72	September/ October	Operations and Algebraic Thinking The Number System	4.OA.4 6.NS.4	Practice of conventional notation of factorization.	Conventional Factorization Notation
102	November	Operations and Algebraic Thinking	5.OA.3	Describe rules in words and an algebraic equation that relates one set of values (in-values) to another set (out-values).	*Guess My Rule*
109	November	Geometry The Number System	5.G.1 6.NS.6b	Plot points on a coordinate graph; identify and articulate how and where a graph relates to the function, equation, and T-chart it represents.	Coordinate Graph Exploration

(Continued)

Page	Month	Domain	Standard	Focus	Activity
120	November	Operations and Algebraic Thinking	5.OA.3 6.OA.6b	Explore and represent a growth pattern.	*Growing Caterpillars*
133	November	Operations and Algebraic Thinking The Number System Geometry	5.OA.2 6.NS.6b 5.G.2	Explore and represent a linear function in a literature context.	*Five Dog Night* by Eileen Christelow
137	November	Operations and Algebraic Thinking The Number System Geometry	5.OA.2 6.NS.6b 5.G.2	Explore and represent a nonlinear function in a literature context.	*Minnie's Diner* by Dayle Ann Dodds
142	November	Operations and Algebraic Thinking	5.OA.1 5.OA.2	Explore the meaning of the equals sign.	True, False, Open Number Sentences
144	November	Operations and Algebraic Thinking	5.OA.1 5.OA.2	Explore the order of operations in a game context.	*Three Strikes and You're Out*
161	December	Operations and Algebraic Thinking	4.OA.1 4.OA.2 4.OA.3	Investigate, classify, solve, and create multiplication and division problems according to their structure.	Classification of Multiplication Story-Problem Structures
169	December	Operations and Algebraic Thinking	4.OA.1 4.OA.2 4.OA.3	Create and solve multiplication and division problems according to an identified structure.	Multiplication and Division Storybooks

(Continued)

Page	Month	Domain	Standard	Focus	Activity
178	December	Operations and Algebraic Thinking	5.OA.2	Solve more complex problems by using what they know about simpler related problems.	Silent Multiplication
		Number and Operations: Base Ten	5.NBT.2		
182	December	Number and Operations: Base Ten	5.NBT.5 5.NBT.6	Apply multiplication and division strategies within a problem-solving context.	*Where Does 100 Land?*
186	December	Number and Operations in Base Ten	5.NBT.5	Explore, practice, and apply alternative as well as standard multiplication algorithms.	Multiplication Algorithms
217	January	Number and Operations: Base Ten	5.NBT.5 5.NBT.6	Explore the relationship between multiplication and division in a literature context.	*Esio Trot* by Roald Dahl
219	January	Number and Operations: Base Ten	5.NBT.6	Practice division computation in a game context; reason about the significance and relationship of dividends, divisors, and resulting remainders.	*Leftovers*
224	January	Number and Operations: Base Ten	5.NBT.6	Practice division computation in a game context; think flexibly about division and multiplication as divisors and dividends are built.	*Seth's Game*
228, 235	January	Number and Operations: Base Ten	5.NBT.6	Interpret and represent remainders in story problem and problem-solving contexts.	Remainder Explorations: Story Problems and Riddles
239	January	Number and Operations: Base Ten	5.NBT.6	Explore, practice, and apply alternative as well as standard division algorithms.	Division Algorithms

(Continued)

Page	Month	Domain	Standard	Focus	Activity
267	February/ March	Number and Operations: Fractions	4.NF.1 4.NF.2 4.NF.3 4.NF.4 5.NF.1 5.NF.2	Represent and compare fractions with a linear model.	Fraction Kit
271	February/ March	Number and Operations: Fractions	4.NF.1 4.NF.2 4.NF.3 4.NF.4 5.NF.1 5.NF.2	Explore, identify, and articulate parts of a whole in a game context (Fraction Kit Activity).	*Cover the Whole* and *Cover the Whole: The Sequel*
274	February/ March	Number and Operations: Fractions	5.NF.1 5.NF.2	Explore equivalence and compare magnitudes of fractions in a game context.	*The Comparing Game*
277	February/ March	Number and Operations: Fractions	5.NF.1 5.NF.2	Investigate fractional parts and how they relate to the area of a given shape; Explore the area model of fractions.	*How Much Is Blue?*
282	February/ March	Number and Operations: Fractions	5.NF.1 5.NF.2	Compare and order fractions with like and unlike denominators.	*Put in Order*
284	February/ March	Number and Operations: Base Ten	5.NBT.1 5.NBT.2 5.NBT.3	Explore and identify decimal representations of fractions.	*Decimal Gardens*
290	February/ March	Number and Operations: Base Ten	5.NBT.1 5.NBT.2 5.NBT.3	Construct, visualize, and represent decimal numbers with a physical model.	*Place-Value Round Robin*

(Continued)

Page	Month	Domain	Standard	Focus	Activity
298	February/March	Number and Operations: Base Ten Ratios and Proportional Relationships	5.NBT.1 5.NBT.2 5.NBT.3 6.RP.3c	Construct and estimate percentages created on a hundreds grid.	*Percent Designs*
304	February/March	Number and Operations: Fractions	5.NF.1 5.NF.2	Explore, create, and defend strategies for adding and subtracting fractions.	Models for Addition and Subtraction
325	April	Geometry	5.G.4 6.G.1	Investigate fixed area and how it is related to perimeter; i.e. Shapes with the same area can have different-length perimeters.	*Area Stays the Same*
328	April	Geometry	5.G.4 6.G.1	Investigate fixed perimeter and how it is related to area; i.e. Shapes with the same length perimeter can have different areas.	*Perimeter Stays the Same*
330	April	Geometry	5.G.4 6.G.1	Explore area and perimeter and the relationship of one to the other in a problem-solving context.	*Dog Yards*
334	April	Geometry	5.G.3 5.G.4 6.G.1	Calculate areas of irregular polygons.	*Paving Patios*
335	April	Geometry	5.G.3 5.G.4 6.G.1	Calculate and generalize about the areas of triangles and squares within squares.	*Bear Paw Borders*
335	April	Geometry	5.G.3 5.G.4 6.G.1	Predict, measure, calculate, and generalize about the areas of triangles resulting from the partitioning of a rectangle.	*Criss-Cross*

(Continued)

Page	Month	Domain	Standard	Focus	Activity
337	April	Operations and Algebraic Thinking Geometry	5.OA.3 5.G.1	Predict, calculate, and generalize about perimeters of growing areas of linear banquet tables	*Banquet Table Problem*
339	April	Measurement and Data	5.MD.3 5.MD.4 5.MD.5	Construct and articulate predictions and generalizations about objects (boxes) and their volumes.	*Filling Boxes*
340	April	Measurement and Data	5.MD.3 5.MD.4 5.MD.5	Explore and calculate volume of irregular solids.	*The Painted Cube Problem*
344	April	Measurement and Data	5.MD.3 5.MD.4 5.MD.5	Explore and calculate the dimensions of a solid when the volume is doubled.	*Doubling the Number of Cubes*
346	April	Measurement and Data	5.MD.3 5.MD.4 5.MD.5	Estimate and compare magnitudes of volume of containers of varying sizes and volumes.	*Put in Order*
350	April	Geometry	5.G.4 6.G.1	Explore, construct, and defend invented and standard formulas for areas.	Calculating Area
363	May	Data Analysis and Probability	5.MD.2 6.SP.1 6.SP.2 6.SP.3	Explore and identify the measures of central tendency of a given data set: mode, median, and mean.	What Do You Mean?
369	May	Statistics and Probability	6.SP.1 6.SP.2 6.SP.3 6.SP.4 6.SP.5	Explore and identify the median, mode, and mean of a collected set of data.	Exploring the Mean

(Continued)

Page	Month	Domain	Standard	Focus	Activity
371	May	Statistics and Probability	6.SP.1 6.SP.2 6.SP.3 6.SP.4 6.SP.5	Construct and articulate predictions and generalizations about collected sets of data.	*Data About Us*
373	May	Statistics and Probability	6.SP.1 6.SP.4	Read, analyze and interpret collected data in various formats presented in everyday media.	*Graph Round Robin*
376	May	Statistics and Probability	6.SP.1 6.SP.2 6.SP.3 6.SP.4 6.SP.5	Make, collect, and record measurements within a literature context; Identify, compute, and analyze measurement averages: mean, median, and mode.	*A Giant Among Wizards*
395	June	Number and Operations: Base Ten	5.NBT.1 5.NBT.2	Explore the magnitude and representation of numbers beyond one million.	*The King's Chessboard* by David Birch
401	June	Geometry Ratios and Proportional Relationships	5.G.4 6.RP.1 6.RP.3	Explore and make generalizations about the relationship between the area and perimeter as similar shapes grow.	*Rep-Tiles*
408	June	Number and Operations	6.RP.1 6.RP.2 6.RP.3	Compare, identify, and calculate rates by applying proportional reasoning.	A Few Good Problems
409	June	Ratios and Proportional Relationships	6.RP.1 6.RP.3	Compare and determine rates; informally manipulate ratios.	Rate Pictures
411	June	Ratios and Proportional Relationships	6.RP.1 6.RP.3	Solve problems involving proportions in a variety of contexts without dependence on rules or formulas.	Rate Problems
412	June	Number and Operations	5.NBT.1 5.NBT.2	Review and extend multiplication strategies and understandings.	Context: Multiplication and Division Games to Revisit

ACTIVITIES AND GAMES
Connections to NCTM's
Focal Points and *Principles and Standards for School Mathematics*

Page	Month	Strand(s)	Focus	Activity
33	September/October	Data Analysis and Probability	Collect, analyze, and interpret data in a literature context.	*Chrysanthemum* by Kevin Henkes
40	September/October	Number and Operations	Find factors of the numbers 1 to 30; explore the relationship among factors, divisors, and multiples.	*The Factor Game*
44	September/October	Number and Operations	Identify an array's dimensions as the factors of that product; Recognize that factors come in pairs.	Factor Pairs and Arrays
56	September/October	Number and Operations	Investigate odd and even sums and products based upon their respective addends and factors.	*Fair Game 2*
63	September/October	Number and Operations	Explore and identify prime and composite numbers.	*The Sieve of Eratosthenes*
69	September/October	Number and Operations	Multiplication fact practice in a game context.	*Rio*
70	September/October	Number and Operations	Multiplication and division fact practice in a game context.	*Multiplication Tic-Tac-Toe (The Product Game)*

(Continued)

Page	Month	Strand(s)	Focus	Activity
71	September/October	Number and Operations	Investigate the rules of divisibility and why they make sense.	Exploration of Divisibility Rules
72	September/October	Number and Operations	Practice of conventional notation of factorization.	Conventional Factorization
102	November	Algebra	Describe rules in words and an algebraic equation that relates one set of values (in-values) to another set (out-values).	*Guess My Rule*
109	November	Algebra	Plot points on a coordinate graph; identify and articulate how and where a graph relates to the function, equation, and T-chart it represents.	Coordinate Graphing Explorations
120	November	Algebra	Explore and represent a growth pattern.	*Growing Caterpillars*
133	November	Algebra	Explore and represent a linear function in a literature context.	*Five Dog Night* by Eileen Christelow
137	November	Algebra	Explore and represent a nonlinear function in a literature context.	*Minnie's Diner* by Dayle Ann Dodds
142	November	Algebra	Explore the meaning of the equals sign.	True, False, Open Number Sentences
144	November	Algebra	Explore the order of operations in a game context.	*Four Strikes and You're Out*
161	December	Number and Operations	Investigate, classify, solve, and create multiplication and division problems according to their structure.	Classification of Multiplication Story-Problem Structures

(Continued)

Page	Month	Strand(s)	Focus	Activity
169	December	Number and Operations	Create and solve multiplication and division problems according to an identified structure.	Multiplication and Division Storybooks
178	December	Number and Operations	Solve more complex problems by using what they know about simpler related problems.	Silent Multiplication
182	December	Number and Operations	Apply multiplication and division strategies within a problem-solving context.	*Where Does 100 Land?*
186	December	Number and Operations	Explore, practice, and apply alternative as well as standard multiplication algorithms.	Multiplication Algorithms
217	January	Number and Operations	Explore the relationship between multiplication and division in a literature context.	*Esio Trot* by Roald Dahl
219	January	Number and Operations	Practice division computation in a game context; reason about the significance and relationship of dividends, divisors, and resulting remainders.	*Leftovers*
224	January	Number and Operations	Practice division computation in a game context; think flexibly about division and multiplication as divisors and dividends are built.	*Seth's Game*
228, 235	January	Number and Operations	Interpret and represent remainders in story problem and problem-solving contexts.	Remainder Explorations: Story Problems and Riddles

(Continued)

Page	Month	Strand(s)	Focus	Activity
239	January	Number and Operations	Explore, practice, and apply alternative as well as standard division algorithms.	Division Algorithms
267	February/March	Number and Operations	Represent and compare fractions with a linear model.	Fraction Kit
271	February/March	Number and Operations	Explore, identify, and articulate parts of a whole in a game context (Fraction Kit Activity).	*Cover the Whole* and *Cover the Whole, the Sequel*
274	February/March	Number and Operations	Explore equivalence and compare magnitudes of fractions in a game context.	*The Comparing Game*
277	February/March	Number and Operations	Investigate fractional parts and how they relate to the area of a given shape; Explore the area model of fractions.	*How Much Is Blue?*
282	February/March	Number and Operations	Compare and order fractions with like and unlike denominators.	*Put in Order*
284	February/March	Number and Operations	Explore and identify decimal representations of fractions.	*Decimal Gardens*
290	February/March	Number and Operations	Construct, visualize, and represent decimal numbers with a physical model.	*Place-Value Round Robin*
298	February/March	Number and Operations	Construct and estimate percentages created on a hundreds grid.	*Percent Designs*
304	February/March	Number and Operations	Explore, create, and defend strategies for adding and subtracting fractions.	Models for Addition and Subtraction

(Continued)

Page	Month	Strand(s)	Focus	Activity
325	April	Geometry Measurement	Investigate fixed area and how it is related to perimeter; for example, shapes with the same area can have different-length perimeters.	*Area Stays the Same*
328	April	Geometry Measurement	Investigate fixed perimeter and how it is related to area; for example, shapes with the same length perimeter can have different areas.	*Perimeter Stays the Same*
330	April	Geometry Measurement	Explore area and perimeter and the relationship of one to the other in a problem-solving context.	*Dog Yards*
334	April	Geometry Measurement	Calculate areas of irregular polygons.	*Paving Patios*
335	April	Geometry Measurement	Calculate and generalize about the areas of triangles and squares within squares.	*Bear Paw Borders*
335	April	Geometry Measurement	Predict, measure, calculate, and generalize about the areas of triangles resulting from the partitioning of a rectangle.	*Criss-Cross*
337	April	Geometry Measurement	Predict, calculate, and generalize about perimeters of growing areas of linear banquet tables.	*Banquet Table Problem*
339	April	Geometry Measurement	Construct and articulate predictions and generalizations about objects (boxes) and their volumes.	*Filling Boxes*
340	April	Geometry Measurement	Explore and calculate volume of irregular solids.	*The Painted Cube Problem*

(Continued)

Page	Month	Strand(s)	Focus	Activity
344	April	Geometry Measurement	Explore and calculate the dimensions of a solid when the volume is doubled.	*Doubling the Number of Cubes*
346	April	Geometry Measurement	Estimate and compare magnitudes of volume of containers of varying sizes and volumes.	*Put in Order*
351	April	Geometry Measurement	Explore, construct, and defend invented and standard formulas for areas.	Calculating Area
363	May	Data Analysis and Probability	Explore and identify the measures of central tendency of a given data set: mode, median, and mean.	What Do You Mean?
369	May	Data Analysis and Probability	Explore and identify the median, mode, and mean of a collected set of data.	Exploring the Mean
371	May	Data Analysis and Probability	Construct and articulate predictions and generalizations about objects (boxes) and their volumes.	*Data About Us*
373	May	Data Analysis and Probability	Read, analyze and interpret collected data in various formats presented in everyday media.	*Graph Round Robin*
376	May	Data Analysis and Probability	Make, collect, and record measurements within a literature context; identify, compute, and analyze measurement averages: mean, median, and mode.	*A Giant Among Wizards*

(Continued)

Page	Month	Strand(s)	Focus	Activity
382	May	Data Analysis and Probability	Calculate mentally using friendly numbers and number sense.	Mental Computation
395	June	Number and Operations	Explore the magnitude and representation of numbers beyond one million.	*The King's Chessboard* by David Birch
401	June	Number and Operations	Explore and make generalizations about the relationship between the area and perimeter as similar shapes grow.	*Rep-Tiles*
408	June	Number and Operations	Compare, identify, and calculate rates by applying proportional reasoning.	A Few Good Problems
409	June	Number and Operations	Compare and determine rates; informally manipulate ratios.	Rate Pictures
411	June	Number and Operations	Solve problems involving proportions in a variety of contexts without dependence on rules or formulas.	Rate Problems
412	June	Number and Operations	Review and extend multiplication strategies and understandings.	Multiplication and Division Games to Revisit

Chapter 1

Before the Children Arrive

"Manners are not taught in lessons," said Alice. "Lessons teach you to do sums, and things of that sort."

"Can you do Addition?" the White Queen asked. "What's one and one and one and one and one and one and one and one and one and one?"

"I don't know," said Alice. "I lost count."

"She can't do Addition," the Red Queen interrupted. "Can you do Subtraction? Take nine from eight."

"Nine from eight I can't you know," Alice replied very readily: "but—"

"She can't do Subtraction," said the White Queen. "Can you do Division? Divide a loaf by a knife— what's the answer to that?"

"I suppose—," Alice was beginning, but the Red Queen answered for her. "Bread-and-butter, of course. Try another Subtraction sum. Take a bone from a dog: what remains?"

1

Alice considered. "The bone wouldn't remain, or course, if I took it—and the dog wouldn't remain; it should come to bite me—and I'm sure I shouldn't remain!"

Through the Looking Glass and What Alice Found There
Carroll 1986, 189–190

Planning Your Math Program

As you begin planning your math program, please realize that this book presents an overview of the mathematical concepts, procedures, and topics fifth-grade mathematicians may encounter in a given school year. It is not meant to be a prescribed curriculum, but rather a presentation of integrated and interconnected activities and investigations based on topics and units covered in most fifth-grade classrooms, as well as those recommended by two NCTM (National Council of Teachers of Mathematics) landmark publications, *Principles and Standards for School Mathematics* (2000) and *Curriculum Focal Points for Prekindergarten through Grade 8 Mathematics* (2006), as well as the Common Core State Standards (National Governors Association Center for Best Practices and Council of Chief State School Officers 2010). Even though those moments arise in the year when we literally plan day by day (and even minute by minute on those less-than-perfect days), perhaps it is more important that we learn to think about *how* to think about a full year of math instruction and how we can thoughtfully plan for its execution.

Since its initial release, *Principles and Standards* has precipitated a number of extensions and elaborations in the area of curriculum development. *Curriculum Focal Points* describes an approach to curriculum development that focuses on areas of emphasis and descriptions of what NCTM considers significant mathematics within each grade level. Organizing and presenting a curriculum around these described focal points with a clear emphasis on the Process Standards proposed in *Principles and Standards*—communication, reasoning, representation, connections, and problem solving—can provide our students with a connected and coherent body of mathematical knowledge and ways of thinking (NCTM 2006).

Chapter Focus and Time Span

The mathematical content and sequence covered in *Enriching Your Math Curriculum, Grade 5* focuses on the following topics commonly presented in fifth grade and represents the curricular focal points offered by NCTM for grade 5:

Topics	*Suggested Month(s)*
factors and multiples; number theory	September–October (8 weeks)
algebraic thinking	November (4 weeks)
multiplication and its relationship to division	December (3 weeks)
division	January (4 weeks)
fractions/decimals/percents	February–March (6–8 weeks)
geometry/measurement (area/ volume)	April (4 weeks)
data analysis	May (4 weeks)
multiplication and division revisited	June (2–3 weeks)

You may notice fewer content areas in the scope and sequence of the year than in more traditional approaches to a year of fifth-grade mathematics in my attempt to focus the curriculum on those topics requiring and receiving special emphasis. I believe, as does NCTM, that a curriculum offering our fifth graders the opportunity to explore related topics in greater depth will allow them to develop more connected and applicable mathematical understandings. The Curriculum Focal Points and Connections for grade 5 can be accessed by visiting NCTM's website, www.nctm.org/focalpoints/.

The suggested scope and sequence is simply that—suggested. Each school, each district, and each state may present its particular curricular and scheduling expectations that are nonnegotiable. To be an effective teacher is to learn to work within those constraints without losing the vision of what it means to present rich mathematics instruction. Each year I tweak my schedule and its content a bit given the strengths and needs of my particular class. Becoming familiar with the Focal Points has made doing this feel very right. When our focus becomes one of making meaningful connections among the content, schedule, and pedagogy, the students benefit greatly.

Chapter Structure

Each chapter is sequenced in a similar fashion and contains the following sections.

The Learning Environment

Each chapter begins with a discussion of the classroom climate and culture and its importance to the learning of the mathematics. Different topics and procedures often lend themselves to different teaching, learning, and communication routines and practices. Is this a lesson for small-group work? Or is this a lesson for individual paper-and-pencil work? Is this a lesson for student-led discussion? Or is this a lesson for a teacher-facilitated conversation? How will classroom discussions be fostered and nurtured? How will misconceptions be addressed? Research continues to remind us of the importance of context and natural learning environments in the teaching and learning of mathematics (Stoessiger and Edmunds 1993). What real-world and problem-solving contexts will you provide to help your students construct greater meaning from the mathematics? How will you establish expectations in regard to quality of work, achievement, participation, and behavior? A positive, challenging, and comfortable classroom climate not only needs to be established at the beginning of your school year but also needs to be maintained throughout the year—and that can be the tricky part!

The Mathematics and Its Language

As children move through the fifth grade, the process and progress of mathematical learning becomes increasingly entrenched in the content and the language required of it. Because of this, a teacher's understanding and identification of the mathematics being taught, explored, and discovered takes on significant importance. The mathematics of each chapter will be discussed as well as the possible misconceptions that may manifest themselves as students move through the material. It is your understanding of the mathematics and how your students are moving through it that will help to direct lesson planning. The exploring, defining, manipulating, and refining of mathematical language helps students learn with greater understanding and meaning. Students need to speak the mathematics, represent the mathematics, and write the mathematics. Acquiring the necessary vocabulary and language usage will help students to develop the conceptual and procedural skills required for mathematical growth and success. How to consider working through the language of the mathematics of each particular chapter will be addressed in this section as well.

Lesson Planning

Because we are working to make connections between concepts and procedures as well as between content and language, our instruction needs to be deliberate. We need to understand the mathematics we teach and the mathematicians we are teaching. Lesson planning, or what I like to call prethinking a lesson, needs to become part of our daily routine. This section will address the importance of thinking through the mathematical or management issues that may arise as the lesson is presented.

TEACHER-TO-TEACHER TALK ■ **About Lesson Planning** ■ Yes, I have been teaching some thirty-something years—and about twenty-something years in the fifth grade. Yes, I have taught reading, language arts, English, as well as my beloved mathematics. Yes, I have spent hours preparing and prethinking lessons only to have some fail miserably. Lesson planning does not exempt us from botched lessons or just plain bad days in math class. But what it does do is allow and encourage us to reflect on just what went wrong—or even on what went right! I have had many a student save an abysmal lesson by asking a wonderful question or having a wonderful idea. I have also learned to be quite honest about those unfortunate mathematical incidents with myself, my colleagues, and my students. Not that I take out an ad in the school newspaper, but if the opportunity arises for a conversation about why things did not go exactly as planned, I will take the opportunity to do so. I am always reminding my students that learning and understanding develop from processing events and meaningful communication. And the same holds true for us as teachers. Teaching is not a science. It is not predictable, nor is it prescribed. We, too, need to process and communicate what did work, as well as what did not, as we develop our craft and plan and prepare for lessons and mathematical conversations. As teachers of mathematics, we work with ideas, and mistakes, and people . . . most of whom happen to be ten or eleven years old. Perhaps UCLA's John Wooden said it best, "Failing to prepare is preparing to fail."

Investigations, Games, and Literature-Based Activities

Sample investigations, games, and literature-based activities are offered to help support the unit of study. The investigations presented in each unit may also help you to develop or adjust existing activities of your own that may better serve your mathematical objectives and needs.

Good Questions to Ask

Developing and posing good questions can help focus learning on the process of thinking through the mathematics. Good questions help students make sense of mathematics. Asking good questions not only encourages students to apply what they understand about mathematical concepts and procedures, but it also helps them make connections and generalizations. Examples of good questions to ask your students will be presented for each unit of study.

Calculation Routines and Practice

Paper-and-pencil routines and practices will be discussed, explored, and shared in this section. The emphasis is on the *representation* of the calculations and numerical reasoning—not necessarily on the repetition or drill of one specific algorithm. Our fifth graders need to learn to apply their calculation skills as they work to further develop number sense and solve problems efficiently and accurately. The flexibility of moving from one procedure or representation to another given the context or the numbers involved in a problem is equally important. We will discuss calculation routines and practices relevant to each unit of study as well.

Reading, Writing, and Vocabulary

Mathematics can no longer be taught in isolation because of the reading, writing, and vocabulary expectations of mathematical investigations, curricula, and high-stakes testing. How our students understand, interpret, and apply the language of reasoning offers important insights on how they understand and make sense of mathematics. Mathematics *is* a language as much as it requires language. The integration and development of mathematical reading, writing, and vocabulary will be discussed as they relate to each unit of study in this section.

Assessment

Wiggins and McTighe define *assessment* as "the use of many methods of gathering evidence of meeting desired results, whether those results are state content standards or local curricular objectives" (2005, 6). Embedding informal assessment measures into day-to-day routines as well as establishing formal assessment practices helps us to identify and document the evidence of the mathematical growth of our students. Assessment routines can also give us important information about the effectiveness of our teaching and the math curriculum. We need to listen and learn from our students as they tell us what makes sense to them and show us what they can do with the mathematics. Discussions of formal and informal assessment practices will be offered in this section, as well as suggestions on how to use the information gathered for in-house or reporting purposes.

Home and School Connections

Creating a partnership between school and home supports the mathematical education of everyone involved. Communication with families needs to be regular and ongoing in order to report all the meaningful mathematics going on in the classroom. Parents often may be spending time doing mathematics with their children at home, but in a more traditional context within which they feel comfortable. Parents need help understanding what and how you are teaching their children and what they can do to help. Parent information forms, newsletters, formal reports, phone calls, and conferences can all help to establish this working relationship. We have an opportunity (and an obligation, if you will) to educate families about the importance of teaching mathematics with meaning and understanding. Suggestions and samples of home-school communication will be offered in each section.

A month before school starts, I draft my "Back-to-School Parent Newsletter" to the parents of my students (see Figure 1–1). I have been doing this for so many years that I simply revise the previous year's letter, thanks to modern technology. So even if this is your first attempt at such a letter, save it and revise it the following year. It will be well worth the time and effort spent in writing a comprehensive and informative first draft. In my attempt to open a window (or door . . . depending how wide you wish to open it) to our fifth-grade mathematics class for the upcoming year, I present an overview of classroom routines, practices, and expectations. With every newsletter sent home (about four a year), a relevant article or summary of related research is attached. The NCTM journals often have articles that describe and support current best practices in mathematics education that can accompany the newsletters.

FIGURE 1–1
Back-to-School Parent Newsletter.

September 5

Dear Fifth-Grade Parents,

Perhaps it is a sign of old age (*mine*, that is!), but the days between June and September seem to be fewer and shorter with each passing year! I do have to admit, however, that September continues to be my favorite month of the year with all of the hope and promise of the upcoming year. Welcome back.

Now on to the business of math. I must admit that I continue to believe that the fifth-grade year is one of the very best in math education. Fifth graders are ripe for new conceptual challenges, and their creativity runs rampant! I will continue to implement the same curriculum this year as last with teacher-generated units on multiplication and division, volume, and patterns and functions as well. The mathematical thinking abilities of fifth graders never cease to amaze me. Many times I am humbled and in awe of the connections and conjectures they are all able to make.

Please note that a Parent Information and Involvement Form will be posted on the electronic bulletin board under "Lower-School Homework" that explains the goals and expectations of each upcoming unit. A form will be posted prior to the beginning of each new unit in grade 5.

I have included some of my classroom quirks and policies here. Please note that some new pieces have been added to this letter for those of you seasoned veterans. I hope that this information will give you an idea of the structure of our classroom and the expectations that are supported by it. Please feel free to discuss any questions or concerns about your child in math this year with me at your convenience.

Class Policies

- *Homework:* Homework will be assigned three nights a week. I give students an opportunity to start most assignments in class in order for them to ask any necessary questions. I ask that you give *little* parental supervision to your children as they complete their math homework. Please refer to the handout in your child's registration packet for further "helpful hints" about helping with math homework. If children are having a tough time with the assignment, please have them stop, and send in a note with them the next morning. (Email works fine, too!) I would rather *not* have them "dissolve" over an assignment after a long day of school! The fifth grade will have "Marvelous Monday" each week—a no-math homework night.

(Continued)

- *Pencils: All classwork and homework is to be done in pencil.* The end.
- *Math notebooks:* I will ask all students in fifth grade to keep a math notebook. I have already distributed the three-ring binders to students in class. This notebook will become a valuable tool as they move through the year. Quizzes, homework, seatwork, and other written activities are completed in their notebooks. A quick look at the notebook will give you an excellent reference about what we have done in class and the degree of progress that your child is making.
- *Unit archive:* At the end of each unit, ask each student to clean out the completed work and archive the unit. We will remove our unit text, all lab sheets, assessments, and handouts and place them in a manila folder during class. I am asking each student to create a filing system at home (plastic crates work well or a filing drawer in a desk) in which to place their completed folders at year's end. This archiving system will be extremely helpful for students as they move through the upper school math curriculum. Completed units will be a great resource for future units of study. Archived units will be housed in my room until May, and then they will be sent home with your child.
- *Evaluation:* Evaluation is a constant process in our classroom. ACE questions and Mathematical Reflections are evaluated carefully—not necessarily by a grade, but in my comments, corrections, and suggestions. Occasionally, I ask children to redo an assignment. This is by no means a punishment. My expectations of mathematical writing are high. I am looking for thoroughness and clarity, and not always the "right" answer! Often misconceptions will manifest themselves in the students' writing, and I need to understand and see those as well.
- *Exams:* I have always thought of my exams as opportunities for students to shine. I give unit exams after the completion of each major unit and I will *always* hand out study sheets two or more days prior to *every* exam. With the use of a study sheet, each and every student can be well prepared for each and every test. No surprises will appear on the test: what is on the study sheet is what is on the test. Test self-reflections follow every exam and are stapled to the front of each exam. The finished product is then filed in the children's math binders. They are asked to assess their preparation and performance on their test reflection sheet. I have actually learned more about the students from reading these sheets than by correcting their tests. They are often brutally honest and right on the mark as they self-reflect.
- *Partner quizzes:* These will be new to students this year. They will have their first partner quiz as we move through the number theory unit. Each student is assigned a partner with whom they work through the quiz. The quiz is collaborative and based on shared ideas and procedures. We will have three or four partner quizzes this year. Study sheets are given out prior to the quiz. Students will not know who their partner is until the day of the quiz. Students are assigned different partners for each of the three quizzes. I give careful thought and consideration to the partner assignments.

FIGURE 1–1 (Continued)

- *Grades:* This will be your child's first experience with end-of-term numerical grades. Written work, class work, small-group work, participation, effort, evaluations (tests and projects), and homework completion all contribute to the grade for the term.

- *Calculators:* I love playing with calculators, and the students do, too. In these more technological times, it is important for our children to know their way around a calculator. We use calculators in class when I am not as concerned about the calculations as I am about the *process* of reaching a solution. We are now using the TI-15 in class. It is not necessary to have the same calculator at home. I would actually prefer to have students learn to use other styles and brands as well. Please keep your chosen calculator simple, however.

- *Written expectations:* A great deal of writing is required and expected in this particular curriculum. Most assignments will be based on the end-of-investigation questions. The students will answer all questions in their math notebooks. We will spend much of September discussing how to write a "good" math solution. The explanation of one's thinking is crucial in this curriculum. One young man admitted last year that his thinking became much clearer as he wrote, and that he often changed his position right in the middle of an assignment because he realized that it did not make sense mathematically. Developing self-awareness and insights such as these are what makes this program so strong.

- *Language demands of the mathematics:* The exploring, defining, manipulating, and refining of mathematical language can help children learn with greater understanding and meaning. Children need to speak the mathematics, represent the mathematics, and write about it. Acquiring the necessary vocabulary and language skills will help your fifth grader develop the conceptual and procedural skills required for mathematical growth and success. Working through the mathematical language of each particular unit of study will be a primary teaching and learning objective. One section of each student's math notebook will be designated for the vocabulary and language applicable to each unit.

- *Heffalumps and Woozles:* As most of you already know, Heffalumps and Woozles are the *optional* problem-solving activities posted in my room every two weeks. Students are encouraged to pick up problems and work on them on their own, with a friend, or even as a family. I have received some wonderful family solutions! I have been collecting solutions to these problems for the past three years and have begun to use them as I work with teachers over the summer. Please remind your children that they *must* show or explain their thinking when completing their problems.

Additional Supplies
- colored pencils
- mechanical pencils

FIGURE 1–1 (Continued)

I have included two articles about current practices in the teaching of elementary mathematics. Mathematics education has changed, and it will continue to change as our world becomes hungrier for problem solvers and mathematical thinkers. The first article, titled "Teaching Children Mathematics," discusses possible units of study and why it may all "look" different from our days in fifth grade. This is a chapter from the book *Beyond Arithmetic*, written by a research group out of Cambridge (Mokros, Russell, and Economopoulos 1995). I have also included a second article addressing the same issues that was recently published in *Mathematics Teaching in the Middle School*, a monthly journal published by the National Council for the Teaching of Mathematics (NCTM; Martinie 2004). Both articles are written for parents as we all redefine the role of mathematics education. These articles are included to highlight some of the theory and practice behind these necessary changes in the classroom. I think you will find them interesting and hope that you will take a few minutes out of your busy schedule to read them.

I would like to close this epic with a paragraph from *Raising Cain: Protecting the Emotional Life of Boys* (Kindlon and Thompson 1999). Even though this book explores the emotional life of boys, it provides insights into the development of all young people.

> The most important thing to remember, the guiding principle, is to try to keep your son's self-esteem intact while he is in school. That is the real risk to his success and to his mental health. Once he's out of school, the work will be different. He'll find a niche where the fact that he can't spell well, or didn't read until he was eight, won't matter. But if he starts to hate himself because he wasn't good at schoolwork, he'll fall into a hole that he'll be digging himself out of for the rest of his life. (36)

My goal as a teacher (and as a mother of two sons) is to send all of our fifth graders off into the mathematical world feeling confident and self-assured. They may struggle sometimes with fractions or remainders, but they will also realize that they have the strength and courage to wrestle with these concepts, knowing that understanding will come in time. I cannot praise this book enough. I laughed, I sighed, I even wept while reading certain chapters. I rarely say this about a book, but it is a must-read if you have sons, know sons, or are a son.

Thank you all—children and parents—for your continued support. This is a very difficult job to do well, and it would be all the more impossible without your support.

Mathematically yours,

Lainie Schuster

Lainie Schuster
Teacher of Mathematics Most of the Time
Student of Mathematics Always

FIGURE 1–1 (Continued)

Resources

Wonderful mathematical resources are on the market—some for which we search, and some over which we accidentally and fortuitously fall! A resource listing at the end of each chapter offers additional materials to support the concepts and procedures covered in that unit. This section may also offer additional resources containing extensions that you may wish to explore with some or all of your students. The extensions follow an investigative format that allows for creative and open-ended approaches to solving the problem or answering questions. Understanding the needs of your students and the targeted mathematics will help you seek out relevant and valuable resources. The bibliographic citation for each is listed in the References.

TEACHER-TO-TEACHER TALK ■ **About Teacher Resources** ■ Let's not get into how many hundreds of publications I have purchased over the years in the search for that I-can't-teach-without-this resource! But the good news is that I have found a few:

- *Math Matters: Understanding the Math You Teach: Grades K–8, Second Edition* (Chapin and Johnson 2006) What makes this reference so invaluable is its depth, practicality, and user-friendliness. This reference will help to clarify and support *your* understanding of the mathematical concepts you teach.

- *About Teaching Mathematics: A K–8 Resource, Third Edition* (Burns 2007) This comprehensive reference includes more than 240 classroom-tested activities, as well as information necessary for teachers to teach math through problem solving, to understand the math they are responsible for teaching, and to understand how children best learn mathematics. *About Teaching Mathematics* offers the guidance teachers need to make appropriate and effective instructional decisions.

- *Making Sense: Teaching and Learning Mathematics with Understanding* (Hiebert et al. 1997) This resource presents best practice and research-based ideas on how to design classrooms that help students to learn mathematics with understanding. The authors describe the essential features of such classrooms.

- National Council of Teachers of Mathematics journals: *Teaching Children Mathematics* and *Mathematics Teaching in the Middle School*. Both are monthly journals offering activities, lesson ideas, teaching strategies, and problems through in-depth articles, departments, and features. Both journals provide activities and lessons helpful to fifth-grade teachers. They can be accessed at the NCTM Web site: http://nctm.org/publications/index.htm#journals.

A Note About Homework

Homework will *not* be addressed in this year overview. Homework policies can be district-based, school-based, discipline-based, or teacher-based. My homework routines have remained simple over the years and have largely been influenced by the homework practices set forth in Annette Raphel's *Math Homework That Counts* (2000). I assign homework three nights a week: Tuesday, Wednesday, and Thursday. In my classroom, Monday night is designated as "Marvelous Monday"—a no-math-homework night. Because of the reading and writing demands of our language arts curriculum, I ask students to spend time organizing and focusing their attention on their language arts work for the week on Monday evenings, which allows them to free up time on the following evenings to complete their math assignments.

Setting Up Your Classroom

When we value mathematical communication and sense making, we need to pay attention to the organization of our classrooms. Furniture arrangement, availability of supplies, and the organization of student and teacher materials become routines and practices that need to be addressed. "How is this best helping my students learn mathematics?" can be a guiding question as you search for and implement organizational systems and practices.

Furniture Arrangement

Because mathematical talk, communication, and cooperative problem solving are so valued in my classroom, students are seated at tables in groups of four. The seating is rotated every two weeks—an every-other-Monday routine. Random seating practices such as choosing cards or colored Popsicle sticks can facilitate the seating assignments. Small-group rules and expectations are given to students in those first few days of school. Three rules are in operation when students work in small groups and are posted in my classroom:

1. You are responsible for your own work and behavior.

2. You must be willing to help any group member who asks.

3. You may ask the teacher for help only when your group has the same question.

You may wish to refer to *About Teaching Mathematics* (Burns 2007) for a more extensive discussion of managing a classroom for problem solving.

I also give fifth graders mathematical communication guidelines in addition to the small-group rules. (See Figure 1–2.) Suzanne Chapin, co-author of *Math Matters* (2006) and *Classroom Discussions* (2009), developed these guidelines for use in our middle school. I have adapted them for use in my classroom. Each student receives a set of guidelines, which are housed in their math notebooks (see the "Student Materials" section of this chapter).

Mathematical Communication

Discussions regularly occur in mathematics classes. As part of any classroom discussion, students have certain *rights* and *obligations* in regard to how they talk together about math.

Rights

- Students have the right to make a contribution to an attentive, responsive audience.
- Students have the right to ask questions.
- Students have the right to be treated civilly.
- Students have the right to have their ideas discussed, not themselves.

Obligations

- Students are obligated to speak loudly enough for others to hear.
- Students are obligated to listen for understanding.
- Students are obligated to participate constructively in class discussions.
- Students are obligated to agree or disagree (and explain why) in response to other people's ideas.

FIGURE 1–2
Math Classroom Communication Guidelines.

I send copies of these guidelines home to parents as well. I make comments about the students' willingness and ability to conduct themselves during classroom conversations in report cards and conferences. I want parents to know that I expect and value meaningful and respectful participation from each and every child. It is extremely helpful for parents to be aware early on in the year of the expectations for such classroom practices.

Teaching Materials

Math Manipulatives and Tools

Although my choice of manipulatives has stayed fairly consistent over the years, my organizational practices and containers change fairly frequently. In my earlier days of teaching, I stored manipulatives in dishpans in open shelving. I have since changed to clear plastic containers with locking lids. The contents of the containers can be easily identified and just as easily stacked and stored. In an active mathematics classroom, certain materials need to be available and accessible at all times. Over the years I have found that giving students immediate access to materials encourages independence and creativity in the problem-solving process. The organization of materials is a personal choice, but one that needs to be shared with your students. Establishing routines early in the year for use, organization, and cleanup will be well worth your time and effort.

Your choice of manipulatives should rely on instructional purpose. How will their use help support the teaching and learning of the mathematics? Although I use linking cubes when we investigate volume later in the year, I do not use them enough to warrant having a set housed in my classroom. Each year I borrow several sets from the first- and second-grade classrooms when we move into our work with volume. Pooling materials with other teachers can help stretch your budget and allow for a greater selection of materials.

Here is my personal "must-have" classroom list of manipulatives followed by a "nice-to-have/borrow-from-others" list.

Must-Have Manipulatives

- color tiles
- pattern blocks
- transparent counting/bingo chips
- dice
- fraction dice

I have found that commercially produced fraction dice have a greater shelf life than those we create ourselves with stickers or permanent markers—although those certainly can be made! Many companies produce them. Two sets of the dice with the appropriate markings are recommended:

Set 1: $\frac{1}{2}, \frac{1}{4}, \frac{1}{8}, \frac{1}{8}, \frac{1}{16}, \frac{1}{16}$

Set 2: $\frac{1}{2}, \frac{1}{3}, \frac{1}{4}, \frac{1}{6}, \frac{1}{12}, \frac{1}{12}$

Two sets of fraction dice accompany the Fraction Kit® (Burns 2003c) produced by Math Solutions and are appropriate for each fraction activity requiring dice presented in this publication.

Number Card Decks

You may find that your prescribed curriculum offers card decks. Decks are made up of four of each of the numbers 0 through 12. Have enough for one deck per pair of students and a few extra decks for card replacements. Playing card decks also work well, substituting the 2 of the face cards with values of 11 and 12.

Nice-to-Have/Borrow Manipulatives

- Cuisenaire rods
- decimal cards (see Chapter 6, "Fractions, Decimals, and Percents," for reference information)
- linking cubes

Calculators

The use of calculators in the upper-elementary grades is controversial. It is important for you to establish your philosophy about calculator use before the school year begins in order to help students, parents, and administrators understand your reasoning in support of their use. In my classroom, students have access to calculators at all times—except during the multiplication and division units. In those units, the use of calculators needs to be requested and approved because of the respective mathematical objectives of the instruction. Over the years, I have collected various makes and models of calculators. Once upon a time, I felt the need to offer the students one brand and model for consistency of instruction. I am now more concerned with students' flexibility in being able to use any calculator because so many models are available outside of school. I always find it interesting that as the year goes on, the more basic four-function models continue to be the calculator of choice. Calculators are housed in one drawer of a three-drawer plastic unit. This particular chest of drawers houses calculators, six-inch rulers, and twelve-inch rulers. The drawers, as well as all other containers, are labeled for quick reference and easy access. Our primary school colleagues have much to teach us!

I am blessed with the use of a document camera and an LCD projector. These two pieces of technology have greatly changed the mathematical discussion and sharing that are carried out in my class. The students have immediate access to each other's work, and I can work right along with them as we complete written work in class. This type of modeling and the accompanying discussions have enriched the mathematical experiences of everyone in the class. However, for some lessons, the overhead projector still takes center stage (literally and figuratively). I continue to make overheads to support our work in class. Projecting them on the whiteboard allows us to write directly on the board and offers a larger work space than the document camera's projections. I have a supply of overhead pattern blocks that the students and I prefer when their use is warranted. I can, however, be easily overwhelmed technologically, and my students are greatly entertained by that. They giggle as I move from one piece of equipment to the other—without plugging either one of them in—and then get confused about which piece I am using.

TEACHER-TO-TEACHER TALK ■ **About Color Blindness** ■ When was the last time you thought about color blindness? I am a visual learner and have always utilized color in my instruction . . . colored pencils, colored pattern blocks, colored markers for the whiteboard. Several years ago I was working on a fraction activity one night at home on our kitchen table with pattern blocks. My husband wandered in the room and made a face. "And you think I could do that?" he asked. I chuckled—he is always reminding me of his mathematical limitations. "No, I am serious!" he protested. Knowing that he was color-blind, I shuddered. We had a very important discussion that night

---

(Continued)

about what he can and cannot see and how instruction continues to be hard for him when color is involved—the worst being the use of those red laser pointers in lectures! I immediately got online and researched color blindness. Approximately one in twelve people will have some sort of color deficiency. Yikes! For years I had been using color and referring to colors for whole-class instruction with no awareness of the possible students who were color-blind. Although I continue to use color for instructional purposes, each September I check in with my class and the nurse about the presence of color blindness and make adjustments if necessary. Several years ago I discovered that I had two boys in my class who had been diagnosed with red-green color deficiency. I would never have thought to seek out that information to adjust my presentation to their needs had it not been for my husband's protests at the kitchen table that one night.

Supplies

As with your choice of manipulatives, supply choices and accessibility should rely on instructional purpose and budget. How will students record their day-to-day math? How will you organize math writing? What paper will you use if students will be making posters or presentations? Will these materials be exclusive to mathematics, or can they be shared with the other disciplines you teach? Organization and storage will also need to be addressed as you determine class and logistical needs and constraints.

My paper supply is perhaps my most costly line item in my yearly order. In my classroom, paper is organized in a five-tier tray, which saves considerable space on the countertop. Quarter-inch graph paper, 1-cm graph paper, plain white paper, and lined notebook paper fill the tiers. I keep a roll of 1-inch graph paper on hand for projects requiring larger work areas. A supply of 16-by-24-inch newsprint for poster making and presentations is also handy. I also keep tablets of lined and gridded chart paper available for use with whole-group instruction. I do not have room for a freestanding easel for the chart paper, so I just mount individual sheets on the whiteboard when necessary. Three-by-three-inch sticky notes are also available for each table grouping. Several years ago, a few of my students began to apply the annotations practiced in reading to their work in math. We had begun to post annotations made on sticky notes on the literature we were reading at the time. This particular group of students found this routine extremely helpful when new mathematical vocabulary, concepts, or procedures were introduced within lessons. Some students make better use of this practice than others, but the sticky notes are available for all to use.

Art supplies such as scissors, glue sticks, colored pencils, and markers are also available and found in plastic bins on the countertop as well. Colored pencils and markers are boxed for table groupings so that each table has access to a box of each type. Over the years, the students and I have agreed that markers are best suited for poster making, but colored pencils are better for day-to-day work. Colored pencils do not bleed and can be sharpened. I ask that only colored pencils be used in paper-and-pencil activities.

Student Materials

We all know teachers who have developed ingenious systems for students' organization of materials. I was not one of them! It has taken me thirty-something years to develop and implement an organizational system for my class that works for all of us. But what I now have, I love! Instead of asking myself what I wanted the students to have in terms of organizational skills and system, I finally began to think about what disrupts the students and our work together as far as the accessibility—or inaccessibility—of their materials. Here is my list:

- loose papers
- no pencils
- math homework stashed in other folders
- inaccessible class work from the previous day
- corrected homework, class work, and exams lost in the black holes of lockers or book bags
- misplaced textbooks/workbooks

I began to collect sample notebooks, binders, and folders over the summer to construct a math binder that would give all of us easy access to necessary materials. I was very pleased with that summer's work and continue to implement the use of the math binder.

Each student receives a three-hole view binder. I create a name page for each student that he or she will decorate on the first day of school. The name page is slipped into the plastic sleeve on the front of the binder for easy identification. Inside the binder are the following materials:

- pencil pouch (three-hole punched)
- class text (workbook style, three-hole punched by publisher)
- spiral graph paper notebook, quarter-inch ruled, for class work and homework; pages are never torn out. This notebook becomes a well-documented representation of a year of mathematical work.
- a top-loaded plastic sleeve with the rights and obligations of mathematical communication (see page 13).
- three dividers made of cardstock-weight paper that students label and decorate

    handouts for student worksheets

    returns for corrected homework, classwork, or tests

    vocabulary (see the designated section that follows)
- pocket folder, three-hole punched, for loose papers and packets

Top-loading plastic sleeves sold in boxes of one hundred are also available to house important reference sheets throughout the year. These sheets remain in the math notebook all year for easy reference and accessibility. Although I distribute the sleeves when needed, students often ask if they can place a particular paper in a sleeve if they find it helpful and applicable to other work done in class.

Such a math binder can become an excellent resource and organizational tool for our fifth-grade mathematicians. It does take some vigilance, however, to implement its use and continued organization, but the time and effort will be well worth it. Early in the year, I check notebooks daily at the end of each class to ensure that all papers and materials are housed appropriately and in the prescribed order. I become a tad obsessive about these binders because I know how valuable this organizational tool can be for students. For my students, this is often their first experience with a class binder and an organizational system that can easily be applied in later years and even to other disciplines. I want students to be successful with its implementation.

Vocabulary

TEACHER-TO-TEACHER TALK ■ About the Importance of Language ■

Disclaimer: I am passionate about language. When the language of mathematical reasoning and reflection is used explicitly and mindfully in the classroom by teachers, students are empowered to use the same language in their thinking, articulation, and problem solving. If the truth be known, my years of being a student of literature and writing have served me well as a learner and teacher of mathematics. Ken Goodman (1986) argues that language learning in schools can either be made accessible, or interfered with, as explained in the following chart:

It is easy when:	It is hard when:
■ It's real and natural.	■ It's artificial.
■ It's whole.	■ It's broken into bits and pieces.
■ It's sensitive.	■ It's nonsense.
■ It's interesting.	■ It's dull and uninteresting.
■ It's relevant.	■ It's irrelevant to the learner.
■ It belongs to the learner.	■ It belongs to someone else.
■ It's part of a real event.	■ It's out of context.
■ It has a social utility.	■ It has no social value.
■ It has a purpose for the learner.	■ It has no discernible purpose.
■ The learner chooses to use it.	■ It's imposed by someone else.
■ It's accessible to the learner.	■ It's inaccessible.
■ The learner has the power to use it.	■ The learner is powerless.

The implementation of meaningful work with vocabulary can support our students as they apply the language of mathematics in their thinking, reasoning, and problem solving.

I am constantly reminding my students to "watch your language!" Our yearlong work with vocabulary has purpose and protocol. We choose and use words carefully and mindfully as we talk and write. My fifth graders do not take too long to realize my passion for the language—and I like to think that my students begin to develop an appreciation for the same.

The vocabulary section of my students' math binders has several components: a page of double-meaning entries (see Figure 1–3; see also Reproducible 1.1), a word bank, and alphabetized pages of entry words. Vocabulary pages are not archived at the end of each unit. The vocabulary section stays intact throughout the year as we continue to enter relevant words with each unit of study.

Many math words have double meanings: those that we use in everyday conversation and those relevant to mathematics. These meanings can be confusing to students when first introduced in mathematics. These

▶ REPRODUCIBLE 1.1
Double-Meaning
Word Entries

FIGURE 1–3
Double-Meaning Word Entries.

Double-Meaning Word Entries

Many math words have a *math meaning* and another meaning in regular conversation. Keep a list of these *double-life* words and how they can be used in various contexts.

Word	In math it means . . .	It usually means . . .
Proper	Proper factor factors of a number except itself	Right way, correct way
Decompose	To break down a number	It rots or breaks down
Odd	Not even	Strange, awkward
Product	Answer to a multiplication problem	Merchandise; something that is produced

Source: From *Writing About Mathematics: An Essential Skill in Developing Math Proficiency, Grades 3–8* (O'Connell 2002)

double-meaning words can also cause some difficulties for English language learners. Keeping a list of these words can support students as they identify and incorporate words with double meanings into their working vocabularies. Adding words to this list is always a favorite activity in my class. Students are often intrigued by the confusion language can pose—especially if they themselves provide the words to discuss and notate.

A word bank is a useful tool to help students organize the words to be defined and explored. (See Figure 1–4; see also Reproducible 1.2.) My class is always surprised at how many P-words there are in our yearlong study and is forever wondering if we will enter a word for every letter. Although my list of desired words is available whenever we work on vocabulary, I often ask the students to provide words that they feel would be helpful to enter. Their words are often right in sync with mine!

REPRODUCIBLE 1.2   ◀
New Math Words in
My Vocabulary

FIGURE 1–4
New Math Words in My Vocabulary.

A-Words	B-Words	C-Words
abundant number		composite number

D-Words	E-Words	F-Words
divisor		factor
deficient number		

G-Words	H-Words	I-Words

J-Words	K-Words	L-Words

M-Words	N-Words	O-Words
multiple		

(Continued)

P-Words	Q-Words	R-Words
product prime number proper factor perfect number		
S-Words	**T-Words**	**U-Words**
sum		
V-Words	**W-Words**	**X-Words**
	whole number	
Y-Words	**Z-Words**	**Symbols**

FIGURE 1–4 (Continued)

Entry words are entered in much the same way as words in a glossary. (See Figure 1–5; see also Reproducible 1.3.) Each page starts with the beginning letter of each entry word. Students use a thin marker to identify the letter of the page, but all entries are completed in pencil. You may wish to specify cursive or manuscript according to your classroom handwriting guidelines. I allow students to choose between cursive or manuscript, only asking that they use their neatest writing and be consistent for all entries. As words are identified, the definitions are discussed, double checked in the glossaries of our text, and paraphrased for all to understand. We create an example or diagram for each entry. We also post the entry word on a word wall in the classroom under the heading of the particular unit. The word wall remains up throughout the year with the cumulative words posted under their respective units. Having immediate access to all vocabulary words makes spelling less of an issue and helps students make connections between word usages in our varied units of study.

When I first implemented this vocabulary routine, I was not sure how the children would respond. Would I hear groans from the tortured or cheers from the converted? Each year I am somewhat surprised by the students' appreciation of the time spent with vocabulary development. Initially, it may be due more to my fascination with mathematical language and etymology than theirs, but in time they are equally as intrigued!

► REPRODUCIBLE 1.3
Vocabulary/Entry
Words

FIGURE 1–5
Vocabulary/Entry Words.

REPRODUCIBLE 1.3
Vocabulary/Entry
Words ◀

Vocabulary/Entry Words

D

Entry Word: Divisor

Definition: a number that divides into another number

Example:

7 × 5 = 35; 5 is a divisor of 35. 7 is a divisor of 35.

Entry Word: Deficient number

Definition: a number whose proper factors add up to less than itself. (prime numbers will always be odd)

Example:

10: 1, +2, +5, +θ $\sum$ (proper factors) = 8
8 < 10

P

Entry Word: Product

Definition: an answer to a multiplication problem

Example:

(factors)   (factors)
21 = 7 × 3   350 = 50 × 7
(product)   (product)

Entry Word: Prime number

Definition: a number with 2 factors, 1 and itself

Example:

7: 1, 7   2: 1, 2   9: 1, 3, 9

Entry Word: Proper factor

Definition: the factors of a number *except* the number itself

Example:
12 : 1, 2, 3, 4, 6, 12

Organization of Student Work

Young teachers bring so much to our practice. Jessica Girouard, a young fourth-grade teacher new to my school, developed a self-reflection proto-col and portfolio system that both the fourth and fifth grades now use. Although I have always valued portfolio work, its standardization among disciplines and implementation has always been elusive and cumbersome to me. But not so much anymore thanks to Jess!

We place all math work in math binders until the end of each unit. At that time, we remove all relevant handouts and returns from the students' binders and archive them in manila folders that eventually will be sent home. Students are asked to choose two pieces of work from that unit for written analysis and self-reflection. Although most students will choose two of their best pieces of work to write about, some may choose lesser pieces of work and compare and contrast what they know now to what they did not know then. These particular entries can be extremely insight-ful and meaningful. The students complete the self-reflection handout for all disciplines, which creates efficient standardization and implementation. (See Figure 1–6; see also Reproducible 1.4.) Each discipline's reflection sheets are copied on different colors of paper for easy identification and organization within the portfolio.

► REPRODUCIBLE 1.4
Presentation of
Work

Completed reflection sheets and relevant work are housed in each student's portfolio until the end of the year. These portfolios can be easily accessed for parent or student conferences and progress checks. The remainder of the unit work can then be sent home.

Organization of Teaching Materials

As we gain years of experience, we begin to develop our own organiza-tional systems for teaching materials. I used to keep numerous files of student handouts, unit projects, and activities. I still do, but I now keep the bulk of my unit planning in a three-ring binder—one for each unit. Each binder has the unit printed on the spine and on the front. Similar dividers in each binder designate:

- *Lesson Plans and Teaching Notes:* I usually type these up on Friday afternoon from the previous week. They are cryptic, but address the mathematics of the lesson and contain important text page numbers, homework given, and personal notes about the success of the lesson.
- *Vocabulary:* I use the same vocabulary masters that the students use. I keep a listing of each unit's relevant words, definitions, and exam-ples. Even though the students craft class definitions that are posted in their notebooks, I continue to find it helpful to explore and review the vocabulary myself prior to class.
- *Student Handouts:* I keep copies of handouts given in class either for in-class or out-of-class work. They are referenced in the Lesson Plans and Teaching Notes.

FIGURE 1–6
Self-Reflection Handout.

REPRODUCIBLE 1.4
Presentation of Work ◀

Presentation of Work

Piece 1

Subject Area: Math _____

Work Being Presented: Partner Quiz _____

Date Completed: Winter Term _____

Why is this piece an example of quality work (as defined by the fifth grade)?

This piece is a example of quality work because I studied hard for the quiz and cooperated with Vinay throughout the test. This resulted in a good grade.

I chose this piece of work to show how much I have improved at:

Working in a group. I now cooperate better in a group and honor my partner's ideas.

I would like you to notice:

How much I have improved my mathematical writing and vocabulary from fourth grade.

What I learned in the process of completing this piece of work:
    About the subject/area/topic:

    I learned mathematical strategies used to find factors and multiples.

    About myself as a learner:

    I learned that if I work with someone who thinks like me or has the same strategies as me then we work well together.

If I did this project again, I would . . . (What would you do differently?)

Study harder because it never hurts to be ready.

- *Parent Handouts:* Newsletters that have been sent home during that unit are filed in this section, as well as the Parent Information Form for that particular unit.

- *Unit Project:* If a project is assigned in this unit, I file the student information sheets and rubrics for it here.

- *Formal Assessments:* Copies of study sheets, quizzes, and the unit test are filed in this section.

- *Reference Articles:* I may come across an article in an NCTM journal or have been given an article by a colleague that supports the teaching of a particular unit. These are filed here.

This binder becomes my teacher's manual for that unit. Personally, I have found that this notebook system makes referencing activities, articles, and dates of material covered much easier and more accessible from year to year. I add to the notebook each year and remove and archive dated material. Each unit will quickly become your own as you collect materials to support and document your teaching and progress.

Literature Display

No child is ever too old for picture books. And if they say they are, do not believe them! I have yet to meet a fifth grader who did not delight in yet another reading of Kevin Henkes's *Chrysanthemum* (1991), was not enthralled with Eileen Christelow's *Five Dog Night* (1993), or was not totally entertained by Susan Meddaugh's *Martha Blah-Blah* (1996). A book display rack is a handy thing in any classroom, but a math display is a special treat. I continue to collect mathematical titles whenever I come across them, and they are all housed in my book display rack. Marilyn Burns, in conjunction with Scholastic Publications, has developed a mathematical library of twenty-six titles and related lessons for use in grades 4 through 6 (Burns 2005). If you do not have access to mathematical titles, this library might be a good place to start. Another place to start is your local bookseller. I have spent many a Sunday afternoon on the floor of a bookstore in the midst of a pile of picture books. I discovered Greg Tang on such an afternoon many years ago. I also have a passion for picture books about baseball. The mathematics of the sport intrigues me—but so does the history. We read about Shoeless Jo Jackson in September and Lou Gehrig in April and of their numbers and contributions to baseball history. These particular books live on a special shelf in my classroom, but are always accessible to the students. Book collections and displays are wonderful places to explore your own passions as well as those of your students!

The classroom is a world unto itself. We work to create a mathematical culture supported by its routines and practices as well as our values as teachers. This task is not easy, nor one that should be taken lightly. I am always amused at the comments of previous students when they come back to say hello in later years. "Hey! You changed the picture!" or "Why did you move the calculator drawer?" or "Now I don't know where to go to find a ruler!" They remember their world as fifth graders and cannot figure out why anyone would want to change it to fit the needs of anyone else!

Chapter 2

Welcome Back Activity/
Factors and Multiples

Prime numbers are what is left when you have taken all the patterns away. I think prime numbers are like life. They are very logical but you could never work out the rules, even if you spent all your time thinking about them.

the curious incident of the dog in the night-time
Haddon 2003, 12

The Learning Environment

Create a Safe, Supportive, and Engaging Mathematical Culture

Much of September is devoted to developing the mathematical culture of your classroom as well as establishing communication, problem-solving, and reflection routines and practices. If we define a mathematical classroom as a community of learners, then expectations and norms need to be established for all of its members. Opinions need to be heard. Alternative strategies need to be explored. Informal mathematical proofs need to be offered. Mistakes need to be made and examined. And all need to be carried out within a safe and supportive culture. Teachers play a central role in the creation of such an environment. As we guide mathematical instruction, activities, and conversation, we need to honor our students as thinkers and mathematicians. We also need to hold them to high communication standards as we guide them in the process of making sense of the mathematics.

Understand and Value the Mathematics You Teach

The mathematical content of the fifth-grade year is significant. It not only builds on the foundation of the previous four years, but it also requires increased proficiency and conceptual understanding. A strong fifth-grade curriculum expects the same of its teachers. Our mathematical knowledge allows us to ask students good questions and to provide and guide learning experiences that are mathematically significant. Reviewing the content of upcoming units with other fifth-grade teachers, a math coach, or a math curriculum specialist may help to solidify your understanding of the concepts and procedures to be covered. Spending time with others actually doing the math will also help you to better understand the nuances and importance of the language, the tasks, and the desired understandings. According to the authors of *Making Sense: Teaching and Learning Mathematics with Understanding* (Hiebert et al. 1997), knowing mathematics means understanding it. Knowing a subject means getting inside it and seeing how concepts and procedures work, how they are related to each other, and why they work like they do.

Model and Facilitate "Math Talk"

Mathematical communication is not just recommended, it is essential. It is not a question of *whether* students should interact about mathematics, but rather *how* they should interact.

As teachers, we elicit responses from our students in various ways—with questions, commands, hints, jokes, and so on. When students become familiar with our inventory of phrases and expressions, they usually know what we expect of them. Although we rarely stop to think about our most common conversational prompts, they are among our most important instructional tools (Chapin, O'Connor, and Anderson 2009).

The authors of *Classroom Discussions: Using Math Talk to Help Students Learn* (Chapin, O'Connor, and Anderson 2009) present five effective talk moves that can support mathematical thinking and learning. They are as follows:

1. Revoicing: "So you're saying that seventeen is a prime number."

2. Asking students to restate someone else's reasoning: "Can you repeat what he just said in your own words?"

3. Asking students to apply their own reasoning to someone else's reasoning: "Do you agree or disagree and why?"

4. Prompting students for further participation or clarification: "Would someone like to add on?"

5. Using wait time: "Take your time . . . we'll wait."

These talk moves are user friendly and promote listening skills that can support our children as they make sense of the mathematics. Mindful implementation of these moves is necessary to establish an environment in which meaningful mathematical discussion is valued and expected. Establishing expectations for courteous and respectful talk is imperative. It may be necessary to remind students frequently that when we disagree in math class, it is with another person's *idea*—and not with the person. Each student has an obligation to listen attentively as others talk. Listening allows others to participate in the ongoing discussion. I remind my students often that listening is hard work—but listening *well* is *really* hard work!

The Mathematics and Its Language

Children Investigate the Relationships among Factors, Multiples, Divisors, and Products

Exploring and articulating relationships among factors, multiples, divisors, and products help students to construct beginning understandings of number theory. The concepts of factor and multiple are interdependent: if A is a factor of B, then B is a multiple of A. Fifth graders will often use the terms *factor* and *multiple* interchangeably and will need guidance and correction as they apply these words in conversation and writing. Several statements can be made about the relationships in the number model $5 \times 4 = 20$. We can say the following:

- 5 is a factor of 20.
- 4 is a factor of 20.
- 20 is a multiple of 4.
- 20 is a multiple of 5.
- 4 is a divisor of 20.
- 5 is a divisor of 20.
- 20 is a product of 4 and 5.

It is important for the students to learn to use the language of number theory with meaning.

Children Develop Strategies for Finding Factors, Multiples, Least Common Multiples, and Greatest Common Factors

Children need repeated and varied activities that require them to identify whole number factors of given numbers. Games, paper-and-pencil tasks, and rich mathematical discussions can help children create, adopt, and apply meaningful strategies as they factor. It is important for students to distinguish between and identify properties of numbers with many factors and those with only a few. Venn diagrams can be introduced as a tool to help students identify common multiples and common factors. Factoring numbers with only a conventional notation may also be a required objective of your particular school, district, or state standards.

Children Recognize and Articulate Properties of Even and Odd Numbers, Prime and Composite Numbers, and Square Numbers

Classifying numbers by certain characteristics helps identify number patterns and leads to generalizations about numbers (Chapin and Johnson 2006). We can sort, compare, contrast, and classify numbers as prime, composite, odd, even, square, abundant, deficient, or perfect. A deep understanding of number relationships develops over time and relies upon the experiences of the previous years. Teachers play an important role in scaffolding the understanding of number relationships and properties.

Children Make Connections between the Area and Dimensions of Rectangles with Products and Factors

Rectangular arrays can represent models for numbers and their factors, the product being the area of the array and the factor pair being the dimensions of the rectangle. The orientation of the rectangles begins to be questioned. Is a 2-by-5 array the same as a 5-by-2 array? Giving rows first, then columns is the mathematical convention. For example, 2×5 can be interpreted as two groups of five that are represented by the first array below. Story problems can also help to illustrate the "same but different" scenario of turnaround facts. For example, five bags of two apples is quite different from two bags of five apples. Although the products are the same, the orientations of the two arrays are different.

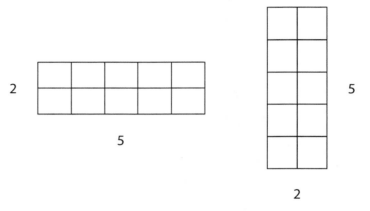

When the turnaround facts are included (5×2 and 2×5), the number of factor pairs of a given number equals the number of factors. Including the turnaround facts also helps to illustrate the commutativity of multiplication. For example, the rectangular arrays for ten are the following:

    1 by 10
    10 by 1
    2 by 5
    5 by 2

The conventional notation for the factorization of ten is as follows:

    10: 1, 2, 5, 10

Ten has four distinct factors and four distinct rectangular arrays.

Children Explore and Apply Divisibility Rules or Tests

Rules regarding divisibility are related to factors and divisors. Fifth graders are often aware of the divisibility rules of 1, 2, 5, and 10, but may need to spend some time articulating those rules and justifying why they work. The divisibility rules of 3, 6, and 9 are a bit more complicated, but extremely useful nonetheless (see the section "Calculation Routines and Practices"). Asking students why and for what types of numbers certain divisibility rules work contributes to our students' ability to make sense of numbers.

Children Review the Basic Multiplication Facts

As students complete mathematical tasks requiring the application of the basic multiplication facts, the fluency and relational understanding of those facts become more important. Identifying factors also requires an understanding of how multiplication relates to division within a context that explores number relationships.

Children Apply Their Understanding of Factors, Multiples, and the Use of Mathematical Models as They Create Strategies to Solve Problems

Problems are posed, solved, and shared that engage the children in using their knowledge of primes, factors, factor pairs, multiples, and square numbers.

TEACHER-TO-TEACHER TALK ■ About the Study of Factors of Multiples ■

As I teach this unit each year, I am struck by its importance and connection to just about every other unit in the fifth grade. I hear myself saying to the children, "Remember this— you will be seeing this again!" or "We will come back to this again when we work through our fractions unit." Mac blurted out one day that " . . . she thinks *everything* in this unit is more important than anything else we have learned in math so far!" And in some very real ways, I do. In this unit, bits and pieces of knowledge and instruction from the previous years are now connected and useful. When students realize that they are going to explore odd and even numbers, some of them groan. "We have done that for three years already!" is often the cry of the tortured! But when students begin to explore the structures of even and odd numbers, they are intrigued. Knowing that 8, 12, 34, and 566 are all even numbers is no longer enough. We now ask why they are even and discuss how the evenness or oddness may affect a computation. We ask that conjectures be proved with mathematical models, and offer investigations that allow connections to be made and understandings to be justified. Each year when we investigate the products of even and odd numbers, someone always shares with the class that they always wondered why so many products were even numbers in the multiplication table. Michael said he remembered thinking once upon a time that *all* products were even and that the only way you could get an odd number was to find a sum! The arithmetic of this unit is simple, but the mathematics is not. The structure of numbers is important—not just to me, but to the study of mathematics. And I take every opportunity to remind my students of that. It becomes a bit of a mantra by November. "We know, we know . . . this is important, too!"

Lesson Planning

Identifying the mathematical objectives of this first unit of a fifth-grade year of mathematics instruction will be of great help and support as you plan lessons and activities. The objectives noted at the beginning of this chapter may or may not align themselves with the objectives of your prescribed curriculum. Teacher's manuals and state frameworks are important resources from which this information can be gleaned. Other fifth-grade topics in a unit on number theory may include:

- factor strings and prime factorizations
- exponential notation
- squaring and unsquaring numbers (square roots)

Take advantage of the opportunities that will present themselves as you help, encourage, and support your students in identifying and articulating connections that can be made between concepts and procedures. Be mindful and deliberate in these conversations. The following list of good questions may help to make those connections accessible and visible:

- Where have we seen this before?
- How does this relate to our work with ____?
- How are these two ideas or procedures related?
- Is there something that we have discussed recently that could help us solve this?
- Can knowing x help you to know y?

Pay special attention to the language of your students. It is not uncommon for fifth graders to have difficulties applying the words *factor*, *multiple*, *product*, and *divisor* when speaking or writing. The language is important!

Speaking of important, so is mastery of the times tables—and I do mean *mastery!* It will help to be aware of those students who have achieved fluency with the multiplication facts and those who have not. You may need to develop minilessons for small groups of students in order to increase their facility with the tables. Mastery of these facts is not optional at this point in a student's mathematical career: it is necessary.

All students need to continue to construct physical models. Having color tiles available for all class investigations and assessments involving arrays can offer continued accessibility of the mathematics for some students. If you are using array models to introduce factor pairs, remember to connect the mathematical conjectures constructed by your students and class discussions with the physical models even if a majority of the class has moved on from their use.

Possible Difficulties or Misconceptions

The concept of *factor* may be new to some. As lessons are carried out that require factoring, ask for the strategies that the students are applying in the process. Asking for generalizations about factors will also help students be more efficient in their factoring. For example, some fifth graders may not realize that all even numbers have 2 as a factor. If and when that is evident, have the class list all the factors of several even numbers. Ask the students to articulate what all the factorizations have in common. Push for a generalization about even numbers and their divisibility by 2.

Some divisibility rules are apparent, while some are not. Most students will recognize that all multiples of 5 end in 5 or 0. All multiples of 10 end in 0. Multiples of 10 are divisible by 2 (because they are even), by 5 (because they end in 0), and by 10 (because they end in 0). Beginning with what students know helps to engage their curiosity about what they do not know. The divisibility rules of 3, 6, and 9 initially may be elusive to students. As the class investigates and has conversations about the structures of numbers, even these unfamiliar rules may become more apparent. You will need to present opportunities and make connections that require and illustrate the application of those rules in meaningful contexts. See the "Calculation Routines and Practices" section of this chapter for additional discussion of divisibility rules.

Investigations, Games, and Literature-Based Activities

Chrysanthemum

Duration: 2–3 Class Periods

Hope and anticipation often accompany the first days of school. But for those students new to your school or to each other, the first days can also be a bit overwhelming. Beginning the school year with a favorite children's book and a data-collection activity about class names can help to establish working relationships among your students as they develop a mathematical community. This investigation offers students opportunities to

- collect, represent, and analyze data
- review statistical landmarks such as mean, median, and mode
- make assumptions and predictions based on the collected data
- engage in mathematical discourse
- develop problem-solving protocols and strategies

Materials
- *Chrysanthemum* by Kevin Henkes (1991)
- newsprint, 1 sheet per group

NCTM Connection

Strand: Data Analysis and Probability

Focus: Collect, analyze, and interpret data in a literature context.

Context: *Chrysanthemum* by Kevin Henkes

- linking cubes, enough for each student to correspond with the number of letters in his or her first name
- chart paper, 1 piece

Vocabulary

maximum, mean, median, minimum, mode, range, sample size

Children's author and illustrator Kevin Henkes (1991) tells a wonderful tale about a mouse named Chrysanthemum and her first days of school. Chrysanthemum always thought that her name was absolutely perfect . . . and then she started school. Henkes's story describes Chrysanthemum's not-so-pleasant experiences during those first few days of school with the likes of Victoria, Jo, and Rita. Mrs. Twinkle arrives on the scene, and the story takes a delightful turn.

Begin the activity with an oral reading of *Chrysanthemum*, sharing each and every picture with your class. The watercolor illustrations are exquisite! Some of your students will be familiar with the book—and some will not. You may wish to take the time to discuss the importance of rereading literature, informing students that they may be reading and rereading pieces of literature two and even three times as they move through their educational careers. (I think I read *To Kill a Mockingbird* [Lee 1960] three times . . . then later read it out loud to my own sons . . . and loved it more with each reading!)

TEACHER-TO-TEACHER TALK ■ About the Beauty of Picture Books ■

I adore the use of children's literature in the teaching of mathematics—and in particular, picture books. I have yet to meet a ten-year-old who does not have a favorite! The beauty of good literature is that it can be read over and over again. I establish this bias early in the school year with my class. When I hold up a book, they know to huddle in and enjoy! Without any prompting, my students often leave their tables to sit at my feet or move their chairs around me. We never read books without discussion. If some students are familiar with the book, they often share stories capturing early memories. We may examine illustrations, explore the point of view, or discuss the plot. Because I am explicit and deliberate with the connections I make between literature and language and their use in math class, the students often look for the connections even before I ask for them. Once we read a book, we place it on the marker tray of the whiteboard for several days for revisiting.

Does this practice take time away from the lesson of the day? Sometimes, but it is time well spent. Personally, I often like to blur the lines between reading and math. Language is as important to mathematics as it is to reading. Both reading and mathematics require thinking. When we ask students to make sense of mathematics, we are asking them to think, reflect, question, and imagine—just as we ask them to do when reading. And how exactly do we do that? With language.

Inform the students that they will be investigating name lengths in this activity. They will work to identify the typical name length of their class. You will need to lay down some ground rules, however, in regard to name choices. Will full names be used? Can nicknames be used? I open up this discussion to the students in order for them to take ownership of the constraints of the activity. My class usually agrees to use full first names because we always seem to have a few interesting ones. The students always tell a few interesting stories, as well, about name choices and the circumstances that decided them. Have these conversations! You might even have a story to tell yourself! Shared stories unite a community.

I provide newsprint for each table group and give students the following directives:

What is the typical first name length of our class?

1. In your group of four, collect, organize, and chart the length of the first names of your classmates.
2. On your newsprint, write two summarizing statements about your class or classmates.

You may wish to post this task on chart paper prior to the investigation for class reference. Having the task posted gives the class immediate access and reference to the task. I have found this practice to be extremely helpful in that it is the first mathematical task of the year and one with which I want to establish comprehension, problem solving, and talk routines and practices. Processing the task in a whole-group setting also gives you the opportunity to make your expectations known and deliberate. Informing your students that this is the purpose of your modeling can be equally helpful.

In a whole-group setting, I ask students to read the guidelines silently. Then I ask for a volunteer to read the task aloud. The class discusses the task and its question in table groups. A volunteer summarizes the task and restates the question being posed. Once the summary has been delivered, asking if any student wishes to "add on" to the summary gives you the opportunity to move into your class discussion repertoire.

Because this is their first mathematical task of the year, the students may be a little sloppy with their language. Deborah substituted the word *average* for *typical* when rephrasing the question. When I pushed her to explain her use of the word *average*, she faltered. "Well, the average—the average name length. You know . . ." I look forward to this scenario—and it happens almost every year—because it allows me to make the first of many moves as devil's advocate. "No, I don't know. Can you tell me more about what you mean by *average?*" Opening up such a discussion allows me to implement other talk moves. Asking if anyone wants to add to

Deborah's description or if anyone disagrees with Deborah's description can help the modeling process. Informing the students of your reasons for holding the discussion will not only help them focus on the language of the mathematics but also focus on the talk formats that you will implement throughout the year. You may need to be vigilant in these first few weeks of school about the expectations of class members as they carry out mathematical discussions. Referring to the rights and obligations on the math communication handout (see Figure 1–2, page 13) may be helpful or necessary.

Once the class agrees that the word *typical* allows for greater interpretation of the data than the word *average* and that they understand the guidelines, students work in their table groups to complete the task. In order to foster independence and efficiency, I remind students to refer to the problem and its question frequently throughout their data collection and representation in order to focus their thinking and writing on the task at hand. Ten-year-olds are capable of offering wonderful answers to interesting yet unasked questions!

As you circulate around the room, you will undoubtedly notice small-group dynamics in action as the students set out to complete the task. Some groups will be more efficient than others. Some will not know where to begin. Some groups will struggle with leadership. Some will lose their focus easily. We expect to see all of these dynamics in September. Because this is the first opportunity for your students to work together, their understanding of how work groups need to operate in math class may be fragile at best. If a particular group is having difficulties, do step in and try to problem solve with the students by asking them to reflect on their behavior, rather than offering solutions, as in the following:

- Why is this task becoming so difficult for your group?
- What is it that you are being asked to do? What is your goal?
- Is there another way to begin the task?
- Can you break the task down into smaller components? How could you implement that with each other?
- How can everyone have a chance to contribute to the completion of the task?
- What can you do if you have a question? Posting small-group rules (see page 13) in your classroom can give the group access to possible solutions for that issue.
- How will you know when you have finished and are ready to share?

Offering time constraints may be helpful in keeping students focused on completion of the task. Calling the class together for a quick check-in after about fifteen minutes of work can give you the opportunity to do so.

Guiding questions such as the following can help students assess their group's progress:

- Where are you in the data collection?
- Have you decided on a plan for representing the data?
- Have you begun to make some generalizations about the names of your classmates?
- How much more time do you think you will need to finish the investigation?

Given the responses to the previous questions, offer a time constraint to the class such as, "You have twenty minutes to finish your investigation and written work. At that time we will get together and share our findings. I will call you together at nine thirty."

It is extremely important to circulate through the class as the students are working on this initial investigation. The personalities of your students begin to make themselves known, as do their mathematical reasoning strengths and needs. Who plows forward and who holds back? Who offers leadership and who prefers to follow? Who speaks and who listens? Who cooperates and who resists? Each classroom is a community of learners. Communities are defined, in part, by how children relate and interact with each other (Hiebert et al. 1997). As we guide and facilitate the communication and mathematical learning of the school year, we always need to be aware of the personal and social gifts and nuances of our students as well as their mathematical abilities.

When I sense that all groups are close to completing their written work, I often give them a two-minute warning. When I call the time, I ask students to clean up their areas, be ready to share their presentation with the class, and be prepared to focus on a whole-class discussion. This preparation for processing time quickly becomes routine when the class carries out investigations. The students soon realize that completing the investigation is only part of the task; the other no-less-important part is the discussion and sharing of ideas that will follow.

Mathematical talk can support, promote, and develop student learning both directly and indirectly (Chapin, O'Connor, and Anderson 2009). Classroom discourse can provide students with direct access to ideas, relationships, and the connections found between them, as well as with strategies, procedures, and conjectures. Classroom discussions can also support student learning indirectly through building a social environment—a community of learners—that supports and encourages mathematical learning. Whole-group discussions offer students opportunities to treat each other with respect in thinking, conjecturing, exploring, and sharing mathematical ideas.

I ask each group to share their findings and generalizations about typical name lengths with the class. Once a group has presented, their poster is posted on the whiteboard for future reference. Once all the groups have presented, I ask my favorite question: "What do you notice?" The open-endedness of this question is completely deliberate—and can move the class in surprising directions. Asking students to share their observations with a partner prior to opening up the discussion to the whole group will give all students a chance to talk and listen. Once I call the group together, the class shares the following three observations:

- No one uses nicknames in our class—except Mrs. Schuster!
- It's a good thing we didn't use last names because our last names are so much longer than our first names—and hard to spell!
- Only two groups represented their data in a bar graph (something unexpected)!

As a class member shares an observation, I ask the class if anyone else has something to add to that particular observation. I ask the students to speak to each other rather than to me: "If you are adding on to Jared's and Nick's observations, please speak directly to Jared and Nick." This talk move is intentional and one that may need to be modeled. Reminding students to address each other and respond to each other respectfully is necessary if classroom conversations have not been part of your students' previous mathematical experiences.

Keeping in mind the objective of this lesson can help to move the conversation forward. As the class discusses, agrees on, and adds on to generalizations, students will be better able to see commonalities in their thinking and with others in their new learning community. (See Figure 2–1.)

FIGURE 2–1
Caroline, Ian, and Seth's Collected and Generalized Name Data.

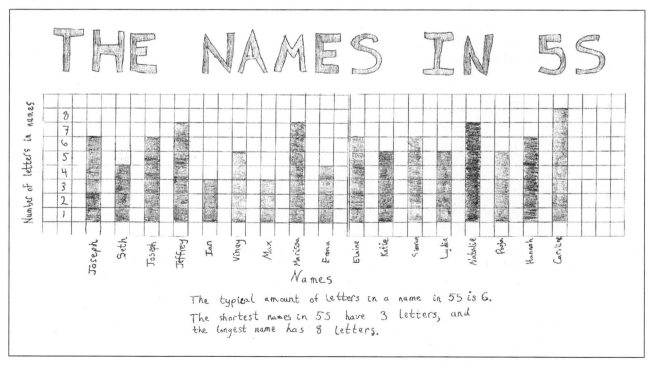

The term *typical* may continue to be problematic for some students. Many students will have had some experiences with data analysis from previous grades, so a discussion of the *median* and *mode* of a data set may help establish some consensus about the term *typical*. Organizing the data set into an organized list can help to identify the median as well as the mode. If we agreed that the typical name length was determined by the median of this data set, what might the name of a new class member be? If we agreed that the typical name length was determined by our mode, would that name of the new class member be the same? If not, what might it be now? The *mean* name length of the data set, however, can often be elusive. Many students may use the word *average* freely without really understanding that an average can represent the median, mode, or mean. The following minilesson can help establish some understanding of the mean.

I distribute a tub of linking cubes to each table group. Then I ask students to link together the number of cubes that corresponds to the number of letters in their first name, and I ask them to line up in an organized manner. We can easily identify where the median name falls in the class by counting off. The physical manipulation of the data offers an opportunity to discuss what will need to happen when that middle value falls between two values, as will be the case when there is an even number in the sampling. Identifying the mode is also helpful, especially if there are several even numbers.

Once we have discussed the median and mode, we can turn our attention to the mean. A question such as, "If everybody had the same name length, how long would that name length be?" can begin the distribution process. If no one offers the suggestion to share cubes, I can ask the student with the minimum number and the student with the maximum number how they can balance their letter amounts. Students will quickly realize that the student with the maximum value can share a few cubes with the student with the minimum value in order to even out the name lengths. So students talk among themselves as they share in and even out the letter amounts. This can be a little chaotic, but the chaos can support the process—honest! In some years this process becomes much like the trading game of Pit, where students are shouting their name lengths so that others can know what they have to offer or need.

Once we agree on a mean name length, posing a question such as, "If a new student walked into our class right now, what might their name be?" can give closure to the activity and elicit some creative thinking. Asking how and where a proposed name would fit into the data set will help keep the conversation focused on the purpose of the investigation . . . or not. Ava offered that a "Robert" could walk through the door. When I questioned her about why Robert, she quickly responded. My expectation was that she would explain that Robert had six letters in his name, which was our agreed-upon typical name length. I should have known to expect the other-than-expected when it came to the creative responses so often offered by Ava. "Well . . . ," she began, "every class I have ever been in up until this year has always had at least one Robert in it—so why not this one?"

NCTM Connection

Strand: Number and Operations

Focus: Find factors of the numbers 1 to 30; explore the relationship among factors, divisors, and multiples.

Context: The Factor Game

REPRODUCIBLE 2.1
The Factor Game
Directions

REPRODUCIBLE 2.2
The Factor Game
Game Board for 30

REPRODUCIBLE 2.3
The Factor Game
Game Board for 49

The Factor Game

Duration: 2–3 Class Periods and Played Throughout the Unit or Year

Playing the *Factor Game* provides an engaging format in which students can become familiar with the factors of numbers from two to thirty by playing a two-person board game. This investigation offers students opportunities to:

- review multiplication and division facts
- relate dividing and finding factors of numbers
- classify numbers as prime or composite
- recognize that some numbers are rich in factors while others have few
- recognize that some products are the result of more than one factor pair
- identify and articulate the relationship between factors and multiples

Materials

- *Factor Game* directions (see Reproducible 2.1)
- *Factor Game* game boards, 1 overhead copy and 1 copy per pair of students (see Reproducibles 2.2 and 2.3)
- colored pencils, 1 color per player

Vocabulary

factor, factor pair, multiple, product

Games can be an important instructional tool in every mathematics classroom. Not only are games engaging, motivating, and challenging for students but they also contain and support mathematical knowledge and help students to further develop procedural and reasoning skills. Playing games helps students deepen their mathematical understandings and fine-tune skills and strategic thinking. In playing the *Factor Game*, each player chooses a number while the other player finds the sum of the available factors of that number.

While playing this wonderfully simple and effective game, students explore the factors of numbers from two through thirty as well as their properties. Students quickly realize that prime numbers are poor choices after the first move of the game, although they may not be able to define the numbers as such . . . yet. They realize that larger numbers are not necessarily the best choices. They learn that some numbers are deadly choices because they have so many factors. They understand that some odd numbers are good choices and that even numbers can be poor choices. But above all, students learn that the ability to factor a number relates to their understanding of multiplication and division.

My method of introducing the *Factor Game* to my class is not standard. Many texts suggest that you discuss the term *factor* and how it relates to this game. Although this works, I wondered if the students could identify the relationships between the numbers chosen and the points scored without telling them the objective of the game, which would allow *them* to identify the game's purpose. Several years ago I purposefully introduced the game on the overhead with no instructions other than we would be keeping score and the team with the most points would "win." The title of the game board was available to students, but they paid no attention to it. I constructed a T-chart on the board to keep track of the points scored.

Mrs. S.	Fifth graders
29	1

I told students that I would go first . . . after all, I was the teacher! I told them that I was choosing 29 and earned those 29 points. I crossed 29 off on the game board. Then I told them that they would receive 1 point as the result of my choice and crossed off 1. Now it was their turn to choose.

The class worked together to choose a number—and invariably chose 30. After all, it was the largest number on the board! I crossed off 30 and posted it on their side of the T-chart while keeping a running total. The class now had 31 points. I deliberately thought out loud as I calculated my points. "Let's see—I get six and five, two and fifteen, oh yeah, and three and ten. That gives me a total of forty-one points!" Tortured cries came from the class. As I was thinking out loud, the students were buzzing about how I was earning my points—and how they were losing theirs!

I then chose 25—knowing that the students had to earn points for at least one factor in order for the move to be "legal." So I posted 25 and asked the class for their choice. They broke out in animated mathematical conversation. Some students were aware of some of the rules of the game at this point. They realized that when one player chose a number, the other player earned points related to the numbers multiplied together to get that particular number.

The language of *factors*, *multiples*, and *products* was not yet being used, but that was fine at this point in the game. When I first began to play the game in this manner, I was astounded at the inefficiency of the discussion accompanying the game without the availability of this terminology. What a great lesson to learn about the power of mathematical language!

As we played one or two more rounds, I began to share a few of the rules—the first being that when you choose a number, the other player must be able to earn points. If the other player can earn no points from your choice, you lose your turn. The language of *prime* and *composite* had not yet been introduced, but students quickly learned that they needed to stay away from prime numbers after that first move because they could not earn any on the resulting move.

After several rounds, I introduced language that would be helpful as students discussed potential moves. As words were discussed, I wrote them on the board for accessibility. The class was familiar with the term *product*, but not at ease with its application in their casual mathematical conversations. Walk-by interventions, as I call them, are crucial early in the school year. If I hear students playing and referring to "answers" in multiplication problems, a hand on the shoulder and a reminder to use the work *product* helps to focus the mathematical conversation, making it more efficient and concise. The game title identified the new term *factor* and its meaning in reference to the game being played. You can also introduce *multiple,* but be prepared for its misuse. Because of the newness of the language, many fifth graders will interchange *factor* and *multiple*. They will often use *factor* correctly in isolation, but run into difficulty when asked to construct a sentence with both *factor* and *multiple*. (Refer to the "Reading, Writing, and Vocabulary" section of this chapter for further discussion of the scaffolding for appropriate use of these terms.)

An entire class period was devoted to this introduction of the *Factor Game*. I was delighted with the mathematical observations, insights, and discussions that occurred within this format. The language of *factors*, *multiples*, and *products* was immediately meaningful because it supported students as they discussed and analyzed their number choices. They also learned an important lesson about the importance of implementing appropriate mathematical language. Kira reminded us several times that it was just plain easier to use the word *product* than the phrase "the answer to a multiplication problem."

Once the initial games are played, students can set off with partners to play a game or two on their own. As students play the game, circulate through the room making note of interesting strategies. You may also want to note who continues to struggle with the recall of their basic multiplication facts. A lack of fluency with the multiplication tables can make playing this game difficult and tedious. As you move around the room, you may wish to visit with some of the pairs and ask them the following questions:

- Is it better to have the first move when you start the game? Why?
- What is the best first move? Why?

- What is the worst first move?
- How do you know when the game is over?
- How do you know when you have found all the factors of a number?

Pulling the class together for a processing session is important and necessary after students have had the opportunity to play several rounds of the game. Processing the game gives mathematical meaning to the activity. Students need to realize that although games can be great fun, as this one certainly is, good mathematical games also have purpose.

Crafting, asking, and answering good questions can further the mathematical understanding of just about any activity. Good questions can set the stage for meaningful classroom discussion and learning. Students are no longer passive receivers of information when they are asked questions that deepen and challenge their mathematical understandings and convictions. Good questions

- help students make sense of the mathematics;
- are open-ended, whether in answer or approach;
- empower students to unravel their misconceptions;
- not only require the application of facts and procedures, but encourage children to make connections and generalizations;
- are accessible to all students in their language; and
- lead children to wonder more about a topic (Schuster and Anderson 2005).

Questions such as those that follow can help to scaffold and articulate new understandings that have come about as a result of playing the *Factor Game*. Processing questions in a whole-class format also gives you the opportunity to implement talk moves. Asking students to restate classmates' ideas or strategies can help to keep them focused on the mathematics of the game, while asking them to add on to others' ideas can deepen insights and observations. You can help to establish respectful discourse by asking for agreement or disagreement. Revoicing can emphasize important mathematics, insights, or strategies:

- Is it better to go first or second? Why?
- What is the best first move?
- What is the worst first move? Why?
- How do you know when you have found all the factors of a number?
- How do you know when the game is over?
- Is there a way to finish the game with all the numbers circled on the game board?

- What was your strategy for choosing numbers?
- After the first round, what types of numbers did you stay away from? Why?

You can now have follow-up lessons that draw upon the understandings constructed from the *Factor Game*. Lessons exploring prime and composite numbers, odd and even numbers, and square numbers take on greater meaning because of the students' exposure to and application of these concepts while playing the *Factor Game*. My class explores perfect, abundant, and deficient numbers as well because of the connections they can make to number choices on the *Factor Game* game board. Exploring and applying divisibility rules also now have a place and purpose in the curriculum. Being mathematically proficient goes far beyond being able to compute accurately and proficiently. It involves understanding and applying various relationships, properties, and procedures associated with number concepts (Chapin and Johnson 2006). The *Factor Game* and the lessons that it subsequently supports can do just that.

NCTM Connection

Strand: Number and Operations

Focus: Identify an array's dimensions as the factors of that product; recognize that factors come in pairs.

Context: Factor Pairs and Arrays

Factor Pairs and Arrays: Introduction to Factoring

Duration: 3–4 Class Periods

Rectangular arrays can help to scaffold multiplicative understandings as students work to make sense of area models of multiplication. Arrays are useful in making the relationship between products (area) and factors (dimensions) visible and accessible. Conventional factorization representation is explored further in the "Calculation Routines and Practices" section of this chapter. This investigation offers students opportunities to

- construct and make sense of area models of multiplication (arrays);
- identify the dimensions of an array as that product's factors;
- recognize that factors come in pairs;
- develop strategies for finding the factors of a given number;
- compare and contrast numbers based on properties such as odd, even, prime, composite, and square;
- explore the use of Venn diagrams to represent number classifications;
- articulate and apply the commutative and identity properties of multiplication; and
- apply reasoning related to number relationships in problem-solving situations.

Materials

- webbing template (see Reproducible 2.4)
- centimeter grid paper (see Reproducible 2.5)
- Venn diagram templates (see Reproducibles 2.6 and 2.7)
- color tiles
- colored construction paper for charting arrays (in a single color; blue works well)
- colored construction paper for squares: red 3-inch squares for composite numbers, yellow 3-inch squares for prime numbers, and 1 white square for the number one
- chart paper
- math notebooks or graph paper
- glue sticks

Prior to the Lesson

The red, yellow, and white squares will need to be cut and marked. If you are planning to represent the numbers one to thirty, each composite number will need to be marked on the red squares, the prime numbers on the yellow squares, and the number one marked on the white square. House the cards in a paper bag or bin until their use is required so that the students can randomly select the numbers. Any range of numbers can be selected: one to forty works just as well—just make sure that you have the wall space to post each array chart.

Vocabulary

array, composite number, consecutive, dimensions, divisible by, divisor, factor, factor pair, multiple, product, proper factor, prime number, square number, Venn diagram

This lesson is introduced to the class with a purpose and direction. Once students are familiar with the *Factor Game*, they will have developed some beginning understanding of factors. Starting the lesson with a "What do we know about factors?" whole-class discussion can set the stage for several investigations about factors. Posting the question on chart paper and scripting students' responses will document the understanding of the class at that point in time. You can also use a webbing activity. Posting the initial responses in one color, and then returning at the end of the investigations to modify and add new understandings in another color can make a nice representation of what the students have learned. (See Figure 2–2; see also Reproducible 2.4.)

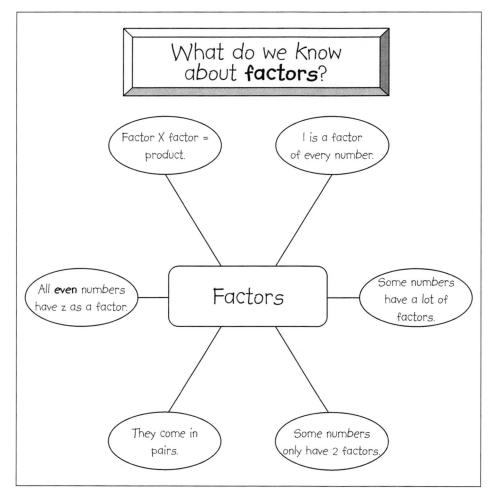

FIGURE 2–2
What Do We Know About Factors? Web.

Distribute color tiles to each table. I love introducing my dog, Maxx, to the class. He appears in many word problems and class investigations throughout the year. Although he is entirely loveable and somewhat of a mess—as all Siberian Huskies are—Maxx also can offer engaging contexts for mathematical investigations! I introduce my dilemma to the class: I need to build a dog pen for Maxx. Electric fences do not work well for Huskies, and he loves being outside in the snowy weather (which we seem to have forever in New England!). I ask students to work in pairs and to make as many rectangular dog pens as they can for Maxx out of twelve tiles.

Before students start making dog pens, we have a discussion about how the dog pens are represented. Even this early in the school year, students quickly realize that mathematical thinking needs to be documented in some way. Because students have had previous experiences with arrays and immediately recognize this as an array investigation, they suggest representing the pens with multiplication number models. Rebecca was quick to remind the class that the products will all be twelve because we are dealing with twelve tiles.

I ask students to make all the dog pens that they can with these twelve tiles. They should be able to do this in a relatively short period of time. As with most math investigations, the students will need some time for processing the task.

I quickly call the class back together to process the arrays and number models. As students offer a possible dog pen configuration, I post it on the whiteboard. Before too long the question of using turnaround facts comes up. Are 3 × 4 and 4 × 3 the same pen?

In my classroom, I treat the turnaround facts as separate arrays—and both arrays need to be represented. Even though their factors and their products are the same, their orientations are not. Changing the context can help model the possible difference between the two facts. Is having three bags with four marbles in each bag the same as having four bags with three marbles in each? Not really, the students agree. You still have twelve marbles, but they are not "packaged" in the same way. We agree as a class to include the turnaround facts of twelve.

Including the turnaround facts also gives the class an opportunity to discuss the commutativity of multiplication . . . and addition. We often assume that our fifth graders understand the property of commutativity, but whether they can articulate it becomes the bigger question. Asking students to generalize about turnaround facts may be helpful at this point in the discussion. A number sentence may also help to make the mathematics visible and accessible:

$$4 \times 3 = 3 \times 4$$

The question "Is this true for *all* multiplication facts?" can move students to a discussion not only about multiplication, but also to a conversation about addition, division, and subtraction, as well. "Order matters" becomes the mantra for both subtraction and division. This becomes the first of many conversations about retaining and using the mathematics they have learned from the earlier grades. They might already know about turnaround facts from first or second grade. In the fifth grade, however, it is increasingly important for them to make generalizations about numbers and *how* and *why* they "work." It is the *how* and *why* thinking that makes our work mathematically important in the fifth grade.

I post a list of all of Maxx's possible dog pens on the board:

3×4
4×3
2×6
6×2
1×12
12×1

An interesting conversation about the 1×12 or 12×1 pen comes up each year, which makes this context a particularly meaningful and useful one. Does a 1×12 or a 12×1 dog pen make sense? For a Husky, yes! They love to pace—and a long narrow dog pen is actually perfect for Maxx.

My favorite question for beginning a class discussion has become "What do you notice?" Its simplicity offers accessibility to the mathematics and participation in the discussion for the entire class. As students offer observations, I encourage them to be clear in their language and word choice. The introduction of the words *factor* and *product* in their observations helps students to integrate these new words into their existing mathematical vocabulary. Once again students recognize that each factor has a partner. Asking them to represent each array with its dimensions on graph paper will help them to visualize and access the relationship between the dimensions of an array and the factors of that product. (See Figure 2–3.)

FIGURE 2–3
Marissa's Arrays and Dimensions of Twelve Tiles.

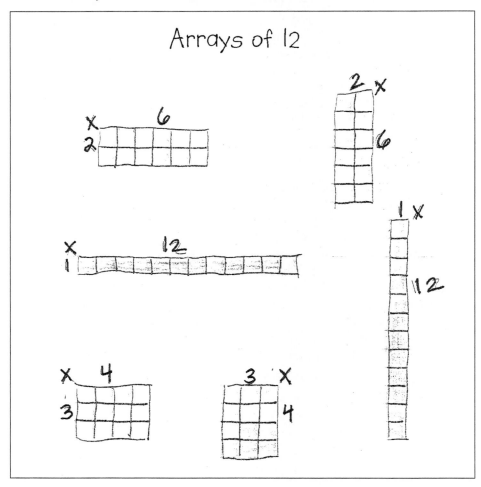

Making references to the *Factor Game* as you discuss factors and multiples can offer students a model from which to think about factors of numbers from one to thirty. Having a *Factor Game* game board available for students to reference can support the mathematical talk that can accompany questions such as:

- While playing the *Factor Game*, did you find numbers that did not have many factors? What were those numbers? What were their factor pairs?

- Did you come across numbers that had a lot of factor pairs? What were those numbers? What were their factor pairs?

- What can you tell me about the number one?

- After the first move in the *Factor Game*, did you find numbers that should not be chosen? Why did you stay away from those numbers?

Now you can give the class their next task. Each student will randomly choose a number from one to thirty (or one to forty) to represent on a sheet of construction paper, using the number's arrays and dimensions of the arrays. Prior to the lesson, print the numbers on yellow (primes) or red (composites) construction paper squares and house them in a paper bag from which students will choose. *Students will include turnaround facts and their arrays on the posters.* My reason for including the turnaround facts is the eventual generalization that students can make about the number of arrays of a given number being equal to the number of factors of that same number.

Factor Pairs of 12

3×4
4×3
2×6
6×2
1×12
12×1

Factors of 12
1, 2, 3, 4, 6, 12

The children will color and cut out each array for their given number using centimeter grid paper (see Reproducible 2.5). I prefer to use crayons for this particular activity because I laminate each poster and then post it in the classroom. Students mount the number and its arrays on the construction paper, and then they write the dimensions of each array in magic marker. The posters stay up not only for the remainder of this unit, but for the entire year as well. Students learn to refer to these representations for much of their work throughout the year. The use of factors becomes

▶ REPRODUCIBLE 2.5
Centimeter Grid
Paper

connected and accessible to other work we do throughout the remainder of the year—in particular our later work with fractions.

You will need to make a conscious decision about posting the conventional factorization on the poster. Some curricula suggest this, while some do not. I prefer *not* to have the factorization posted. The number of arrays on a poster can help students determine quickly whether they have the correct number of factors for a given number. If they have the need to access a particular factor pair, then they need to reference the array and its posted dimensions, which I much prefer to simply referencing the numerical factorization. (See Figure 2–4.)

TEACHER-TO-TEACHER TALK ■ **About the Posting of Student Work** ■ I do not have too much wall space in my classroom, but that was a trade-off I was willing to make when my classroom was moved into our new math and science wing. I have a bank of windows that overlooks a soccer field and windows on either side of my whiteboard because I have an end room. It is filled with natural light and airy even on the dreariest of February days. But because of all of the windows, I have limited wall space and have learned to be very selective about what I post in my classroom. These array posters are displayed above and below my whiteboard and stay up all year. When I first began implementing this activity, the posters went up and then came down when the next unit began. Several years ago, one of my students wanted to reference what we did in the first months of school to our work with fractions. "I could show you what I mean (about common factors) if only those posters were still up . . . ," Diana commented. Hmmm . . . good point! Keeping the posters up all year helps me to help students make those important connections between factors and just about everything they do in the fifth grade! Students refer to the array posters when dividing, finding common factors, simplifying fractions, making number riddles, or when 8×7 becomes elusive yet again. We teach our fifth graders to reference primary sources in social studies and to reference texts when answering questions in reading. Our students need to know when and how to do the same in their study of mathematics. These posters become an important reference for our yearlong study of mathematics—as do the students' texts and math notebooks. Encouraging our students to reference their materials is just is not enough, however. We need to model how this can be done. They need to see us referencing the array posters, checking something out in the text, or referring to something we did in class last week that is notated in their math notebooks. Reference materials are important and meaningful even in math class. They allow us to access information and to make meaningful connections among concepts, procedures, and the language of mathematics.

Once students begin pulling their numbers from the paper bag, be prepared for the groans of the tortured and cheers of the victorious. When Matthew pulled out 24, he just about fell off his chair. "OK—who is going to help me?" he called out. "There is no way I can get all those arrays done by myself!" Matthew knew from playing the *Factor Game* that 24 had a plethora of factors. Brad cheered when he pulled out 29, his new favorite number. "I always win the *Factor Game* with this first move!" Brad much preferred to make two arrays rather than eight. Those students who pull

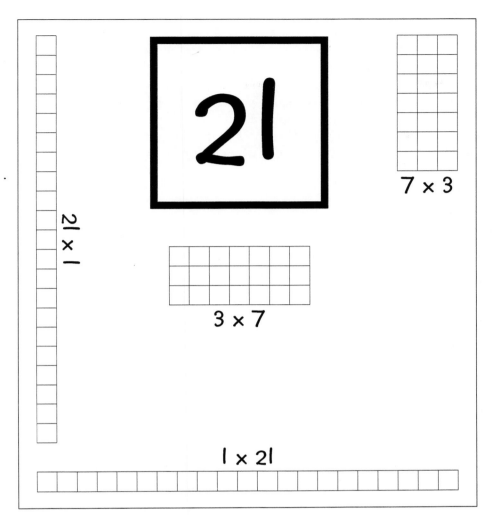

FIGURE 2–4
Pooja's Representations of 21.

prime numbers are encouraged to help out those who have composite numbers with many factors after they are finished with their own posters. It is rewarding and validating to observe students access their understanding of factors from playing the *Factor Game*. They know which numbers have many factors and which numbers have few. They know which numbers have an even number of arrays and which numbers have odd—even though they may not understand why . . . yet. Your students know a lot; remind them of that!

Follow-Up Lessons

You can and should implement follow-up lessons, such as the following, once the array posters have been completed in order to process the mathematics exposed by the activity.

Sorting

Posting the array cards on the whiteboard with tape or magnets prior to displaying them more permanently on the wall can allow the students to sort the numbers by common properties. Asking students to work in table groups to identify possible sorts of the array cards can help them focus on the properties of the represented numbers. Students may opt to sort the numbers in the following ways. You will need to ask processing questions after every sort to identify the organizing principle and to highlight the mathematical importance of these number characteristics.

Odds and Evens

- How do you know when a number is even? (They always have a two-by-something array.)
- How do you know when a number is odd? (They never have a two-by-something array).
- What do you notice about the factors of all the even numbers? (Two is a factor of every even number.)

Primes and Composites

- How do you know when a number is prime? (It only has two factors or arrays.)
- What numbers between one and thirty are prime?
- Which pairs of consecutive prime numbers differ by exactly 2? (3 and 5, 11 and 13, 17 and 19. These pairs are called *twin primes*.)
- How do you know when a number is composite? (It has more than two factors or arrays.)
- Can even numbers be prime? Why does this make sense? (Two is the only even prime number. All other even numbers have two as a factor, which makes them composite.)

Square Numbers and Nonsquare Numbers

- Which numbers have an odd number of factors? Why? (Square numbers—their squared factors are only listed once, which makes their total number of factors odd.)
- Which numbers have an even number of factors? Why? (Nonsquare numbers have factors paired with other factors—*factor pairs*.)

The Number One and All the Other Numbers

- How many arrays does the number one have? Why is this significant? (The number one has only one array—a 1 × 1. It does not have a turnaround fact, which does make it a square number, but neither a prime nor a composite number.)

■ What do you notice about the number one and all the other numbers? (Every number has one as a factor.)

Venn Diagrams

Venn diagrams can help students to sort, record, and communicate characteristics of various number classifications. You can introduce this activity in a *Guess My Rule* framework. Prior to the sorting activity, generate a class list of the possible sorts that can be made from the array cards. The following list can be posted on the board and in math notebooks for further reference. You may wish to add a few sorts that the students overlook. I like adding in the "numbers with six as a factor" to further conversations about divisibility.

■ odd numbers

■ even numbers

■ numbers with two as a factor

■ numbers with only two arrays or factor pairs

■ numbers with five as a factor

■ prime numbers

■ composite numbers

■ square numbers

■ numbers with three or more arrays or factor pairs

■ numbers with three as a factor

■ numbers with six as a factor

Although you can draw Venn diagrams on the board, I prefer to use multiple blank two- and three-circle Venn diagram templates (see Reproducibles 2.6 and 2.7) prepared as overheads. As conversations break out about sorting and properties, you can easily reference the Venn diagrams. It continues to be important for students this age to have visual or concrete anchors from which to speak and think. I begin to sort various numbers according to two sorts unknown to the students. As I place the numbers in various areas of the Venn, I ask the students to identify and justify my sort. Remember to include a few numbers that do not fit either sort so that they can be placed outside of the Venn. (See Figure 2–5.)

When the class reaches consensus about the sort, ask for other numbers that can be placed in or outside of the Venn and ask why they belong where they do. You can develop various worksheets such as the ones in Figure 2–6 that ask the students to sort numbers or to identify the sorts. Including both types of sorts will help students develop flexibility in identifying and articulating number characteristics.

▶ REPRODUCIBLE 2.6
Two-Circle Venn
Diagram Template

REPRODUCIBLE 2.7
Three-Circle Venn
Diagram Template

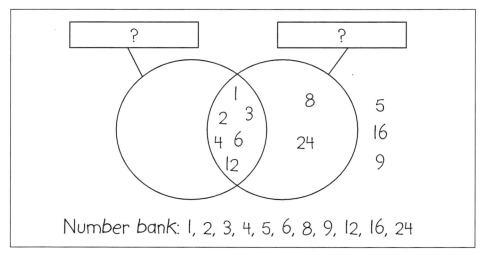

FIGURE 2–5
Sample Venn with Sorting Criteria Unknown to Students.

FIGURE 2–6
Examples of Sorting by Number and Sorting by Property.

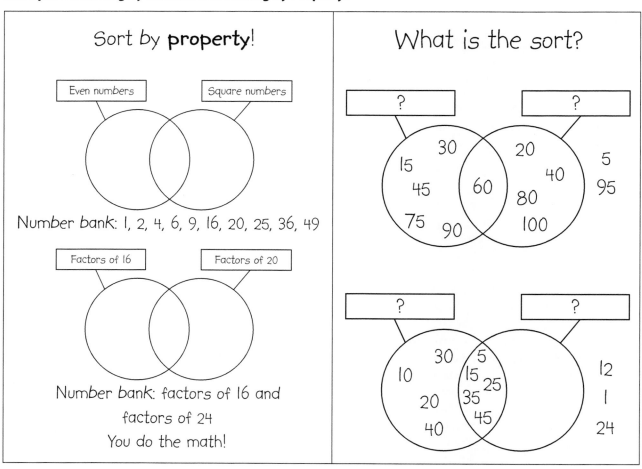

Number Classification Explorations

Duration: 3–4 Class Periods

You will need additional investigations to offer students the opportunities to classify numbers by their characteristics. As students move through the upper-elementary grades, it becomes increasingly important for them to be able to generalize about sets of numbers. These investigations offer students additional opportunities to

- compare and contrast numbers based on characteristics such as odd, even, prime, composite, and square;
- determine where a sum is even or odd based on its factors;
- determine where a product is even or odd based on its factors;
- identify numbers as perfect, abundant, or deficient based on the sum of their proper factors; and
- apply reasoning related to number relationships in problem-solving situations.

Materials

- *Fair Game 2* directions and materials (see Reproducible 2.8)
- *Sieve of Eratosthenes* directions and template (see Reproducibles 2.9 and 2.10)

Vocabulary

abundant number, addends, composite, conjecture, deficient number, even, factors, multiples, odd, perfect number, prime, product, proper factors, square number, sum

As students move into the upper-elementary grades, they are beginning to understand that ideas about mathematics and classifications of numbers can be generalized. They are also learning how to formulate and articulate those generalizations as they make conjectures while reasoning about mathematical concepts and procedures. Encouraging, supporting, and modeling the development and articulation of conjectures become increasingly important in our teaching routines and practices in the fifth grade. Investigations that ask students to justify classifications of numbers can offer contexts in which fifth graders can generalize and support their thinking.

Classifying numbers by certain characteristics helps students identify number patterns. The more students know and can articulate about a set of numbers, the more powerful they are in making sense of numerical situations (Chapin and Johnson 2006, 9). Fifth graders have been classifying numbers as odd or even since the first grade. Simply identifying a number as odd or even is no longer enough in the world of fifth-grade mathematics. We need to offer experiences to our students in which

► REPRODUCIBLE 2.8
Fair Game 2
Directions

REPRODUCIBLE 2.9
The Sieve of
Eratosthenes
Directions

REPRODUCIBLE 2.10
The Sieve of
Eratosthenes
Template

they can make sense of and generalize the "evenness" and "oddness" of numbers.

NCTM Connection

Strand: Number and Operations

Focus: Investigate odd and even sums and products based upon their respective addends and factors.

Context: Fair Game 2

REPRODUCIBLE 2.8 ◄
Fair Game 2

Fair Game 2

Fair Game 2 (Burns 2007) (see Reproducible 2.8) offers a game context in which students can make conjectures and generalizations about the result of operations on odd and even numbers. The game asks students to hypothesize and test whether a sum is odd or even based on its addends and whether this game is fair or unfair based on the evenness or oddness of the rolled sums. The game then moves to multiplication and the effect of the product based on the evenness or oddness of the factors.

The beauty of *Fair Game 2* is that it offers a context within which students can write and chart their thinking. The directions for *Fair Game 2* can be posted on chart paper for class reference throughout the game and then saved for future years' use. Once you have presented the directions for the game, you can ask students to make predictions in their math notebooks about the potential fairness of each game. (See Figure 2–7.) You may need to discuss what constitutes a *fair* game—one that offers an equal chance of winning or losing—even though most fifth graders will assume that fair games are those in which they themselves win more often than not! Offering sentence starters such as the following can help those students who find it difficult to self-start when given a writing task.

Playing Fair Game 2 *with addition will be fair or unfair because . . .*

Playing Fair Game 2 *with multiplication will be fair or unfair because . . .*

Once partners have been assigned or chosen, the public sharing of predictions between partners can happen prior to playing the game. Allow students to stand by their misconceptions—at least initially! Many will make the assumption that if the game for addition is fair (or not), the game for

FIGURE 2–7
Jake's Predictions About the Outcomes of *Fair Game 2*.

> Prediction: Is fair game 2 fair with addition?
>
> I think the game isn't fair because I think there are more ways to get an even sum then an odd sum.
>
> Fair game 2 with multiplication
>
> Prediction: Will fair game 2 be fair w/ multiplication?
>
> I think it will be fair with multiplication because addition and multiplication are pretty similar.

multiplication will follow suit. You may notice that students will tend to focus on the outcome of the operation, rather than the components—the addends or factors. This misconception helps to differentiate the work our fifth graders have done in previous years on odds and evens with the present. The evenness or oddness of the addends or factors determines the evenness or oddness of the respective sum or product—not the other way around! This task and game pushes students to look beyond the solution and what they already might think they know about even and odd numbers.

You will need to make an instructional decision about how prescriptive to be in the format of charting written work. Written documentation of the sums and products of number pairs will be important as students work to prove or disprove their conjectures. Their written work can serve as mathematical proof for their generalizations. I explain this process to my students. I want them to know that charting games can be important and will serve a purpose when we later process the investigation. And yes, neatness and organization matter! If we want to develop organized and logical thinking (and we do), we need to establish organized and logical written routines. I tend to be quite prescriptive in these early weeks of school and try to offer varied models that make sense given the task at hand. As the year progresses, students will then have a range of charting options from which they can choose based on the investigation.

You can hold a class discussion about the task and what we are being asked to investigate. Asking students to restate the objective of the investigation several times during the conversation will keep the mathematics of the task visible and available. We will be rolling dice and identifying whether the sum or product is odd or even—and then we need to determine if the game is fair or unfair based on the outcomes of the rolls. So how best can we chart the game and the outcomes? A multicolumned T-chart works well for this particular game. If students do not come up with this option, I present, the following table to the class:

ADDITION

Number Model	Sum	Player A (even sum)	Player B (odd sum)

Although you can chart both players' data in one table, both players are expected to track the game in their own notebooks. (See Figure 2–8.) Not only do math notebooks document what goes on in class each day, but they can also serve as a reference and offer models for later investigations and tasks.

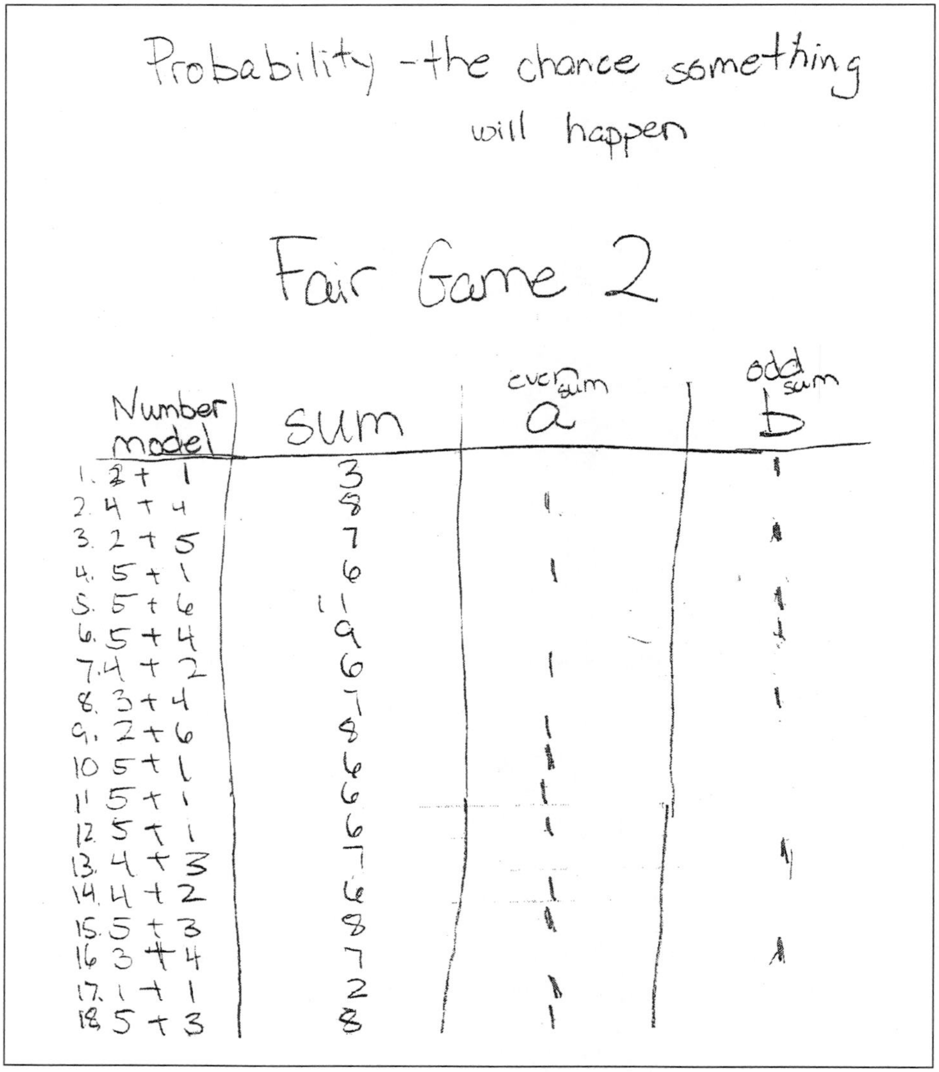

Probability – the chance something will happen

Fair Game 2

Number model	sum	even sum a	odd sum b
1. 2 + 1	3		l
2. 4 + 4	8	l	
3. 2 + 5	7		l
4. 5 + 1	6	l	
5. 5 + 6	11		l
6. 5 + 4	9		l
7. 4 + 2	6	l	
8. 3 + 4	7		l
9. 2 + 6	8	l	
10. 5 + 1	6	l	
11. 5 + 1	6	l	
12. 5 + 1	6	l	
13. 4 + 3	7		l
14. 4 + 2	6	l	
15. 5 + 3	8	l	
16. 3 + 4	7		l
17. 1 + 1	2	l	
18. 5 + 3	8	l	

FIGURE 2–8
Norah's Game Data.

Once students have completed *Fair Game 2* played with addition, I ask them to talk with their neighbor about the fairness of the game. Was it fair? Did Player A and Player B have an equal chance of winning? How do you know? Did your data support your conjecture? Be aware that students have not had much opportunity to practice their articulation skills since this is still early in the school year. Their conversations might be short and void of much, if any, mathematical proof. Modeling such a conversation with a pair of students once all the addition games have been played will offer them an opportunity to observe a meaningful mathematical conversation.

TEACHER-TO-TEACHER TALK ■ **About Our Students' Observations** ■ There is something very good about growing old in this noble profession. It is good that we acquire wisdom. Wisdom does, in fact, accompany years of good learning and teaching. As teachers, we are constantly reminded by the powers that be that our students need to articulate and defend their reasoning in mathematics. In other words, they need to think and act like mathematicians. If these are our goals, then our classrooms need to be communities in which students can observe, practice, and refine the fine art of conjecturing, defending, and justifying. Learning how to develop and support mathematical ideas does not occur in a vacuum. Our students need to observe their teachers making conjectures, wondering out loud, posing questions, justifying results, and developing generalizations. We need to be as actively involved in the mathematical process as the students—perhaps even more so. As the school year progresses, I often hear my students speaking, thinking, and questioning just as I do when they solve problems and play games. They ask each other, "Why do you think that?" or "Could we think about this in another way?" as they solve problems. They ask for mathematical proof and question the answers when the results do not seem to make sense. They learn from watching us—even when we think they are not. Our students become all the wiser when they have engaged and passionate teachers of mathematics. Everyone is the wiser.

Be prepared for students to be animated as the games begin. You will once again need to make decisions about how to address the misconceptions and the disequilibrium that will follow when conjectures are proved to be false. I support allowing students to get a *little* lost in the messiness of their thinking—the operative word here being *little*. I also want to be there, however, to help them make use of what they now know in order to make adjustments to what they thought they knew prior to playing the game.

Many students will assume that the game with multiplication will be as fair as the game with addition. Not so much! As students compare their games and scores, they will begin to see that the addition game is *fairer* than that of multiplication. A minilesson on theoretical probability can help to differentiate what should happen with the game playing with the experimental probability and, what actually did happen.

Asking students about methods in which they can organize the possible sums will engage them in discussing and thinking about the need to represent the theoretical probability of the number of odd and even sums. Because of their previous experiences with addition and multiplication tables, some students may suggest the matrix format. A matrix can help to represent the theoretical probability of rolling odd and even solutions in both games. Because we are playing with two dice, the probability of rolling any sum or product is 1 out of 36 because $6 \times 6 = 36$. But what does that look like in a matrix?

+	1	2	3	4	5	6
1	2	3	4	5	6	7
2	3	4	5	6	7	8
3	4	5	6	7	8	9
4	5	6	7	8	9	10
5	6	7	8	9	10	11
6	7	8	9	10	11	12

This matrix confirms that when playing with addition, the chances of rolling an even number are 18 out of 36—the same as rolling an odd number. An abbreviated matrix such as the following will also prove the even distribution of odd and even sums.

+	Odd	Even
Odd	e	o
Even	o	e

This abbreviated matrix further illustrates the possibility of odd and even sums. The theoretical possibility of rolling an even number is 2 out of 4, and an odd number is 2 out of 4 as well. Therefore, *Fair Game 2* played with addition is a fair game. If students begin to question why their experimental data does not align itself with the theoretical probability, you can have a conversation about the importance of a larger sample size. A greater sample size and more data will push the experimental data closer to the theoretical data. If time permits, you may want to pool the class data and in doing so, examine a greater sample size.

Students may also suggest the use of an organized list, as well as the matrix. If they do not mention it, you may wish to introduce this additional tool as another way to represent the theoretical probability of these two games and other tasks involving two variables—in this case, each of the numbers on two dice. (See Figure 2–9.)

Before the class begins the game with multiplication, offer students the opportunity to independently revise their initial conjecture about the fairness of this new game, allowing them to apply what they now know about addition and probability to what they want to know: Is *Fair Game 2* fair or unfair with multiplication? Be mindful of the importance of revisiting the question posed by the investigation several times as pregame and postgame processing is taking place. Doing so helps to keep the conversation and thinking focused on the mathematics and instruction. If students are

1 + 1 = 2	2 + 1 = 3	3 + 1 = 4	4 + 1 = 5	5 + 1 = 6	6 + 1 = 7
1 + 2 = 3	2 + 2 = 4	3 + 2 = 5	4 + 2 = 6	5 + 2 = 7	6 + 2 = 8
1 + 3 = 4	2 + 3 = 5	3 + 3 = 6	4 + 3 = 7	5 + 3 = 8	6 + 3 = 9
1 + 4 = 5	2 + 4 = 6	3 + 4 = 7	4 + 4 = 8	5 + 4 = 9	6 + 4 = 10
1 + 5 = 6	2 + 5 = 7	3 + 5 = 8	4 + 5 = 9	5 + 5 = 10	6 + 5 = 11
1 + 6 = 7	2 + 6 = 8	3 + 6 = 9	4 + 6 = 10	5 + 6 = 11	6 + 6 = 12

FIGURE 2–9
An Organized List.

going to revise a conjecture, I ask that they label their reworked conjecture as "Revised Conjecture," or something of this sort, in their notebooks. Doing so allows students to document and witness the progression of their thinking, We can and are encouraged to change our minds in the study of mathematics!

You may find varying degrees of sophistication in the revised conjectures. Some students may opt to go straight to the matrix to identify what should happen and some may not. I ask students to share their new conjectures with their partners before they begin their multiplication games. It will be important to remind students to chart their games just as they did with addition. (See Figure 2–10.)

As the games come to a close, you can hold a whole-class discussion to process the games and the mathematics. The class will wholeheartedly agree that *Fair Game 2* played with multiplication is just plain unfair! Offer both matrixes representing the theoretical probability as further proof of both conjectures.

FIGURE 2–10
Max's Charting of *Fair Game 2* with Multiplication.

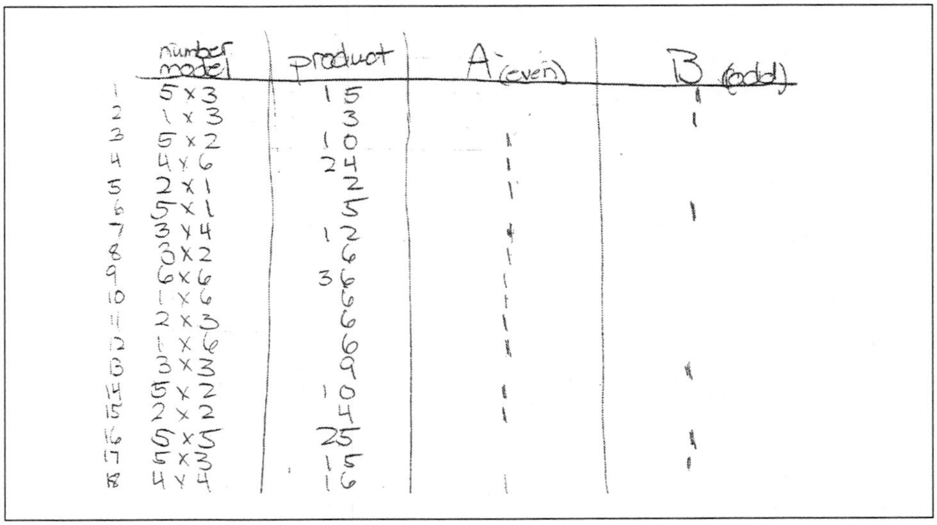

×	1	2	3	4	5	6
1	1	2	3	4	5	6
2	2	4	6	8	10	12
3	3	6	9	12	15	18
4	4	8	12	16	20	24
5	5	10	15	20	25	30
6	6	12	18	24	30	36

x	Odd	Even
Odd	o	e
Even	e	e

Both matrixes represent 27 out of 36, or 3 out of 4, the chance of rolling an even product when playing with two dice. Yikes!

As they process the multiplication version of *Fair Game 2*, students complete matrixes in their notebooks while we talk and compare conjectures and games. This will be a challenge for some—simultaneously writing, thinking, listening, and talking. Taking a few anecdotal notes following the processing may help you assess those students for whom this was a struggle. Some may find it difficult to keep up with the pace of the class. Some may find it hard to keep their work organized on the page. Some may be unsure of the language and find it difficult to make connections to the written work. There is no question that this all becomes a balancing act. As we are modeling the matrixes and facilitating a discussion about the fairness of both games, we need to be mindful of the pace of the class and the level of engagement. We are not only processing the mathematics but we are also creating and nurturing the mathematical culture and community in which we will work for the year.

Posing questions such as the following can help to guide and facilitate the mathematics uncovered by students:

> *Is* Fair Game 2 *with addition fair or unfair? How do you know?*
>
> *Is* Fair Game 2 *with multiplication fair or unfair? How do you know?*
>
> *What could you do to make* Fair Game 2 *fair with multiplication?*

This is actually a very interesting question. Some students may suggest the option of scoring three points when you roll an odd product, instead of one. I have even had classes opt to make a new die. One die will have the digits 1–6. The other die will only have odd numbers: 1, 3, 5, 7, or 9. If time permits, students can play the multiplication game once again with these adjustments—and then check out the results and the fairness of the new games.

- What have we learned about odd and even sums, products, addends, and factors?
- What can you tell me about all even numbers? All odd numbers?

- Why is knowing the evenness or oddness of the addends important when predicting the evenness or oddness of the sum?
- Why is knowing the evenness or oddness of the factors important when predicting the evenness of oddness of the product?

Without Doing the Math ...

- What can you tell me about the sum of 137 and 42?
- Can you tell me if the sum of 137 and 42 is divisible by 2?
- What can you tell me about the product of 45 and 59?
- Can you tell me if the product of 45 and 59 is divisible by 2?

Asking students to complete a lesson summarizer such as "A Ticket to Leave" (Saphier and Haley 1993) can help to give closure to the lesson. I ask students to write something brief in their math notebooks related to the lessons learned from the investigation. Depending on the time available, students can

- share their "ticket" with the class so everyone has the opportunity to hear many ideas generated from the lesson;
- explain their "ticket" to you as they are walking out the door—if they are going to another class; or
- turn in their "ticket" and math notebook to you as they leave class.

You may wish to post a writing prompt on the board, such as: *Name one important thing that you learned today in class* or *Ask one question about today's investigation* to help the process along.

The Sieve of Eratosthenes

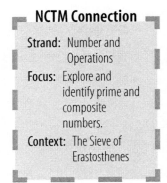

NCTM Connection

Strand: Number and Operations

Focus: Explore and identify prime and composite numbers.

Context: The Sieve of Erastosthenes

For centuries, mathematicians (and fifth graders!) have been interested in prime and composite numbers because they are the building blocks of whole numbers. The Fundamental Theorem of Arithmetic tells us that every whole number greater than one can be renamed as a unique series of prime factors—what we commonly refer to as prime factorization. Around 300 B.C., the Greek mathematician Euclid proved that there is no largest prime number. No matter how large a prime number you find, there will always be prime numbers that are larger. Ever since Euclid's time, people have been searching for more and more prime numbers.

A Greek mathematician by the name of Eratosthenes, who lived around 200 B.C., devised a rather simple method for finding prime numbers. His strategy was based on the premise that every multiple of a number is divisible by that number as well. In other words, a whole number is a factor of every one of its multiples. A hundreds chart is used to identify all the multiples of the factors two through nine. I am not sure if Eratosthenes color-coded his sieve, but it works quite well as we sift out the prime numbers.

REPRODUCIBLE 2.9
The Sieve of
Eratosthenes
Directions

REPRODUCIBLE 2.10
The Sieve of
Eratosthenes
Template

Copies of the sieve, nine different colored pencils, and a highlighter for each student or pair of students are required for this task. It is also helpful to provide extra sieves for each table—mistakes are easy to make! Although this task requires nothing more than skip counting, remind students to stay focused while counting and x-ing. The sieve can get very busy after several sets of multiples are marked.

Refer to Reproducible 2.9 for directions for completing the *Sieve of Eratosthenes*. You don't need to duplicate the directions for students. This task is better implemented orally—with close monitoring. Completing a sample sieve with students either on the overhead or under a document camera is extremely helpful. I have also found it useful for all students to complete the sieve in the same format and colors. I supply plastic sleeves into which students can slide their completed sieves in order to house them in their math notebooks. I encourage my fifth graders to reference their sieves whenever it makes sense to do so. Students use their sieves not only in this particular unit of study, but also when they are multiplying, dividing, or working with fractions. You might wish to be mindful of other opportunities in various lessons throughout the year for which the sieve might be helpful. A little aside such as "Hm . . . I wonder what Eratosthenes would do in this situation?" will not only make students smirk but will also encourage them to refer to their sieves. The *Sieve of Eratosthenes* can be a valuable tool, but only as valuable as students deem it to be! We need to offer guidance to our students and model the use of the sieve when applicable and appropriate.

As you work through the completion of the sieves, take the time to pause and pose the question, "What do you notice?" You may also wish to ask some guiding questions such as the following in order to help students make connections between the task and the targeted mathematical concepts.

- What numbers are "crowded?" What does that tell us about that number?
- What do you know about the number fifty-one? (That it is *not* prime!)
- Are all the multiples of two also multiples of four? Why does that make sense?
- Why are multiples of ten also multiples of five?
- Is the reverse true? Are multiples of five also multiples of ten? Why or why not?
- If we were playing the *Factor Game* on a 1–100 chart, what would be the best first move? Why? What would be the worst first move? Why?

REPRODUCIBLE 2.3
The Factor Game
Board for 49

Once the sieves have been completed, you may want to try another round of the *Factor Game*. You may wish to use the 49-board (see Reproducible 2.3) for this particular game. Encourage students to use their sieves when stumped about possible factors or to doublecheck their factoring.

If your curriculum includes the instruction of prime factorization, the sieves can be equally helpful in that process as well. Remind students that the sieve is a tool and a reference, not a crutch or a cheat sheet. The sieve cannot, or should not, take the place of understanding how, why, or when to factor.

Perfect, Near-Perfect, Deficient, and Abundant Numbers—Revisiting the *Factor Game*

The sum of the *proper factors* (all the factors of a number excluding the number itself) may be greater than, less than, or equal to the number being factored. Ancient mathematicians applied this idea to classify numbers as *abundant*, *deficient*, or *perfect*.

The *Factor Game* can be a wonderful reference for classifying numbers in this way. When students are asked about potentially bad first moves on a 1–30 *Factor Game* game board, they will often respond with the choices of 24 or 30. If the students have had multiple opportunities to play the game, they should recognize and articulate that these numbers give the opponent more points than the number chosen. If you choose 30 as your first move, your opponent receives 42 points! If you choose 24, your opponent receives 36 points. Numbers such as 24 and 36 can be classified as *abundant* numbers because the sum of their proper factors exceeds their value.

Post three circles on the board with the following labels:

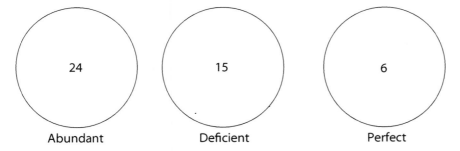

Ask students to make sense of the labels and the numbers posted in them using what they know about abundant numbers from the *Factor Game* and the previous discussion. You can then ask students to place the whole numbers from two to thirty in the appropriate circles. They should also be prepared to justify their placements based on the sum of each number's proper factors. You may want to determine how this task will be performed—independently or with a partner—before giving the assignment to students. Your decision may need to be based on the factoring proficiency of your class by this time in the unit. You may want students to make their placements independently, and then compare their placements with tablemates for confirmation and justification.

Once students have made all the placements, further class discussion can continue about number placements and classifications. Carefully crafted questions can help to guide the conversation and expose targeted mathematical ideas and concepts. As students respond to the questions, ask them to "watch their language" as they speak about various numbers and their properties. Students should use their newly acquired vocabulary as they describe numbers and their classifications. If you make use of a mathematical word wall, referring to the posted words and reminding students to incorporate them when appropriate will help to bring greater clarity to their language and ideas. The following list of possible questions may help guide the conversation. Possible student responses follow each question. Following up on a student's response with a "How do you know?" question can support the student as he or she learns to develop and deliver justifications of his or her mathematical statements.

- What do you know about abundant numbers?
  - They are all composite.
  - They are all even.
  - They cannot be prime.
  - Stay away from abundant numbers when playing the *Factor Game*.
  - Abundant numbers can be terrible first moves in the *Factor Game*.
- What do you know about deficient numbers?
  - There are more deficient numbers than abundant and perfect numbers from two to thirty.
  - All the prime numbers are deficient.
  - All the square numbers from one to fifty are deficient.
  - They are even and odd.
  - Deficient numbers are good numbers to choose when playing the *Factor Game*.
- What do you know about perfect numbers?
  - There are not many!
  - They are even. (A note to the interested: no odd perfect numbers have been identified as of the writing of this book!)
- In which circle does 36 belong? 55? 97? How do you know?
- What is your opponent's score if you choose four? What if you choose sixteen? Four and sixteen can be classified as *near-perfect* numbers. Why does that classification make sense? Can you find other near-perfect numbers?

Revisiting two- and three-circle Venn diagrams can further support students' understandings of number relationships and their ability to analyze and sort numbers based on their characteristics. You can ask students to sort numbers according to the classifications of even, odd, prime, composite, square, abundant, deficient, perfect, and near-perfect. You can also include sorts according to factors and divisibility.

As in the previous Venn lesson, assign sorting tasks by identifying the sort as well as showing the sort and asking for the classification properties. Lately I have been asking students to choose one number to place outside the Venn with a written explanation of why it does not belong in any of the classifications. (See Figure 2–11; see also Reproducible 2.6.)

▶ REPRODUCIBLE 2.6
Two-Circle Venn
Diagram Template

Good Questions to Ask

- Toby says the *Factor Game* could also be called the *Divisor Game*. Do you agree? Why or why not?

- Willy says that twenty-four is the worst first move on the *Factor Game* game board. Brad says thirty is the worst move. With whom do you agree? Why?

- Joan says that all the factors of twelve are also factors of twenty-four because twelve is a factor of twenty-four. Will every multiple of twelve contain the factors of twelve? How do you know? Support your thinking with examples or models.

- Using the terms *factor*, *multiple*, *product*, and *divisible by*, write as many sentences as you can about the number model $6 \times 4 = 24$.

- Can a rectangular array be created for every multiplication number model? If so, why does this occur?

For more good questions, see *Good Questions for Math Teaching: Why Ask Them and What to Ask, Grades 5–8* by Lainie Schuster and Nancy Anderson (Math Solutions 2005).

FIGURE 2–11
Nick's Completed Venn Diagram and Explanation.

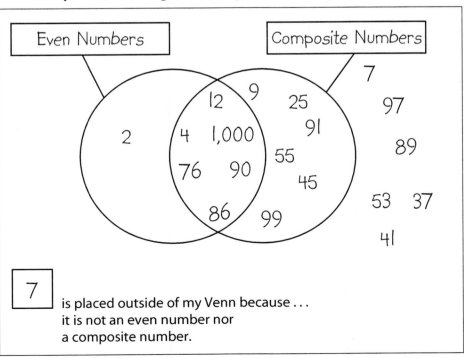

- ■ The greater the product, the greater its number of factors.
  - ● Is this a true statement? Why or why not?
  - ● Use number models and examples to support your thinking.
- ■ If *even × odd = even*, can we then assume that *even ÷ odd = even*? Why or why not? Will this be the case when *any* even number is divided by an odd number? Support your thinking with words and number models.
- ■ Consecutive numbers are whole numbers in numerical order, such as 5, 6, 7 or 22, 23, 24.
  - ● For any three consecutive numbers, what can you say about odd and even numbers? Explain your thinking. Support your thinking with number models.
- ■ On a 1–49 *Factor Game* game board, Ben says forty-eight is the best first move because it is the largest *even* number. Mac says forty-eight is the worst first move because it is the largest *abundant* number. With whom do you agree—and why?

Calculation Routines and Practices

As our fifth graders make sense of the structure of and relationships between numbers, they are developing new and useful strategies for finding factors and multiples of whole numbers. Proficiency with the multiplication tables quickly becomes imperative as students work to factor numbers. As the unit progresses, those students who are not proficient quickly become apparent. Building multiplication minilessons for review and practice into your weekly plans may be helpful to some as well as necessary for others. Traditionally, review and practice have been synonymous with drills and worksheets full of problems. Memorization was often the objective rather than understanding and application.

The following activities can offer meaningful fact practice to your students. They can be used as class warm-ups or as options at choice time. You may also wish to supply your library or resource center with sets of fact triangles and Rio and Product game boards for further practice if students have extra time in these settings. Web sites are also an option for continued practice, which can take place in the school setting or be sent home with students as additional opportunities to fine-tune the fluency of fact recall. Listings of possible Web sites are noted in the "Resources" section of this chapter.

Fact Triangles and Families

Fact triangles may be thought of as a "new and improved" version of flash cards. In my opinion, fact triangles are more effective than flash cards because they emphasize fact families and the relationships between operations.

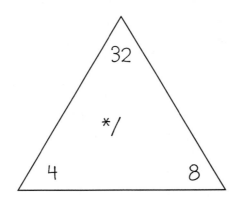

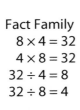

Fact Family
8 × 4 = 32
4 × 8 = 32
32 ÷ 4 = 8
32 ÷ 8 = 4

One student can place a thumb over one of the numbers in the vertices of the triangle, and the teacher asks the other student to identify the missing number of that particular fact family. Students can also sort the fact triangles into facts that they know and those they still need to master. Fact triangles can be purchased through the Everyday Math Learning Corporation or other educational publishing resources.

Rio

Rio is a multiplication game that is played by two or three students and offers them the opportunity to practice and apply one multiplication table at a time. (See Reproducibles 2.11 and 2.12 for the *Rio* game board master, directions, and materials.) You create boards for the tables you wish students to practice. I have three game boards for each of the four through nine tables available for students. (See Figure 2–12.)

NCTM Connection

Strand: Number and Operations
Focus: Multiplication fact practice in a game context.
Context: Rio

► REPRODUCIBLE 2.11
Rio Directions

REPRODUCIBLE 2.12
Rio Game Board Template

FIGURE 2–12
A Sample *Rio* Game Board for the Multiples of 6.

Rio			
12	18	24	30
36	42	Free Space	48
54	60	66	72

Journal Writes

Asking students to write about multiplication strategies can help to solidify their thinking, reasoning, and understanding of multiplication. Assigning the following journal writes can illuminate a student's facility with multiplicative thinking and understanding. Processing journal writes following their completion can offer valuable instruction for students by students. Asking students to publicly share their writing and strategies can encourage them to assess the quality and value of their own thinking. Some students may opt to discard their own strategy for one that is offered that makes more sense to them.

- How can knowing 4×8 help you to understand and calculate 4×16?
- How can knowing 4×6 help you to understand and calculate 12×6?
- How can knowing 9×11 help you to understand and calculate 9×12?
- How can knowing 6×7 help you to understand and calculate 60×7?

TEACHER-TO-TEACHER TALK ■ **About Mastery of Multiplicaton Facts** ■

So when do we move on from reviewing and worrying about the fluency of the multiplication tables? I am not sure if we ever do as fifth-grade teachers, but as the year progresses, so too do the focus and time constraints of what is important to address in class and what needs to move to an out-of-class responsibility. My expectation is that my students will be fluent in their multiplication tables once they enter the fifth grade. That is my expectation, mind you, but not always the reality of the situation! I do spend the first days of the school year reviewing tables and having fun with the fact "demons" that students seem to come up against so often. I will pose a problem to someone as they are walking down the hall, or in the pick-up line, or waiting for a drink at the water fountain. I will ask someone for a factor pair of 24, or 42, or 63 when they are waiting in the office. Students are well aware of my intentions; they just have to know these tables! Once we begin factoring, I take stock of who knows what. There will always be a few students for whom mastery will be eternally elusive. At this point, I enlist the help of parents or resource teachers to help those students in need. I encourage the parents and resource teachers not only to continue to review the tables, but also to work with students on using available reference materials housed in their math notebooks such as a multiplication matrix. All my students have access to such tools at all times. Sarah had mastered her times tables—and was very proud of her fluency with each and every table. Yet she loved her matrix and pulled it out every day—and did so throughout the year! I asked her about that one morning. She told me that she liked her matrix and thought it was important to have it there for reference. "Sometimes I just like to make sure!" I would far rather the students wrestle with the concepts presented in an investigation than the product of eight and seven at this point in their mathematical careers.

Multiplication Tic-Tac-Toe

You use a game board displaying products up to eighty-one. *Multiplication Tic-Tac-Toe*, also commonly referred to as the *Product Game*, offers students the opportunity to practice and recall multiplication and related division facts. This game also pushes students to move flexibly between multiplication and division in order to identify products, factors, divisors, or quotients. (See Reproducibles 2.13 and 2.14 for the *Multiplication Tic-Tac-Toe* game board master, directions, and materials.)

Divisibility Rules

I can certainly not speak for you, but I remember questioning the use and abhorring the practice of memorizing the divisibility rules when I was a child. It was only after years (and years!) had passed that I found meaning in those rules. Several teachers gave me these rules many years ago with no apparent purpose for their use—or at least not one that was made clear and deliberate to me. Only when the class explores and discusses the divisibility rules within meaningful contexts will they be used, applied, and remembered. I certainly get that now!

Playing the *Factor Game* offers a context within which to discuss divisibility rules—those the students already know and those that will be helpful for them to learn. Divisibility rules are related to factors and divisors as is the *Factor Game*. You can then apply these rules to the students' work with arrays and continued work with factoring. Divisibility rules and their applications are also visible in the *Sieve of Eratosthenes*.

A majority of our fifth graders have already come up against the divisibility rules of 2, 5, and 10. I find that many students are often intrigued by the divisibility rules of 3, 4, 6, and 9, especially if there is reason to apply them.

NCTM Connection

Strand: Number and Operations

Focus: Multiplication and division fact practice in a game context.

Context: Multiplication Tic-Tac-Toe (The Product Game)

▶ REPRODUCIBLE 2.13 Multiplication Tic-Tac-Toe Directions

REPRODUCIBLE 2.14 Multiplication Tic-Tac-Toe Game Board

NCTM Connection

Strand: Number and Operations

Focus: Investigate the rules of divisibility and why they make sense.

Context: Exploration of Divisibility Rules

Rules Regarding Divisibility

Divisibility by 2: The number is even.

Divisibility by 3: The sum of the digits is divisible by 3.

Divisibility by 4: Either the last two digits are 00 or they form a number divisible by 4.

Divisibility by 5: The number ends in 0 or 5.

Divisibility by 6: The number is even (divisible by 2) and the sum of the digits is divisible by 3.

(Continued)

> **Divisibility by 8:** Either the last three digits are 000 or they form a number divisible by 8.
>
> **Divisibility by 9:** The sum of the digits is divisible by 9.
>
> **Divisibility by 10:** The 1st digit of the number is 0.

Although I present the divisibility rules for 4 and 8, students rarely apply them without the aid of a written explanation. I have found that fifth graders easily apply the divisibility rules for 3, 6, and 9 because they make sense to the students and are easy to manipulate. I also prepare these rules as a handout. As with the *Sieve of Eratosthenes,* students place it in a sleeve and house it in their math notebooks as a reference tool for future investigations . . . particularly those with fractions (I wish someone would have let me in on that little tip many years ago!). I encourage students to access these rules at any time. As with many other newly introduced mathematical routines, we need to carefully model the application of these rules. Choosing tasks that require their application within meaningful contexts will push students to access and apply what they know about divisibility. Directives such as the following can push students to think creatively beyond standard questions such as "Is one hundred twenty-three divisible by six?"

- Name three three-digit numbers that are divisible by six. What do we know about these numbers?
- Name two four-digit numbers that are divisible by nine. What do we know about these numbers?
- Name three two-digit numbers that are divisible by two and five. What do we know about these numbers?

NCTM Connection

Strand: Number and Operations
Focus: Practice of conventional notation of factorization.
Context: Conventional Factorization Notation

Conventional Factorization Notation

Conventional routines certainly continue to have their place in the study of mathematics. Although I do present the conventional notation of factoring, I do so only after the students have had the opportunity to play several rounds of the *Factor Game,* explore divisibility rules, and investigate arrays, their dimensions, and their subsequent factor pairs. Offering students an organized method of recording factors becomes useful when they begin to investigate properties of numbers based on their factors.

Choose a friendly number from which to work. Twelve always seems to be a good choice. As I am working at the whiteboard, students are working in their math notebooks. We start by noting the number we are factoring, followed by a colon.

12:

Rather than just beginning with the number one, I ask students how they get started in the factoring process. By this time in the unit, many students have already devised systematic methods of finding factors, the most common one being that they start with one and then move up through the numbers in numerical order until they reach the number they are factoring. "Hmmm . . . ," I say. "Sounds like a great way to start . . . but I think you may be doing too much work!" That comment certainly intrigues students! So we begin the process that was suggested:

12: 1, 2, 3, 4

I have students stop at four. I then ask the ever-popular question, "What do you notice?" Mac noticed that when you multiply those last two numbers, you get the number being factored. So we "rainbow" those two numbers:

12: 1, 2, 3, 4

Now comes the easy part. All we have to do is pair up the previously noted numbers with their respective factor-pair partners. Two is paired with six. And one is paired with twelve.

12: 1, 2, 3, 4, 6, 12

Many curricula refer to this method of factoring as the "rainbow method." Although it is not foolproof because students can sometimes miss an entire factor pair, this method does help them keep track of the initial factors and their partners as they move numerically from one to the number being factored.

Once we have explored the conventional notation, students need to apply it. Organized notation is helpful when classifying numbers as abundant, deficient, perfect, and near-perfect. It is equally helpful when students are identifying common factors and common multiples. A student of mine years ago coined this method of notating common factors and common multiples as the "peanut" method. When you draw rings around the common factors, they often resemble peanuts—hence the label. For example, the common factors of 12 and 24 are 1, 2, 3, 4, 6, and 12 with 12 being the greatest common factor as represented by the "peanuts."

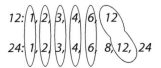

12: 1, 2, 3, 4, 6, 12
24: 1, 2, 3, 4, 6, 8, 12, 24

Least-common multiples can also be identified with the peanut method. For example, the least-common multiple of six and eight is twenty-four as represented by the peanut once again.

$$6: 6, 12, 18, 24$$
$$8: 8, 16, 24$$

Michael was lobbying just last year for a new label of the "pickle" method, but the majority ruled in favor of the peanut label for yet another year! Who likes pickles anyway?

Reading, Writing, and Vocabulary

The National Council of Teachers of Mathematics (NCTM) has long advocated curricular instruction with a clear and deliberate emphasis on the processes involved in and required by the teaching and learning of meaningful mathematics. Through the process standard of *communication*, students are able to test their thinking, clarify misconceptions, discover alternative ideas, and extend their understanding. Communication skills can be separated into those requiring receptive and expressive proficiencies. When children read and listen, they receive and process information. When children talk and write, they express that information to others. Through communication, children gather, refine, and express their understanding about mathematical concepts and procedures (O'Connor 2007).

When we ask our students to read about number relationships, we are asking them to interact with what they read and make sense of it. When we ask our fifth graders to write about number relationships, we are asking them to make visible their understanding of those relationships. In order to read and write well, our fifth graders first need to understand what they are being asked to do. Understanding the language and mathematics of the problem being posed or the question being asked is critically important.

Modeling and assessing mathematical writing with your class will be important early in the year as you establish writing routines and expectations. Responding to open-ended questions or journal prompts can offer contexts in which students can discuss, conjecture, record, generalize, and justify their thinking and reasoning. Many curricula tout the importance of mathematical writing and communication. Many high-stakes tests require proficiency in these areas, as well. So if our students are being asked to write about the mathematics they know and understand, we need to be vigilant about providing the teaching and learning structures that need to be in place in order for them to do so. If we want our students to write as mathematicians and to write well, they will need to spend time writing, talking about their writing, and receiving feedback to improve their writing.

Modeling

Establishing writing routines and practices early in the year will allow you and students more time to focus on the mathematics of the writing rather than on the format and expectations that you will cover later in the year. My students write in their graph paper notebooks, which allows them the space and structure for mathematical models to support their thinking.

You will need to make an instructional decision when you choose that first question or prompt for the class. It also helps to tell students your reasons for modeling a response with the entire class. Although our students do not need to be privy to the reasons for all the instructional decisions that we make, in this case it makes sense. You will need to have your convictions in place about the role of writing in your class before you engage students in this conversation and task. One of my favorite phrases about mathematical writing is that it makes understanding visible and real—in much the same way that love affects the nursery toys in *The Velveteen Rabbit*, and I use that metaphor! The process of mathematical writing helps students reflect on what they know, what they do not know, and what they need to know. I have also found that adding a personal touch to this discussion with the class goes a long way. I love to write and always have. I value language and how thoughts are constructed and strung together to make meaning. And just as with any other process, we will be learning along the way as we refine, revise, and adjust our mathematical reasoning and language.

You may wish to choose a published question, use a prompt from your curriculum, or create a question based on a mathematical idea that students have already explored in class. Just be mindful, however, that the language and mathematics of the question and its answer will need to be manageable and accessible to the entire class. Post the question on the board for reference throughout the session. Because students are familiar with the *Factor Game* and its associated mathematics, I often choose or create a question such as the following:

Willy says that 4 is the worst first move on the Factor Game *game board. Brad says 0 is the worst move. With whom do you agree? Why?*

Asking a student to read the question out loud can begin the modeling process. You can then ask students to discuss the question (not the answer) with a partner. You may wish to post the following prewriting questions on the board or on chart paper for reference throughout the year:

- What is being asked?
- Are there multiple parts to the question?

- Can you each restate the question in your own words?
- Are there any words whose meaning you are unsure of in the question?
- Is there any work or thinking that would be helpful to do before beginning to answer the question?

Once partners have had a chance to discuss the question itself, you can call the class back together to review the question and its components. With this particular question, some work needs to be done before the class can answer it. This question was created with that in mind. It is often helpful for students to have models from which to write. We can then brainstorm about what needs to be done before we begin the writing process. The class will quickly agree that we need to figure out how many points each player receives when they choose twenty-four as the first move—and then when they choose thirty as the first move. I ask students to represent the points in their math notebooks once their page is headed and dated, making sure to identify Willy and Brad's choice of numbers. (See Figure 2–13.)

What I particularly like about this question is that there are a few ways to think about the answer—and a great deal of applicable vocabulary can be used. Twenty-four and thirty are both *abundant* numbers. Therefore, the opponent is going to get more points than either boy— sixteen more points, to be exact. So in essence, both twenty-four and thirty are bad moves—but are they equally bad? This new question can open up a potentially interesting conversation with the class. Once again I ask students to turn to their partner and discuss their opinion

FIGURE 2–13
Kelsey's Work.

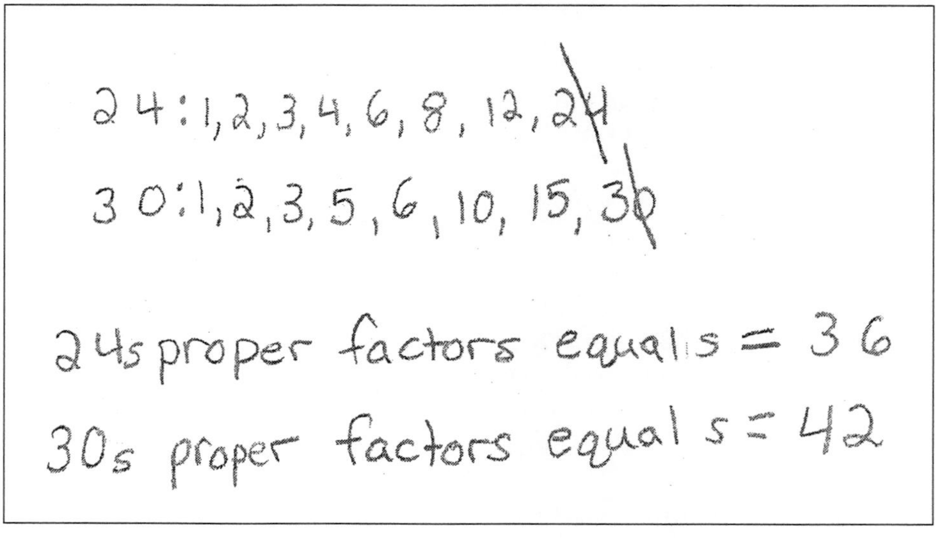

about this new question, making sure to support their thinking with the mathematical proof they have just constructed. I remind students that they need to take a stand! As students will quickly see, more than one "right" answer to this question may exist, which makes answering it all about the ability to support and prove a position. In other words, I am asking students to think and respond like mathematicians.

TEACHER-TO-TEACHER TALK ■ **About Talk** ■ A great deal of talking needs to accompany writing. I am not sure I really understood this until I watched, really watched, the cooperative writing (a process my class seems to reinvent each year) that seems to happen a lot in my classroom. Each time I present a prompt, conversation erupts! The first reaction of my students is to turn and talk to each other about the prompt. This is not something I ask students to do—they just start talking! When talking about mathematics is valued, practiced, and routine in a classroom, it becomes a mathematical tool that students use to solve problems and answer questions, in much the same way a calculator or reference is used. Research suggests that students who have had practice in talking at length with their peers and teacher about solving mathematics problems tend to persist longer in trying to understand a new problem (Gavin, Chapin, Dailey, and Sheffield 2007). They are more engaged with the mathematical task and more willing to persist. I have also found students to be more willing to try out new ideas verbally before they put them on paper. So I gladly let them talk!

Now for the writing. Because I have access to a document camera, I set myself up to write in the middle of the class with blank graph paper and pencil with the projection of my work to be done with the document camera. Using an overhead projector or writing on the board works just as well. The important factor here (no pun intended) is the students' experience of seeing you write, not the technology used to do so.

I ask someone in the class to rephrase the initial question once again in their own words. We quickly review what the question is asking us to do. As a class we can now brainstorm the information that may be helpful as we work to answer the question. We all brainstorm on our papers. I like to use bullets when brainstorming, which is what my students are accustomed to in science and social studies. As students share ideas, I create bullet points just as I expect them to do. Because this is a whole-class activity, you will need to remind students that they will have to come to a consensus about an answer so that we can craft our response together. Depending on the potential lawyer types in your class, you might have a heated discussion on your hands! I smile when this happens; I adore seeing students passionate about their mathematical ideas. But eventually you may have to step in and rule on the answer that you are going to use just to get through the process. (See Figure 2–14.)

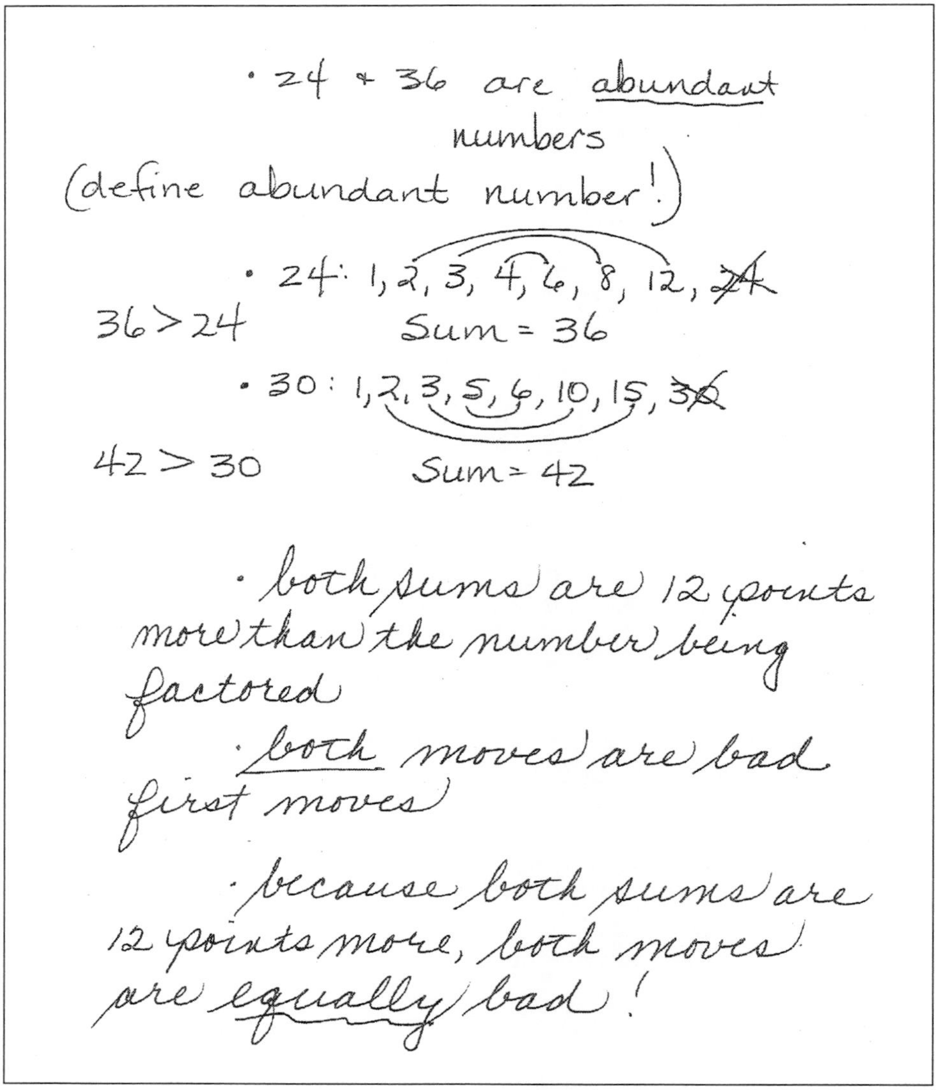

- 24 & 36 are abundant
numbers
(define abundant number!)
- 24: 1, 2, 3, 4, 6, 8, 12, 24
36 > 24   Sum = 36
- 30: 1, 2, 3, 5, 6, 10, 15, 30
42 > 30   Sum = 42

- both sums are 12 points
more than the number being
factored
- both moves are bad
first moves
- because both sums are
12 points more, both moves
are equally bad!

FIGURE 2–14
Mrs. Schuster's Work.

By this time, we have scaffolded the writing. We have a model, language, and an agreed-upon solution from which to write. So we write. Although students are using pencil and can erase, I choose to cross out words and use carets in my version. I want the editing and rethinking process to be visible to the class. Good writing does not just happen!

As students offer introductory sentences, we continually refer to the initial question. Are we working toward an answer characterized by clarity and thoroughness? Are we answering the question? Is each component of our answer offering proof of our reasoning and position? Is our word choice appropriate and representative of the mathematics being discussed?

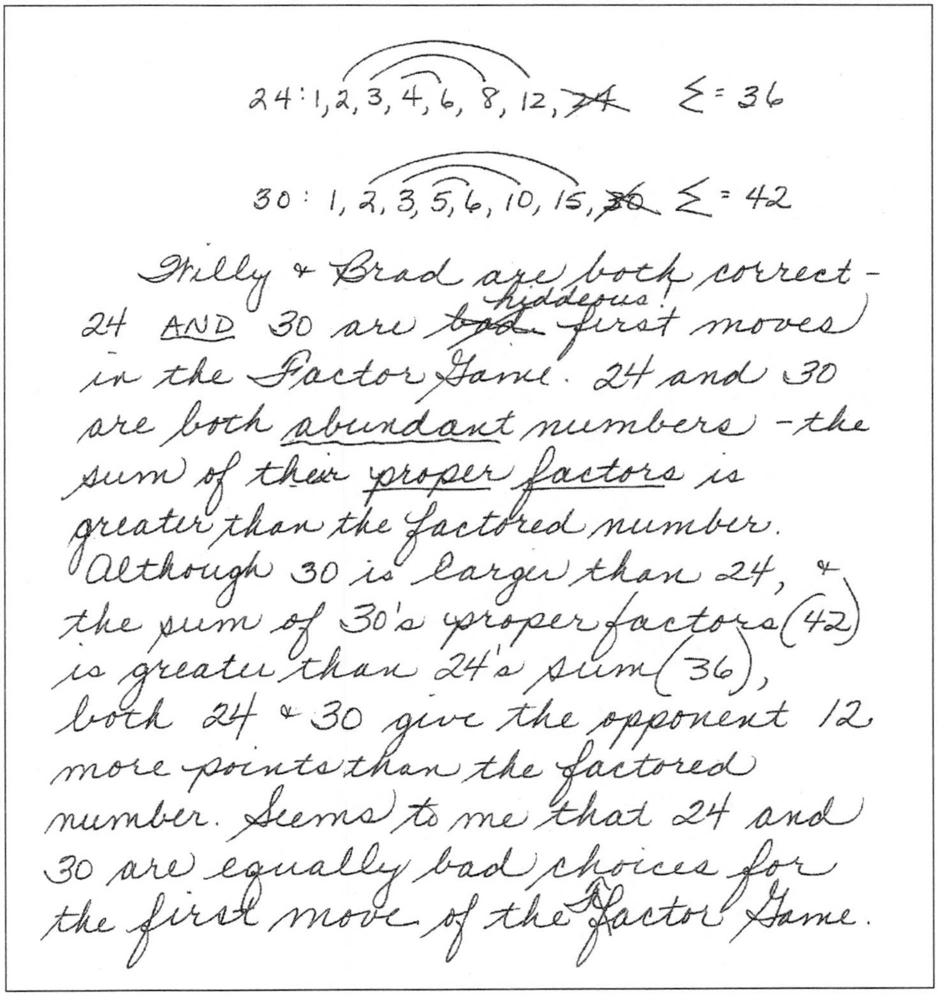

24 : 1, 2, 3, 4, 6, 8, 12, ~~24~~ $\Sigma = 36$

30 : 1, 2, 3, 5, 6, 10, 15, ~~30~~ $\Sigma = 42$

Willy & Brad are both correct — 24 AND 30 are ~~bad~~ *hiddeous!* first moves in the Factor Game. 24 and 30 are both *abundant numbers* — the sum of their *proper factors* is greater than the factored number. Although 30 is larger than 24, & the sum of 30's proper factors (42) is greater than 24's sum (36), both 24 & 30 give the opponent 12 more points than the factored number. Seems to me that 24 and 30 are equally bad choices for the first move of the Factor Game.

FIGURE 2–15
Class Write.

As we craft our response, we revise and edit along the way until we reach the final class group writing. (See Figure 2–15.) Marilyn Burns writes of writing:

> The process of writing requires gathering, organizing, and clarifying thoughts. It demands finding out what you know and don't know. It calls for thinking clearly. Similarly, doing mathematics depends on gathering, organizing, and clarifying thoughts, finding out what you know and don't know, and thinking clearly . . . the mental journey is, at its base, the same—making sense of an idea and presenting it effectively. (Burns 1995)

Once the document has been completed, the class can begin a conversation about what constitutes good mathematical writing. This will undoubtedly be a yearlong conversation—and should be! I suggest that these initial characteristics be posted on chart paper so that they can be revised and added on to as the year progresses. You may wish to reproduce this initial list and have students house it in their math notebooks to revise and add to, as well. This list of characteristics and expectations can help support and guide students as they write in and outside class, keeping in mind that offering such a list as a reference is only as good as the frequency with which it is used, accessed, revised, and refined. A beginning list may look like the following:

Traits of Good Mathematical Writing in the Fifth Grade
- Answers the question being asked.
- Is thorough.
- Uses strong mathematical language.
- Uses examples or models to support thinking.
- Is neat and organized.
- Has few spelling errors.

Why, when, and how to assess mathematical writing is addressed in the "Reading, Writing, and Vocabulary" section of Chapter 3.

Assessment

As teachers, we are diagnosticians of student growth and achievement. In order to assess meaningfully and teach well, we need to understand the thinking of our students. This is neither a simple nor an isolated charge. As September and October come and go, we understand more about the students we teach with every conversation, observation, piece of writing, and written representation of concepts and procedures. Being curious about and interested in the reasoning and learning of your fifth graders will help you to effectively assess their thinking and mathematical growth on an ongoing basis. Understanding how your students comprehend and perform mathematics will also allow you to make meaningful curricular decisions and choices that will guide future instruction and learning.

The authors of *Beyond Arithmetic: Changing Mathematics in the Elementary Classroom* (Mokros, Russell, and Economopoulos 1995) propose a "checking-in" process in which students are asked to talk about and explain their thinking, strategies, and ideas. This practice is grounded in the process of learning rather than being the product of testing. As we circulate, observe, and talk to our students, the following questions may help to frame how we assess their thinking and learning:

- Do students come up with their own strategies for solving problems, or do they rely on the strategies or suggestions of others? What do their strategies tell me about their mathematical understanding?
- Do students understand that there are different strategies for solving problems? Do they articulate and explain their strategies? Do they listen to the strategies offered by other students? Are they able to apply strategies other than their own?
- Do students seek out tools and materials to help them work? Do they use these tools and materials effectively?
- Do the students have ideas on how to record their work, or does the process of representing their thinking seem difficult for them?

Answers to these questions give us different types of information than that gleaned from formal, written, and more traditional assessments. Documenting these answers about what and how your students are learning will help you formulate necessary judgments as you plan and adjust instruction. I use a spiral notebook with tabs for each student to date and notate observations and conversations. On certain days I try to comment on the same skill or work habit so that I can have a standard for comparison. I can then assess each student individually as well as make judgments about the entire class. I can report on data collected from student conversations and observations in much the same way as for more traditional assessments. You may find that your prescribed curriculum offers materials with which to document and archive anecdotal notes, as well.

Yes, this process of checking in with students and documenting your observations is daunting. This is not a daily routine in my class, however, and I cannot get to every student on any given day very often. While checking in with our students supports the practice of ongoing assessment, so too does the *examination* of student work, which is different from merely *checking* student work! I discuss the examination of student work in the "Assessment" section of Chapter 3.

Formal written assessments continue to have their place and purpose, but teachers and administrators need to treat them as just another ongoing assessment, not as the sole indicator of a student's proficiency in that particular unit or with that particular skill. I do give unit tests and approach them with great seriousness, but the students are well aware that this is just one more piece of information that we all can use to understand their strengths and needs as fifth-grade mathematicians. We have this conversation early in the year—and prior to each written assessment. The format of my written assessments varies throughout the year; I use unit tests, unit projects, partner quizzes, and chapter check-ups. Some assessments require a lot of writing, while some require straight calculation. Some are completed individually and quietly, while others incorporate partners and discussion. I link the assessment to the instruction as well as to the concept or skill being studied. Different units dictate different formats. The purpose and format of each assessment makes sense to students. Because of that, they exhibit far less anxiety surrounding a particular event than might be expected.

Each formal assessment that I give in my class has some consistencies, however. I share these, too, with the students. They know what they can expect in advance with each assessment, and there is some comfort in that for all of us! For every formal assessment:

- I distribute study sheets several days prior to a test or distribute project guidelines prior to a project's due date.
- The assessment contains required sections as well as sections with a question bank from which students can choose a specified number of questions to answer.
- The students complete self-reflections after I have reviewed and returned the assessments.

Unit Tests

I give two formal assessments to my fifth-grade class in the months of September and October. I assess students with a partner quiz midunit as well as with an end-of-unit exam (see the "Assessment" section of Chapter 7 for an explanation of partner quizzes).

Unit tests can be characterized as summative assessments, those that measure student learning upon completion of an instructional unit. I give a unit test at the end of this particular unit on factors and multiples. It is an individual assessment and one that requires a quiet classroom. I distribute extensive study sheets to students about a week prior to the test. I outline all that will be on the test as well as attach practice and review pages. Because I do so little workbook or worksheet work during daily class time, I can easily copy the applicable reproducibles from my prescribed curriculum to attach as the additional practice pages. I give no written assessment without a study sheet. In my world, the preparation for the quiz or test takes on a life of its own and is just about as important as the quiz or test itself.

Each unit test contains a required section and a question bank from which students can choose a specified number of questions. There are significant benefits to having students make such choices. They not only have to read and comprehend what each question is asking but they also have to be able to assess what is involved in solving and representing the problems before deciding which problems to solve. Understanding the mathematics required of each question helps students choose problems with greater ease, ownership, and confidence. A great deal of reading, underlining, and note taking in the margins goes on before students make their final decisions. Further discussion of the process of comprehending mathematical problems can be found in the "Reading, Writing, and Vocabulary" section of Chapter 6. You may wish to refer to this section of the next chapter if you are considering adding a free-choice component to your assessments.

TEACHER–TO–TEACHER TALK ■ **About Accessible Resources** ■ All the unit exams in my class are open book and open notebook with the exception of the multiplication and division procedural exams. I worry that our students can too easily choose to become passive learners. They learn, or have already learned, to wait for needed information to come their way. Mathematical resources are important. It is equally important to offer students opportunities to seek out the resources and to make informed decisions about what resources can help support the reasoning required of their work. As students work to complete partner quizzes and unit tests, I often see them flipping through their math notebooks searching for the sieve or removing the sheet of divisibility rules for easy access. The students quickly realize that offering "open book" opportunities does not necessarily make the thinking any easier. What it does allow, however, is time for students to focus on the concept or the big idea of the question. Referencing their sieves or their sheets of divisibility rules will help them to formulate, articulate, and support ideas based on what they understand and can apply to the question being asked. A seventh-grade math teacher new to my school last year found his way into my classroom with a sieve in his hand—a very worn-out and well-loved sieve! One of my fifth graders, now a seventh grader, had filed it away in her sixth-grade math notebook and in her seventh-grade notebook, as well. The teacher was amazed, and even a little impressed, at Ellie's ability and continued willingness to access the information found on her sieve as she solved problems, answered questions, and constructed new understandings in the seventh grade. My fifth graders also have frequent access to calculators, but find their need to access them more reliant on their understanding of when an exact answer is required or when an estimate will do. I continue to believe that it is important for them to make informed decisions about what will be helpful and when. And sometimes it is just about the ideas. No sieve, calculator, or partner will need to be accessed. It is just about them and the mathematics!

A student's capability and willingness to assess their own progress and learning is one of the greatest gifts students can develop. Mathematical power and fluency come with how much we know and knowing what to do to learn more (Stenmark 1989). Self-assessment offers students the time and opportunity to think and reflect upon their experiences as learners, to understand and articulate their strengths and needs in order to monitor and enrich their learning experiences. You can give self-assessment inventories throughout the unit—perhaps after an extensive investigation, or after a new concept has been introduced and explored, or after a unit exam. Meaningful self-assessment should move students to think beyond describing how they feel about a learning experience. Open-ended questions such as the following can help students begin to participate in such a reflective process:

- What did I need to know in order to do this task?
- What was familiar about this task? Where have I seen something like it before?
- How did I feel doing the task?
- What is getting easier?
- How would I describe my strengths?
- What is still hard for me?
- What would help me improve?
- What did I learn about the mathematics? About myself?
- If I did this again, what might I do differently?

My fifth graders complete a written test reflection following the unit exam. Before I return the tests, I take time to discuss my general observations about their performance. Each test may warrant a different conversation. In this particular unit, I often find that I comment on students' study habits, their willingness to access helpful resources, as well as on common misunderstandings . . . and there always are a few! One year about half the class classified nine as a prime number. Oops! That was obviously an important conversation waiting to happen! Once I hand the tests back to the students, I ask them to look them over before they begin to write and respond. Students will get very good at this by the end of the year. You may find that they become less interested in the problems they did correctly and more interested in those they missed . . . and why. That is when you know you are doing something very right! Students do test reflections privately and quietly. I do review the reflections upon completion; at times I may make comments to a particular student in a margin and other times not. Students are often brutally honest, admitting when they did not study enough or that their lack of fluency in the multiplication tables really affected their work on a particular section of the test. Others may admit that they did not understand some of the questions. I learn a great deal about the students as I read through their reflections. At times I have picked up the phone to call a parent after reading either something really wonderful or something equally concerning. Completing a test reflection takes the emphasis off the test itself and places it in the process of learning and understanding.

In *Finding the Connections: Linking Assessment, Instruction, and Curriculum in Elementary Mathematics* (Moon and Schulman 1995), the authors remind us that a child's metacognitive capability needs to be guided and practiced if it is to develop to its full potential. Self-reflective practices need to become routine and respected. If we want our students to become aware of their own learning and know why that awareness is an important dimension of learning, then we need to offer ongoing opportunities for students to identify and understand the relationship between learning and assessment. (See Figure 2–16; see also Reproducible 2.15.)

REPRODUCIBLE 2.15 ◄
Unit Exam Analysis
and Reflection

Unit Exam Analysis and Reflection

Unit: *Prime Time*

Total Number Points on the Exam: 60

My Total: 65   **My %:** 100 +

Range of scores in entire grade: 31-65

Mean raw score: 56/94%

What did you learn about numbers and their properties from *Prime Time:*

1.) I learned about exponents. _____

_____

2.) I learned a ton of vocabulary. _____

_____

3.) I learned about cycle problems. _____

_____

Did you prepare properly for this test?

I prepared very well for the test, I know I prepared well because the test seemed easy.

_____

What part of the test or concept was difficult for you?

I did not know what "relatively prime" meant, but I was smart to avoid the question with them.

_____

What did you do really WELL on the test?

I did really well on GCF and LCM problems because I am very good at factoring.

_____

I contributed to the classroom discussions and understanding of *Prime Time* when I... (give examples)

I shared my homework with Ian and we caught each other's mistakes.

_____

_____

FIGURE 2–16
Patrick's Factors and Multiples Test Reflection.

Home and School Connections

Making the mathematics we teach more visible within a school has the valuable side effect of modeling for parents and families the kind of mathematics that happens in school (Mokros, Russell, and Economopoulos 1995). Yes, parents can be skeptical and question what may seem to them a foreign approach to the teaching of mathematics—and rightly so. These same parents may be spending time doing mathematics with their child at home, but with worksheets and drills rather than the meaningful mathematical activities that promote and support making sense of concepts and procedures. Regular and ongoing communication with families will help to establish a relationship that will support and benefit everyone involved throughout the year.

Communication venues such as Parent Information Forms can inform families of pending units and the concepts and procedures that will be addressed. These information forms will take some time to construct initially, but will be well worth the time and thought for years to come. Thanks to modern technology, my Parent Information and Involvement Forms are saved in a folder on my computer at school. Prior to each unit, I can pull up the previous year's form and review, adjust, and print it. I send home a Parent Information Form prior to the beginning of each new unit of study. (See Figure 2–17; see also Reproducible 2.16.)

REPRODUCIBLE 2.16
Parent Information and Involvement Form ◀

Parent conferences may be in your near future as they are in mine. Just as we are getting to know our students as mathematicians (and readers and scientists and historians), parents need to share their understandings of their children with us and to have those understandings heard. Parental insights can answer many questions we may have about a child or uncover a child's hidden affinity or passion. Conferences are a rare opportunity: a time and place to focus on the needs and abilities of each child as an individual (Litton 1998).

Early in the year, my conferences focus on goal setting. Prior to conference time, I ask my students to establish two goals for the academic school year. More often than not, one of their goals is connected to mathematical progress or achievement. I spend time with each student reviewing that individual's goals and offering one of my own. In my school's August back-to-school mailing, I include a memo alerting the parents of this goal-setting process of which they, too, are a part. I ask them to formulate a goal or two for their child prior to conference time. (See Figures 2–18 and 2–19 on page 88; see also Reproducibles 2.17 and 2.18.)

REPRODUCIBLE 2.17
Parent Goal Setting Information ◀

REPRODUCIBLE 2.18
Student Goal Setting Information

When the parents sit down for their conference, I have their child's goals available as well as my goal for their child. I do not share these goals with the parent(s) until we have a conversation about the goal(s) they have formulated for their child. Following the conferences, each student is presented with a printout of the three goals: theirs, mine, and those of their parent(s). They copy all the goals on a master sheet that will be revisited frequently throughout the year as they monitor their progress in regard to achieving their goals. This goal-setting practice is outlined in greater depth in *Developing Grading and Reporting Systems for Student Learning* (Guskey and Bailey 2001).

Parents want to know how to help their children at home with routines and practices that may not be familiar to them. They want to help and be supportive of the teaching and learning going on in school, but often do not know how. Having handouts available at conference time that outline how parents can offer help at home can be extremely useful and appreciated. The specific handouts I have available for parents may vary from year to year, but their topics remain consistent. I have one handout about

▶ REPRODUCIBLE 2.16
Parent Information
and Involvement
Form

Parent Information and Involvement Form

From: Lainie Schuster
Re: Mathematics Curriculum
Unit: Factors and Multiples

During the next unit, the major topics we will be studying are

- factors
- multiples
- prime and composite numbers
- even and odd numbers
- square numbers
- greatest common factors
- least common multiples

My goal in studying these topics is for the students to be able to

- understand relationships among factors, multiples, divisors, and products
- link the area and dimensions of rectangles with products and factors
- recognize numbers as prime, composite, odd, or even based on their factors
- develop strategies for finding factors and multiples of whole numbers
- recognize situations in which problems can be solved by finding factors and multiples
- develop and apply vocabulary related to the study of number theory

---

Parents can help at home by

- reviewing the times tables up to 12×12
- playing the *Factor Game* and the *Product Game* with your child. After playing, ask your child about his or her strategy and why it did or did not "work."
- if your child is stuck when answering a question, ask him or her if the question is similar to a problem that was done in class. Helping your child to make that connection will help them to apply newly constructed strategies and "big" ideas.

FIGURE 2–17
Parent Information and Involvement Form: September/October.

homework help, one about good questioning techniques, and one about the practice of mathematical proficiency. (See Figures 2–20, 2–21, and 2–22; see also Reproducibles 2.19, 2.20, and 2.21.) The NCTM journals *Teaching Children Mathematics* and *Teaching Mathematics in the Middle School* often offer informative articles that address these issues and can easily be used as handouts. Your prescribed curriculum may offer parent newsletters that can be used as handouts for this same purpose. You may also find it helpful to keep a file of articles that may be used for parent education in general. As I come across articles, I archive them by topic, such as "Back to School," for future reference.

▶ REPRODUCIBLE 2.19
Helpful Things to
Say When Your Child
Asks for Help with
Math Homework

REPRODUCIBLE 2.20
How Can I Help My
Child to Become
Mathematically
Powerful?

REPRODUCIBLE 2.21
Good Questioning
Techniques for
Parents

FIGURE 2–18
Two Samples of Completed Parent Goal Setting Information Sheets.

Parent Goal Setting Information
Academic Year 2008–2009

Please respond to the following questions to help us work with and support your child throughout this academic year. Teachers and students will also be doing a similar goal-setting exercise. At Parents' Weekend we'll be discussing all responses.

1. What do you feel was the most important goal that your child accomplished in school last year?

   Made tremendous progress working independently and working with her peers. Socially, she learned to respect the differences among her friends and how to deal with them.

2. What new goals, academic or social, do you have in mind for your child this year?

   __ is a perfectionist. Her fear of making a mistake prevents her from working independently. We would like to see her work towards overcoming this fear.

[Please return this form to your child's homeroom teacher at your earliest convenience. Thanks!]

Parent Goal Setting Information
Academic Year 2008–2009

Please respond to the following questions to help us work with and support your child throughout this academic year. Teachers and students will also be doing a similar goal-setting exercise. At Parents' Weekend we'll be discussing all responses.

1. What do you feel was the most important goal that your child accomplished in school last year?

   Making some new friends and enjoying their company.

2. What new goals, academic or social, do you have in mind for your child this year?

   Become more of an independent reader.

[Please return this form to your child's homeroom teacher at your earliest convenience. Thanks!]

REPRODUCIBLE 2.17
Parent Goal Setting
Information

REPRODUCIBLE 2.18
Student Goal Setting
Information

FIGURE 2–19
Natalie's Completed Student Goal Setting Information Sheet.

Goal Setting for 2008–2009
Grade 5

My goal for myself this year is:

to increase my typing skills, to improve my vocabulary.

My parents' goal for me is:

to broaden my circle of friends; to continue to gain confidence in my academic abilities and achieve to the best of my ability.

My teachers' goal for me is:

to continue to strive for academic excellence; to stay focused on personal academic goals.

FIGURE 2–20
Parent Handout Addressing Help with Homework.

Helpful Things to Say When Your Child Asks for Help with Math Homework

In order to help your child to become a strong and flexible problem solver, we assign a variety of math activities as homework.

Often your child will receive homework that is directly connected to our math curriculum in the Lower School. You will begin to recognize Home Links (grades 1, 2, and 3), Study Links (grade 4), and ACE questions (grade 5) as the year progresses. All are connected to the texts in their respective grades. Other assignments may be teacher generated or adapted from other relevant sources.

Games may also be assigned for homework. We use games as motivating ways to help our students learn and master concepts. We play these games in school and ask that you play them at home with your child, too. Games are to be taken seriously. When your child asks you to play a math game, notice that your child has to remember and explain rules; create, articulate, and justify a strategy; and use math, as well. Yikes! Often a lot more mathematical thought goes into playing a game than completing a worksheet!

We also assign open-ended problems (multistep story problems) or performance tasks (collecting data). Open-ended problems often challenge your child to try to use much of his or her math knowledge to solve an unfamiliar problem. Sometimes children complain that "the teacher did not teach me how to do this." And in a way, they are correct. We cannot teach your child how to do every kind of problem. Instead, we focus on problem-solving strategies and making connections between similar types of problems and possible strategies used to solve them.

When you child asks you for help, please try not to jump in with an answer no matter how tempting that may be! Instead, try using some of these prompts to support their thinking and perseverance:

- Does this remind you of other problems that you have done in class?
- What have you come up with so far?
- Where do you think you should start?
- What is the problem asking you to do?
- Would drawing a diagram or picture help?
- Why do you think your answer is not correct?

Implementing a well-balanced homework policy takes into account the various needs and expectations of children. This is a tricky business! It requires mathematics teachers to be thoughtful, purposeful, and respectful in their assignments. The ultimate goal of any homework assignment is to offer opportunities for meaningful mathematical conversations between parents and their children.

▶ REPRODUCIBLE 2.19
Helpful Things to Say When Your Child Asks for Help with Math Homework

REPRODUCIBLE 2.20
How Can I Help My
Child to Become
Mathematically
Powerful?

FIGURE 2–21
Parent Handout Addressing Mathematical Proficiency.

How Can I Help My Child to Become Mathematically Powerful?

Money

Encourage your child to

- participate in making family budget decisions
- participate in grocery shopping
- begin to manage his or her allowance
- make decisions about how much the allowance can buy

Counting/Number

Encourage your child to

- count past 500 by different multiples (count past 500 by 50s, or count past 650 by 20s)
- make connections between factors and multiples (If I can run one mile in five minutes, how many miles can I run in thirty minutes?)

Math Facts

- By the beginning of grade 5, your child should know the multiplication facts up to 10×10.

Time

These are some of the time concepts that you can help your child learn at home:

- how to read an analog clock (with an hour and minute hand)
- how to schedule time. If you need to do four specific things, how much time will you need? If you have four things to do and they each take twenty-five minutes, how much time will you need to complete them all? What could those four things be?

Measurement

Involve your child in measurement activities that encourage measurement like

- cooking (fractions, volume, cups, teaspoons, and so on, following step-by-step instructions)
- reading a thermometer
- estimating temperatures (It will be 60° today, will you need a coat for recess?)
- estimating area and perimeter, and identifying the difference between the two!

Problem Solving

Pose meaningful problems attached to real-world contexts whose solutions allow for varied approaches. Follow up solutions with questions such as:

- How did you figure that out?
- How do you know if your answer is correct?
- Can your answer be an estimate or does it have to be an exact number? Why?

Good Questioning Techniques for Parents

Careful, intentional, and mindful questioning is one of the most powerful tools a skillful teacher possesses (from *Activating and Engaging Habits of Mind* by Costa and Kallick 2000). So what do careful, intentional, and mindful questions look like?

- They help students *make sense* of the mathematics.
- They are *open-ended*, whether in answer or approach. They may use multiple answers or multiple approaches.
- They empower students to *unravel their misconceptions*.
- They not only *require the application of facts and procedures*, they also encourage students to *make connections and generalizations*.
- They are *accessible to all students* in their language and offer an entry point for all students.
- Their answer *leads students to wonder more about a topic* and to perhaps construct new questions themselves as they investigate this newly found interest.

The list below offers a generic set of questions that may help guide and facilitate discussions with your children about the mathematics they are studying:

- Why do you think that?
- How did you know to try that strategy?
- How do you know you have an answer?
- Will this work with every number? Every similar situation?
- When will this strategy not work? Can you give a counter example?

(Source: *Good Questions for Math Teaching: Why Ask Them and What to Ask, Grades 5–8* by Lainie Schuster and Nancy Anderson, Math Solutions 2005.)

▶ REPRODUCIBLE 2.21
Good Questioning Techniques for Parents

FIGURE 2–22
Parent Handout Addressing Good Questioning Techniques.

I explore conferences that address student achievement and progress in the "Home and School Connection" section in Chapter 3. Sometimes you need to raise academic concerns early in the year. You may also wish to refer to Chapter 3 for a discussion of parent conferences that focus on mathematical achievement and progress.

Back-to-school night may loom large in your world in these first weeks of the school year. Many schools organize back-to-school nights by moving through a daily school-day schedule, rotating classes within a given increment of time. If your evening is scheduled in this way, find out how long your math period will be with parents in order to schedule your time appropriately. Many parents will be interested in the nuts and bolts of your curriculum, the book (curriculum) being used, and the scope and sequence of the year. You can easily address this information in a handout. Parents may ask questions about homework, about how students are assessed, and about how your work will prepare their children for future mathematical endeavors. It is important for you to address communication with parents, whether the question arises or not. Parents need to know how to contact you and you them. If you plan on implementing Parent Information Forms, explain their purpose and format. I now post my forms electronically, so it is important for me to tell parents how to find the forms on my school Web site.

Although the previous information is important, over the years I have come to prefer spending the majority of my time with parents in this back-to-school format solving a math problem, time permitting—and I make sure that it does! It is important for me to convey how we work in math class: what goes on and how and why it can affect a fifth grader's mathematical growth and progress. Engaging in a mathematical problem does just that. One of my favorite problems to present to parents is *The Horse Problem* (Burns 2007).

Dealing in Horses

A man buys a horse for $50.
He sells it for $60.
The man buys the horse back for $70.
He sells the horse for $80.
What is the financial outcome of these transactions for the man?

The context is engaging, the language accessible, and the problem can be approached with various strategies. I prepare the problem on an overhead and provide a handout. Parents have access to paper, pencil, and even paper money. I like to make the point with parents that what is perplexing about this problem is not the numbers—they can be easily manipulated. What becomes the more important and interesting issue is how to go about solving the problem.

Parents may opt to work backward, approach the problem algebraically with equations, or act it out. However parents decide to proceed with the problem, they will more than likely offer several solutions. What becomes important about the processing of this problem with parents is not necessarily a discussion of the solution, but rather a discussion of the process of coming to a solution. The emphasis becomes one of sound mathematical thinking. Some parents may not be convinced that the answer is a gain of $20! And that is okay. Let them know that wondering about a solution—and a process—is a good thing and something that you support and encourage in your class. One of my favorite lines to use with my students is, "Not knowing is different from not knowing *yet!*" I offer this thought to the parents with the explanation that they may need more time to think about the problem, just as their children sometimes do.

TEACHER-TO-TEACHER TALK ■ **About Engaging Parents** ■ Dealing with parents and other adults looking from the outside in can be a tricky business. And let's be honest, good and effective teachers feel comfortable with children; we really enjoy them and may even prefer to deal with them more than with most adults! These first few weeks are perhaps the most important of the school year. We are working hard to establish learning communities and a culture in which children value, explore, and discuss mathematics. Even though students are our first and favorite priority, we also need to be mindful of the adults with whom we will engage throughout the year: parents, colleagues, and administrators. Over the years I have found it helps to distinguish between justifying and explaining what I do, and I much prefer to explain. I am a professional. I am well-read, experienced, and passionate about the mathematics I teach.

When parents or administrators question me about a teaching practice, unit of study, or method of assessment—and believe me, they do—I rely on my understanding of how children learn and why it makes sense to do what I am doing. I will often answer questions with examples of student work and anecdotes of children learning. I would far rather *explain* what and why I do what I do, rather than justify. There is a difference.

Resources

About Teaching Mathematics: A K–8 Resource (Burns 2007)

A comprehensive resource for teachers that offers classroom-tested activities as well as information necessary to support teachers as they teach math within a problem-solving context.

Part I: "Raising the Issues"
A thorough discussion of the teaching and learning issues in a mathematics education based on sense making and understanding within a problem-solving context.

Math Matters: Understanding the Math You Teach, Grades K–8 (Chapin and Johnson 2006)

A resource for teachers that examines mathematical concepts covered in grades K–8 that can help us clarify our own understanding of the mathematics we teach. It also helps us to pose better questions, explain ideas more accurately, and stress important relationships and concepts.

Chapter 1: "Number Sense"
In-depth discussion about the classification and understanding of numbers and their relationships.

Good Questions for Math Teaching: Why Ask Them and What to Ask, Grades 5–8 (Schuster and Anderson 2005)

A comprehensive collection of open-ended questions and teaching notes that promote students' mathematical thinking, understanding, and proficiency. The questions are organized by mathematical topic and grade level.

Minilessons for Math Practice, Grades 3–5 (Bresser and Holtzman 2006)

A collection of minilessons designed for instructional teaching time of five to fifteen minutes to reinforce math skills, concepts, and procedures. Offers activities that broaden the perspective of what it means to provide practice in mathematics.

Groundworks: Reasoning with Numbers, Grade 5 (Greenes, Findell, Irvin, and Spungin 2005)

A collection of reproducibles that can provide students with an increased awareness of how numbers and operations are related.

Web Sites for Additional Fact Practice

www.mathplayground.com

www.oswego.org/staff/cchamber/techno/games.htm

http://illuminations.nctm.org/ActivitySearch.aspx

Please note that the NCTM Illuminations Web site offers electronic versions of the *Factor Game* and the *Product Game* (*Multiplication Tic-Tac-Toe*).

Chapter 3

Algebraic Thinking

SUGGESTED MONTH: NOVEMBER

The street lights were fuzzy from the fine rain that was falling. As I made my way home, I felt very old, but when I looked at the tip of my nose I could see the fine misty beads, but looking cross-eyed made me dizzy so I quit. As I made my way home, I thought what a thing to tell Jem tomorrow. He'd be so mad he missed it he wouldn't speak to me for days. As I made my way home, I thought Jem and I would get grown but there wasn't much else for us to learn, except possibly algebra.

To Kill a Mockingbird
Lee 1960, 282

95

The Learning Environment

Acknowledge, Support, and Celebrate Effort

Putting forth consistent effort in and out of class is a habit of mind and one that every child can develop. Speaking openly about the value and consequences of thinking and learning with effort can help to make our expectations explicit. When students approach their mathematical work with effort, perseverance is not far behind as they work to make the concepts and procedures their own. Although measuring effort is highly subjective, we need to be mindful of its impact and the importance it can play as we make instructional assessments, choices, and decisions.

Voice and Model the Importance of Making Mistakes and Taking Risks

Mistakes happen. As students work to make sense of mathematical concepts and procedures, they will miscalculate, make errors in reasoning, come to faulty conclusions, and make fragile generalizations. Mistakes are a natural part of the learning process; they are outcomes of methods and thinking that need to be improved (Hiebert et al. 1997). If students (and teachers) are to engage in serious mathematics, they need an intellectually and socially safe environment in which to take risks and try out new ideas.

> **TEACHER-TO-TEACHER TALK ■ About Making Mistakes ■** I applied for a teaching position in a district a few towns over a while back—for no other reason than I thought it might be time for a culture change. This particular district asked its applicants to teach a lesson while being observed by several teachers and administrators. My charge was to teach a lesson about angles to a group of sixth graders who were just finishing up a study of geometry. Prior to the session I was informed that students would have protractors with them and pages of angles to measure in their textbooks. But I didn't go there. Instead, I developed a lesson about the generalizations that you can make about angle measurement when angles meet at a vertex of tessellating regular polygons. It was a lesson I had used before, and to be quite honest, I found the idea of measuring angles in the book rather boring—and something I just didn't want to do nor liked to do very much. The long and the short of it is that as we were developing a chart of the sums of angle measures, I made a mistake . . . but did not realize it until we began to process the data in the chart. One sum did not fit the pattern . . . and panic began to set in. What to do? So I stayed true to myself and did what I always try to do when I make a mistake: enlist students to help me find it. Now this was a new task for this particular class, and I certainly had their attention when I admitted publicly that I had made a mistake somewhere. The numbers did not add up (literally), and I not only

needed to find the mistake, but I was rather curious about why I had made the mistake in the first place. The focus of the lesson then completely shifted, as you can well imagine. A few students even admitted that they had made the same mistake in their charts. I once again realized that we not only have an obligation as teachers to make mistakes a part, an important part, of the process of learning mathematics, but also to develop and support communities and cultures in which this practice is safe.

The Mathematics and Its Language

Children Engage in Explorations That Support Algebraic Thinking

Algebraic reasoning involves representing, generalizing, and formalizing patterns in all areas of mathematics (Van de Walle 2004). When we ask students to think algebraically, we are asking them to predict, generalize, and symbolically represent patterns and functions. Modeling geometric and numerical growth patterns and representing that growth in T-charts, graphs, and symbols can offer experiences that will scaffold the algebraic thinking required of students as they move on in their mathematical careers.

Children Investigate Growing Patterns That Connect Numeric, Symbolic, and Geometric Representations

Understanding patterns is essential to algebraic thinking and fluency. We need to offer students in the fifth grade experiences in which they can create, extend, and represent growing patterns. Students need to describe the patterns verbally and then represent those same patterns numerically on tables (T-charts), symbolically using equations with variables, and geometrically in graphs. It is equally important for our fifth graders to recognize the connectedness of these representations of growth. A graph, a T-chart, words, and a picture can all tell the same story.

Children Continue to Investigate, Articulate, and Represent the Relationship of Equality

Even in the fifth grade, the meaning of the equals sign can continue to be fragile and elusive. Although the equals sign denotes the relationship between two equivalent or equal quantities, many fifth graders continue to view the equals sign as a command to carry out an operation. Tasks and conversations that move students to identify, explain, and apply the relationship that the equals sign represents will help to support and develop a deeper understanding of this symbol.

Children Continue to Investigate the Meaning and Use of Variables

Variables are symbols that represent unknown quantities in algebraic expressions, equations, and inequalities. Fifth graders may be accustomed to the use of boxes and triangles to represent unknown values. Although this practice can continue, you need to introduce and apply the convention of using letters for unknown values. Algebraic equations and inequalities that involve variables, also known as open sentences, can be classified as true or false once a value is substituted for the unknown. Work with algebraic sentences offers students opportunities to evaluate and calculate as they make sense of the symbols and mathematical conventions, such as the use of parentheses and other operational notations such as the dot used to represent multiplication ($5 \cdot 4 = 5 \times 4$).

Children Explore, Generalize, and Represent Functional Relationships

A *function* is a relationship or rule that uniquely associates one member of the first set with exactly one member of the second set. When students generalize this unique relationship called a *function*, they are exploring one of the most important topics that will be covered in high school and college algebra (Chapin and Johnson 2006). Identifying, discussing, and representing functional relationships in T-charts can be very helpful in scaffolding the understanding and mathematics necessary to manipulate and describe these cause-and-effect relationships.

Children Construct and Provide Informal Proof of Conjectures and Generalizations About Fundamental Properties of Mathematics

Fifth graders have developed a great deal of implicit knowledge about the fundamental properties of mathematics, but have not often been given the opportunity to make that knowledge explicit (Carpenter, Franke, and Levi 2003). For example, ten-year-olds know a lot of things about zero. They know that when zero is added to a number, the sum is always the number they started with ($a + 0 = a$). They also know that when a number is multiplied by zero, the product will always be zero ($a \times 0 = 0$). It is important for students to articulate and examine the fundamental properties that are true for all numbers. Articulating these properties in words and symbols can help to attach meaning to the principles and manipulations students will be asked to apply as they move through their future study of algebra.

Lesson Planning

- Please keep in mind that the lessons, activities, and conversations encountered at this stage are focused on the development of algebraic *thinking*. Students can and should be introduced to algebra as a way of thinking, rather than as a formalized unit of study. When we ask students to predict, continue, and articulate patterns, functions, and generalizations, we are asking them to think algebraically.

- You can embed valuable arithmetic practice in lessons focusing on algebraic thinking. Take advantage of the opportunities to revisit addition, subtraction, multiplication, and division routines when working with equations, rules, and functions. You can introduce or review work with parentheses and practice that in the same venues. Many lessons focusing on algebraic thinking can also support, enhance, and extend students' understanding of geometry. When we ask students to think algebraically, we are asking them to make deliberate connections among arithmetic, geometry, and algebra.

- Listen for and honor divergent thinking. Not all students will see a pattern growing in the same way. Class discussions and careful listening will help to expose and support the different ways that students can interpret growth. For example, Craig offered a rule of $2s + 2$. Ava said her rule was $2(s + 1)$. Both rules simplify to $2s + 2$. What is important is to be able to identify how the unsimplified rule matches the growth of the pattern *as the student sees it*. Both rules simplify to $2s + 2$, but the *picture* of the growth may be different.

- Play around with the mathematics before you introduce the lessons. If you are working with true or false, open-number sentences, work out the arithmetic yourself before you present the lesson to the class. If you are working with function tables, work out possible in-values and out-values that fit the given rule. Remember to offer out-values that will ask students to reverse their thinking as they identify the corresponding in-value. Do not shy away from using fractions, decimals, or negative numbers. Adding these values can differentiate your instruction for those students who are able and willing to manipulate these different classifications of numbers.

REPRODUCIBLES
3.1 and 3.2
Growing Patterns
Templates 1 and 2

- Make deliberate connections between the various representations of growing patterns. Using the Growing Patterns Templates (see Reproducibles 3.1 and 3.2) can help students connect one representation with another. The graph, T-chart, picture, words, and equation (rule) all tell the same story. Ask students to identify where the rule is in the picture, or where the values in the T-chart show up in the graph, or how the words can be transformed into the rule. It is no longer enough to ask fifth graders simply to extend a pattern geometrically or numerically. Our fifth graders need to be able to identify and describe the different representations of growth.

- You may notice that most lessons begin in whole-class formats with guided discussion and questioning. You also may find yourself asking the same types of questions for each lesson:

  - What do you notice about this pattern? What is happening from stage to stage (or term to term if working through a T-chart)?

  - What do *you* see staying the same in each stage? Where is the *constant* in the pictures? In the T-chart?

  - Where do *you* see the growth? Where is the growth in the pictures? In the T-chart?

  - Can you describe the growth of the pattern in words? How could we use symbols or construct a rule to describe the growth? What might that rule look like? Will it work for every stage (or every term)?

  - Where do you see the growth represented in the picture of the pattern? In the T-chart? In the graph?

  - Can you predict values or pictures of subsequent growth based on this pattern?

    When you ask similar questions in several lessons, students begin to expect these questions and ask them of themselves. Each year, the *Five Dog Night* lesson practically teaches itself!

- Deciding which written representation best supports the thinking required of the task is an important instructional decision when lesson planning:

  - Students can work with a partner as they represent their thinking about the presented pattern in conversation, then on paper.

  - Students can present multiple representations of patterns on newsprint, large sheets of white construction paper, or on one of the Growing Patterns Templates (see Reproducibles 3.1 and 3.2)—whatever best fits the mathematical needs of the lesson and the availability of supplies.

  - T-charts representing growth patterns often include the first five terms, a jump to ten, and then to one hundred. Many T-charts will take on the following format:

In-Value ($\square$) (*x*)	Out-Value ($\triangle$) (*y*)
(0)	
1	
2	
3	
4	
5	
.	
.	
.	
.	
10	
.	
.	
.	
100	
(any stage)	

- You will need to make an instructional decision about the inclusion or discussion of Stage 0 for particular patterns. Sometimes it makes sense to do so; sometimes it does not. You may also wish to include "any stage" as the final in-value. You would then write the generalized rule for the pattern as the out-value for that final entry. You may wish to refer to this lesson format as you choose, construct, and carry out your lessons.

Possible Difficulties or Misconceptions

Some students may wrongly generalize that all growth patterns can be simplified to one specific rule, perhaps one that you covered in class. Several years ago I worked through two growth patterns with my class; both patterns could be represented by the rule *s* + 2. Yikes! Many of the students assumed that *all* growth patterns could somehow be simplified to *s* + 2! Now I introduce two different patterns with two very different rules in order to keep students from making that generalization.

Deciding how to deal with the order of operations can be tricky. Some curricula formally introduce the order of operations and some high-stakes tests assess students on their ability to apply it. Opportunities to explore the mathematical convention of PEMDAS (Please Excuse My Dear Aunt Sally—Parentheses, Exponents, Multiplication, Division, Addition, Subtraction) are important. (See Figure 3–18, page 146.) That being said, however, I worry that fifth graders may rely more on the acronym than on their understanding of the purpose of operational order. You may wish to refer to the "Calculation Routines and Practices" section of this chapter for ideas and activities that will expose the need for order when calculating and the importance of that understanding.

Investigations, Games, and Literature-Based Activities

Guess My Rule: Exploring Functions

Duration: 2–3 Class Periods and Can Be Revisited Throughout the Month

When you ask students to investigate and study the relationships between two sets of numbers or values, they are exploring and constructing their own understanding of functions and functional relationships. This investigation offers students opportunities to

- describe rules in words and in algebraic equations that relate one set of values (in-values) to another set (out-values);
- apply the use of T-charts to represent in- and out-values;
- apply and manipulate reverse operations to compute in-values when given out-values; and
- create functions, T-charts, and values for classmates to investigate, identify, and articulate in words and symbols.

Materials
- color tiles or pattern blocks
- math notebooks or paper

When students explore patterns and generalize relationships between and among numbers, they are developing informal understandings of one of the most important topics in high school and college algebra: functions (Chapin and Johnson 2006, 205). A *function* is a relationship in which two sets of values, commonly referred to as *in-values* and *out-values*, are linked by a rule that pairs each value of the first set with exactly one value of the second set. In other words, for every in-value, there is exactly one out-value.

You can represent functions using concrete objects or pictures, in words, on T-charts, with equations, and on graphs. Most fifth graders have been exposed to functional relationships as represented in T-charts from previous years of math instruction. It is important for the teacher to build from those understandings, but also to introduce additional representations of those same functions. Making deliberate the connections between representations is one of our greatest tasks when developing and presenting lessons on functional relationships. Fifth graders are often introduced to multiple representations in isolation. They know how to construct a T-chart. They know how to construct an equation or rule. They know how to graph. What they often do not know is how all the representations are related and tell the same story!

Because of my school's prescribed curriculum, my fifth graders have completed work in grades 1 through 4 with T-charts. They understand that the first column represents the in-value, and the second the out-value. They understand that a rule connects the two values. They understand that if the out-value is given, you reverse the rule to attain the in-value. You need to base instructional decisions on previous understandings and knowledge so that learning can move forward. You may need to supplement the following lesson with minilessons that will offer opportunities to support students as they develop strategies with which to think about functional relationships and how they work.

Prior to introducing this lesson, I share previous years' work with the students. I take pages from the texts of grades 1 through 5 that focus on T-charts and the relationships between the targeted in- and out-values. The students recognize many of the activities and always enjoy sharing their memories of earlier grades and work. I tell students that they will be continuing this work with T-charts and will need to apply what they already know about them to the work we are about to do in class.

We then discuss T-charts, focusing on the following ideas:

- T-charts have two values: the in-value and the out-value.
- A rule is associated with moving from the in-value to the out-value.
- A rule is reversed when moving from the out-value to the in-value.
- Rules can be described in words and in symbols.

I draw a T-chart on the board with an in-value and an out-value:

In	Out
2	5

Choose values that can represent a number of relationships. For example, the rule for these two values could be:

$$In + 3 = Out$$

or

$$(In \times 2) + 1 = Out$$

or

$$(In \times 3) - 1 = Out$$

Sean was confused by the rule options. "You said there can be only one rule! And now we have three! What is that about?" By this time in the school year, students should be comfortable and willing to express their confusion. Sean's confusion led us to a discussion about the necessity for additional in- and out-values so that we could rule out (no pun intended!) rules that did not apply. We added two more values to the T-chart:

In	Out
2	5
3	7
4	9

As soon as I posted the second set of values, each table group began a discussion. The class quickly began to eliminate rule options. "It can't be *plus three* because three plus three equals six, and four plus three equals seven. Out-values of six and seven don't fit." "And it can't be *times three minus one* because when the in-value is three the out-value would be eight, and not seven." The class quickly agreed that the rule for this set of values seemed to be "times two plus one" because that rule fit all three sets of values. I posed this question about adding another set of values: Would another set of values confirm their conjecture about the rule? The class agreed unanimously. So we decided to add another set of values.

I asked students what they wanted the in-value to be. Just about everyone agreed that they wanted five to be the in-value. "What if I posted seven as the in-value? How about thirty-three? How about nine and a half? Would the rule stay the same with numbers not presented in numerical order? Would the rule apply to values with fractions?" I must admit that I greatly enjoy playing devil's advocate with fifth graders. At first they are horrified at your feigned ignorance, but quickly realize that you are pushing them for something more. The arithmetic that this rule presents is accessible to all, but the concept of a generalized rule that will work for all values may not be. I ask students to turn and talk to their neighbors about this idea: Would any in-value confirm our rule?

Again, the group came to a consensus that any value would confirm the rule. Since I was "keeper of the rule," I added two more values. I did not, however, add an in-value of four because I wanted students to think beyond the *recursive* rule and to identify an *explicit* rule. An explicit rule is one that relies on the *relationship* between any given in- and out-value. You may have fifth graders in your class who prefer to think recursively. When students do so, they rely on the pattern presented by the previous value to determine the next. Some students may recognize that the out-values are increasing by two as you increase the in-value by one. Recursive thinking becomes less efficient as you move to an in-value that is out of numerical sequence. Students who are rooted in the need to operate with a recursive rule will need to list the in- and out-values up to ten in order to predict the eleventh. As students move through the fifth grade, we need to introduce them to the importance of looking beyond the recursive rule— but not require them to do so. Some will just not be developmentally ready. Please be cognizant of those students who are not yet ready to move beyond their need to think recursively—and you will certainly have some. These students may be able to see the benefit of explicit rules, but they are not just ready to move in that direction yet!

In	Out
2	5
3	7
4	9
.	.
.	.
.	.
10	21
.	.
.	.
.	.
100	201

The class was fairly convinced that the rule was "times two plus one" because it fit all five sets of values. I asked the class for a description of the rule in words and posted it below the T-chart. I reminded them that I wanted precise language. Gracie offered her words: "Take the in-value and double it. Then add one. Then you will have the out-value."

We spent time analyzing the language. Could we be more specific? Were there mathematical terms that we could use to make the meaning of those words clearer and more precise? The class agreed that the word "double" made sense, but that perhaps saying that we "multiply by two" would be more sophisticated. I smiled. Not only were students thinking like mathematicians, they were sounding like them, too! I asked the class to what were we adding the one? Gracie reminded us that the answer to a multiplication problem was called a product, so maybe we should say "add one to the product." Our revised rule in words took the following form: "Multiply the in-value by two. Add one to the product. That will give you the out-value."

Because we were all pleased with the revision, we were now ready to take the time to move from words to symbols. This process supports the introduction of ☐ and △ labels—or x and y, depending on the mathematical maturity of your class. Because my class was familiar with the ☐ and △ labels, we began there. However, at this time the x and y labels are introduced, as the labels that students will be seeing exclusively as they move into middle school. Some students will opt to stay with what they know, and some will be ready to move on to the x and y. Those holding on to the ☐ and △ labels are often ready to let them go as we move through several investigations requiring the use of a T-chart. We make the transitions when students are ready.

We are now ready for a discussion about algebraic sentences and generalized rules—a discussion that may take longer than you expect. Take the time! As students move from words to symbols, their understanding of algebraic language needs to be nurtured and developed. You can add additional labels to the T-chart to help students articulate their generalization algebraically.

In $\square$ x	Out $\triangle$ y
2	5
3	7
4	9
.	.
.	.
.	.
10	21
.	.
.	.
.	.
100	201

Now you can translate the students' words into symbols:

Multiply the in-value by 2.	$\square \times 2$
Add 1 to the product.	$(\square \times 2) + 1$
That will give you the out-value.	$(\square \times 2) + 1 = \triangle$

Our generalized rule is $(\square \times 2) + 1 = \triangle$ or $(x \cdot 2) + 1 = y$.

Once our rule is agreed on, we can test it with existing and additional values. You need to give the out-values as well and ask the students to solve for the corresponding in-values in order to develop the flexibility to do and undo operations depending on the values given. A completed T-chart may look like the following:

In $\square$ x	Out $\triangle$ y
2	5
3	7
11	23
9	?
?	33
?	9
10	?
25	?

As the students study and evaluate the in- and out-values, they may recognize that all of the out-values are odd numbers. If they do not, you might wish to ask them a "What do you notice?" question about the in- and out-values. Given your work in September and October with properties of odd and even numbers, you may have some interesting conversations about why all the out-values are odd numbers. Whenever you double an even or odd number, the result is even. Therefore, the final step of plus-one will always cause the out-value to be odd. Press the students to identify and articulate previously investigated concepts and how they relate to what they are now studying. They will be delighted with their ability to apply previous understandings and to make sense of observations and conjectures in relationship to the function being analyzed.

Adding a final out-value of twenty and posing the question, "What do we know about the in-value when the out-value is even?" will cause some well-intentioned confusion. Moving from whole numbers to fractions and mixed numbers offers opportunities for those students ready for a challenge. Be prepared to support those ready and willing to make conjectures about fractional numbers without calculating. Some students may be ready to make the generalization that out-values will only be odd when whole numbers are the in-values. But what happens when in-values are fractions or mixed numbers? How about an in-value of one-half? How about $5\frac{1}{2}$? $6\frac{1}{2}$? Identifying relationships within relationships can be intriguing and worth another investigation!

Your prescribed curriculum may offer lessons and practice pages supporting work with functions, T-charts, and identifying or applying rules. In addition to offering practice, these pages can also offer models from which students can work as they create their own functions and T-charts for classmates to investigate. (See Figure 3–1; see also Reproducibles 3.3 and 3.4.) You may wish to alter the directions to stretch the students' thinking to further engage and challenge them.

Once students have had some additional experiences examining functions presented in T-charts, you can ask them to create T-charts with in- and out-values that you can then ask their classmates to extend. Over the years I have learned that open-ended tasks like this certainly have their creative purposes, but you may need constraints to streamline the process. I have also learned that engaging students in developing the constraints helps to keep the them focused on the mathematical purpose of the task. It also helps for you to have set of constraints in mind before opening up the discussion to the class. You wish to set parameters that can be rolled into students' suggestions. You will also need to determine whether this work will be completed independently or with a partner.

▶ REPRODUCIBLE 3.3
What Is the Rule?

REPRODUCIBLE 3.4
Complete the
Missing
Representations

REPRODUCIBLE 3.3
What Is the Rule?

REPRODUCIBLE 3.4
Complete the Missing Representations

What is the rule?

in	out
0	0
3	9
4	12
—	15
10	—
101	—
$\frac{1}{3}$	—

in words:

in symbols:
out =

□	△
0	1
1	11
2	21
3	—
6	—
—	91
—	201
7	—

in words:

in symbols:
△ =

Complete the missing representations

x	*y*
8	—
14	—
—	49
—	1
9	—
2	—
—	16

in words:
multiply the *x*-value by 3 and then add 1 to get the *y*-value

in symbols:
$y =$

x	*y*
10	—
—	10
26	—
—	26
2	—
100	—
1	—

in words:

in symbols:
$y = (x \div 2) + 4$

FIGURE 3–1
Examples of Rules and Representations Practice Charts.

As a class, discuss what needs to be represented on and with each T-chart. You may wish to offer some of the following guiding questions as you move through the process:

- How many ins and outs should be represented?
- Do the initial values need to be in numerical order? Should there be a range for those first values (1–10? 1–20?)?
- Can fractions be included?
- Can negative numbers be included?

Keep in mind that including fractions and negative numbers can help differentiate the instruction for those students who are ready for a challenge. As you move around the room, suggest a fraction or negative number as an in- or out-value to students willing and able to manipulate such numbers.

As students work, chart and post the agreed-upon suggestions for reference. A possible set of guidelines may look like the following:

T-chart Guidelines

- Construct a T-chart of five in- and out-values.
- Post five in- or out-values that require your classmates to solve for the corresponding value.
- Include space at the bottom of the T-chart for your classmates to add additional in- and out-values.

On the back of the paper:

- Describe your rule in words with the following sentence starter: To get the out-value, you . . .
- Write your rule in symbols.

You may need to set time parameters before students set off to create their T-charts and rules. Your understanding of the class will determine how much time you will want to give them for the task.

Once the class has completed the T-charts, I collect them. I spend time reviewing the rules and values and then organize the class work into two piles. For one pile, students will identify the rule from the given values. For the other pile, students will apply the rule to calculate out- from in-values and in- from out-values. The number choices or complexity of the rules often determine into which pile the T-charts go. We can spend the next class period sharing T-charts or rules. I can write them on the whiteboard, reproduce them as handouts, or place them under a document camera. I ask the fifth-grade mathematicians responsible for the work to facilitate the class discussion about their particular function. I ask students exploring the function to represent their work and thinking in their math notebooks.

Coordinate Graphing Explorations

Duration: 1–2 Class Periods

Functional relationships can be represented graphically. In these investigations, students explore the coordinate graphing system developed by Rene Descartes (1596–1650). Reading *The Fly on the Ceiling* following the graphing activities gives students a context within which to enjoy their

NCTM Connection

Strand: Algebra
Focus: Plot points on a coordinate graph; identify and articulate how and where a graph relates to the function, equation, and T-chart it represents.
Context: Coordinate Graphing Explorations

understanding of graphing. These investigations offer students the opportunities to

- plot points on a coordinate graph;
- make generalizations and predictions based on the shape of a graph;
- informally explore the concept of *slope* and *y-intercept;* and
- identify and articulate how and where a graph relates to the function, equation, and T-chart it represents.

Materials

- *The Fly on the Ceiling: A Math Myth* by Julie Glass (1998)
- Graphing *Tic-Tac-Toe* One-Quadrant Grids (see Reproducible 3.5)
- Graphing *Tic-Tac-Toe* Four-Quadrant Grids (see Reproducible 3.6)
- graph paper, $\frac{1}{4}$ in. or 1 cm
- grid chart paper for class graphs
- lined or unlined chart paper or newsprint for the "Things That Come in Groups" charts

Vocabulary

axis, horizontal, vertical, equation, graph or linear graph or function, coordinates, ordered pair, plot, interval, scale, quadrant, positive number, negative number

The use of coordinate geometry makes it possible to represent functions graphically. Graphing a function calls for using ordered pairs to locate place points on a coordinate grid. Many curricula introduce coordinate graphing in the earlier grades. In order to make informed and appropriate instructional decisions, be cognizant of how much exposure and experience your students have had with coordinate graphing. Be aware that prior knowledge may vary from year to year given the makeup of your class. You can refer to *Lessons for Algebraic Thinking, Grades 3–5* (Wickett, Kharas, and Burns 2002) for leveled explorations with graphing. See the "Resources" section of this chapter for specific chapter and exploration explanations.

Because my students have had experiences with coordinate graphing in the fourth grade, our explorations begin with a quick review of the coordinate graphing system and a game of *Tic-Tac-Toe.* On a gridded piece of chart paper, we construct a quadrant I coordinate graph, discussing the placement of the axes and which is which. We continue to use the ☐ and △ as we label the *x*- and *y*-axes. We pay special attention to the language used to describe the axes, such *horizontal, vertical, intersecting,* and *origin.*

REPRODUCIBLE 3.5
Graphing Tic-Tac-Toe One-Quadrant Grids

REPRODUCIBLE 3.6
Graphing Tic-Tac-Toe Four-Quadrant Grids

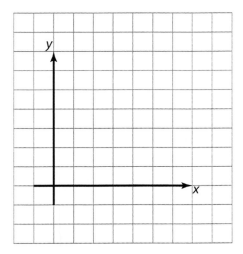

The conversation then moves to a discussion of ordered pairs and the mathematical convention of plotting points: (x, y). As we prepare to plot points, I pose questions such as the following about labeling the intervals of both the x- and y-axes.

- Is the origin always $(0, 0)$?

- Do we have to count by ones?

- Can we skip-count the intervals?

- Can we skip a chunk of numbers and then resume counting once again?

- Does the x-axis have to have the same interval length or scale as the y-axis? Why or why not?

When you distribute premade graphs to students, these questions and their answers are relatively meaningless. However, when students construct their own graphs, they exhibit greater interest and intrigue about these issues and the possible constraints.

Although the lessons do not need to center on the use of scale, it is an aspect of graphing that you can touch on in the fifth grade. The scale of the intervals on the x- and y-axes should be related to the range of values for each variable.

The decisions that you make about selecting a scale can lead to distortion in the data as shown by three different graphs. (See Figure 3–2.) Although all three graphs display the same data, posing questions to the students about the assumptions that they may make based upon the scale used in each graph can be helpful in highlighting the importance of scale. You can have conversations about the need to select an appropriate scale that will represent the data accurately. It may help to reference your prescribed curriculum to see how this topic is approached—or not! Over the years, I have decided to have this discussion, but to inform students that for our purposes, we will use scales with intervals of one because a scale of one aligns with the mathematical objectives of our explorations and their subsequent data sets.

▶ REPRODUCIBLE 3.5
Graphing Tic-Tac-Toe One-Quadrant Grids

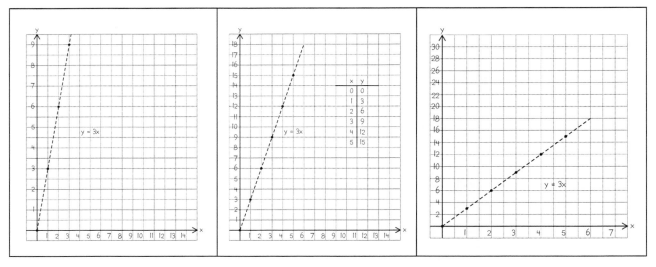

FIGURE 3–2
Three Graphs, All Showing the Same Values with Different Scales for the *x* and *y* Axes.

▶ REPRODUCIBLE 3.7
Graphing Tic-Tac-
Toe Directions

Once we have constructed our class coordinate grid, I introduce the directions for *Tic-Tac-Toe* (see Reproducible 3.7). I play an introductory game with students to model marking the Xs and Os as point locations are chosen. Because many of the students are familiar with the board game *Battleship*, they often need reminders about the placements of the points. In the game of *Battleship*, students place their markers in spaces on a grid; when graphing on a coordinate grid, the points are placed on the intersections of the *x*- and *y*-axes. In this game, I ask students not only to plot their points as they play but also to keep a T-chart of their ordered pairs as well. In another version of this game, students record their ordered pair in the T-chart *first*. The other players then hold that player to that recorded ordered pair. This practice will encourage students to be more thoughtful about their recording as well as their partner's recording—because the order of the ordered pair matters. The placement of (8, 3) is very different from (3, 8)!

After they play several games, I ask students to return their attention to the class coordinate graph and further discuss the structure of the coordinate graphing system. I pose several guided "What do you notice?" questions about the axes. When students can identify the axes as number lines, their understanding begins to develop around the idea of numbers that can be represented beyond the graph.

As the class discusses the ideas of negative values for *x* and *y*, we construct a four-quadrant graph. Negative numbers are very real to fifth graders—they may not understand how to manipulate them, but they are well aware of their presence and potential use. Constructing a four-quadrant graph and playing *Tic-Tac-Toe* on this grid can present new challenges and the need for new strategies. I distribute four-quadrant *Tic-Tac-Toe* grids (see Figures 3–3 and 3–4; see also Reproducible 3.6), and students play several more games.

REPRODUCIBLE 3.6   ◀
Graphing Tic-Tac-
Toe Four-Quadrant
Grids

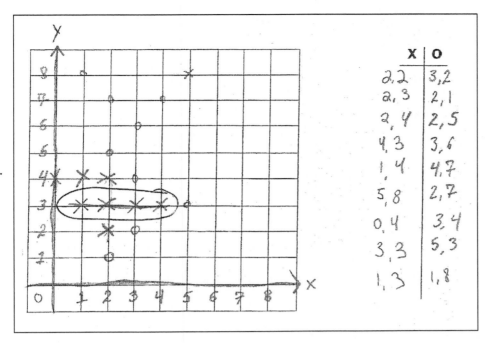

FIGURE 3–3
Harriet's and Ellie's Completed Game.

FIGURE 3–4
Harriet's and Ellie's Completed Four-Quadrant Game.

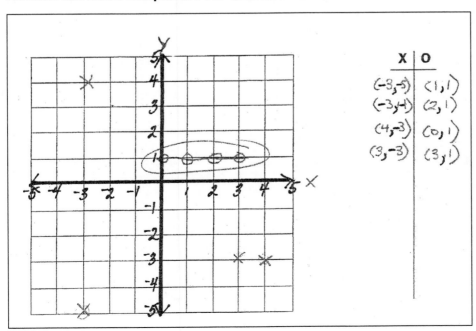

Things That Come in Groups

This activity, presented and discussed in many Math Solutions publications, is often a third-grade activity. However, fifth-grade data collected from charting things that come in groups can offer opportunities for students to investigate functions in the real world. The class can then graph and discuss these functional relationships. You can scaffold an informal understanding of *slope* as students discuss the rates of growth represented in the graphs. (The original write-up of this activity contains student vignette and author commentary [Burns 2007].)

TEACHER-TO-TEACHER TALK ■ **About Revisiting Previous Learning** ■ I have a theory regarding revisiting the previous years' activities and work in mathematics. For lack of a better title, let's just call this practice *retroactive metacognition*. I have found great value in asking students to reflect on the work they have done in previous years, especially work that they liked. I am very aware of the work that our third grade does as they move through their unit on multiplication because I helped to develop it. The third grade has adopted many of the practices and routines proposed in *Teaching Arithmetic: Lessons for Extending Multiplication, Grade 3* (Wickett and Burns 2001). They play *Circles and Stars*, investigate candy boxes, and create lists of *Things That Come in Groups*. Because I know these tasks well and understand the mathematics supporting them, I am willing and able to reference them in later years. We see things differently and often with greater understanding as we grow older—and that even includes ten-year-olds! You may be amazed at the insights students now have about *Circles and Stars* and *Things That Come in Groups* in the fifth grade compared with their understandings of the same activities when in the third! (Stay tuned—because we will revisit *Circles and Stars* in the next chapter!) You can make those connections and transferable understandings visible and accessible with meaningful classroom conversation, good questions, or writing prompts. Casual conversations with your colleagues teaching in the third and fourth grades can also be significant. Each year I take note of those landmark activities of each unit in both the third and fourth grades in order to assess how I might access them in the fifth. When scaffolding those conversations with your class about previous years' tasks, remember not only to ask about what they *thought* they understood way back then, but also to ask about misconceptions that they might have had and how those misconceptions have been resolved over the years.

You can introduce the lesson with a discussion of things in our everyday world that come in groups as class charts go up; Things That Come in Twos, Things That Come in Threes, and so on up to nine. I ask students why the grouping of things is helpful as we move through our lives. Although many ideas can be tossed around, the common theme seems to be that grouping things together makes them easier to count. Students are reminded once again that counting is a huge mathematical requirement of our world, and the need to count efficiently is very important whether you are six, ten, or fifty-two years old!

I instruct students to work with a partner to post items that come in groups on the various charts around the room. I ask students to think outside the box a bit, but not to forget to post the more obvious things as well, such as the days of the week or the number of tennis balls in a can. (See Figure 3–5.)

Because my students use graph paper notebooks, the following graphing task can be posted right in their notebooks. If you do not use graph paper notebooks, you will need to distribute graph paper to each student—one piece of graph paper per representation. Once the charts have a variety of postings, I call the class back together to describe the task.

Moving from a T-chart to a graph can be a challenge for some students—and for some adults! Too often the concepts and procedures that connect the two representations are not made visible to students. Textbooks often present and teachers often teach the representations in isolation. Moving from a list of things that come in groups, to a T-chart, and then to a graph will empower students to connect the representations. In doing so, they will begin to perceive one as just another representation of the other.

FIGURE 3–5
Sample Listing of Things That Come in Sixes.

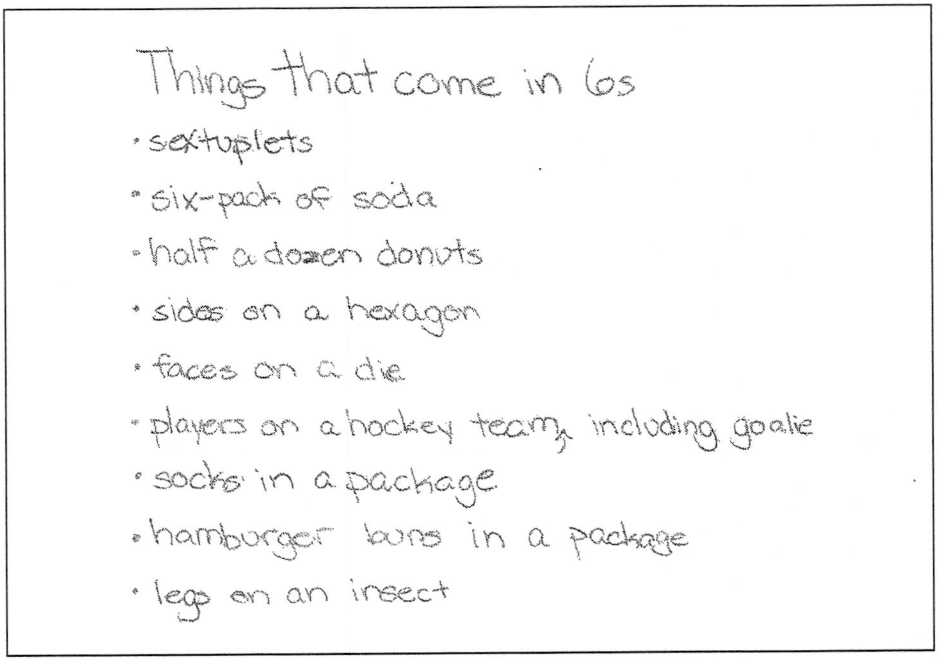

Things that come in 6s
- sextuplets
- six-pack of soda
- half a dozen donuts
- sides on a hexagon
- faces on a die
- players on a hockey team, including goalie
- socks in a package
- hamburger buns in a package
- legs on an insect

I select a grouping from a chart to model the activity from beginning to end with the class. They will work in their notebooks as I work under the document camera or on a piece of chart paper. Because so many of my students play ice hockey or pickup games of pond hockey, I often choose the number of hockey players on the ice as my grouping, and given our geographic location, this is always a popular choice! We head our papers: "Things That Come in Sixes." (And please note: We came to consensus as a class that six players were on the ice on a hockey team. We have two goalies in the class, and they did not like being left out of the count—because they often are! It is always important to keep your audience in mind!)

Although students may prefer to start their T-charts with an in-value of one, the class needs to have an important discussion concerning an in-value of zero. Does it make sense to have an in-value of zero? What does that mean in this context of teams and total number of hockey players? Elise was quick to offer that it most certainly made sense. "If you have no teams on the ice, then you have no players! So if we have zero teams, then we have zero players!" Discussions accompany all postings that follow the guidelines presented in the "Lesson Planning" section of this chapter.

I make the connection between the class charts and the T-chart deliberate and visible. The class chart offers us information in words, and the T-chart offers us that same information in numbers. Adam reminded us that the T-chart gives us more information in a more usable format. Questions such as "Why would that be important?" and "Who might use this information?" can push students to use and interpret the mathematics. Our conversation moved from the number of pairs of hockey skates needed for so many players to how much hockey skates cost to the ridiculous cost of hockey sticks all in about fifteen minutes! One year I had a student whose father worked for Bauer, a hockey equipment distributor. Lo and behold, several days after our lesson, a spreadsheet appeared on my desk that had been used to project and estimate the number and cost of the skates needed for a Boston area college hockey team for the upcoming season. Very cool!

As we discuss and analyze our T-chart, I ask questions about other activities in which T-charts have been used. Because my students have been working with T-charts representing functional relationships since first grade, they quickly make the connection between this T-chart and a set of in- and out-values. I place a label of *in* and *out* on our T-chart. I ask students to make sense of these labels with a neighbor. (See Figure 3–6.)

When the class reaches consensus about the use of the in and out labels, I ask students if any other labels could be placed on the two columns. The class quickly agrees that the box (☐) and triangle (△) can be used as labels, as well as x and y. You can ask guiding questions to scaffold the understanding of the functional relationship that exists between the two sets of

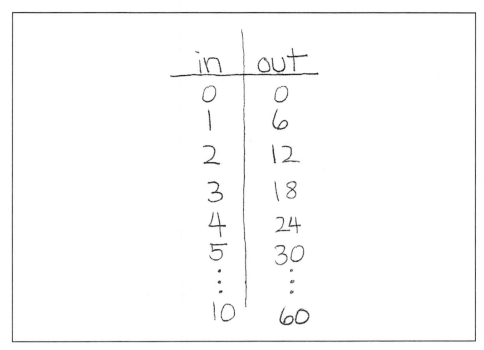

FIGURE 3–6
Adam's T-chart Labeled with *In* and *Out*.

values. When we agree on a rule for this set of values, we add it to the T-chart as the *y*-value for any number of teams (*n*). (See Figure 3–7.)

Coordinate graphs can also represent functional relationships. The big idea that graphs are *representations* of relationships often eludes young mathematicians. As teachers of mathematics, we need to make those connections and generalizations deliberate and visible to our fifth graders. As we discuss the T-chart and the functional relationship that it represents, we also need to pay attention to the coordinate graph and how it can represent that same relationship.

We can now turn our attention to the coordinate graph. Some students will begin to make the connection between the in-values of the T-chart and the *x*-axis of the coordinate graph and between the out-values and the *y*-axis. Constructing a coordinate graph and titling the axes can help to support and scaffold this understanding. Agreeing on the scale of the *x*- and *y*-axes will also help. All the graphs will need to have the same scale on both axes for ease of comparison. (See Figure 3–8.)

Students can now access the T-chart to help identify the *x*- and *y*-values of this function. As you plot the points, you can have discussions about the shape of the data. This may happen without much facilitation on your part! Some students will notice that each time you go over one on the chart, you go up six. They are able to plot points simply by following the

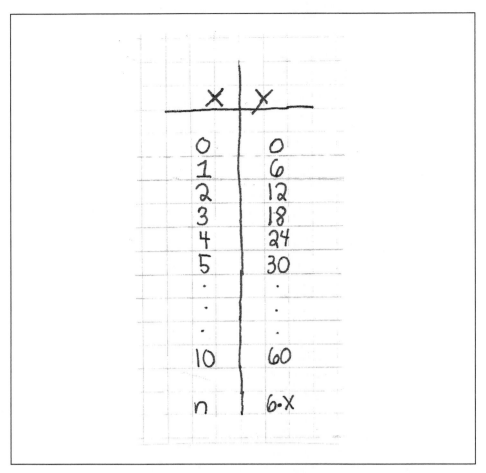

FIGURE 3–7
Adam's T-chart with the Added x-Value of n and $6x$.

pattern of *over one* and *up six* rather than referring to the T-chart. In doing so, these students are making sense of the rate of change (or *slope*) of the growth of this $6x = y$ pattern. Although I do not give a formal definition or discuss slope, I tell students that mathematicians refer to this rate of change pattern as the *slope of function*. They will spend more time investigating slope as they move into the later grades.

Once the class has constructed the graph, you can have several conversations. One is a discussion about the shape of the graph. The graph makes a line and represents a *linear* function. The linear format of the graph is not a coincidence. Patrick reminded us that as far as he could see, not much in math was! I ask students to discuss the linear nature of the graph and why that makes sense. Because the growth of this pattern is constant and predictable, the representation of the growth is linear and can be represented by a straight line.

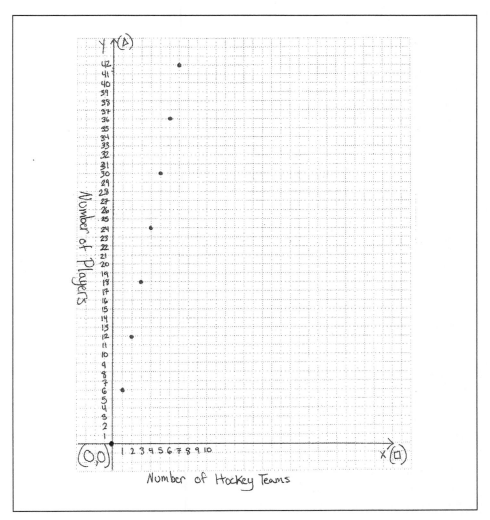

FIGURE 3–8
Labeled Coordinate Graph.

The other discussion that can follow is one pertaining to connecting the values. Do we connect the points—or not? According to mathematical convention, when points are connected, each and every point along that line is a solution. So we decided to test a few out. What if we played around with fractions? What if we had $1\frac{1}{2}$ teams on the ice? How many players would that be? Would that value make sense? One and a half teams would be equivalent to twelve players. And yes, that does make sense. But what about one and one-third teams? That would mean ten and two-thirds players . . . and you cannot have two-thirds of a player! So we agree that the values should not be connected because not all points along the line would make sense given the context of our grouping.

Our representation of *Things That Come in Sixes* is now complete. We have a T-chart, a rule, and a graph, all telling the same story. I ask students to work with a partner on representing other things that come in groups. Although the work will be done with a partner, each student is responsible for his or her own paper. The format will be the same as the one modeled that will be the scale for the graph.

Once students have had the time to prepare two or three representations, I ask them to compare and contrast their graphs at their table groupings. The purpose of this discussion is to elicit conversation about the shape and rate of growth, or slope, of the various graphs.

- Are all the graphs linear? Why does that make sense?
- Some graphs have a steeper set of points than others. Why is that so? And why does that make sense?
- Where does your graph start? Do all the graphs start at the same point? Why or why not? Why does this make sense?
- Can you make a prediction about the steepness of a set of points? What if we investigated things that come in twelves? What would that set of points look like? How about things that come in twos?
- What is the relationship between the steepness of a line and the number of items in a group?

Although this informal discussion about slope and the *y*-intercept is just that, encourage your fifth graders to be as explicit as possible with their observations and explanations. Do not be surprised at the mathematical sophistication demonstrated by their responses! They are learning to think like mathematicians as you are supporting and facilitating that learning.

An oral reading of *The Fly on the Ceiling* (Glass 1998) can give closure to the lesson and reinforce the time spent plotting ordered pairs on a coordinate graph. The story of Rene Descartes and his resolution to the dilemma of one very messy house will engage and entertain your students.

Growing Caterpillars: Investigating Growth Patterns I

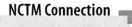

NCTM Connection

Strand: Algebra
Focus: Explore and represent a growth pattern.
Context: Growing Caterpillars

Duration: 4–5 Class Periods

In this investigation, students use pattern blocks to model a geometric growth pattern. Students are asked to predict, extend, and represent the patterns in words, on T-charts, with equations (rules), and on graphs. This investigation offers students opportunities to

- explore, predict, and represent patterns that grow;
- connect geometry, number, and algebra;
- explore equivalent expressions and equations;
- represent patterns with pictures (geometry), words, numbers (T-charts), symbols (equations), and graphs; and
- move flexibly from one representation to another.

Materials

- centimeter grid paper (see Reproducible 2.5)
- *Growing Patterns Templates* 1 or 2 enlarged for 11-by-18-inch paper (see Reproducibles 3.1 and 3.2)
- pattern blocks
- 12-by-18-inch white drawing paper or construction paper
- lined paper
- colored pencils
- optional: pattern blocks for the overhead
- optional: overhead

▶ REPRODUCIBLE 2.5
Centimeter Grid
Paper

REPRODUCIBLES
3.1 and 3.2
Growing Patterns
Templates 1 and 2

Vocabulary

conjecture, constant, core, explicit thinking or rule, growth pattern, iterative thinking or rule, multiple representations, repeating pattern, slope, *x*-axis, *y*-axis, *y*-intercept

In *About Teaching Mathematics: A K–8 Resource,* Marilyn Burns reminds us that patterns are key factors in understanding mathematical concepts. The ability to recognize, create, and extend patterns is essential for making generalizations, seeing and articulating relationships, and understanding the order and logic of mathematics (Burns 2007). In this investigation, we will explore growth patterns as students create and represent growing caterpillars. One geometric model of a growing caterpillar can offer a context within which to explore two different functions—an interesting concept in itself! We will explore and represent the number of blocks needed to make each successive caterpillar as well as the perimeter of each.

Many fifth graders have had experiences with growth patterns in the previous grades, but may not have had opportunities to identify, think about, or articulate the differences between repeating patterns and those representing growth. A kinesthetic approach to comparing and contrasting repeating and growth patterns works well. I begin a repeating pattern of clap—snap—clap—snap—clap—snap. I ask students to join in once they can identify the pattern. We have a quick conversation about this pattern, which begins with my favorite question, "What do you notice?"

Rebecca pointed out that the pattern repeated. Norah added that it was an A—B—A—B—A—B pattern. I posed the following question to the class:

If this is an A—B—A—B—A—B pattern, with A representing the clap, can you predict what the fifteenth term of the pattern would be? Would it be a clap or a snap? How do you know?

Mac responded that all even-number terms would be Bs, or snaps, and that all odd-number terms would be As, or claps. So the fifteenth term would be a clap because fifteen is an odd number. I asked the class if they needed to test out Mac's conjecture. Although no one responded, I could tell that a few students were a little unsure of this prediction. So I suggested that we try it out, just to make sure. We clapped and snapped up to the fifteenth term—and it was, in fact, a clap. Then we discussed the power of prediction. If we could, in fact, predict whether a term was a clap or a snap based on the oddness or evenness of the term number, then we did not need to try it out. The students agreed that this idea of prediction was pretty cool—it saved time and work!

I told students that this type of pattern can be identified as a *repeating pattern*. The clap-snap of the pattern is called the *core*, the part of the pattern that repeats over and over. If students can identify the core, they can continue the pattern and make predictions about what comes when.

You can then introduce a new pattern such as the following:

(C = clap, S = snap)

C—S—C—S—S—C—S—S—S—C—S—S—S—S—C—S—S—S—S—S

I asked students to join in once they could identify the pattern. And once again, I asked them the "What do you notice?" question.

Matthew mentioned that this pattern was different from the previous one. This pattern grew. Evan responded that you had to count carefully with this pattern because the number of snaps was different after each clap. Willy made a connection to our work with predictions with the previous repeating pattern. He had some reservations about his ability to predict the fifteenth term in this pattern. He was fairly sure that he would have to continue clapping and snapping until the fifteenth term before he could be sure whether that term would be a clap or a snap. "But you know," Willy began, "chances are that the fifteenth term would be a snap because there are more snaps than claps." A few students were quietly clapping and snapping as Willy was sharing his idea. The class erupted when they realized that the fifteenth term was actually a clap!

I asked students for a label for this type of pattern; one that grows. Norah called it a *growth pattern*. And right she was! Nonrepeating patterns can be more difficult for students both to understand and predict. Students not only must identify what comes next in the pattern, but also must begin to generalize about the relationships apparent in the pattern. The numbers, objects, letters, or geometric figures that make up the sequence are called the *terms, steps*, or *stages* of the sequence (Chapin and Johnson 2006).

TEACHER-TO-TEACHER TALK ■ **About Taking an Algebra Class** ■ Several years ago, I sat in on an honors algebra class for eighth graders that was being offered down the hall from my classroom. I was greatly enjoying my work with algebraic thinking in the fifth grade and felt it was time to rethink all that I thought I knew about algebra. A phenomenal math teacher taught the class, and some of her students had been students of mine when they were in the fifth grade! Now Shivani and Sophie were helping *me* with *my* homework! I could not attend every class due to my own teaching responsibilities, but word got around fast that I was taking Ms. Chapin's algebra class. There was something very right about this exercise in humility. And I was humbled by how much algebra instruction had changed in thirty years! Or had I changed? Now I was looking for connections everywhere. Now I was trying to make sense of rules and routines. But even better, I was asking myself questions. Is there a more efficient way to solve this problem? Would writing the rule out in words first help me to understand the equation? Could I solve this problem in another way? Would working from a T-chart help me better understand the problem? Would a graph be a better representation for me to work with? I was beginning to experience the formal study of algebra as a connected body of concepts, procedures, practices, and routines. We do not create graphs, T-charts, words, and pictures or solve problems in isolation as we used to do so many years ago. I had been given a gift—and to think that it had always been just down the hall.

I tell students that they will spend some time investigating a growing pattern represented with pattern blocks. When the pattern block tubs are placed on the tables, students cheer! Year in and year out, pattern blocks continue to be my class's favorite manipulative. I have also learned over the years that the class needs free exploration time prior to any lesson using pattern blocks with the reminder that when time is called, they push the blocks to the center of the tables—and we are ready to begin the planned investigation.

Once students have put the blocks away, I present the context of the investigation. Students are going to be investigating the growth of a caterpillar that will be made out of pattern blocks. A one-year-old caterpillar is created on the overhead (see below). I ask each student to make a one-year-old caterpillar at their tables.

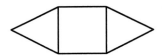

A one-year-old caterpillar

Next I ask students to think about what a two-year-old caterpillar might look like. As they share their ideas about how this caterpillar might grow, I take the opportunity to implement and practice talk moves. Asking students to repeat what their classmates have said will keep the focus on the thinking of another student. Asking students to add on to their classmates' ideas will help them to extend the thinking of another student. Asking them to repeat or add on to the opinions of others offers opportunities for them to make sense of the thinking and language of classmates.

I introduce students to this particular task's *constraint*, or the predetermined limitation to this problem. In this task, we need to agree on the growth of the caterpillar—where it will be and what it will look like. I construct a two-year-old caterpillar on the overhead next to the one-year-old so that we can make comparisons:

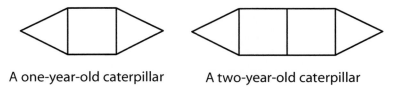

A one-year-old caterpillar   A two-year-old caterpillar

I ask students once again to turn and talk to their neighbor about how and where they see the growth of this caterpillar. The power of pattern is in its predictability. Because of this, I can ask students to predict what a three-, four-, and five-year-old caterpillar would look like.

Although conversations that help to scaffold the articulation of the rules of this pattern will become extremely important, at this time in the lesson it is more important for students to manipulate, discuss, and draw the pattern before they attempt to create rules from the words and symbols. We often jump too quickly to the symbolic representation of patterns without allowing students ample time to construct their own understandings and articulations of growth patterns. When students can make sense of a pattern and its growth, the rule can fall out of the words that students use to articulate the growth as they see and understand it. Questions such as the following can help students *see* the growth in the geometry:

- Where is the caterpillar growing? Can you show me?
- How is the growth related to the birthday? How are the number of squares (the growth) related to the birthday?
- How are the *total number of blocks* related the growth of the caterpillar?
- Is there something *constant* about each caterpillar? Something that every caterpillar at every age has that is the same?
- Can you predict the caterpillar's age if I show you a picture of that caterpillar? How can you do that? Why does your method of prediction make sense?

Jake became animated when he realized that there was a "plus two" in each birthday as he calculated the total number of blocks in each birthday represented by the head and the tail of the caterpillar. He raced up to the board to describe his thinking—being careful not to dismantle any of his classmates' aging caterpillars, of course! "So all I have to do for any birthday is line up the number of squares that equals the number of years. Then I add a head and tail—and bingo! See—here is the plus two." (See Figure 3–9.)

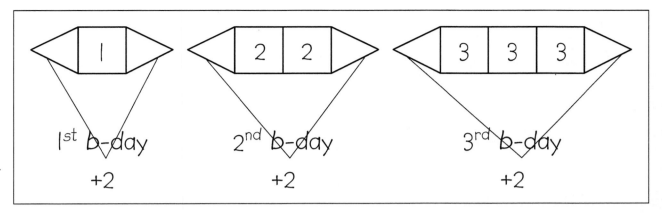

FIGURE 3–9
Jake's Thinking.

This idea of the "plus two" representation of the head and tail is a wonderful one for students to discover. This "plus two" represents the *constant* of the pattern; every caterpillar at every stage will have a head and a tail. Because of that, every number model for every stage will either begin or end with the "plus two." Posing questions and supporting conversations that offer students opportunities to connect the meaning of *constant* in everyday language to its meaning in mathematics will help them to make sense of the rule that is falling out of their speech.

I ask students to construct the first five birthdays of this caterpillar with pattern blocks. You can ask students to build in pairs if there are not enough pattern blocks for each student. As students are building, I distribute white construction paper to each table group. I ask each student to draw and color the first five birthdays of the caterpillar at the top of their paper. I usually ask students to draw the squares and triangles freehand. If this is problematic for your class, tracing the blocks or using pattern block templates are options, although they are more time-consuming. I also ask students to label each birthday.

Modeling is an important practice and one that will support many, if not all, of your students' learning styles. Prior to this lesson, you can start a poster with the first five stages of this caterpillar's growth drawn and labeled just as you have instructed students to do. As students are working to complete their drawings, you can post your poster on the whiteboard for reference. You can add more representations to your poster as students do the same to theirs. Having a model from which to work often allows students to answer those questions dealing with protocol or procedure themselves.

Language can help to move students from drawings to more abstract representations of this growth. I often introduce the term *stage* at this point in the lesson as a word that mathematicians use to identify the sequence of a pattern—or in this case, to represent the birthdays of a growing caterpillar. Often students will take it upon themselves to add

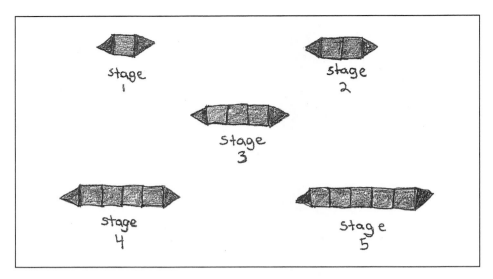

FIGURE 3–10
Noah's First Five Caterpillar Birthdays.

the labels of Stage 1, Stage 2, Stage 3, Stage 4, and Stage 5 to their drawings. They are thinking like mathematicians! (See Figure 3–10.)

After students draw and label the first five stages, we begin a conversation about the purpose of our investigation. I inform students that they
will be investigating the relationship between the birthday number of each
caterpillar and the total number of blocks they will need to make that
particular caterpillar. In other words, we are exploring the relationship
between the stage number and the total number of blocks.

It is important for students to understand that pictures are just one way
of representing this pattern. This pattern can also be represented numerically. Because my students are familiar with T-charts, the move to a numerical representation in a T-chart is quick and comfortable. We construct a
T-chart on our posters below the pictorial representation of the growth of
this pattern. The class constructs the T-charts with a great deal of discussion. They quickly come to a consensus about the labels of the in- and out-
values based on the relationship we are studying. The in-value (x) will be
labeled Stage Number. The out-value (y) will be labeled Total Number of
Blocks. Because of previous experiences, my students are also acquainted
with the labels of $\square$ and $\triangle$ and x and y, which can be used to represent the
in- and out-values of any T-chart. We agree to add these labels to our
T-chart. In time, students often drop the $\square$ and $\triangle$ labels. However, I hesitate to suggest to those students comfortable with these labels that they
drop them for those of x and y. If this is students' initial experience with
multiple representations of a growth pattern, familiar labels such as $\square$ and
$\triangle$ often help them make sense of the relationships found in the T-chart.
These familiar labels help connect the understanding of this pattern to

previous knowledge and can and will, in time, be discarded for more conventional labels.

You can introduce a three-column T-chart at this point in the lesson. Because students are aware of the labels and purposes of the In and Out columns, a middle column can now be added to represent the number models for each stage. Students can begin to focus their attention on the numerical representations of what grows and what stays the same (constant) in this particular pattern. The addition of this middle column can be helpful for a variety of reasons. The middle column can

- represent the calculation;
- concretely represent the constant of the pattern (What is the constant in this pattern? In any pattern? Where do we see it in the geometry of this pattern? Where do we see it with numbers?);
- offer opportunities to connect the stage number with what is happening mathematically (Where is the stage number found in our number model? Why does that make sense?); and
- scaffold the abstraction of a rule.

Stage Number (Birthday) □ x	What Is Happening?	Total Number of Blocks △ y
1		
2		
3		
4		
5		

A question such as, "Can we predict how many total blocks will be needed for Stage 10 without building or drawing that stage?" can begin conversations that require students to articulate and subsequently apply a generalization or rule for the growth of this pattern. Jake had taken on the role of the "Keeper of the 'Plus Two' Rule" and was quick to offer a generalization. "It's all about the plus two," he began. "Find the stage number, or the birthday. That is how many squares you will need to use. Then add the plus two for the head and tail—and there it is!" When I asked the class about Stage 100, they broke out in conversation. They all agreed with Jake's generalization: just take the stage number and add two more blocks for the head and tail. You can then add values of 10 and 100 to the in-values with the use of ellipses to represent the skipped values. I ask students to create and complete T-charts to represent the numerical growth of this pattern. (See Figure 3–11.)

□ Stage # (Birthday)	What is happening?	△ Total # of blocks
1	1 + 2	3
2	2 + 2	4
3	3 + 2	5
4	4 + 2	6
5	5 + 2	7
⋮	⋮	⋮
10	10 + 2	12
⋮	⋮	⋮
100	100 + 2	102

FIGURE 3–11
Patrick's T-chart.

Now students are ready to construct and formulate symbolic representations of this pattern in words as well as with an algebraic equation. If this is an initial experience with putting a pattern to words, you might consider working through this process within a whole-class format. It is extremely helpful for students to observe and be part of the process of putting thoughts to words to symbols.

I ask students to turn and talk to their neighbor about how they see this caterpillar growing. You will need to remind them of the importance of language and to be consistent with the language that they have used throughout this process. As they share ideas, you will also need to remind students to stay true to *their* perceptions—how *they* see the pattern growing. Some will begin with the head and tail. Others will begin with the number of blocks in the body. It is important for students to be able to articulate what they see as a *constant* in the pattern—and what they see as *growth*. The middle column of each student's T-chart should document this perception.

I ask students to take a partner and craft a written description of how they each see the growth, keeping in mind that they may not see the growth in the same way. I ask the them to think aloud to each other so that the words and phrases can be tried out and tested for sense. I encourage students to revise their descriptions as they talk to each other. Just as we do in reading, I ask students to close their eyes and visualize the caterpillar growing as their partners read their descriptions. As your partner reads, can you see it growing? What stays the same? The students then share individual descriptions in a whole-class format. For the sake of modeling,

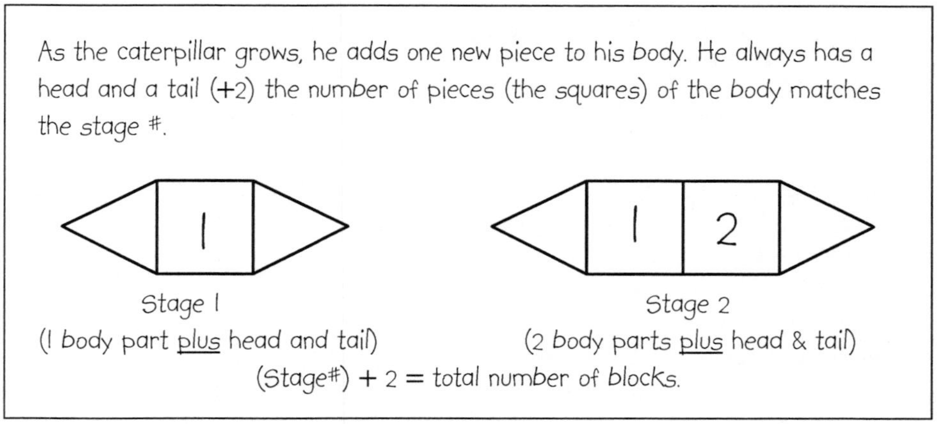

As the caterpillar grows, he adds one new piece to his body. He always has a head and a tail (+2) the number of pieces (the squares) of the body matches the stage #.

Stage 1
(1 body part <u>plus</u> head and tail)

Stage 2
(2 body parts <u>plus</u> head & tail)

(Stage#) + 2 = total number of blocks.

FIGURE 3–12
A Whole-Class Description of the Growth in Words.

we agree on a description that seems to be fairly common and craft a class description. As I work under the document camera, each student writes with me as we compose a class description, paying close attention to the precision of our language. Once the description is complete, I ask students to close their eyes and visualize the growth of this caterpillar as I read the description out loud. We can now add the description to the posters. (See Figure 3–12.)

Once each student has crafted a description of the growth in words, we can work on putting those words in symbols. Moving to the algebraic equation from the written description offers the opportunity for further abstraction of the pattern. I ask students if they can think of a way to represent the growth of any caterpillar at any stage using mathematical symbols and numbers. I often introduce *Stage n* at this point in the lesson to represent *any* stage. I notate on the board as we begin to formulate the equation:

$$n =$$

Jake was quick to announce that this was his rule:

$$n = (head + tail) + (age)$$

If students begin the process with words, I script the words. The words anchor the pattern in the geometry and offer a visualization of the pattern that can be important for some students as they move from the concrete to the abstract.

The students can work from this representation to a more conventional representation using the symbols found in the labels of their T-chart. The class agrees that the (head + tail) can be represented as + 2 and that the age can be presented by the in-value or ☐ or x. The equation can now be represented as the following:

$$n = 2 + \square \qquad or \qquad y = 2 + x$$

If the *n* or the *y* continues to create confusion for some students, the term *any stage* can be easily substituted:

$$any\ stage = 2 + \square \qquad or \qquad any\ stage = 2 + x$$

We then refer to the T-chart to try out some values to make sure our equation makes sense. Our agreed-upon equation is then posted on the poster. We try some values documented on the T-chart, and some that are not. Asking students to close their eyes and to visualize a caterpillar at age thirty-three can reinforce the comprehension of the pattern and rule. "That is one long caterpillar!" reported Jake.

The pattern of moving from the pictures to the numbers to the words to the equation has set the stage for the move to the graph. (See Figure 3–13.)

I distribute centimeter graph paper to students. I tell them to construct the axes and labels of their graphs based on the labels of the in- and out-values on our T-chart. You may need to be mindful of the uses of $\square$ and $\triangle$ or *x* and *y* with various students as you move about the room to ensure alignment of the labels being used. Even after many years of working through this lesson, I find that this representation continues to be elusive to many. Making a deliberate connection between the T-chart and the

FIGURE 3–13
Multiple Representations of a Pattern.

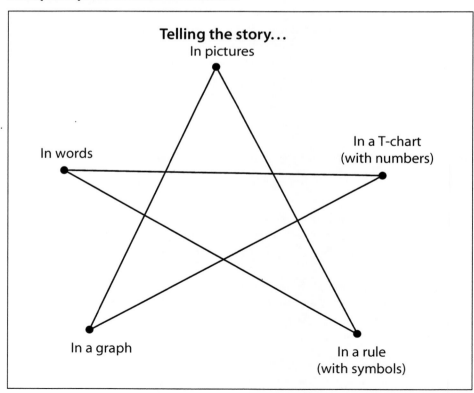

graph is important to help ground students in the context and growth of the pattern and how it can be represented on the graph.

As we graph the first five stages and their respective *x* and *y* values, I pose questions and field answers:

- What happens every time we go to the next stage?
- Is the rate of change or growth constant? Is it consistent? How do you know? Where is that constant growth in the graph? Where is it in the T-chart? Where is it in the geometry?
- Do we connect the points? Why or why not?

The final question regarding connecting the points is worth another class discussion. The context of this problem determines whether we connect the points or not. When we connect points on a graph, we assume that every point along that line is a solution. Can we have an age of two and a half? Yes, *but* can we have half blocks within this context? The students will invariably argue that the blocks can be broken into halves, but given this context and the pattern blocks that we are using, there are no half blocks. So our points will remain discreet and we will not draw a line.

My favorite conversation in this entire lesson is the one that focuses on the *plus two*. Because Jake had been so focused on the plus two throughout the lesson (and someone every year always is!), I asked him where he could see that plus two in the graph. That question threw him for a loop— because he could *not* see it. Jake became quite exasperated. "But it *has* to be there—it is in the picture—we wrote about it and it is in the rule. So it has to be there somewhere!" We hope for a Jake in every class every year. Jake was desperately trying to make sense of the graph. Every other representation had made sense to him. There was something problematic about this graph, or his thinking, or so the class thought!

I asked students to think about the graph and where it started. The class agreed that this graph—and the T-chart and the geometry—all started at Stage 1 (1, 4). My question, "Could this pattern start at another value or at another place?" moved them to think beyond the pattern that had been represented.

Questions about the possibility of a Stage 0 began to fly around the room. Some students realized that the graph could be extended to intersect the *y*-axis. We would plot a Stage 0 value where we intersected the *y*-axis. At Stage 0, the *y*-value would be 2. "There he is!" shouted Jake. "So the plus two is just where the graph starts!" Jake was quite pleased with himself, and the class agreed unanimously that he was brilliant!

We discussed and explored the concepts of *slope* and *y-intercept* without putting labels to these concepts during this conversation. Fifth graders do not need to understand the complexities of either at this point in their mathematical careers, but I do introduce the terms to students as words that they will encounter as they move through the middle grades. We quickly refer to slope as the rate at which the pattern is growing. In the case of the growing caterpillar, every time we go up a stage, the total number of blocks increases by one; so every time we go "over" one, we are going "up" one. We refer to the y-intercept, the starting point on the graph, as Stage 0 when the in-value, ☐-value, or x-value is 0. And we leave it at that for the time being.

Once students have completed the graphs, we post them on the posters. Once again, I refer to the importance of being able to connect one representation to the other and to move flexibly among representations. These multiple representations tell the same story, the story of an aging caterpillar. (See Figure 3–14.)

As students explore and represent these new concepts, one experience with growing patterns is often not sufficient for them. You can present additional patterns in a menu format or as individual assignments. As the class constructs and explores growth patterns, you can provide a template that students can use to represent their patterns (see Reproducibles 3.1 and 3.2). Students can work independently or with a partner, within class time or free-choice time, in school or out of school. The growing caterpillar investigation can be extended as the class explores another function: the relationship between the age of the caterpillar and the perimeter of its shape based on the same growth pattern. What

FIGURE 3–14
Maisie's Completed Poster.

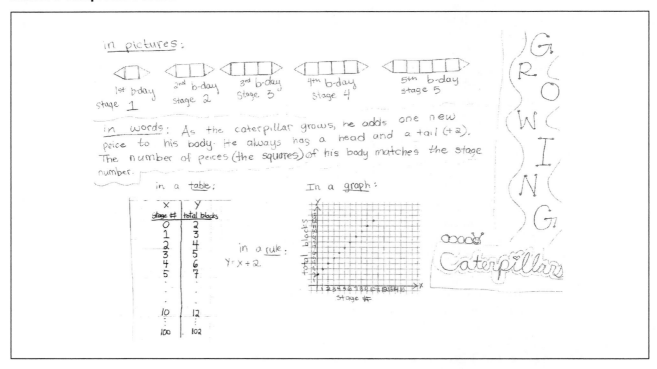

students often find intriguing is that a different rule comes out of this new relationship, which is grounded in the same geometric growth pattern. *Lessons for Algebraic Thinking, Grades 3–5* (Wickett, Kharas, and Burns 2002) presents additional growth pattern investigations. Further reference to these activities can be found in the "Assessment" and "Resources" sections of this chapter.

Literature Investigations

Engaging children's literature can offer meaningful contexts within which to explore patterns and functions. I have yet to meet a fifth-grade class that does not delight in the sharing of a picture book . . . especially in math class! I always introduce each lesson with an oral reading and sharing of the respective book.

Five Dog Night: Investigating a Linear Function

Duration: 1–2 Class Periods

This book presents a context within which a linear function, representing the number of feet in Ezra's bed depending on the temperature of the night, can be enjoyed and explored. This lesson offers students opportunities to

- identify, articulate, and represent a linear growth pattern;
- organize information on a T-chart;
- construct a rule that represents the growth of the pattern; and
- create a linear graph.

Materials

- *Five Dog Night* (Christelow 1993)
- Growing Patterns Template 2, enlarged for 11-by-18-inch paper (see Reproducible 3.2)
- colored pencils

Vocabulary

linear function

NCTM Connection

Strand: Algebra
Focus: Explore and represent a linear function in a literature context.
Context: *Five Dog Night* by Eileen Christelow

▶ REPRODUCIBLE 3.2
Growing Patterns
Template 2

In *Five Dog Night* (Christelow 1993), a cantankerous Ezra teaches his nosy neighbor Betty that a bed full of dogs can be just as warm as a pile of blankets as winter approaches and settles in. The story is charming and the illustrations endearing. And the context within which to investigate the relationship of dog nights (x) to the number of feet in Ezra's bed (y) is wonderfully algebraic! After the story is read out loud, the class will no doubt chatter about the story—about poor Betty, about grumpy Ezra, and

REPRODUCIBLE 3.2
Growing Patterns
Template 2 ◄

about all the dogs in the bed. A question about what is growing in the story can embed the mathematics into the context and set the stage for the lesson.

The Growing Patterns Template 2 (see Reproducible 3.2) is a helpful tool for this and other literature activities. With it, you can present and connect all the varied representations. I have found that for this particular task, starting with the T-chart helps support the thinking necessary to move through the representations. Please note that there is no "What Is Happening?" middle column on the template. I recommend that you post a three-column T-chart on the whiteboard from which to work. That middle column will greatly support the students as they think their way to a rule that will connect the x- and y-values. I have found that this "What Is Happening?" column of the three-column T-chart supports the words and rule of this particular pattern. That middle column also supports a move from additive thinking to that of multiplicative as the students work to make their description more efficient.

For this particular context, using Stage 0 (Ezra's feet) makes very good sense and is worthwhile to pursue. Although students may wish to start at Stage 1, I want to eventually move them to include Stage 0 as the discussion plays out. The class may decide to add Stage 0 without any guidance on your part. Feel good about that! Students are making sense of the mathematics within the context.

Dog Night	What Is Happening?	Number of Feet in the Bed

Students will want to connect the coldness of the night to the number of dogs in the bed, but may need some support as they work to articulate the functional relationship that is found in the story. Offering the x and y labels of the T-chart can be an entry point.

As the class offers the stages (the "dog nights") and discusses the number of feet in the bed, do not forget Ezra! Students may focus on the feet of the dogs but very well forget Ezra. The following questions will support a Stage 0 entry in the T-chart:

- What about a warm night?
- What if there are no dogs in the bed?
- How many feet are there now?
- Whose feet are those?
- Does a Stage 0 make sense? Why?

As the class describes each stage, I post the growth in the bed in very simple terms and with conversation. The class agrees that each dog is worth four feet. So I post it as such.

Dog Night	What Is Happening?	Number of Feet in the Bed
0	2	2
1	2 + 4	6
2	2 + 4 + 4	10
3	2 + 4 + 4 + 4	14
4	2 + 4 + 4 + 4 + 4	16
5	2 + 4 + 4 + 4 + 4 + 4	20

There is a very nice visual representation of the growth of this pattern in the form of a triangle. This T-chart also represents the constant (Ezra's feet) and the growth nicely, as well. Students quickly agree that in this particular pattern, the constant is Ezra—we have to start with him since it is, after all, his bed! Then as the night gets colder, he adds an extra dog. Some students may quickly make the connection between the dog night and the number of dogs, or groups of four. A question such as "Where do you see the dog night represented in the *What Is Happening* column of the T-chart?" can support that necessary connection.

If your students have had several experiences working with rules in words and symbols with previous patterns, you can ask them to turn and talk to their neighbors as they then construct a rule representing this growth first in words, then in symbols. If your students are a bit fragile in their facility to move from a T-chart to the rule, a class discussion with opportunities for partner talk may better serve the class. (See Figure 3–15.)

FIGURE 3–15
Paige's and Jessica's Joint Rule in Words and Symbols.

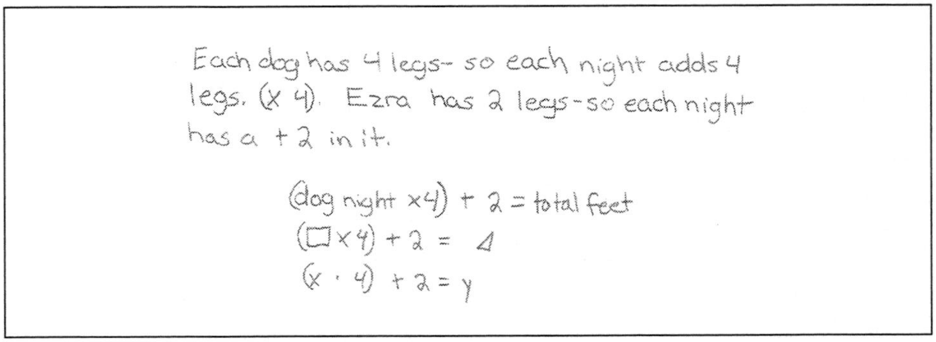

Each dog has 4 legs- so each night adds 4 legs. (x 4). Ezra has 2 legs-so each night has a + 2 in it.

(dog night x4) + 2 = total feet
($\square$ x 4) + 2 = $\triangle$
(x · 4) + 2 = y

An interesting discussion opened up as we discussed Paige's and Jessica's rule in words and symbols, because they differed just a bit. Jake (the "plus two" young man from the *Growing Caterpillar* investigation) noticed that Jessica's and Paige's description in words began with Ezra, so shouldn't we present the symbolic rule in the same order? We spent some time debating the need to represent the symbolic rule in the same order as it was described in words. Once again, the commutativity of addition comes into play and should enter into the discussion somewhere. And the conversation was guided in such a way to ensure that it did! We agreed that order did not necessarily matter if we were looking at the symbolic representation in isolation. But to be true to our description in words, perhaps we could better represent the rule as $2 + (x \cdot 4)$. The push to represent what we are seeing with what we are saying was salient. Although this may seem to be a minor nuance, the practice of transcribing one representation into another with increased clarity will eventually help many students as they move through the middle grades.

Moving to the graph is a natural progression and one students can do independently. You may need to discuss the scale of the y-axis in order to represent the first five stages of this pattern on the graph paper provided on the template. This pattern and rule also lend themselves to further discussion about the y-intercept. Because my class had already agreed that the pattern started with Ezra, the y-intercept of two made complete sense. (See Figure 3–16.)

REPRODUCIBLE 3.2 ◄
Growing Patterns
Template 2

FIGURE 3–16
Jessica's Completed *Five Dog Night* Template.

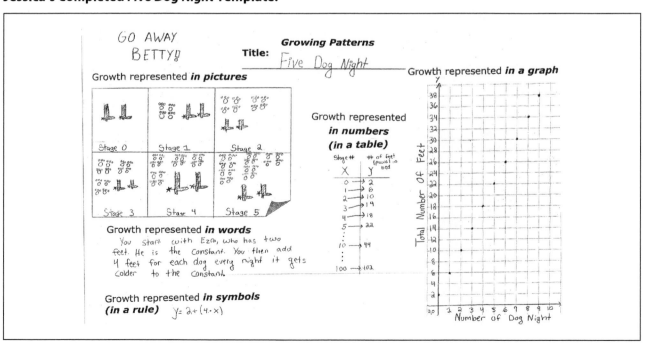

Minnie's Diner: Investigating a Nonlinear Function
Duration: 1–2 Class Periods

Algebraic growth does not always occur in a constant or regular manner. It can also be exponential. Like linear growth, exponential growth is predictable. But unlike linear growth, the rate of growth from stage to stage is not constant. This lesson offers a context in which to explore a pattern that presents a nonlinear function and graph. (The original write-up of this activity contains student vignette and author commentary [Schuster 2008].) This lesson offers students opportunities to

- identify, articulate, and represent a nonlinear growth pattern;
- organize information on a T-chart;
- discuss a rule that represents the growth of the pattern; and
- create a nonlinear graph.

Materials
- *Minnie's Diner* (Dodds 2004)
- Growing Patterns Template 2 enlarged for 11-by-18-inch paper (see Reproducible 3.2)

Vocabulary
nonlinear function

Minnie's Diner (Dodds 2004) is a delightful story about the McFay boys and their inability to resist the aromas from Minnie's kitchen. One by one they succumb to the sweet aromas with each brother being twice as hungry as the brother before. When Papa McFay realizes that his boys are gone and the chores are not done, he heads off to Minnie's only to be enticed by her cooking as well. Students are immediately engaged by the illustrations and cadence of the book. They also become aware of the growth pattern of the menu items as each brother orders from Minnie. You will undoubtedly hear groans and giggles around the room as each brother places his order in the diner.

Because this story represents an exponential function, $y = 2^{(x-1)}$, the sets of ordered pairs generated by the T-chart will not fall in a line when graphed. You can call this type of function a *nonlinear function*. Yes, the rate of growth of an exponential pattern is predictable, but not constant. The number of items ordered on Minnie's menu depends on each brother. The *x*-value will be labeled *McCay* and the *y*, *number of menu items*. (See Figure 3–17 for the T-chart and graph representing the growth of this function.)

Additional family members can easily be added to extend the pattern. What if Mama came to fetch everyone from Minnie's? (And my guess is that she would be none too happy!) If she succumbed to the irresistible aromas and Minnie's wonderful hot cherry pies, how many menu items would Mama order? What if Uncle Fred happened to stop by?

NCTM Connection

Strand: Algebra
Focus: Explore and represent a nonlinear function in a literature context.
Context: *Minnie's Diner* by Dayle Ann Dodds

▶ REPRODUCIBLE 3.2
Growing Patterns
Template 2

◄

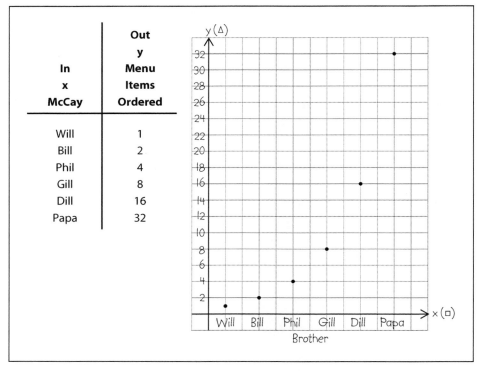

In x McCay	Out y Menu Items Ordered
Will	1
Bill	2
Phil	4
Gill	8
Dill	16
Papa	32

FIGURE 3–17
McCay T-chart and Graph.

Some students may ask about the rule, $y = 2^{(x-1)}$; a rule most will be unable to construct. However, carefully scaffolded conversation, can help them understand the relationship between the doubling growth of the *y*-values and how many times to double it based on the *x*-values. I inform students that for our purposes right now, the rule is not necessarily the most important piece of this pattern. The ordered pairs and the shape they make on the graph are what differentiates this representation from others that we have seen and discussed.

Good Questions to Ask

For more good questions, see *Good Questions for Math Teaching: Why Ask Them and What to Ask, Grades 5–8* by Lainie Schuster and Nancy Anderson (Math Solutions 2005).

- What is the difference between an *equation* and an *expression*? Give an example of each. How can you turn one into the other? (**Hint:** You may wish to discuss the root word of *equation* in your explanation!)
- My bird feeder is set up for the winter. On the first day, six finches come to the feeder. On the second day, eleven finches come to the feeder. On the third day, sixteen finches show up. Each day, the number of finches increases by five more than the day before. At this rate, how many finches will arrive at the feeder on the tenth day? Create a chart to represent the pattern. Explain the pattern in words and

with a rule to represent how many finches would show up for a meal on any given day.

■ The pattern continues. Fill in the blanks. Describe the pattern. What will the equation look like when the first term is 25? 62?

$$2 \times 4 + 1 = 3 \times 3$$

$$3 \times 5 + 1 = 4 \times 4$$

$$4 \times 6 + 1 = \underline{} \times \underline{}$$

$$\underline{} \times 7 + 1 = \underline{} \times \underline{}$$

$$\underline{} \times \underline{} + \underline{} = \underline{} \times \underline{}$$

■ Complete the chart. What is the rule? Add three more pairs of ins and outs.

In	Out
aardvark	a
giraffe	a
hippo	o
?	?
?	?
?	?

■ Using color tiles, create a pattern that fits this T-chart, describing its growth.

■ Be able to identify what stays constant in your pattern and where and how the pattern is growing. How many total tiles will be in Stage 10? Stage 100? Any stage? How do you know?

Stage Number	Total Tiles
1	3
2	6
3	9
4	12
5	15

■ What do you know about each set of points with the following coordinates? Sketch the line that these points would make if connected. Why does your sketch make sense? Can you make generalizations about the shape of the line given the progression of the *x*- and *y*-values?

Set A	*Set B*	*Set C*	*Set D*
(3, 2)	(23, 5)	(2, 1)	(10, 6)
(3, 3)	(26, 5)	(3, 2)	(11, 5)
(3, 4)	(29, 5)	(4, 3)	(12, 4)
(3, 5)	(32, 5)	(5, 4)	(13, 3)

Calculation Routines and Practices

You can embed valuable calculation routines and practices in work supporting the growth and development of algebraic thinking. Working with true-false and open-number sentences can offer opportunities to introduce and apply useful mathematical conventions as well as explore, develop, and ground our students' understanding of the equals sign.

Equations are mathematical sentences with an equals sign. Those sentences without an equals sign are referred to as *inequalities*. In an equation, the expressions on either side of the equals sign represent equivalent values or quantities. Equations can be considered *true* or *false* once we evaluate the expressions on either side of the equals sign.

Algebraic equations involve a variable and therefore are not true or false. We refer to them as *open sentences*. An open sentence is open to a decision about whether it is true or false until we decide on a value for the variable.

Equations	*Inequalities*	*Expressions*	*Open Sentences*
$4 \times 3 = 12$	$4 \times 3 < 5 \times 3$	4×3	$4 \times \square = 12$
$12 = 4 + 8$	$5 \times 3 > 4 \times 3$	$\square + 8$	$4 \times 3 = \square + 8$

We often make assumptions about our fifth graders' understanding of the equals sign that may or may not be warranted. We would like to assume that our fifth graders interpret the equals sign as a symbol of balance: the expressions or quantities found on either side of the equals sign are of equivalent value. Many of our fifth graders, however, continue to interpret the equals sign as an indicator of "the answer is coming." Some might interpret $12 = 4 + 8$ as a false statement. Based on their misconception, the equals sign cannot come at the front end of an equation. Some students might also have difficulty explaining whether $4 \times 3 = 4 + 8$ because they want to see a 12 following the 4×3. These students are not viewing the equals sign as an indicator of balance, but awaiting the product 4×3. Instead of viewing the equals sign as a *relational* symbol, the equals sign is being viewed as one that is *operational*. Misconceptions about the equals sign limit students' ability to learn basic arithmetic concepts and procedures with understanding and restrict their flexibility in representing those ideas. This misconception can create even more serious problems as our children eventually move on to algebra (Carpenter, Franke, and Levi 2003).

TEACHER-TO-TEACHER TALK ■ **About the Equals Sign** ■ Several years ago, I polled my class of fifth graders about their understanding and interpretation of the equals sign. Some focused work on the equals sign had been carried out in the previous year with many of the students due to some prodding on my part with the fourth-grade teachers. The teachers had supplemented the fourth-grade prescribed curriculum with additional true/false/open-number sentence explorations with several activities presented in *Lessons for Algebraic Thinking, Grades 3–5* (Wickett, Kharas, and Burns 2002) (see the "Resources" section of this chapter for recommended chapters and lessons).

The prompt was, "What does the equals sign mean?" Here is a partial listing of the class's varied responses:

- sum of two numbers;
- equal to the word before you say the answer;
- the same thing in looks and values;
- the sign before you put before a math problem sum;
- exactly the same thing;
- is; and
- adds, subtracts, multiplies, or divides up to something.

There was some understanding there (thank you to the fourth grade!), but students continued to have misconceptions about the equals sign that needed to be addressed and explored. I had some work to do!

Some of these responses bothered me more than you might realize because I began to wonder (and still do) about the assumptions that we make about our students—and how our instructional decisions are based on those assumptions. As a result of this experience, I began to offer *Checking for Understanding* tasks and questions before I moved too far into any unit of study. You can find more information about these types of tasks in the "Assessment" section of the Chapter 5.

In *Thinking Mathematically: Integrating Arithmetic and Algebra in Elementary School* (Carpenter, Franke, and Levi 2003), the authors suggest

NCTM Connection

Strand: Algebra

Focus: Explore the
meaning of the
equals sign.

Context: *True, False,
Open-Number
Sentences*

that in order to help students develop an appropriate and working conception of equality, we must place students in positions that challenge their existing conceptions. Carpenter, Franke, and Levi also suggest that true/false and open-number sentences offer a context in which to do so. Exploring mathematical sentences can give us additional opportunities to explore important mathematical properties and identities that students need to generalize and apply as they move toward a more formal study of algebra in the later grades.

Strings of intentional number sentences can help students develop a deeper understanding of equality. The concept of true/false number sentences may be familiar to your students. If not, you can have a quick discussion about the process of identifying and justifying a number sentence as true or false. You can pose a sentence such as $8 \times 3 = 24$. Questions such as "Is this number sentence true?" and "How do you know?" can begin the conversation and the relational thinking required of the responses. As you discuss number models, you can place them in a T-chart that classifies them as true or false.

True	False
A. $8 \times 3 = 24$	$8 \times 4 = 30$
B. $21 = 7 \times 3$	$12 = 6 + 5$
C. $(5 \times 4) + 5 = 25$	$5 \times (4 + 5) = 25$
D. $3^3 = 27$	$3^3 = 9$
E. $17 + 8 = 7 + 18$	$17 - 8 = 8 - 17$
F. $18 \times 3 = 3 \times 18$	$18 \div 3 = 3 \div 18$
G. $38 = 3 + 7 \times 5$	$50 = 3 + 7 \times 5$

By this time in the year, common student calculation errors are undoubtedly on your instructional radar. Constructing number models that address these common errors can give students the opportunity to confront their miscalculations and fragile understandings. Number sentences can address

- the use of parentheses (example C);
- calculation with exponents (example D);
- the Commutative Property (examples E and F); and
- the placement and meaning of the equals sign (examples A through G).

Working with false number sentences offers fertile ground for thinking and explaining what we know about numbers and operations. For one thing, constructing false number sentences is harder than you think! When we work to create a false number sentence, we first need to have a true sentence in mind. My students often admit that once they have created a false number sentence they automatically ask themselves, "Now what can I do to make it true?" And if they do not offer that information as they are sharing their false sentences, I ask for it. Every discussion around a false sentence concludes with options of how the sentence can be made true.

In addition to addressing what students do (and do not) know about the structure of numbers, properties, and operations, true/false number sentences also offer opportunities to explore and support the meaning of equality. Again, strings of true/false sentences can support the relational thinking and conversation necessary to scaffold consistent understanding.

A. $8 + 7 = 15$

B. $15 = 8 + 7$

C. $15 + 0 = 8 + 7$

D. $9 + 6 = 8 + 7$

E. $9 + 6 - 5 = 8 + 7 - 5$

F. $9 + 6 + 13 = 8 + 7 + 13$

G. $(9 + 6) \times 2 = (8 + 7) \times 2$

H. $(9 + 6) \div 3 = (8 + 7) \div 3$

Moving from Example A to B can engage students in thinking about the placement of the equals sign. It may also help to ask students for a phrase that can replace (or is equivalent to) the equals sign, such as *the same as*. The language of *fifteen is the same as eight plus seven* often makes more sense to students in this context. The language of *the same as* represents the balance and equivalence required of a true equation.

It may surprise you how many fifth graders continue to interpret the equals sign as an operational symbol, one that requires them *to do* something or *to operate*. Making a conscious effort to write number sentences throughout the year in which the equals sign falls at the front end of the equation will help students view the symbol as one representing balance and equivalence.

Adding a zero to one side of the equation (Example C) can encourage students to accept a number sentence in which an expression appears on both sides of the equation. Students can develop a deeper understanding of equality when working with *equivalent* expressions and the language used to represent quantities of equal value, but with different representations. Examples C and D present equations with equivalent expressions on both sides of the equals sign. Both sides of both equations are of equal value (fifteen), but are represented with different number models. When the term and concept of *equivalence* are used and applied with greater frequency, students are better able to make sense of other equivalent quantities. For example, the equation $\frac{1}{2} = 0.5$ represents *equivalency*—same value, different representation. We refer to $\frac{1}{2}$ and $\frac{4}{8}$ as *equivalent* fractions because they represent the same value, but with different representations.

Adding, subtracting, multiplying, or dividing the same values from both sides of an equation preserves equality as represented in Examples E, F, G, and H. Students may initially want or need to do the math in order to identify each example as true or false. In time, however, we expect our fifth graders to be able to make generalizations about the equivalence of expressions based on actions that are performed on both sides of an equation without the need for calculation.

Your state algebraic thinking standards or prescribed curriculum may also include work with *open-number sentences*. You can use *open-number sentences*, algebraic number sentences that contain an unknown, to illustrate many of the same ideas as true/false sentences. Open-number sentences are *open* to a decision about whether they are true or false until you make a substitution for the unknown.

I cite several resources in the "Resources" section of this chapter if you wish to explore lessons and further information about open-number sentences.

Order of Operations

The parentheses used in mathematical sentences indicate that you should perform the operations in the parentheses first. If no parentheses are included, you must apply the mathematical convention called the "Order of Operations." Many of us use the mnemonic PEMDAS, or **P**lease **E**xcuse **M**y **D**ear **A**unt **S**ally, to help us remember the order of operations: Parentheses, Exponents, Multiplication, Division, Addition, and Subtraction. While applying PEMDAS may certainly be helpful as students calculate, they also need to be aware of why they need such a convention. The problem $2 + 5 \times 7$ can result in the answers of 49 or 37, depending on whether the calculation carried out was $(2 + 5) \times 7$ or $2 + (5 \times 7)$. Posing such a problem without parentheses can easily create some confusion . . . and I intentionally do just that. Students will quickly realize and articulate the need for such a convention.

A game such as *Four Strikes and You're Out* (Tank and Zolli 2001) can provide a context for the application of the order of operations. You introduce the game by writing the following on the board:

NCTM Connection

Strand: Algebra

Focus: Explore the order of operations in a game context.

Context: Four Strikes and You're Out

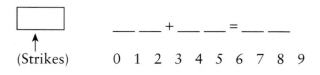

(Strikes)   0 1 2 3 4 5 6 7 8 9

You will write an equation hidden from the students' view. The students will offer digits from zero to nine. If the digit is in the equation, you write it in its appropriate place or places. If the digit is not in the equation, the class earns a strike. You cross off the digits as they are offered and add the strikes to the strike box when they are received. The object of the game is for the class to reason their way through the identification of the equation before they earn four strikes. I remind the students that many possible equations can be used, but they have to guess the one that I have selected.

If my equation was $24 + 48 = 72$, and the students selected a 2 on their first guess and a 4 on their second, the partial equation would look like the following:

$$\underline{2}\ \underline{4} + \underline{4}\ \underline{\ \ } = \underline{\ \ }\ \underline{2}$$

$$0 \quad 1 \quad \cancel{2} \quad 3 \quad \cancel{4} \quad 5 \quad 6 \quad 7 \quad 8 \quad 9$$

The students could then use their reasoning skills to identify the eight and the seven. Once students understand how to play, you can choose an equation that will offer opportunities to discuss and apply the order of operations.

Choose an equation such as $5 + 3 \times 4 = 17$. You would write the following equation on the board:

$$\underline{\ \ \ } + \underline{\ \ \ } \times \underline{\ \ \ } = \underline{\ \ \ }\ \underline{\ \ \ }$$

$$0 \quad 1 \quad 2 \quad 3 \quad 4 \quad 5 \quad 6 \quad 7 \quad 8 \quad 9$$

Some confusion will undoubtedly exist about which operation to perform first: do you add first, or multiply? As students begin to ask these questions, and ask they will, you can make references to the order of operations.

There are always those students who ask if we can add parentheses to the equation. "If the parentheses were there, I wouldn't have to think about the order!" Kelsey announced to the class this year. Initially I was not prepared for this comment, but it seems to come up each year. I remind students that parentheses are mathematical punctuation marks (they like that reference!), and for this activity, we will be working without them. They must decide which operation to do first based on the convention of the order of operations and the number sentence with which they are working. I give students a handout that they keep in a plastic sleeve in their math binders for reference throughout the school year. (See Figure 3–18.)

I keep a list of possible equations for quick reference to use for *Four Strikes and You're Out* for games at the end of lessons or as class warm-ups. Students often refer to this game as *Mathematical Hangman* and enjoy playing it throughout the year.

Order of Operations
a.k.a. PEMDAS

P   Parentheses

E   Exponents

MD   Multiplication or Division (perform whichever operation comes first, from left to right)

AS   Addition or Subtraction (perform whichever operation comes first, from left to right)

"Please Excuse My Dear Aunt Sally"

Some expressions to simplify:

1. $8 \times 4 \div 8 + 2^2$
2. $64 - 3 \times 4 + 10$
3. $12 \div 6 \times 3 - 1$
4. $6 + 4 \div 2 - 6$
5. $10 \times 2 + 5 \div 5$

6. $5 - 3 + 8 \times 3$
7. $5 - 12 \div 6$
8. $4 \div 4 + 4 \times 4$
9. $2 \times 14 - 3 \div 3$
10. $2 + 11 - (13 - 4)$

FIGURE 3–18
Order of Operations Handout.

Multiplication Fact Review

Any opportunity to offer games and activities as continued multiplication fact review is always a good practice and routine. In my yearlong math program, the study of multiplication follows our work with algebraic thinking. In that unit and by this time in the fifth grade, I expect fluency in the multiplication tables up to twelve. I take note of those students who continue to struggle with the recall of their basic facts throughout our work with algebraic thinking. I set up plans for review and reteaching, if necessary, with those students. I am fortunate to have the aid of resource teachers to help me with the extra support these students might need. I have conferences with those students individually to remind them of my expectations and their academic responsibilities.

Familiar games such as the *Factor Game* and the *Product Game* are convenient resources to have on hand. I have a set of laminated multiplication bingo boards within easy reach, as well as reproducibles of multiplication riddles and puzzles that I have collected over the years. *Seek and Cover* (Childs and Choate 2000, 145–46), for example, is a partner game that focuses on substitution work with variables that also supports fact recall and review.

All of the algebraic thinking activities in this chapter provide additional opportunities for fact review and recall. You can construct or adapt number sentences, functions, and patterns to support the review of particular facts based on the needs of your students.

REPRODUCIBLE 2.1   ◄
Factor Game

Reading, Writing, and Vocabulary

Some well-deserved airtime is now being given to comprehension in the teaching and learning of mathematics. According to Arthur Hyde, author of *Comprehending Math: Adapting Reading Strategies to Teach Mathematics, K–6* (2006), as students work to understand mathematical concepts, they must use language, the quintessential characteristic of human cognition. Proficient readers interact with what they read. They do not passively receive meaning, they construct it.

> They use what they know about the content of the text, about the text being described, about how texts of this kind are structured (their format), and about the particular vocabulary (including specialized terms). They must continually draw inferences about the meaning of words. They must make assumptions about missing pieces, things implied but not there on the page. (5)

The same can be said of proficient mathematicians. They, too, must actively construct meaning and comprehend in much the same way that proficient readers do. Like good readers, good mathematicians are aware of how meaning evolves. They understand what it means to understand!

When we ask students to turn and talk with a partner within a lesson, we are asking them to think aloud, a comprehension strategy that supports monitoring for meaning. When we ask students to think aloud or implement partner talk, we are asking them to attend to their understanding as they solve problems. Students need to be aware of the purpose of the task and how to change their thinking when meaning breaks down. As teachers of mathematics, we can model this think-aloud process so that students have the opportunity to listen in as we reveal how and when our comprehension is thrown off track and what we do to get it on track once again (Keene and Zimmerman 2007, 49).

Moving to an explicit or symbolic rule can initially be a challenging task for many fifth graders. Asking good questions can certainly help the process along. Answers to good questions can help students identify connections and relationships that will allow an explicit rule to come from the words and thinking used to describe a specific pattern. For students, watching you think aloud through this process can be equally powerful.

I will often carry out a think aloud with the *Growing Caterpillar* investigation. I have available the T-chart and the pictures of the first five stages of the growing caterpillar. I ask and answer many of the questions that are referenced in the "Lesson Planning" section of this chapter under "Lesson Format." My major purpose of this think aloud is for students to observe the connections that I make between the stage number and the growth I see between each stage. It might sound something like this:

> Let's see . . . I see the constant like Jake does—the head and the tail. So for each stage, there will always be a constant of two. So I am going to start my rule with two because that's how I see it.
>
> For Stage 1, there is one square in the body. Now for Stage 2, there are two squares in the body. And in Stage 3—oh look! Each stage is equivalent to the number of squares in the body.
>
> So if I start with two for any stage, I can just add the stage number to get the number of squares in the body.
>
> So for Stage 7, I would start with two for the head and the tail, and add seven squares for the body.
>
> Hmm . . . let me extend my T-chart here just to make sure. I know Stage 5 will have seven total blocks because $2 + 5 = 7$. So Stage 6 should have one more block because the numbers in the out-column of my T-chart always increase by one for each stage. So Stage 6 should have eight blocks. Let's see if that fits. $2 + 6 = 8$. Yep, it fits. Now for Stage 7. I will start with two, and then add seven more blocks for the body: $2 + 7 = 9$, and that is one more block than Stage 6. Yep, that makes sense, too.
>
> Cool—so I can predict that for any stage, the total number of blocks will be two plus the stage number. I could rewrite that with symbols as
>
> 2 + Stage # = total blocks
>
> And I could rewrite it again with box and triangle as
>
> $$2 + \square = \triangle$$
>
> And if I really wanted to be fancy, I could use the variables x and y:
>
> $$2 + x = y$$
>
> Very cool. There's my rule!

I am very careful to apply the language and vocabulary that we have used in class, as well as the representations that we have worked through together. I must also admit that some theatrics are included. Not that this is any song and dance, but I want students to observe me pondering—to observe me making a statement—and then revising that statement to improve word choice and clarity. I also want students to understand that achieving meaning is the purpose of this task. The rule needs to make sense according to how I see and think about the pattern of growth. My words need to match my thinking. And my thinking and words need to be translated into a rule that will work for any stage.

All students gain something from observing a think aloud. Some will adopt this strategy quickly because of its ease of accessibility. If many of your students understand that their responsibility is to make sense of the mathematics, they will know the questions that they need to ask of themselves. They will also know when the mathematics makes sense and they have achieved understanding.

Those students not quite ready to make that conceptual leap from recursive to explicit thinking also gain something. These students know that good mathematicians need to check their own understanding by asking themselves questions. They need to be able to articulate what they do understand—and what they do not. They need to know when their thinking breaks down—and what to do when it does. You should offer another think aloud to model what happens when thinking does break down—and how we work our way through it.

Assessment

According to Wiggins and McTighe (2005), understanding can be revealed in performance. Therefore, assessment for understanding must be grounded in authentic performance-based tasks that require effective and efficient application and transfer of a repertoire of knowledge, skills, and concepts to negotiate.

Thinking algebraically is a process. Many tasks in this month of study ask students to make connections between and among multiple representations of a growth pattern. We are asking our students to move from informal understandings to more formal written representations of mathematical properties, conventions, concepts, and procedures. We should design and carry out assessments that ask students to apply and transfer these thinking processes.

In *Lessons for Algebraic Thinking, Grades 3–5* (Wickett, Kharas, and Burns 2002), two lessons lend themselves well to a performance-based assessment with a few added tweaks and turns. Both the *Piles of Tiles* lesson and the *Table Patterns* lesson offer additional experiences with growth patterns within different contexts. You can present either one in a project-based format with guidelines and a rubric. (See Figures 3–19 and 3–20.)

What I like about these two assessments is the opportunity for choice. They present students with several tile patterns or several table pattern options and then ask them to choose the pattern they wish to explore. (I usually alternate between the two projects from year to year.) In making that choice, the students will often try out several patterns to see which one they like best and feel most comfortable exploring and explaining.

Piles of Tiles Scoring Rubric		
Criteria	Point Value	Points Earned
I chose my pile and continued the pattern up to pile 5 on my poster.	5	
I made a T-chart to describe its growth. I included the 10th, 100th, and *n*th pile as well as piles 1 to 5.	10	
I used words to describe the growth of my piles.	10	
I created a rule to predict the total number of tiles for any numbered pile—like pile 162!	10	
I graphed the growth of my piles and did *not* connect my points!	10	
My poster is neat, well organized, and really cool!	5	
Total Points	50 Points	My total =

FIGURE 3–19
***Piles of Tiles* Rubric.**

FIGURE 3–20
***Banquet Table* Rubric.**

Banquet Table Scoring Rubric		
Name : _____ Date: _____		
Criteria	Point Value	Points Earned
I chose my banquet table and continued, labeled, and represented the growth of the seating for up to five tables. I posted this on my poster.	5	
I made a *T-chart* to represent the growth of the seating. I included 1 to 5 tables, as well as 10 and 100 tables. I posted this on my poster.	10	
I used *words* to describe the growth of the seating pattern. I posted this on my poster.	10	
I created a *rule* in mathematical symbols and numbers to represent the growth of the seating pattern. I posted this on my poster.	10	
I *graphed* the growth of the seating pattern with a labeled coordinate graph and did *not* connect my points! I posted this on my poster.	10	
My poster is neat, well organized, and really, really cool!	5	
Total Points	50 points	My total:
Comments from Mrs. Schuster:		

This practice of trying out patterns has significant value. When students "own" their patterns, their commitment to thoroughly completing the project is not far behind.

Assessing what your students do and do not understand about algebraic thinking and representation will inform your instructional decisions for the remainder of the school year. You can apply and integrate many routines in the "Calculation Routines and Practices" section of this chapter into other units of study. Understanding equality and equivalence, for example, helps the fifth graders make sense of fractions, decimals, and percents. You may also find that multiplication and division can be enhanced and supported by work with mathematical properties and the continued exploration of functional relationships.

Home and School Connections

Parent Information and Involvement Forms can be sent home or posted electronically for this month of study. (See Figure 3–21; see also Reproducible 2.16.)

▶ REPRODUCIBLE 2.16
Parent Information and Involvement Form

If you choose to use Parent Information Forms, it will help parents if you define *algebraic thinking*. We want parents to be aware of the difference between the process of thinking algebraically and the more formal study of algebra that students will encounter in the later grades.

Placing examples of fifth-grade algebraic thinking on bulletin boards and in hallways can help inform parents about the thoughtful and sophisticated work going on in mathematics classes. Posting student posters displaying the multiple representations of growth patterns not only catches the attention of parents, but that of the younger children as well. I often have students coming in to the fifth grade asking about projects that they have seen in the hallways from previous years. They often ask: "Are we going to do the tiles project?" or "Can we do the posters with the pattern blocks and graphs?"

Conferences are opportunities for parents and teachers to communicate about individual student progress. Whether your conferences are written into your academic calendar or conducted on a need-to-see basis, you need to be prepared to discuss and be knowledgeable about each child's strengths and needs. A small collection of student work can help to highlight and support your assessment of each student. Taking the opportunity to review a student's math notebook before conferencing with a parent can help bring into focus the quality of recent work as well as observations about that student's progress from the beginning of the year. Posting sticky notes annotating the discussion points on various pages of the notebook is also helpful. Do not worry about parents (or students) seeing your sticky notes. They will appreciate the time you took to prepare for the conference. Following the conference, you can remove and archive the sticky notes on your conference write-up for future reference.

REPRODUCIBLE 2.16
Parent Information
and Involvement
Form

Parent Information and Involvement Form

From: Lainie Schuster
Re: Mathematics Curriculum
Unit: Algebraic Thinking

During the next unit, the major topic we will be studying is:

- Algebraic thinking

My goal in studying this topic is for the students to be able to:

- Identify, articulate, and represent numerical and geometric patterns
- Represent growing patterns with words, pictures, graphs, and symbols
- Identify and articulate functional relationships (rules) found in T-charts of growing numerical and geometric patterns
- Plot points on a coordinate graph
- Solve for unknown quantities (variables) in equations and expressions
- Identify number sentences as true or false
- Apply order of operations to equations and calculations

Parents can help at home by:

- Asking your child to explain how he or she *sees* the growth of patterns: *how* is the pattern growing? Expressing how they see growth in words first can then help children to put numbers and symbols to their ideas.
- Asking your child to identify the relationship between the in-value and the out-value of a T-chart in words before moving to symbols and equations. The function rule connecting the in-value with the out-value can often be uncovered and discovered in your child's language!

FIGURE 3–21
Parent Information and Involvement Form: November.

Parents may come to conferences with specific concerns and questions. Even if time is limited, I do try to engage the parents in a conversation about how *they* see their child as a mathematician before we move on to my assessment. Even though a parent's perspective may be somewhat tainted by the love, affection, and goals they have for their child (and we parents are all guilty of that!), their knowledge and insights can help the teacher to better understand their fifth grader.

Parents want to help their children succeed in school. However, they may be dependent on guidance from their children's teachers on how best to offer that support. This feedback may take the form of suggestions about homework completion, class preparation, or review of specific concepts or procedures (the multiplication tables quickly come to mind). You may want to have handouts available, such as the ones offered at back-to-school night. Many prescribed curricula offer a parent handbook or something similar from which you can copy articles and handouts. NCTM's journal *Mathematics Teaching in the Middle School* offers a series of "Families Ask" articles for parent support about a variety of topics. The November 2004 issue offers a "Families Ask" article entitled, "What Type of Algebra Do Students Do in Middle School?" which I have found to be very helpful in my work with algebraic thinking. You can access archived articles online with an NCTM membership. These articles are well worth printing out and having available for parents.

Creating or making use of a school- or district-developed conference write-up document will help you summarize and document what was said, shared, and agreed upon at a conference. If you decide on an action plan, you will need to provide follow-up communication. Email may suffice for quick check-ins, but a phone call or face-to-face conversation is in the best interests of the child when follow-up plans have been put into place.

Resources

About Teaching Mathematics (Burns 2007)

The chapter about patterns, functions, and algebra offers an overview and problem-solving activities that support the teaching and learning of algebraic thinking. You can offer many of the activities as free-choice or menu problem-solving tasks.

Math Matters: Understanding the Math You Teach (Chapin and Johnson 2006)

Chapter 9: "Algebra"
Provides in-depth discussion of the study of algebra and the development of algebraic thinking in the elementary grades.

Lessons for Algebraic Thinking, Grades 3–5 (Wickett, Kharas, and Burns 2002)

A must-have resource that provides lessons, class vignettes, and author narration to help teachers develop and support a wide variety of algebraic topics.

Thinking Mathematically: Integrating Arithmetic and Algebra in the Elementary School (Carpenter, Franke, and Levi 2003)

An exceptional resource that provides author commentary and classroom vignettes illustrating how algebraic ideas emerge in children's thinking. Chapter 2, on "Equality," is especially insightful.

Groundworks: Algebraic Thinking, Grade 5, from the Groundworks series (Greenes and Findell 2006)

An invaluable book of reproducibles focusing on six big ideas of algebraic thinking: representations, balance, function, proportional reasoning, variables, and inductive reasoning.

Additional resources for work with *open-number sentences:*

Lessons for Algebraic Thinking, Grades 3–5 (Wickett, Kharas, and Burns 2002)

Chapter 2: "True, False, and Open Sentences"
Chapter 14: "Identities: Investigating Properties of Numbers"

The sections on shape equations and shape grids, in particular, are useful. Many other sections can be used to support thinking and reasoning about open-number sentences as well.

Chapter 4

Multiplication and Its Relationship to Division

SUGGESTED MONTH: DECEMBER

"You!" the Trunchbull shouted, pointing a finger the size of a rolling pin at a boy called Wilfred. Wilfred was on the extreme right of the front row. "Stand up, you!" she shouted at him.

Wilfred stood up. "Recite the three-times tables backwards!" the Trunchbull barked.

"Backwards!" stammered Wilfred. "But I haven't learnt it backwards."

"There you are!" cried the Trunchbull, triumphant. "She's taught you nothing! Miss Honey, why have you taught them absolutely nothing at all in the last week?"
"That is not true, Headmistress," Miss Honey said. "They have all learnt their three-times table. But I see no point in teaching it to them backwards. The whole object in life, Headmistress, is to go forwards."

Matilda
Dahl 1988, 217

The Learning Environment

Continue to Develop and Implement Good Questioning Routines and Practices

As we work to support the teaching and learning of mathematics with understanding, we need to continue to pay attention to our questioning techniques. As mathematics teachers, we want our fifth graders to not only understand *what* they think but also to articulate *how* they arrived at those understandings. As we work to open up the questions we ask our students, we are engaging them to think deeper about the mathematics. A meaningful study of multiplication requires the marriage of conceptual understanding and procedural proficiency. It also requires us to ask good questions of our young mathematicians, such as:

- Why does this procedure work? Will it work with every number? In every context?
- What makes sense about this procedure? Why? What does not make sense about this procedure? Why?
- Is your solution reasonable? How do you know?
- Who has a different strategy?
- How is your solution or strategy like or different from another student's?
- Who can rephrase or add on to what _____ is saying?

At times a question and its answer may take on a life of their own . . . and a full class period! Please allow that to happen now and again.

Listen—Really Listen

When we listen to, and subsequently learn from, the mathematical observations, insights, and questions of our students, we must understand their points before forming our responses. Questions such as the following can help to focus the process of listening for understanding:

- So what I am hearing is . . .
- Let me make sure I have this right. You're saying that . . .
- Can you repeat what you just said?
- Take your time. We will wait [for your explanation].

Listening, really listening, to your students talk about mathematics is hard work. Strong reasoning and deep thinking as well as misconceptions and fragile understandings can all be apparent in students' mathematical talk when we are mindful enough to hear them. As we listen and learn, we also need to encourage, support, and offer opportunities for our students to listen to each other. When students respond to and connect with each other based on something that they have heard a classmate say or explain, the learning and understanding become personal and meaningful.

The Mathematics and Its Language

Children Continue to Develop Conceptual Knowledge of Multiplication and How It Relates to Division

In the past, procedural knowledge of multiplication has been the focus in elementary school mathematics. Recent research makes it clear that students need to develop strong and deep conceptual knowledge of multiplication and its relationship to division in order to transfer and apply these operations to solve problems (Chapin and Johnson 2006). Our fifth graders soon will be asked to apply their understanding of multiplication to more advanced multiplicative situations such as proportions, measurement conversion, linear functions, and exponential growth as they move into their middle school years.

Children Continue to Explore and Apply Mathematical Properties and How They Apply to Multiplication and Division

Informal applications of mathematical properties are often evident as children compute. By fifth grade, students can articulate that order does not matter in multiplication (and addition), but it does matter in division (and subtraction). They can take apart and combine numbers in ways that make calculating easier. Although fifth graders do not need to label these routines as examples of the commutative property of multiplication (or addition) or of the distributive property, however, they can and should begin to articulate and apply generalizations about computational procedures based on these properties.

Children Choose, Construct, and Carry Out Efficient and Accurate Computational Strategies Based on the Task and the Particular Numbers Involved

Flexible and efficient multiplication strategies require a conceptual understanding of the operation, the properties of that operation, and how that procedure or strategy is related to other operations. As children construct and apply strategies, it is important for them to be able to explain, support, and represent the applied strategies and how they relate to the numbers and situation presented. Making computational choices based on number sense and comprehension of the problem requires our students to look at the numbers first, and then choose and carry out a strategy that is fitting and efficient (Fosnot and Dolk 2001).

Children Identify, Classify, Create, and Solve Story Problems Based on Multiplicative Models

Multiplication story problems can be defined and classified according to their semantic structure: How the relationships within the problem are expressed in words. The semantic structure of problems can differ in regard to the nature of the quantities and the quantity that serves as the unknown (Chapin and Johnson 2006). Students need to work with all types of multiplication and division story problems in order to make sense of the relationships and language as they extend their understanding of these operations beyond mere procedures. See the "Investigations, Games, and Literature-Based Activities" section of this chapter for a listing of story-problem categories and related tasks.

Lesson Planning

- When you are planning for the study of multiplication, you need to balance instruction that has been traditionally focused on procedural proficiency with that of conceptual understanding. Societal, parental, and even district or school expectations tend to emphasize the need for procedural proficiency over all else. We *absolutely* want our fifth graders to compute proficiently and efficiently, but not to the exclusion of understanding the relationships and multiplicative models presented within the procedures as well as within problem-solving contexts.

■ Every year in every class, some students will struggle with the fluency and subsequent recall of some (or more than some) of the basic multiplication facts, and every fifth-grade teacher is well aware of the impact that this can have on computational proficiency. Spending an initial class session talking about multiplication fact expectations and strategies will allow you to move on from review and reteaching.

- Make your expectations known. If you expect automaticity of multiplication facts by this time in the fifth grade, tell them. I do!

- Take time to discuss students' strategies for recalling their fact "demons." I will ask students which fact they find the most difficult to recall, and also ask how they work with related facts that they know to help them figure out the fact that they do not know. For example, 8×7 is always a popular choice. Many students will say that they know their square numbers, and $7 \times 7 = 49$. The problem 8×7 is just one more group of 8 than 7×7. Or maybe the students move back from $8 \times 8 = 64$ and subtract one group of 8. The problem 8×4 is also a common complaint. Many students use the strategy of applying what they know about doubles. Since $8 \times 2 = 16$, some just double 16 to compute 8×4. Having students "listen in" on the strategies of classmates is extremely helpful. Some students may adopt the strategies of others and some may construct strategies of their own after hearing those of their classmates.

- Make public what tools students can access to help them with their facts, if needed. My students have access to multiplication tables (see the "Calculation Routines and Practices" section of Chapter 2) that are housed in their math notebooks in plastic sleeves. What I always find interesting is that few students access them, even though they are well aware that they can. And if and when students do access them, it is often just to double-check a product.

- Offer continued review opportunities in free-choice time by having multiplication board games, fact triangles, puzzles, and riddles available. You may wish to consider a checkout system for games and fact triangles if students wish to practice at home.

TEACHER-TO-TEACHER TALK ■ **About Automaticity** ■ Teaching basic multiplication facts based on *automaticity* is quite different from recall based on memorization. *Teaching facts for automaticity relies on thinking.* When children focus strictly on the quick recall of facts (memorization), they fail to think about the relationships between

---

(Continued)

and among facts. When the focus is on thinking, children are able to articulate how knowing 6×6 can help them with knowing 6×7 or how knowing 3×8 can help them to know 6×8. The more opportunities children have to make and articulate these relationships and connections, the more automatic and fluent they will become with their facts. Every year I hear parents criticize their children's inability to immediately recall facts—and my refusal to teach to this desired outcome. I like to think my students understand their facts and how they relate to one another, and I share this with those concerned parents. By this time in the year, my fifth graders are well aware of the need for fact automaticity and fluency. Some students will easily articulate how not knowing their facts slows down their calculating and impedes their thinking. When I hear these conversations, I know I am doing my job well!

Possible Difficulties or Misconceptions

Students will often tag isolated key words or phrases within a story problem as they decide on a problem-solving or procedural strategy rather than comprehending the context and what is being asked by the problem. Gracie once told me that the question "How many in all?" always meant to multiply, and a question such as "How much does each student get?" tells you to divide—but that is only when you are studying multiplication and division. When I asked her to explain her thinking, she told me that it always mattered what unit we were studying. If we were studying addition and subtraction, she would add when the problem asked "how many in all?"

I asked her, "So it all depends on the unit you are studying? That tells you whether to multiply or divide or to add or subtract?"

"Yep, pretty much," Gracie responded. Generalizations such as this are the risk we take when we teach concepts and procedures in isolation and do not require comprehension of problems, contexts, and procedural expectations.

Many fifth graders come to us with a repertoire of procedures—some that make sense to students and some that may make little sense because they have been memorized depending on learning style and previous instruction. When children memorize a procedure, they often follow it step-by-step without paying attention to the meaning of the process and the numbers that are being used. A meaningful procedure can be re-created—even if students have "forgotten" it. Meaningful procedures are based on a student's understanding of the problem, the numbers, and how and why to apply the procedure. Sometimes direct instruction is helpful and even necessary when you are investigating multiplication procedures. However, your instruction needs to be based on previous understandings and the need for the procedure to make sense. You also need to accompany your instruction with discussion in which you apply reasoning and require understanding of the steps involved.

Investigations, Games, and Literature-Based Activities

Classification of Multiplication Story Problems

Duration: 3–4 Class Periods

Conceptual knowledge based on an understanding of the relationships that represent multiplication and division in story problems needs to share the spotlight with our work with procedural fluency. Being able to perform calculations does not necessarily mean that students understand the relationships and semantic structure (how the relationship is expressed in words) represented in multiplicative contexts. This lesson offers students opportunities to

- investigate, classify, solve, and create multiplication and division problems according to their structure: *grouping, rate, area or array, combination,* or *comparison*;

- investigate and apply the language of multiplication or division inherent in different problem structures;

- explore, identify, and articulate the connection and relationship between multiplication and division; and

- represent contextual situations with number models.

Materials

- Multiplication/Division Story-Problem Structures handout, 1 per student (see Reproducible 4.1)

- math notebooks or paper

- optional: teacher-generated handouts of story problems for each problem structure

> **NCTM Connection**
>
> **Strand:** Number and Operations
> **Focus:** Investigate, classify, solve, and create multiplication and division problems according to their structure.
> **Context:** Classification of Multiplication Story-Problem Structures

▶ REPRODUCIBLE 4.1
Multiplication/
Division Story-
Problem Structures

I have developed a student workbook containing two parts that I use from year to year. Part I of the workbook includes a description and example of each problem type as well as an area for students to construct their own story problem. (See Figure 4–1.) Part II of the workbook is a collection of story problems that students read, classify, and solve. (See Figure 4–2.) Initially creating such a resource takes time, but every year I am thankful for the workbook and thankful that I took the time to create it. I keep a copy of the workbook on my computer desktop, which makes it easy to tweak the problems to include the names of my students and perhaps to add a few new problems or delete a few outdated ones. My students enjoy using a resource that I created, and delight in seeing their names in the text!

REPRODUCIBLE 4.1a
Story-Problem
Structure:
Grouping Problems ◀

Grouping Problems

In grouping multiplication problems, one *factor* tells the number of things in a group and the other *factor* tells the number of *equal-size* groups. For example:

There are 4 hockey teams at the Lawrence Academy Christmas Tournament.
There are 22 players on each team.
How many players are at the tournament?

Number model: _____

Haleigh and Kara are picking apples.
They have 12 baskets. Each basket holds 8 apples.
How many apples will they be able to bring home for apple pies?

Number model: _____

We can also make *division* problems out of these scenarios. For example:

There are 88 hockey players at the Lawrence Academy Christmas Tournament.
Four teams will be formed.
How many players will be on each team?

Number model: _____

Haleigh and Kara picked 96 apples for apple pies.
Each basket holds 8 apples.
How many baskets of apples will they bring home?

Number model: _____

You can easily model grouping problems with pictures or diagrams. Often they are the first types of multiplication problems that we are introduced to as children.

Write your example of a *grouping* story problem below.

Jillian and Caroline went to a birthday party. There were 60 balloons and 20 kids. How many balloons did each kid get?

Solution: 3 balloons
$60 \div 20 = 3$

FIGURE 4–1
Problem Description Page.

Vocabulary

context, divisor, factor, matrix, product, quotient, tree diagram

The following classifications are based on the relationships and semantic structures that can be found in multiplicative contexts. Students need to be able to identify a problem type with regard to the quantities used and the quantity that serves as the unknown (Chapin and Johnson 2006). Not only will identifying quantities and unknowns help students to classify problems,

---

Story Problems for Grade 5

1. Mrs. Bishop loves to buy rewards for the lower-school kids. Recently, she bought 6 packages of holograph pencils. There were 36 pencils in each package. How many pencils did Mrs. Bishop buy?

Problem classification: grouping problem

Solution:

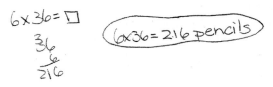

2. Alex is planning a Super Bowl party. He will serve 3 deli sandwiches that are each 5 feet long. The deli charge is $27 per foot. How much will he pay for the sandwiches?

Problem classification: rate

Solution:

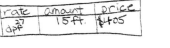

FIGURE 4–2
Story Problem Page.

but this will also help them to operate on the quantities—knowing when and why to multiply or to divide. Although the story problems are classified according to their multiplicative structures, students need to be aware that some problems can be solved with division depending on the unknown. Refer to *Math Matters: Understanding the Math You Teach, Grades K–8* (Chapin and Johnson 2006) for further explanation of problem classifications.

Grouping Problems

These are problems in which one factor identifies the number of things in a group and the other factor identifies the number of equal-sized groups. Equal-grouping problems are often those introduced in the earlier grades. Grouping problems are easy to model with pictures or by using repeated addition:

> *Hayden and Rebecca are going apple picking. The girls place 5 apples in a bag. They go home with 7 bags. How many apples do they have for making apple pie?*

$$7 \times 5 = \square$$

The girls collected 35 apples.

▶ REPRODUCIBLE 4.1a
Story-Problem
Structure:
Grouping Problems

Hayden and Rebecca come home from apple picking with 35 apples. They have placed 5 apples in a bag. How many bags did they bring home?

$$35 \div 5 = \boxed{}$$

The girls brought home 7 bags of apples.

REPRODUCIBLE 4.1b
Story-Problem
Structure:
Rate Problems

◀ ### Rate Problems

These problems involve a rate—a special ratio in which two different quantities are compared. Common rates are miles per gallon, dollars per hour, and points per game. One number identifies the unit rate and the other acts as the multiplier. Rate charts are very helpful when solving rate problems:

Matt and Griffin are going to the Red Sox game. Fenway Franks are $3.50 each. They each buy 2 hot dogs. How much did they pay for their snack?

$$\$3.50 \times 4 = \boxed{}$$

Rate	Total Hot Dogs	Total Price
$3.50 each	4	$14.00

Matt and Griffin paid $14.00 for 4 Fenway Franks at the Red Sox game. How much did each hot dog cost?

$$\$14.00 \div 4 = \boxed{}$$

Rate	Total Hot Dogs	Total Price
$3.50	4	$14.00

REPRODUCIBLE 4.1c
Story-Problem
Structure:
Area/Array Problems

◀ ### Area/Array Problems

These problems require the manipulation of the dimensions or the area of a given array:

The gym is being set up for a concert. There are 8 rows of chairs with 9 chairs in each row. How many people are expected for the concert?

$$8 \times 9 = \boxed{}$$

There are 72 people expected for the concert.

There are 72 chairs set up in the gym for a concert. There are 9 chairs in each row. How many rows of chairs are set up in the gym for the concert?

$$72 \div 9 = \boxed{}$$

There are 8 rows of chairs set up in the gym.

Combination Problems

These problems involve counting the number of possible pairings that can be made between two sets. Tree diagrams (see Figure 4–3) are helpful in identifying all the combinations:

► REPRODUCIBLE 4.1d
Story-Problem
Structure:
Combination
Problems

Ryan is having the boys over for a Super Bowl party. His mom has 4 types of meat and 3 types of cheese available for sandwiches. How many possible combinations of sandwiches can the boys make?

$$4 \times 3 = \boxed{}$$

Ryan and his buddies can make 12 different types of sandwiches.

If Ryan wants to offer 12 different types of sandwiches with 4 different types of meat, how many types of cheese will he have to provide?

$$12 \div 4 = \boxed{}$$

Ryan will need to have 3 different types of cheese available.

Multiplicative Comparison Problems

These are problems in which one number identifies the quantity in one group, while the other number is the comparison factor. The relational language of comparison problems can be problematic for all students. Students often confuse additive language (*five more than* or *five less than*) with that of multiplicative relationships (*five times more than, five times as many,* or *five times less than*):

► REPRODUCIBLE 4.1e
Story-Problem
Structure:
Multiplicative
Comparison
Problems

Harry mowed 5 times more lawns than Nick last month. Nick mowed 4 lawns. How many lawns did Harry mow?

$$5 \times 4 = \boxed{}$$

Harry mowed 20 lawns.

Harry mowed 20 lawns last month. That was 5 times more lawns than Nick mowed. How many lawns did Nick mow last month?

$$20 \div 5 = \boxed{}$$

Nick mowed 4 lawns last month.

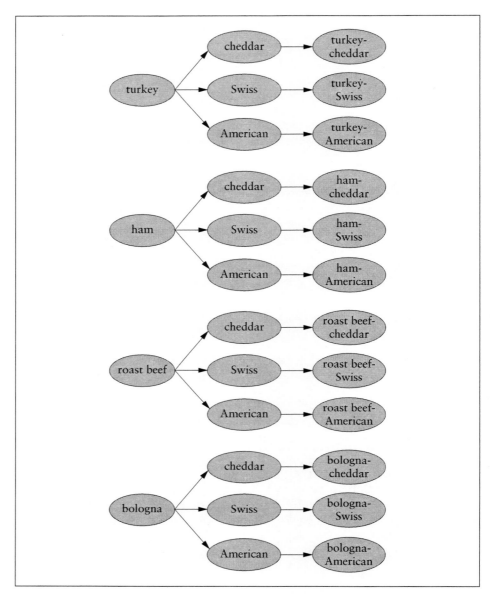

FIGURE 4–3
Tree Diagram for a Combination Problem.

You can and should open this set of lessons with a discussion of why it is important to understand the language of multiplicative contexts. Initially students may have some difficulty understanding the need to classify, construct, and solve problems according to their structure for the simple reason that they have not yet been exposed to this type of thinking about multiplication—its contexts and language. You may be pleasantly surprised with comments such as, "I always wondered how to solve this type of problem!" or "This is a multiplication problem?!" as you move through the instruction.

TEACHER-TO-TEACHER TALK ■ **About Connecting Instruction to Standardized Testing** ■ Our schoolwide standardized tests are administered months after our study of multiplication. I was absolutely amazed at the impact this exploration of multiplication problem structures had on my students' completion of story-problem tasks on their examinations. As I was circulating around the room during the Mathematics portion of the exam, I heard mumblings such as, "Hey! This is a combination problem!" and questions such as, "Can we make a rate chart (or a tree diagram) on our scratch paper?" When I first implemented this instruction, I did not realize the support this awareness and understanding would offer my students as they worked through the standardized test questions. After students completed this portion of their exams, I took the time to look over the test questions. In this particular subtest, I recognized one combination problem, two rate problems, and one comparison problem; I even found myself mumbling, "How cool is this?!" I tell this story to my class every year when we begin our study of problem structures. And what is even more cool is that it repeats itself each and every year as students work through the mathematics section of their standardized tests . . . the mumblings, the rate charts, and the tree diagrams!

I introduce each problem structure with an explanation of the classification and a sample story problem. We examine and discuss the language of that particular structure. We also have a discussion about the mathematical representations and models that support solving the problem. For example, drawings represent equal groupings, rate charts identify the factors or divisors and products or quotients, and tree diagrams display possible combinations. Once we explore and discuss the problem structure, I ask students to solve a problem that represents that particular structure. Each solution requires number models and a summarizing sentence.

Then I ask students to construct their own story problem according to the constraints of that particular problem structure. We share problems and solutions with the aid of a document camera. Students enjoy seeing their own work projected for the entire class to solve and discuss. (See Figure 4–4.)

Although the arithmetic of each problem is important and a correct solution is desired, the continued focus needs to be on the structure and the language of the story problem. The number models are often simple—and that is fine. Asking students to visualize the problem, just as we ask them to do when they read informational text, is also helpful. Questions such as the following can help students construct visual images of the stories.

- Can you group the items in the story?
- Can you visualize a chart, diagram, or array to organize the information?
- Can you label the factors or divisors and the product or quotient of a number model with the information given and asked by the problem?

REPRODUCIBLE 4.1b ◀
Story-Problem Structure:
Rate Problems

Rate Problems

Rate problems involve a *rate*, in which two different quantities or things are compared. Common rates can be miles per gallon, wages per hour, and points per game. The operative word here is *per*. In rate problems, one number identifies the *unit rate* and the other tells the number of sets and acts as the *multiplier*. Check out this problem:

Kelsey is a great babysitter. She makes $12.00 an hour babysitting on the weekends. If she babysat for 8 hours over the weekend, how much money would she make?

In this problem, the rate is $12.00 per hour. We would multiply that rate by 8 hours to get the total amount of money Kelsey made over the weekend.

Number model: ____________

Here is another example of a rate problem:

Nick biked 12 miles at a rate of 6 miles per hour. How long did it take Nick to bike the 12 miles?

Number model: ____________

Rate problems can also be represented by an "RTD" chart (rate/time/distance):

Rate	Time	Distance
6 mph	?	12 mi.

Charting rate problems, as in the case of Nick and the biking problem presented above, can help us to identify the components of the problem and what we have to do to what to get something else!

How would you solve Nick's problem? Multiplication . . . or division? What is the unit *rate*? What would you use as the *multiplier* . . . or the *divisor*, depending on the chosen operation?

We could also chart Kelsey's babysitting problem. But instead of a rate/time/distance chart, we would use a rate/time/total money chart:

Rate	Time	Total Money
$12.00 per hour	8 hours	$96.00

These problems can be difficult to identify because we are not often exposed to them as "multiplication" problems. You will encounter them later on in algebra when you work through rate/time/distance problems. Write your example of a *rate* problem below:

Sim's catering buisness caters 73 parties per week. How many parties would they cater in 3 weeks?

Solution:

73×3=□
219=□
219 parties

Rate	Weeks	total parties
73 *ppw	3 weeks	219

R×W=**TP

*parties per week
**total parties

FIGURE 4–4
Harry's Work with Rate Problems.

Once we have explored the five classifications of story problems, students can begin to work through their collection of story problems. You will need to make an instructional decision about whether to have students complete this task independently or cooperatively. I prefer to have my students work with partners as they discuss, classify, and solve the various story problems. However, each student is responsible for his or her own written work. The following task, Multiplication and Division Problem Storybooks, can give creative closure to the study of multiplication story-problem structures. Once students are familiar with the structures of the various problems, they can create class storybooks of problems and their solutions.

Multiplication and Division Problem Storybooks

Duration: 4–5 Class Periods

Conceptual knowledge of multiplication and division is based on understanding the relationships and contexts that represent multiplication and division. It is through story-problem writing that conceptual understanding of the structures and language of multiplication and division contexts can be developed and assessed. This lesson offers students opportunities to

- transfer and apply developing understandings of the structure and language of multiplication and division contexts to the writing and solving of story problems; and
- practice, apply, articulate, and represent multiplication and division computational strategies.

Materials
- writing paper
- optional: computer access

NCTM Connection

Strand: Number and Operations

Focus: Create and solve multiplication and division problems according to an identified structure.

Context: Multiplication and Division Storybooks

You will need to make some instructional decisions about the final product of this lesson prior to its planning and delivery. Each year, I enlist the support of our technology department to develop electronic templates that students use to type and illustrate with clip art their story problems and solutions. Students drop their files into a class desktop folder on my computer. The stories can then be edited, printed, and collated into a class storybook that has become a very popular fifth-grade rite-of-passage task in my school. Each student takes a copy of the book home, and several others are distributed around the school. Our principal displays the books on a coffee table in her office, the library shelves several copies, and I display several copies, in addition to copies of previous year's books, in my book rack. Although storybooks can be hand-written and illustrated, the use of technology has formalized the integration of this desktop publishing task with my language arts curriculum. We devote two ninety-minute sessions to typing and illustrating the two story problems that I ask each student to write and solve.

REPRODUCIBLE 4.2 Multiplication Story-Problem Book

REPRODUCIBLE 4.3 Description of Multiplication Story-Problem Book Tasks

I introduce the lesson with a discussion of and an informational handout about our forthcoming multiplication and division storybook. The handout explains the jobs, expectations, and responsibilities that I will ask students to carry out. (See Reproducibles 4.2 and 4.3; see also Figure 4–5.)

I expect each student to write and solve two story-problems for two different classifications. You will need an introduction for each classification as well as an overall introduction to the book and project. You will

FIGURE 4–5
Multiplication Story-Problem Book.

Multiplication Story-Problem Book

Class: ____________

Task	*Who?*
Choose a title or a theme	Whole class
Choose or write a dedication	Whole class
Illustrate the cover	____________(1)
Write the introduction	____________(1)
Write, illustrate, and solve two problems	Every student
Write section descriptions or introductions:	
Grouping problems	____________(1)
Rate problems	____________(1)
Area or array problems	____________(1)
Combination problems	____________(1)
Comparison problems	____________(1)
Compile the author list	____________(1)
Self-evaluation	Every student

Description of Multiplication Story-Problem Book Tasks

Introduction

One student in each class will be responsible for writing the introduction to the multiplication book. This task requires a strong understanding of the purpose and mathematical content of the book. The introduction will describe

- what the book is about;
- how we learned about the different types of multiplication problems; and
- what the types are.

The introduction will also explain to readers how to use the book at home and in school to learn more about multiplication, division, and problem solving. The assigned student will write the introduction and then edit it with Mrs. Schuster's assistance.

Section Descriptions

Five students in each class will be responsible for writing brief descriptions of the five types of multiplication/division problems that we covered in class. These descriptions will explain the mathematics involved in solving each type of problem. Students should use narration as well as examples in the explanations.

Author List

One student will compile a list of the story-problem authors in the class. The student will be responsible for the correct spelling for each student's name.

Write, Illustrate, and Solve Two Problems

Each student will write, illustrate, and solve two multiplication/division problems. Mrs. Schuster will assign the category for each problem. Using real-life data and models of interesting, rich problems, each student will write a rough draft for each assigned problem and solution. With editing assistance from Mrs. Schuster, students will revise the problem and solution until they are ready for publication. Each student will type each of the two problems and solutions onto the final template, print his or her name, and attach clip art to match the problem.

Choose a Title

The class will choose a title for their book. The book title should be something a little "jazzy" so that it grabs people's attention. The class should also choose a subtitle that gives an explanation of the book's contents.

▶ REPRODUCIBLE 4.3
Description of Multiplication Story-Problem Book Tasks

FIGURE 4–5 (Continued)

also need a list of authors, dedication, and cover for the book. I ask students to list their choices of extra tasks in numerical order before I make additional assignments. If students have had practice writing story problems and their solutions, they will need minimal instructional support as they craft their storybook entries. However, you may need to sit with those students writing the introductions to offer assistance with sentence structure, word choice, and voice as they craft their pieces.

You will need to make some more instructional decisions about how to carry out the writing process. If you employ the writing workshop format in language arts, you may wish to implement the same process for the writing, editing, and production of both the rough and final drafts. In my classroom, I ask students to write rough drafts that are then read aloud to a classmate as they are proofed and edited. They turn the rough drafts in to me and I make final edits. Students have produced two edited rough drafts before they enter the computer lab. Once in the lab, they type up their story problems and solutions. They add clip art and diagrams to their stories once they have typed up the final drafts. It helps to have another set of hands and eyes in the lab to facilitate as students move through this process. I ask support staff from the technology department—and even our lower school administrative assistant—to join us in these sessions to offer guidance and support. You both can provide minilessons on copying, pasting, and moving clip art as needed for students. The process and product of this project bring great satisfaction to a community of fifth-grade mathematicians. (See Figures 4–6 through 4–11.)

FIGURE 4–6
Kelsey's Final Draft of the Story-Problem Book.

Introduction

Welcome to the wonderful fifth-grade story-problem book. In this book you will find rate, grouping, area array, comparison, and combination story problems. Each one of our mathematician builders had to construct 2 story problems and solve them from those 5 classifications. They could be creative with their ideas, and they were. They ranged from rats coming after Tarun to a penguin collecting frozen fish.

So if there are 15 kids in 5S and each wrote 2 story problems and solved them, how many did we all write? While you're reading our book try and figure it out! I hope you enjoy our book. (No fifth graders were harmed in the making of this book . . . except Nick.) Please enjoy.

FIGURE 4–7
Will's Rough and Final Drafts of a Grouping Problem.

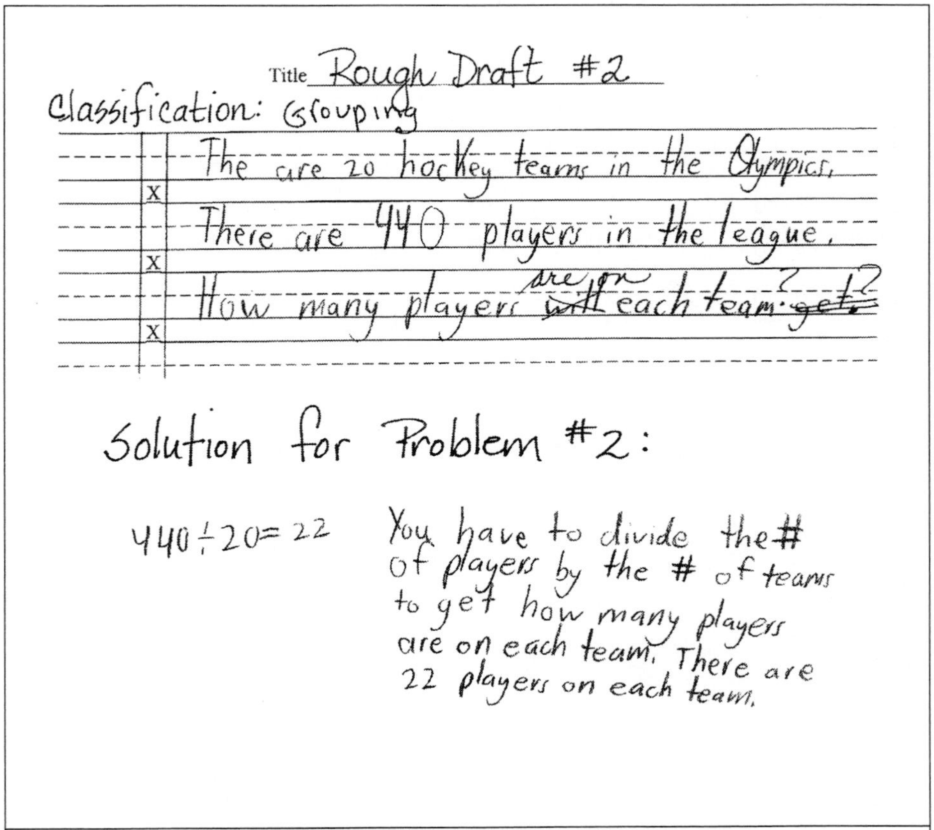

Title _Rough Draft #2_

Classification: Grouping

X The are 20 hockey teams in the Olympics,

X There are 440 players in the league,

X How many players ~~will~~ are on each team? ~~get?~~

Solution for Problem #2:

440 ÷ 20 = 22   You have to divide the #
of players by the # of teams
to get how many players
are on each team. There are
22 players on each team.

Grouping Problems

There are 20 hockey teams in the Olympics. There are 440 players in the league. How many players are on each team?

_____

Solution

440/20 = 22

You have to divide the number of players by the number of teams to get how many players are on each team. There are 22 players on each team.

FIGURE 4–8
Mac's Rough and Final Drafts of a Rate Problem.

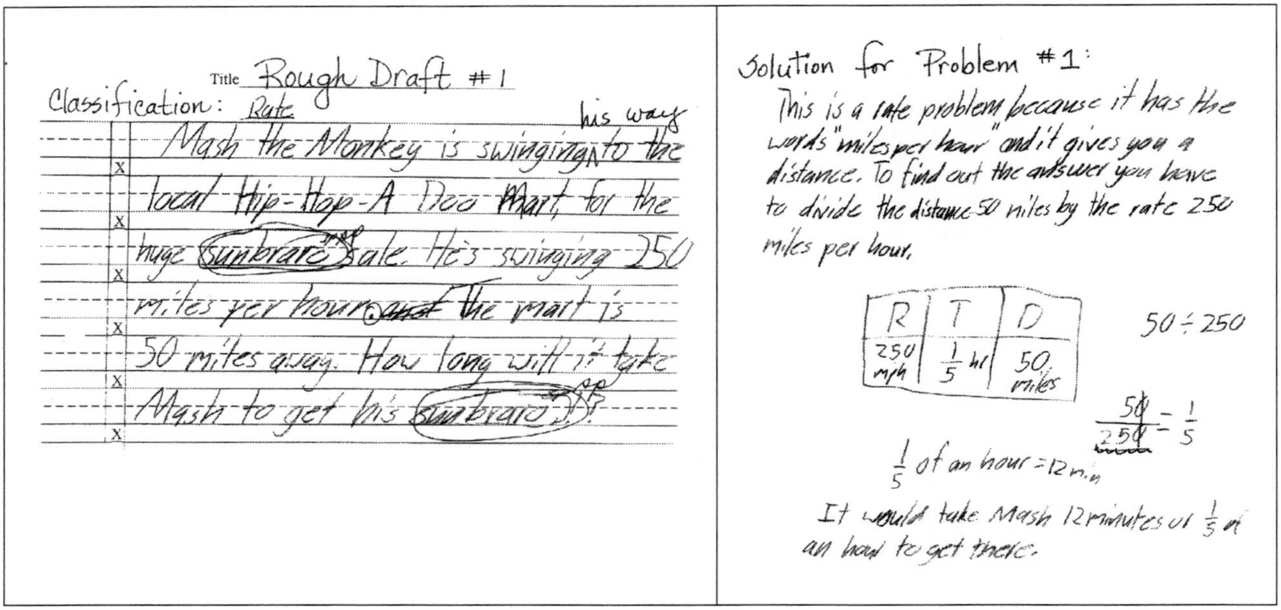

Title _Rough Draft #1_

Classification: _Rate_

Mash the Monkey is swinging into the his way local Hip-Hop-A Doo Mart for the huge ~~sunbrare~~ Sale. He's swinging 250 miles per hour and the mart is 50 miles away. How long will it take Mash to get his ~~sombrero~~?

Solution for Problem #1:

This is a rate problem because it has the words "miles per hour" and it gives you a distance. To find out the answer you have to divide the distance 50 miles by the rate 250 miles per hour.

R	T	D
250 mph	$\frac{1}{5}$ hr	50 miles

$50 \div 250$

$\frac{50}{250} = \frac{1}{5}$

$\frac{1}{5}$ of an hour = 12 min.

It would take Mash 12 minutes or $\frac{1}{5}$ of an hour to get there.

Rate Problems

Mash the Monkey is swinging his way to the local Hip-Hop-a-Doo-Mart for the huge sombrero sale. He's swinging 250 miles per hour. The mart is 50 miles away. How long will it take Mash to get his sombrero?

Solution

This is a rate problem because it has the words _mile per hour_ and it gives you a distance and a rate. To find the answer you have to divide the distance (50 miles) by the rate (250 miles per hour).

$50/250 = \boxed{}$

rate	time	distance
250 mph	$\frac{1}{5}$ hr.	50 miles

$\frac{50}{250} = \frac{1}{5}$

$\frac{1}{5}$ of an hour $= 12$ min.

It would take Mash 12 minutes or one-fifth of an hour to get there.

FIGURE 4-9
Mac's Rough and Final Drafts of an Area/Array Problem.

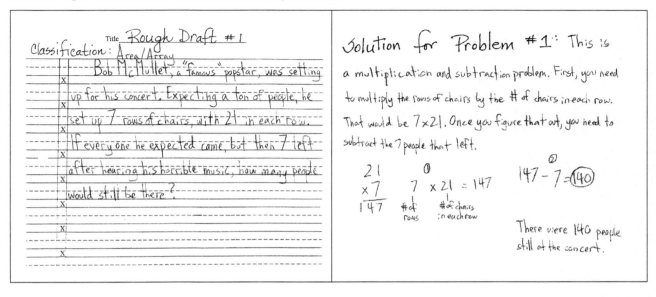

Array Problems

Bob McMullet, a "famous" pop star, was setting up for his concert. Expecting a ton of people, he set up 7 rows of chairs with 21 in each row. If every person he expected came, but then 7 left after hearing his horrible music, how many people would still be at the concert?

_____

Solution

This is a multiplication and subtraction problem. First you need to multiply the rows of chairs by the number of chairs in each row. That would be 7×21. Once you figure that out, you need to subtract the 7 people who left.

$$\begin{array}{r} 21 \\ \times\, 7 \\ \hline 147 \end{array} \qquad 7 \times 21 = 147 \qquad 147 - 7 = 140$$

\# of rows   \# of chairs   There were 140 people still
              in each row   at Bob McMullet's concert.

FIGURE 4–10
Matt's Rough and Final Drafts of a Combination Problem: The Sequel to His Previous Area/Array Problem.

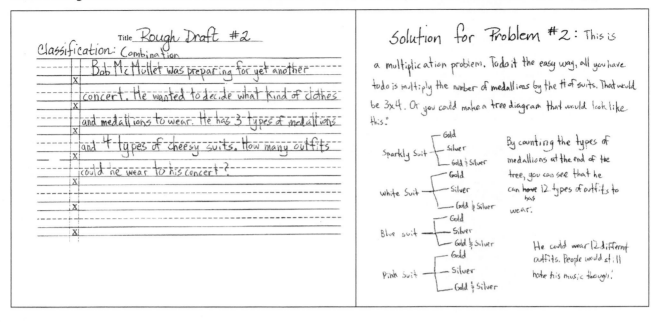

Combination Problems

Bob McMullet was preparing for yet another concert. He wanted to decide what kind of clothes and medallions to wear. He had 3 types of medallions and 4 types of cheesy suits. How many outfits could he wear to his concert?

Solution

This is a multiplication problem. To do it the easy way, all you have to do is multiply the number of medallions by the number of cheesy suits. That would be 3×4. Or, you could make a tree diagram that would look like this:

By counting the types of medallions at the end of the tree, you can see that he has 12 different outfits to wear.

FIGURE 4–11
Jake's Rough and Final Drafts of a Comparison Problem.

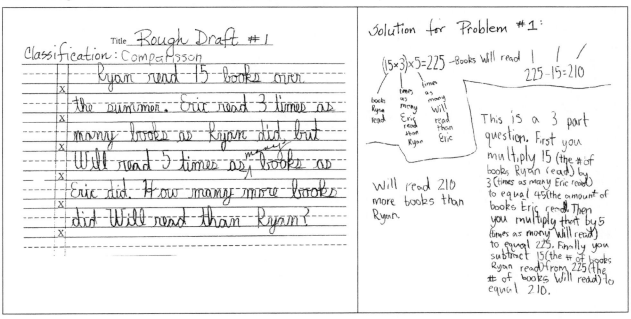

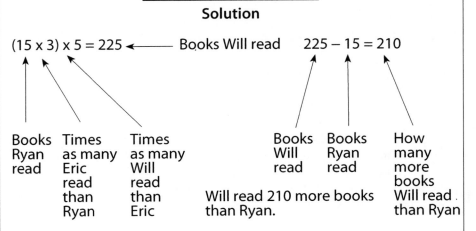

Comparison Problems

Ryan read 15 books over the summer. Eric read 3 times as many books as Ryan did, but Will read 5 times as many books as Eric did. How many more books did Will read than Ryan?

_____

Solution

(15 x 3) x 5 = 225 ◄——— Books Will read   225 − 15 = 210

Books Ryan read	Times as many Eric read than Ryan	Times as many Will read than Eric	Books Will read	Books Ryan read	How many more books Will read than Ryan

Will read 210 more books than Ryan.

This is a three-part question. First you multiply 15 (the number of books Ryan read) by 3 (times as many Eric read) to equal 45 (the amount of books Eric read). Then you multiply that by 5 (times as many Will read) to equal 225. Finally you subtract 15 (the number of books Ryan read) from 225 (the number of books Will read).

NCTM Connection

Strand: Number and
Operations
Focus: Solve more
complex problems
by using what
they know about
simpler related
problems.
Context: Silent
Multiplication

Silent Multiplication

*Duration: 1–2 Class Periods Followed by Shorter Explorations
Several Times a Week*

This lesson, adapted from *Teaching Arithmetic: Lessons for Extending
Multiplication, Grades 4–5* (Wickett and Burns 2001), exposes patterns of
factors and products that will support students as they continue to make
sense of multidigit multiplication. Students develop strategies to solve
increasingly complex multiplications by using what they know about simpler, related problems. This activity offers students the opportunities to

- practice basic multiplication facts;
- explore the commutative, associative, and distributive properties of
  multiplication;
- examine the effect of the product when one factor is halved or the
  other factor is doubled;
- continue to explore the effects on the product when multiplying by
  ten and multiples of ten;
- solve more complex problems by using what they know about simpler related problems; and
- continue to strengthen number sense, computation, and problem
  solving.

Materials

The beauty of this lesson is its adaptability. Initial lessons can focus on just
one idea or procedure at a time and then move on to another for future
lessons. As you continue to use silent multiplication routines throughout
your unit, you can apply multiple concepts and procedures to longer, more
complex strings of multiplication problems. And even though silent multiplication can elicit significant focus and thought from students, it is the
discussion following the activity that is of critical importance as students
work to make sense of the relationships among factors, products, and
open-number sentences while they mentally calculate strings of multiplication problems.

   The activity begins with writing a basic multiplication fact on the board,
such as $4 \times 6 = \square$. Ask the students for the product, then write a related
fact below the initial fact:

$$4 \times 6 = 24$$
$$8 \times 6 = \square$$

Although students will quickly identify the product as forty-eight, I am
more concerned with their awareness of the relationship between the two

equations. How does knowing the product of the first problem help me to calculate the product of the second? Being aware that when one of the factors is doubled, the product will also be doubled is a mathematically powerful observation and generalization. Adding another open sentence to the string of problems that supports this reasoning will help to further develop this generalization:

$$4 \times 6 = 24$$
$$8 \times 6 = 48$$
$$16 \times 6 = \boxed{}$$

Again, the generalization applies. Since we have doubled the previous sentence's factor of 8, we must also double the previous product of 48. So now we know that $16 \times 6 = 2 \times 48$. The next open sentence can offer a doubling of the second factor:

$$4 \times 6 = 24$$
$$8 \times 6 = 48$$
$$16 \times 6 = 96$$
$$16 \times 12 = \boxed{}$$

Conversation is crucial during this first go-round. As you add a new sentence to the string, ask students to turn and talk to their partner about what is happening mathematically to the factors and products in each successive problem. Such partner talk can support the reasoning that is necessary to understand and articulate the mathematical progression of the particular string of equations. My fifth graders love the fact that they can multiply 16×12 without actually carrying out the multiplication. They become quite excited and animated about their ability to solve these more complicated problems by solving and referring to simpler, related problems.

The next open sentence requires students to halve one of the factors. In doing so, the resulting product will be halved as well:

$$4 \times 6 = 24$$
$$8 \times 6 = 48$$
$$16 \times 6 = 96$$
$$16 \times 12 = 192$$
$$8 \times 12 = \boxed{}$$

Many students may notice that the previous product of 16 and 6 is equal to the product of 8 and 12. Why is that so? How is 16×6 the same as 8×12? In these two equations, one factor is halved, and the other doubles. Students quickly identified that—but *why* does it work? And *why* is the product the same?

What began as a "What do you notice?" question quickly became a full class investigation! Matt wanted to look at the factors of both equations.

Because of our previous work with factors and multiples, the class wanted to try to make a connection between what they already knew about factors and products to what they did not know . . . yet! Some students began to factor both sets of factors. Camille was convinced that prime factors would be a better indicator of similarities or differences between the two expressions. Because both products equaled ninety-six, the union of both sets of factors of each equation would have to be the same based on her informal understanding of the Fundamental Theorem of Arithmetic, a theorem that states that every natural number greater than one is either a prime number or can be expressed *uniquely* as a product of prime numbers (NCTM 1989) and one that we touched on in our previous month's work. (See Figure 4–12.)

Camille posted her prime factorizations on the whiteboard. The discussion focused on the similarities between the two sets of factors. And when the factors were written in numerical order, they were exactly the same! Matt noticed that another grouping of the prime factors of ninety-six would result in the factors of four and twenty-four—which *is* a doubling and halving of eight and twelve. As students grouped and regrouped the prime factors of ninety-six, the doubling and halving of factors became visible. (See Figure 4–13.)

Max reminded us that one grouping had been overlooked. He noted that 32×3 could have been the start of this particular doubling and halving string. (See Figure 4–14.)

Although this exploration veered from the instructional sequence that I had originally intended with silent multiplication, we uncovered some sophisticated mathematics and applied this to our work with multiplication strings. Once again, students were impressed and awed by the power of prime factors and how useful they could be! But what I found most interesting about this mathematical digression was the students' concern for and interest in why this string of multiplications made sense. This task of silent multiplication was not magical; it was simply mathematical! The mathematics was intriguing, interesting, and built on previous understandings—a powerful and meaningful lesson learned by ten-year-olds.

FIGURE 4–12
Camille's Prime Factorizations of 16 × 6 and 8 × 12.

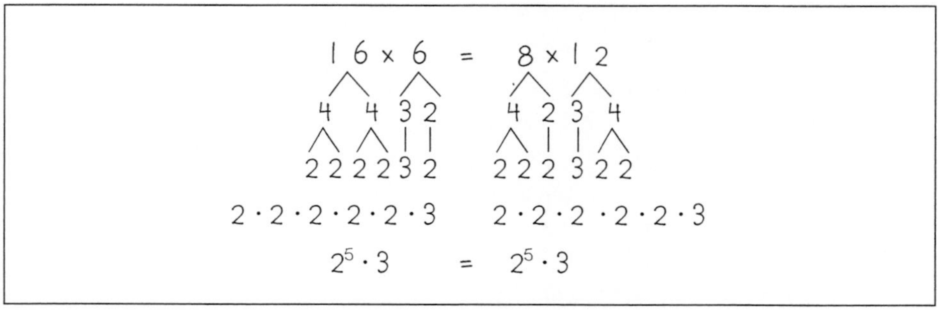

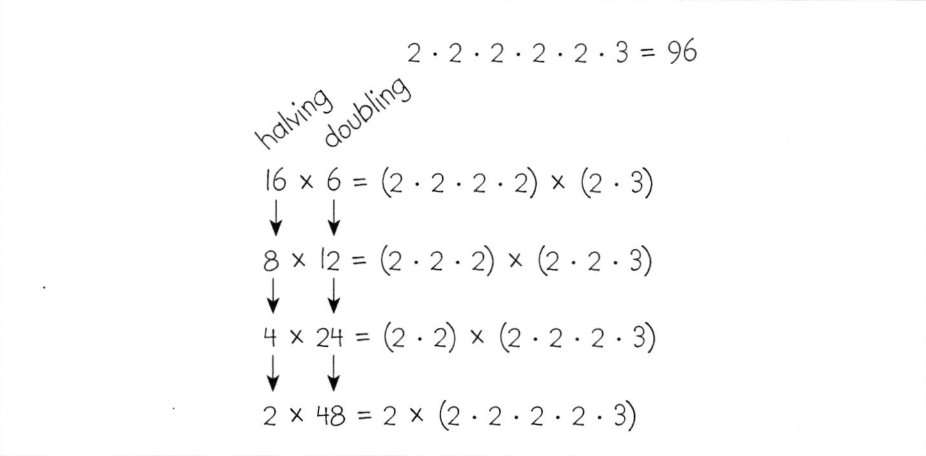

$$2 \cdot 2 \cdot 2 \cdot 2 \cdot 2 \cdot 3 = 96$$

halving *doubling*

$$16 \times 6 = (2 \cdot 2 \cdot 2 \cdot 2) \times (2 \cdot 3)$$
$$\downarrow \qquad \downarrow$$
$$8 \times 12 = (2 \cdot 2 \cdot 2) \times (2 \cdot 2 \cdot 3)$$
$$\downarrow \qquad \downarrow$$
$$4 \times 24 = (2 \cdot 2) \times (2 \cdot 2 \cdot 2 \cdot 3)$$
$$\downarrow \qquad \downarrow$$
$$2 \times 48 = 2 \times (2 \cdot 2 \cdot 2 \cdot 2 \cdot 3)$$

FIGURE 4–13
Patrick's Prime Factor Groupings.

$$32 \times 3 = (2 \cdot 2 \cdot 2 \cdot 2 \cdot 2) \times 3$$

FIGURE 4–14
Max's Factor Grouping.

Not every class will take this activity to this level. And I must admit that I was quite surprised (and impressed!) not only by the thinking but also by the direction in which Matt, Patrick, Camille, and Max moved the class that day. The beauty of open-ended tasks such as silent multiplication and the mathematical discussions that can ensue from them is all about mathematical possibilities. Asking good questions that can be as simple as "What do you notice?" and opening up the thinking of your students can turn a seemingly simple task into a rich and meaningful mathematical opportunity.

You may also find it useful to develop some start numbers for multiplication strings that will eventually address other mathematics, for example, the multiplication of fractions and decimals. A silent multiplication string containing an odd number easily lends itself to multiplication by a fraction or a decimal:

$$5 \times 8 = 40$$
$$5 \times 16 = 80$$
$$5 \times 32 = 160$$
$$2.5 \times 32 = 80$$
$$2.5 \times 16 = 40$$

or

$$7 \times 8 = 56$$
$$14 \times 8 = 112$$
$$14 \times 16 = 224$$
$$7 \times 16 = 112$$
$$3\frac{1}{2} \times 16 = 56$$
$$1\frac{3}{4} \times 16 = 28$$

Although students have not yet been formally exposed to the multiplication of decimals and fractions, they can predict products from what they have already discovered about the doubling and halving of factors. They are trying to make sense of the multiplications with reasoning rather than calculations; a routine with which they are becoming more and more comfortable.

NCTM Connection

Strand: Number and Operations
Focus: Apply multiplication and division strategies within a problem-solving context.
Context: *Where Does 100 Land?*

REPRODUCIBLE 4.4
Where Does 100 Land?

REPRODUCIBLE 4.5
Half-Inch Grid Paper

Where Does 100 Land?

Duration: 1–2 Class Periods

The study of patterns is valuable for helping children discover and develop generalizations about number (Burns 2007, 157). This investigation, which can be referenced in *About Teaching Mathematics: A K–8 Resource* (Burns 2007), not only requires students to investigate patterns, but also asks them to make predictions and generalizations based on their understanding of multiplication and its connection to division. This lesson offers students opportunities to

- investigate arrays of different row lengths and where one hundred will land in respective arrays;
- make predictions and generalizations based on understandings of multiples and divisibility; and
- apply multiplication and division strategies within a problem-solving context.

Materials

- *Where Does 100 Land?*, 1 per student (see Reproducible 4.4)
- half-inch grid paper (see Reproducible 4.5)

Vocabulary

array, column, factor, horizontal, quotient, remainder, row, vertical

You will need to preview and work through this investigation yourself before presenting it to your class. Although the presentation task is not complicated, the construction of a generalization in order to predict in which row and column one hundred will fall can be a challenge. Although we can *see* where one hundred falls in various arrays, the mathematical reason for and subsequent articulation of its placement can be elusive.

This lesson begins with a distribution of *Where Does 100 Land?* (see Reproducible 4.4) to each student. We review and discuss the task in a whole-class format. I inform the students that they will have five minutes of quiet time to work independently on the task, then they will work with a partner to investigate several arrays and possible generalizations that would allow them to predict in which row and column one hundred would fall for any length array. As students construct arrays on grid paper, they are asked to complete the following prompt below each array:

▶ REPRODUCIBLE 4.4
Where Does 100
Land?

In an array of _____ , 100 lands in the _____ row and the _____ column.

Again, the beauty of this particular lesson—and all good mathematical investigations—is its accessibility to all of your fifth-grade mathematicians. As students set off to work, you may be struck by the diversity of responses and work resulting from the task. Some students may:

- create several arrays before they think about the placement of one hundred;
- opt to skip-count by the array length and only represent the final row;
- try to move straight to the arithmetic, but quickly realize that having an array or two in front of them helps to anchor their thinking with a model; or
- begin with multiplication, but shift to a division model as they look for a connection between the placement of one hundred and its row and column.

I moved around the room, offering prompts and help in the wording of generalizations. Initially, as students spoke, I wrote down exactly what they said. Then, together, we would reread and revise what was said in order to clean up the language and the mathematics. As students began to understand and articulate the connection between the multiples of an array and where one hundred would fall, I encouraged them to look at arrays of greater than ten. Would their generalization apply? And what about an array length of ten? Would a special case have to be noted for a multiple of ten? Why would that make sense? (See Figure 4–15.)

You will need to make instructional decisions about when and how often to pull the class together for debriefing and processing. Over the years, I have found that each particular class dictates the time and necessity of coming together. Although I always spend processing time to give closure to the mathematics of the lesson, there are those years when coming together once or twice before the final sharing is helpful and even necessary. A public sharing of "What have you discovered so far?" thirty minutes into the investigation can help students move forward in their strategies and thinking.

REPRODUCIBLE 4.5
Half-Inch Grid Paper

◄

FIGURE 4–15
(A) Grace's Work and "What Do I Notice?" Statements; (B) Generalizations Resulting from Patrick's Work.

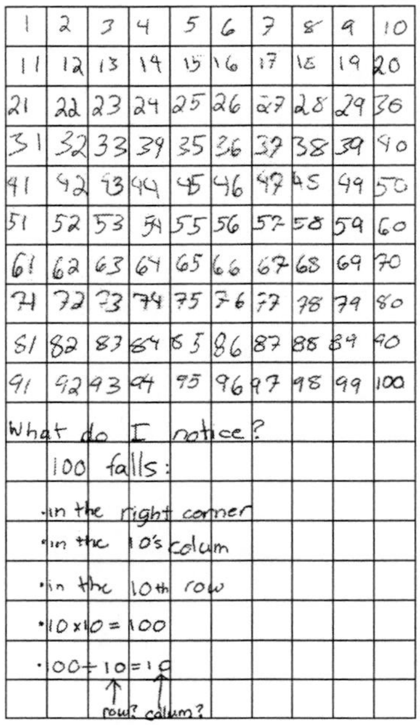

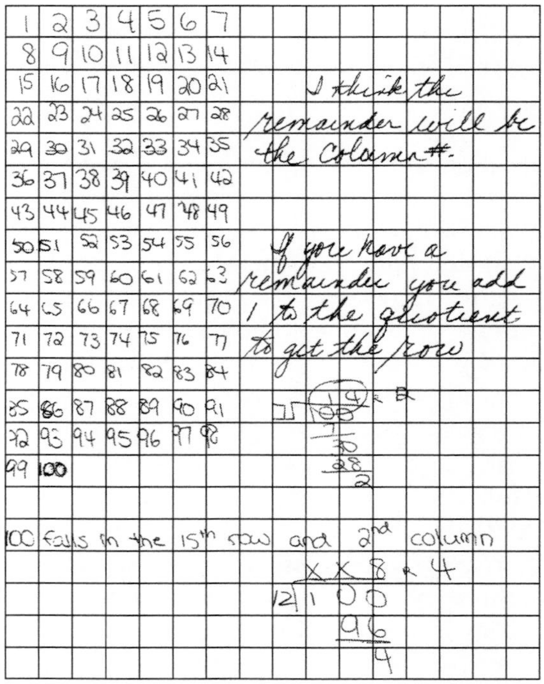

I have found it helps to devote one full class period to the investigation itself, and then another to the processing of the mathematics and generalizations. As students offer generalizations, I post them on the board. As a class, we process the language of each generalization. I solicit suggestions for revision to tighten up the language and make better use of mathematical vocabulary. This year's fifth-grade class offered the following generalizations:

- If you divide one hundred by the array number, your remainder will be the column and the (quotient + 1) will give you the row.

- One hundred will fall in the row number following a multiple of that array that is as close as you can get to one hundred without going over.

- Special cases:

  If the array is a factor of one hundred, the array number will be the column number.

  If the array is a factor of one hundred, the row number will be the other number in that factor pair.

The mathematical language of this investigation is rich. Words such as *factor*, *multiple*, *divisibility*, *quotient*, and *remainder* all help connect the task to formalized generalizations. Meaningful vocabulary can also help to scaffold the connections we want students to discover between the processes of multiplication and division.

In the Groundworks series (Greenes and Findell 2006), the authors offer an algebraic thinking problem set called *Lattice Logic* that is similar in structure to *Where Does 100 Land?* You can use these worksheets as follow-up activities that require students to think about numbers other than one hundred and where they would land in a lattice (array) of a specified row length.

Good Questions to Ask

- Is this equation true or false? Is this equation *always* true or false? How do you know? Use number models to support your reasoning.

$$\square \times \triangle = \triangle \times \square$$

- Is this equation true or false? Is this equation *always* true or false? How do you know? Use number models to support your reasoning.

$$\square \div \triangle = \triangle \div \square$$

- How can knowing $8 \times 4 = 32$ help you to understand $32 \div 4$?
- How can knowing $8 \times 6 = 48$ help you to understand 16×6?

> For more good questions, see *Good Questions for Math Teaching: Why Ask Them and What to Ask, Grades 5–8* by Lainie Schuster and Nancy Anderson (Math Solutions 2005).

- What can you say about 30×24 and 15×48? Is the following equation true or false? How do you know?

$$30 \times 24 = 15 \times 48$$

- Which of the following problems has the largest product? Which of the following problems has the smallest product? Try to figure this out by solving as few problems as possible. How did you choose which problems to do or not do?

42×17	24×12	52×11
40×20	50×24	43×16
36×36	12×14	42×42

- What is different between the two phrases: *four times more* and *four times as many*? Use words and number models to support your thinking.

Calculation Routines and Practices

NCTM Connection

Strand: Number and Operations

Focus: Explore, practice, and apply alternative as well as standard multiplication algorithms.

Context: Multiplication Algorithms

Whole-number computation is the foundation of arithmetic (Chapin and Johnson 2006). Whether the multiplication is embedded in a story problem or required by a naked number calculation, our fifth graders need to make sense of their procedures based on their understanding of multiplicative properties and relationships as well as on the numbers involved.

Algorithms, a structured set of procedures that can be used across problems regardless of the numbers used (Fosnot and Dolk 2001, 102), have an important place in the teaching and learning of mathematics. We certainly want our fifth graders to calculate accurately and efficiently. For that reason, we need to scaffold and embed instruction in students' understandings of the process and meaning of multiplication and division.

It will be important and helpful for you to review your state and district expectations for whole-number calculations before you begin instruction. For example, Massachusetts requires those students in the fifth and sixth grades to

6.N.9 Select and use appropriate operations to solve problems involving addition, subtraction, multiplication, division, and positive integer exponents with whole numbers . . .

6.N.13 Accurately and efficiently add, subtract, multiply, and divide (with double-digit divisors) whole numbers . . . (Massachusetts Department of Education 2000, 20)

Nowhere in the frameworks is the charge to teach the traditional algorithm of either multidigit multiplication or division! Although I do have my students explore and practice both, I also offer several alternative procedures.

Engaging students in thinking about and computing with several partial-products algorithms can continue to ground students in their understanding of place value and number sense. As they decompose, multiply, and then put factors back together again, students can apply their number sense and understanding of place value as they make sense of larger multiplications. Even the traditional algorithm is a partial-products procedure, one that students can make sense of once they have had experiences with other procedures requiring breaking down factors and building products.

Chunking Algorithm

The chunking algorithm provides a concrete structure within which students apply the distributive property. It is a physical as well as conceptual framework within which students can decompose larger numbers into smaller, more manageable parts in order to calculate partial products:

$$426 \times 8 = \boxed{}$$

$\times$	400	$+\ 20$	$+\ 6$
8	3200	160	48

For example, 426 is decomposed into $400 + 20 + 6$. Each number is then multiplied by 8 to calculate the partial products. The partial products are then added together to calculate the final product:

$$
\begin{array}{r}
3200 \\
160 \\
+\ 48 \\
\hline
3408
\end{array}
$$

My students often refer to the grid used in this method as a *chunker*. The label works well. When students discuss strategies and use the chunker terminology, a visual representation of the multiplication is available and easily reproduced. The chunking algorithm also works well with multidigit factors. (See Figure 4–16.)

The number of partial products created by the chunking algorithm compares nicely to the total number of multiplications required by multidigit factors. Students will often look at a more complex multiplication problem consisting of two factors and assume that there are only two multiplications within the calculation. Fifth graders may procedurally equate 7×8 with the same number of multiplications as 76×84. Students *are* making an important generalization, but one that

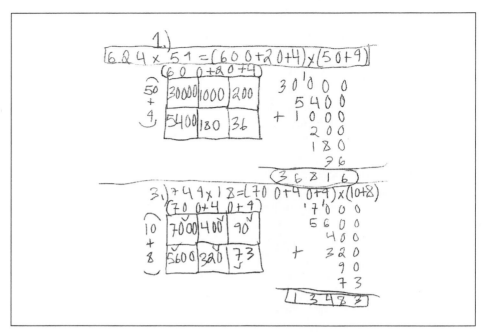

FIGURE 4–16
Gabby's Chunking Calculation.

needs to be readjusted with the aid of the visual reference that chunking provides.

Introducing a multiplication problem containing two three-digit factors such as $326 \times 457 = \square$ can move students to thinking about the efficiency or, even more so, the inefficiency, of such a method as factors become larger. Even Nick, who loved this method of multiplication, complained profusely about the size of the chunker and all the zeros he had to manipulate. As he calculated, the class could hear him musing, "Are you kidding me? I just took up a whole page to do one problem!"

The multiplication of three-digit factors can open up a discussion about the importance of choosing procedures based on the numbers involved. If students have procedural options, this conversation can be one that is meaningful, important, and ongoing as they practice and discuss other multiplication procedures.

After a procedure is explored and discussed, I ask that students evaluate its good and not-so-good points. I distribute a multiplication algorithm evaluation grid (see Reproducible 4.6) to each student to be completed as a class. As students offer opinions, I make a list on the chart for that specific algorithm. It is important to remind students that they may not all agree with every opinion. For example, Nick thought that chunking took up too much paper and was too cumbersome when the factors were large. But Mac liked the structure the chunker provided, which made it less likely to "get lost" in the calculation. Encourage students to evaluate their own opinions of the procedure. If they agree, they can document the articulated

REPRODUCIBLE 4.6
Multiplication
Algorithms: Compare
and Constrast

Multiplication Algorithms: Compare and Contrast

Procedure/Algorithm	Good Points	Not-So-Good Points
Lattice Multiplication	• Multiplacation is easy • kind of fun	• Hard to set up • easy to make mistakes • takes a long time • takes up a lot of paper.
Chunking	• Chunker is easy to make • easy multiplacat-ions • helps to understand place value	• takes up a lot of paper • takes a long time
FOIL Method		
Traditional Algorithm		

▶ REPRODUCIBLE 4.6
Multiplication Algorithms: Compare and Contrast

FIGURE 4–17
Elise's Evaluation of Chunking.

idea. If they do not agree, encourage them to offer their opinion about why they disagree, and document their opinion accordingly. (See Figure 4–17.)

FOIL Method

The FOIL method of multiplication is another application of the distributive property; many of us remember applying the acronym FOIL (first, outside, inside, last) as we multiplied binomials in algebra. The FOIL method also can be used to apply the distributive property as we multiply

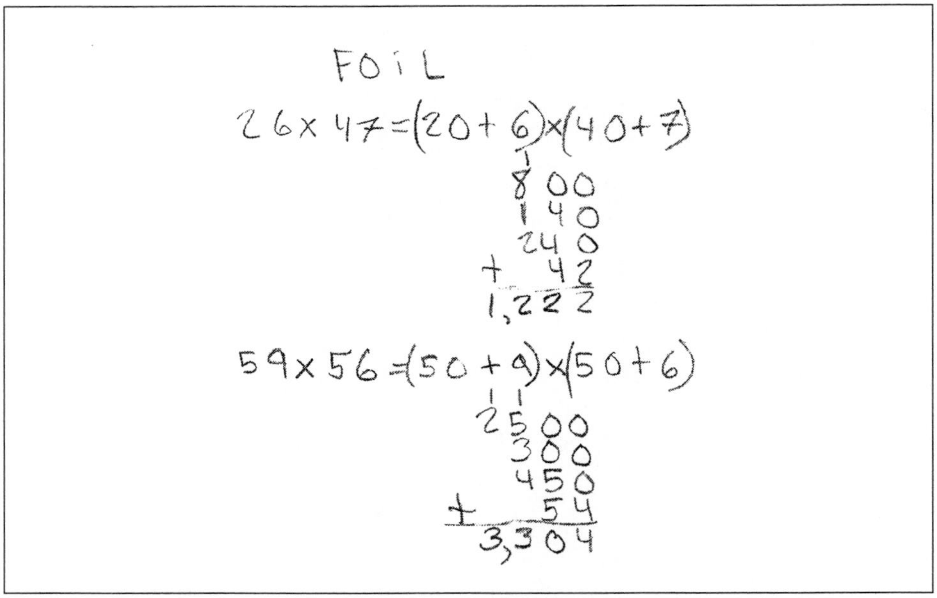

FIGURE 4–18
Matt's FOIL Calculation.

whole numbers and work with calculations requiring the manipulation of two two-digit whole-number factors.

When I introduce FOIL to my students, I begin by telling them that this is a method they will see in years to come; they may already be familiar with the acronym if they have older siblings in a pre-algebra or algebra course.

Next, I present a number model, such as:

$$23 \times 57 = \square$$

As with most multiplication calculations, I prefer to first present the problem horizontally as an open-number sentence. This particular representation does not support or suggest the application of any one algorithm.

The FOIL acronym (First, Outside, Inside, and Last) corresponds with the order of decomposition and calculation. Matt was always pushing us to be better mathematicians and to think a little harder. Matt asked if he could call this procedure FOLI or ILOF or FLIO. "Order doesn't matter in multiplication," he reasoned, "so why not? It is all the same multiplications, just in a different order." Such an insightful generalization allows us the opportunity to be awed and reflective about the mathematical thinking of our fifth graders! (See Figure 4–18.)

Partial Products Algorithm

The partial products algorithm is also based on the distributive property of multiplication. As with the chunking and FOIL methods, students decompose factors and then multiply taking into account the place value of each digit. Then they record the partial products and add them to compute the final product:

$$
\begin{array}{ll}
 & 385 \\
 & \underline{\times 7} \\
(7 \times 300) & 2100 \\
(7 \times 80) & 560 \\
(7 \times 5) & \underline{+35} \\
 & 2695
\end{array}
$$

As with the chunking algorithm, the factor 385 is broken down into hundreds, tens, and ones. Each value is then multiplied by the factor of 7. Students often prefer to begin their decomposing with the greatest place-value digit, moving from left to right through the calculation. This practice will help them keep better track of the place values as well as to construct a systematic written record of this procedure. Again, this big idea of taking apart numbers—operating on them—and then putting them back together is demonstrated by the partial products algorithm.

The partial products algorithm also offers students another estimation strategy, one that encourages students to estimate the magnitude of a number without having to necessarily complete the procedure. For example, when we multiply 385×7, we know that $300 \times 7 = 2100$ and that $80 \times 7 = 560$. The product will therefore be in the 2600 range because $2100 + 500 = 2600$.

As students practice and apply the partial products algorithm, they may begin to find the calculating tedious. Larger factors can cause students to question the efficiency of this procedure.

As students compare and contrast procedures, efficiency invariably becomes a talking point . . . or it should! Fifth graders are apt to "forget" the traditional algorithm because they so often tried to learn the procedure without a conceptual understanding of why and how it works. If your students have had time to explore and practice various partial products methods, you may find that they will be better able to make sense of the traditional algorithm because it, too, is a partial products procedure and another one that requires applying the distributive property.

TEACHER-TO-TEACHER TALK ■ About Making Connections ■ The authors of *Making Sense: Teaching and Learning Mathematics with Understanding* (Hiebert et al. 1997) propose that when we understand something, we " . . . see how it is related or connected to other things we know . . . the more relationships (we) can establish, the better (we) understand" (4). We need to keep this important thought in mind as we move through multiplication algorithms and discussions about those procedures with our fifth graders. We can make connections among all the presented procedures, including the traditional algorithm. They are all examples of partial products procedures as well as applications of the distributive property.

(Continued)

I am not subtle about making these connections with my students; I try to be deliberate and explicit by asking questions such as:

- Where have we seen this decomposition of numbers before?
- How is this procedure like chunking? Or FOIL? Or partial products?
- How do you calculate the partial products?
- Where do you find the partial products in your written representation of the calculation?
- What do you do with the partial products to get your final solution?
- What procedure do you like best? Why?
- What procedure would you be less likely to use? Why?

Posing good questions as procedures are introduced, practiced, and discussed can help make these connections visible and accessible. We cannot always assume that our students are making sense of the connections—or even acknowledging them! We also need to continually remind our students that making connections is important in mathematics. Once we, students and teachers alike, see how the concepts and procedures of multidigit multiplication are related and connected, we can manipulate that knowledge with greater understanding, efficiency, and proficiency. We can then make better decisions about what procedure to apply when. Our decisions become based on the numbers or context of the problem rather than on a memorized procedure based on steps of completion rather than on understanding.

Standard Multiplication Algorithm

If you can lay a conceptual foundation throughout the study of multiplication with plenty of opportunity for students to develop preferred and invented strategies, then you can meaningfully develop the standard multiplication algorithm. As with other algorithms, mathematical conversation and discussion need to occur as the procedure is introduced, practiced, and applied. Questions that push students to compare and contrast procedures, identify smaller problems within a larger one, and estimate will help them to make sense of this traditional approach to multiplication.

Beginning with one-digit multipliers and then moving on to two-digit multipliers seems to be standard fare. Because of my concern with the preservation of place value, I ask students to record each complete partial product, including the zeros:

$$
\begin{array}{r}
41 \\
\times\,58 \\
\hline
328 \\
2050\ (205 \times 10) \\
\hline
2378 \\
\end{array}
$$

Recurrent discussions about why it makes sense for that zero to placed in the partial product helps to keep students focused on the multiplication by ten that the second partial product represents.

Seth preferred to refer to that elusive zero in the second partial product as an "added" zero. It was not until recently that I realized why that language concerned me. That realization led me to rephrase Seth's comment back to the class: "So if I add a 0 to 205, that leaves me with 205 because 205 + 0 = 205. Does this partial product represent 205?" This question opened up a wonderful discussion about what that particular zero represented. It did *not* represent adding zero. It represented *multiplying by ten*. If we just added 0, the written representation would look something like this:

$$
\begin{array}{r}
41 \\
\times\ 58 \\
\hline
328 \\
\underline{205}\ (205 + 0) \\
533
\end{array}
$$

Seth's misconception provided an opportunity for meaningful discussion and thought about one simple zero—which, in reality, was not so simple! We continued to remind each other throughout the rest of the unit why that zero was important in partial products. We also revisited the importance of mathematical language. Instead of using the phrase *add on a zero*, we agreed collectively that *tack on a zero* was a better choice of words.

Each year I am pleasantly surprised at the ease with which students apply the standard multiplication algorithm following our work with other alternative algorithms. If we have had conversations about computational efficiency, students are delighted with an algorithm whose written representation requires minimal space—and one that now makes sense! Making sense of multiplication is not optional in fifth grade; it is imperative for later work with multiplication as our students move on to middle school. According to the NCTM *Principles and Standards for School Mathematics*:

> Students . . . should consolidate and practice a small number of computational algorithms for . . . multiplication . . . that they understand well and can use routinely . . . Having access to more than one method . . . allows students to choose an approach that best fits the numbers in a particular problem. (2000, 155)

Introducing, investigating, practicing, and applying several multiplication algorithms takes time, talk, and patience. It also requires the use of meaningful contexts in which students have the opportunity to choose appropriate strategies. Asking students to share strategies and why it made sense to apply them in that particular context will offer opportunities to talk and think about the numbers—not just the procedure or the final product.

Calculation Practice

Like Annette Raphel, author of *Math Homework That Counts* (2000), I advocate using paper-and-pencil computational practice judiciously as we scaffold understanding and computational proficiency. Calculation practice certainly has a place in our year of mathematical instruction. A problem-solving culture will have little impact without arithmetical proficiency. To be honest, you will not be able to carry out the former without competence in the latter! (See the "Resources" section at the end of this chapter for additional calculation practice resources.)

So what do you do about calculation practice and worksheets? Instructional decisions based on the mathematical objectives of lessons and the needs of your students will allow you to make informed decisions about what constitutes a good worksheet, whether published or self-created. According to Raphel in *Math Homework That Counts* (2000, 9–12), a good worksheet should

- be mathematically rich;
- be interesting;
- stimulate connections;
- be rooted in problem formation, problem solving, and/or mathematical reasoning;
- promote communication;
- advance student understanding;
- not be too intimidating—in format or content; and
- not require students to do arithmetic for arithmetic's sake.

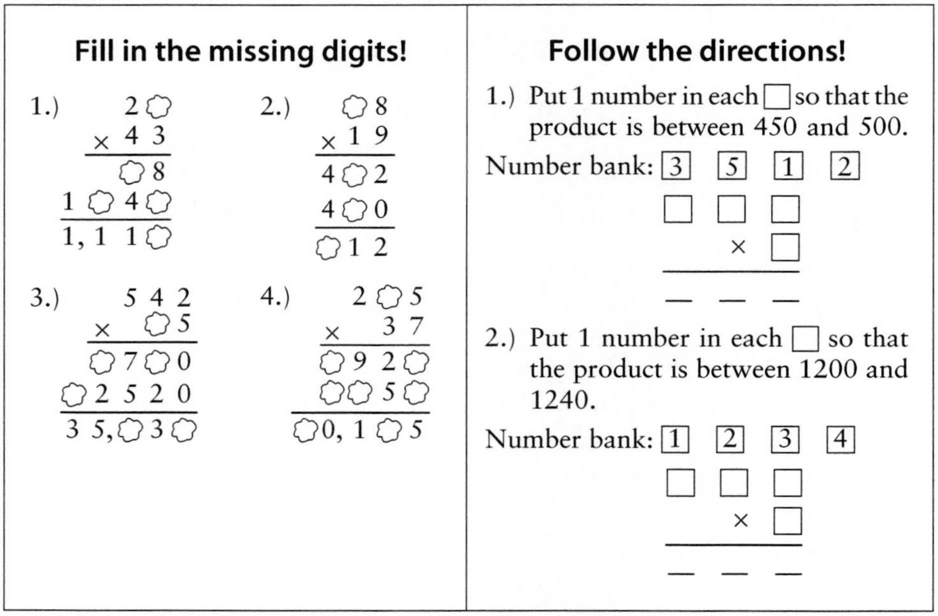

FIGURE 4–19
Source: Adapted from *Groundworks: Reasoning with Numbers, Grade 5* (Greenes et al. 2005).

I would also add that a good worksheet should

- be open-ended whether in approach or solution; and
- offer students some choice.

It is also important for students to be aware of your expectations as they complete their work. You may also be surprised at the preference students will have for the worksheets you have created yourself. Your students will be well aware and appreciative of the effort and time it took for you to create a worksheet with their specific needs in mind. (See Figure 4–19.)

Reading, Writing, and Vocabulary

Reading is thinking. Good readers construct meaning from written text. Good readers interact with what they read and understand. They do not passively receive a text's meaning; they construct it (Hyde 2006, 5). The same could be said for good mathematicians. Like reading, mathematics requires thinking and the construction of meaning. Our strong mathematical thinkers apply what they know about the content of the text, the context being described, how the language of the text is structured, and the particular vocabulary presented in the text.

Reading and comprehending story problems and the structures they present require all of the above. Difficulties with story problems within multiplicative contexts do not occur because students cannot read the words, but because they cannot make sense of the relationships expressed by those words. We can still take the time in fifth grade to address comprehension strategies with our students, and we need to do so even in our mathematics instruction. When we work through lessons requiring the reading of text—especially that presented in a story-problem format—we need to encourage our students to

- make connections;
- ask questions;
- visualize or make mental pictures of what is being said or is being asked;
- infer and predict;
- determine the importance of the information given;
- synthesize, summarize, and retell; and
- monitor their thinking and adjust strategies as they read.

It is our questioning, however, that can help to guide and assess comprehension. Ask the following questions to support this crucial comprehension process:

- Can someone retell the story problem in their own words?
- What do we know for sure?

- What are we being asked to find out?
- Are there any constraints to the problem?
- Do we have all the necessary information?
- How can we proceed with the calculation? How do you know?
- Can someone offer another way to solve the problem?
- Is there only one solution? How do you know?
- Can you draw a diagram or make a model of the problem and/or its solution?

According to Arthur Hyde, author of *Comprehending Math: Adapting Reading Strategies to Teach Mathematics, K–6* (2006), when a class spends time on a discussion in an attempt to gain clarity on a particular task, it is time well spent. There is always danger in *assuming* one knows what is being asked by a problem and then charging ahead to solve what was *not* the problem (29); we have all seen, heard, and read many right solutions to wrong problems!

Writing About a Mathematical Process

When we ask students to write about mathematical processes, we are asking them to reflect on the mathematical decisions they make. The *why* becomes as important as the *how*. When you give them a prompt or task, remind students to focus on the mathematical reasoning involved in their solving the problem or answering the question rather than on just a list of the steps they followed. As students commit their thinking and reasoning to paper, they recognize that they employ specific strategies as they complete specific mathematical tasks.

Matt liked to begin with a number model as he wrote about his thinking and reasoning. "I can use the math to help me think about what and why I did what I did." When he made this strategy public in a whole-class discussion, several other students adopted a similar strategy. Kelsey and Gracie were both strong writers. After hearing Matt's approach, they too realized that they needed a number model to ground their reasoning. Chris preferred to web or brainstorm before he wrote. Chris was more of a "big idea" kind of thinker. The web allowed him to focus on what was important as he noticed repeating ideas or strategies. Having the big picture in front of him allowed him to write about what was important with greater clarity. Nick needed a conversation—it could be with me, a friend, a tablemate, or himself! Nick used this verbal opportunity to fine-tune his thinking and to self-correct. Looking for patterns in their thinking and reasoning enables students to self-assess and monitor their thinking. These metacognitive skills are crucial as our students work to become more proficient problem solvers and mathematical thinkers.

Written explanations of mathematical processes and related concepts also offer us a window through which we can assess understandings, the willingness and ability to apply new skills, as well as fragility in mathematical thinking and language application. Some students will be able to offer a well-organized response, but their explanation reveals a fragile understanding or misconception. Jack's response was extremely well written, with the exception of his use of the phrase *turnaround fact*. He, and most of his classmates, had confused a *turnaround fact* (4×5 and 5×4) with a *related fact* ($20 \div 4$ and 4×5). This is not a minor confusion or misconception—related multiplication and division facts are not commutative nor are they equivalent. This prompt gave us the opportunity to have that important conversation in class the following day. (See Figure 4–20.)

Offering an open-ended prompt or question, such as the one that follows, will allow increased access to the mathematical reasoning required by the concept or procedure. (See the "Assessment" section of this

FIGURE 4–20
Max's Response to "How Can Knowing 9×2 Help You to Know $18 \div 2$?"

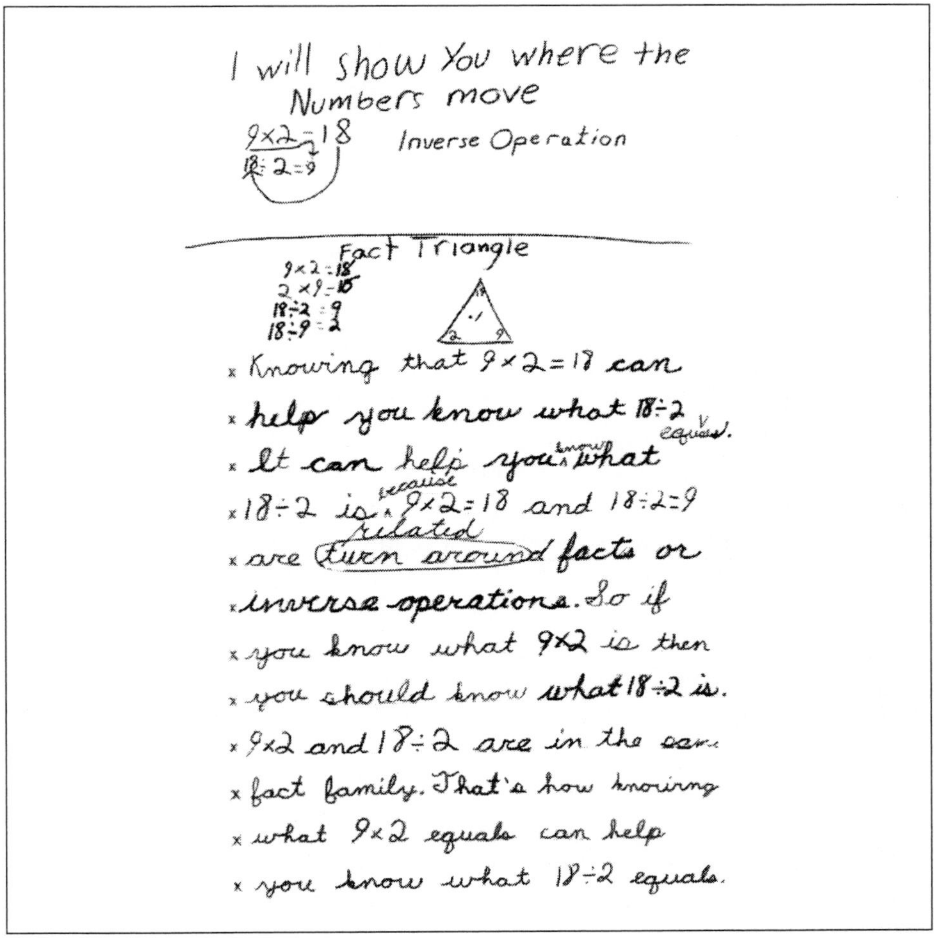

FIGURE 4–21
Gracie's Response.

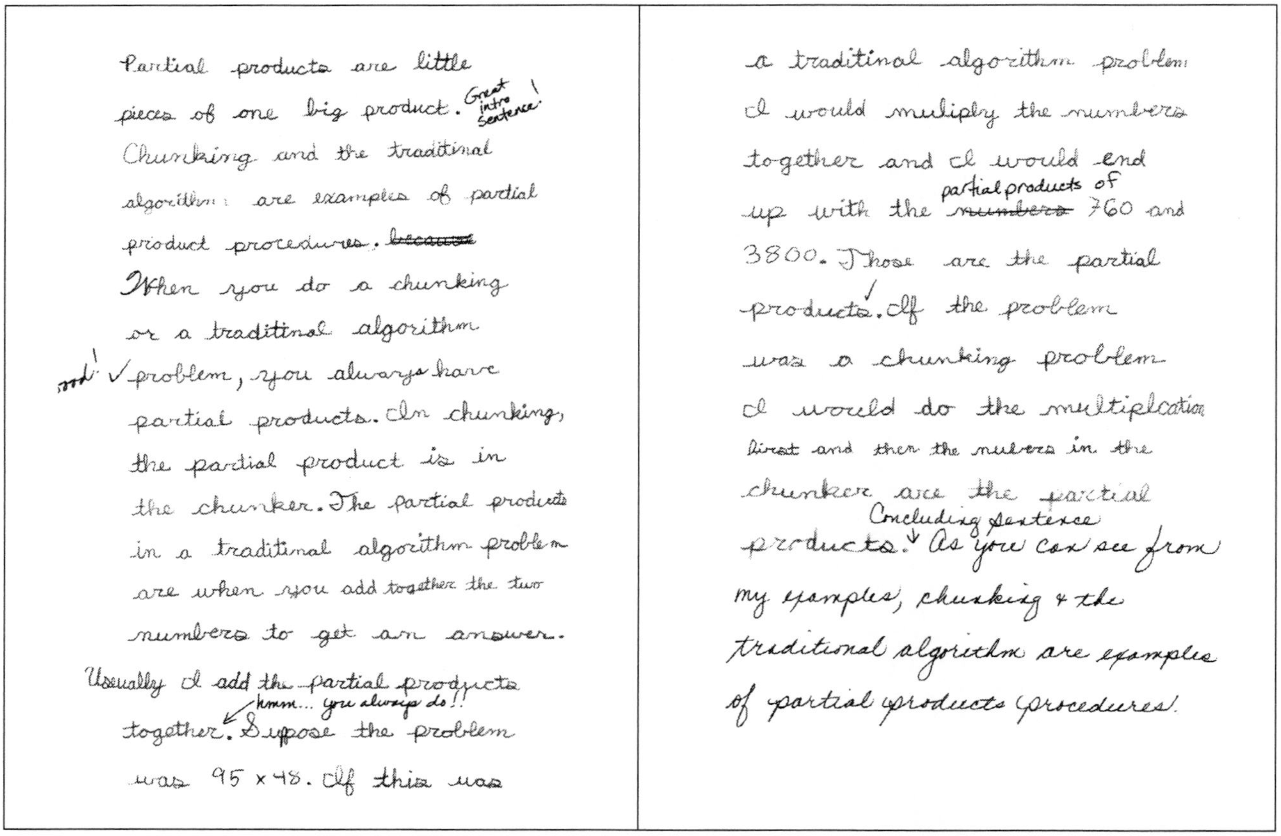

> Partial products are little pieces of one big product. *Great intro sentence!* Chunking and the traditional algorithm are examples of partial product procedures. ~~because~~ When you do a chunking or a traditional algorithm *word!* ✓ problem, you always have partial products. In chunking, the partial product is in the chunker. The partial products in a traditional algorithm problem are when you add together the two numbers to get an answer. Usually I add the partial products *hmm... you always do!!* ✓ together. Suppose the problem was 95 × 48. If this was

> a traditional algorithm problem I would muliply the numbers together and I would end up with the ~~numbers~~ *partial products of* 760 and 3800. Those are the partial products. ✓ If the problem was a chunking problem I would do the multiplication first and then the nubers in the chunker are the partial *Concluding sentence* products. ✓ As you can see from my examples, chunking & the traditional algorithm are examples of partial products (procedures).

chapter; see also Figure 4–21.) Please note that Gracie's response to a prompt I use on my end-of-unit test is exceptional, and not every student will write with such eloquence. Gracie learned quite well how to write for understanding and clarity because she needed to *write to understand*—and she knew it. Never did she look at a writing task as a chore or bother; to Gracie, writing was an opportunity to think and to learn more about how to think. The prompt may ask:

> *Explain* how *and why* chunking, FOIL, or the traditional algorithm are all *examples of* partial product procedures. *What do you do* with those partial *products in order to find your solution? Support your thinking with number models and words.*

Keep in mind that a unit on multiplication is not just about the calculation; many important properties, generalizations, and transferences of previous knowledge need to be in play as fifth graders continue to make sense of multiplication.

Assessment

In designing our teaching and learning experiences . . . our job is not only to uncover the big ideas of content. A great shift requires us to be aggressive in assessing as we teach, uncovering the learners' understandings and misunderstandings. (Wiggins and McTighe 2005, 247)

Assessment practices can be broadly categorized as either *formative* or *summative*. *Formative assessments* are those ongoing formal and informal assessments that allow us to assess developing understandings as the unit progresses. *Summative assessments* can be characterized by their placement at the end of a unit and in their attempt to assess collective and culminating understandings. Although both forms of assessments have their purpose and place in a unit of study, it is the ongoing formative assessments that allow us to mindfully monitor the learning of our students. Without information about the skills, understandings, misunderstandings, and individual approaches to the applicable mathematics, we have little to guide our instructional decisions.

Formative Assessments

Meaningful assessment is varied and carried out over time. Formative assessments such as the following can offer information that informs our practice. We can then take action to improve and support our instruction with that information.

Checking for Understanding Tasks

This task, adapted from *Teaching Arithmetic: Lessons for Extending Multiplication, Grades 4–5* (Wickett and Burns 2001), sets the stage for work with multiplication (preassessment). When you present open-ended prompts with varied numbers randomly throughout the unit, students have the opportunity to think about multiplication and to revisit their initial understandings. The information gathered from these assessments can help to guide, direct, and differentiate instruction. (See Figure 4–22.)

You may wish to vary the number model as the unit progresses in order to assess proficiency and understanding with different types of factors. In some years, I give the same prompt in the beginning, middle, and at the end of the unit. In others, I vary the factor choices because I am interested in gaining additional information. You can also offer students a choice about to what factors and types of numbers they wish to explore and explain. Their choice alone offers valuable information and can inform instruction.

FIGURE 4–22
(A) Preassessment and (B) End-of-Unit Responses from Elise.

A. Please explain what you know about:

$$45 \times 6 = \square$$

You may use words, number models, or pictures to explain your thinking.

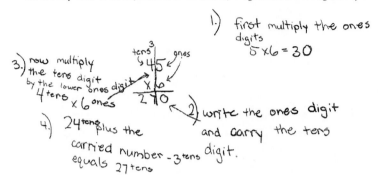

1.) first multiply the ones
digits
$5 \times 6 = 30$

3.) now multiply
the tens digit
by the lower ones digit
4 tens × 6 ones

tens 3
ᵍ45
× 6
2↑0

ones

2.) write the ones digit
and carry the tens
digit.

4.) 24 tens plus the
carried number -3 tens
equals 27 tens

B. Please explain what you know about:

$$721 \times 6 = \square$$

You may use words, number models, or pictures to explain your thinking.

I know that 721 × 6 means 721,
added 6 times. 721 × 6 is
equivalent to 6 × 721 because
order doesn't matter in multiplication.
I also know that 721 × 6 can be
written in several different ways.
Such as 721·6, 721
                    ×6 , or 721+721+ 721+
721+721+721.

You can reverse this equation by
writing - 6)4326̅   or   72)4326̅
           721   6

The   answer to this equation is
           721
           ×6
          4326

Walk and Talk

The role of the teacher and of assessment is quite different in a classroom where students are actively engaged in thinking, learning, and talking about mathematics. In such classrooms, we have the opportunity to observe, listen to, and talk with students about their mathematical thinking and reasoning. We also have the opportunity to ask good questions that can inform what we know about our students and how our instruction may need to be adjusted. (See the "Assessment" section of Chapter 2 for a set of questions to ask when checking in.)

Random Classwork Checks

In order to understand how our students learn, we need to be good diagnosticians of their work (Moon 1997). At least once a week or when I am particularly concerned about the thinking and understanding going on in response to a certain concept or lesson, I study one piece of collected student work. I have a marking pen in hand, which is more for a conversation on paper with the mathematician rather than to correct right and wrong responses. Although I hope to glean meaningful information from the student work that will help to inform my instructional decisions in the days and lessons to come, my major purpose here is to offer meaningful feedback to my students.

TEACHER-TO-TEACHER TALK ■ **About Meaningful Feedback** ■ Erring on the side of substance rather than fluff is always a good thing when giving feedback. Even though a few "Great thinking!" or "Well represented!" comments still slip from my infamous purple pen, I have made a conscious effort over the past few years to offer more meaningful feedback to my young mathematicians. I will often pose questions on their papers such as "Can you tell me more?" or "Could you solve this another way?" I will offer suggestions such as "Perhaps a diagram would work well here" or "Please be more concise with your language." I will comment on errors in their thinking or calculation such as "You are confusing *sum* and *product*" or "Subtraction boo-boo!" My comments are not extensive, but I try to keep my focus on how the student can make the entry or response better. I occasionally use a ✓, ✓+, or ✓– system when correcting student work. The students are always aware of my intentions when I assign work. If I plan on using the ✓, ✓+, or ✓– system, I inform them before they start their work. The ✓, ✓+, or ✓– system also allows me to incorporate habits of mind such as effort, persistence, and creativity in my assessment. I realize that such habits of mind are subjective, but I want students to know that these traits are valued and important in our mathematical community.

Short Writes

The authors of *Content-Area Writing: Every Teacher's Guide* (Daniels, Zemelman, and Steineke 2007) put it bluntly: "Writing breaks are a reminder to me to just shut up every once in a while and let the kids think" (31).

I have to admit that this sentence has remained with me long after I first read it! Sometimes it is important for our fifth graders to just sit, think, and write about what has been going on in class. And just because three or four or five students have been actively contributing to the class discussion, we cannot assume that the entire class "gets" what is going on! A short write can help to identify levels of understanding as well as misunderstanding. If you have established a safe classroom culture (as I am sure you have), students will be willing to be honest and open with their responses. The writing prompts, including those that follow, should be open, general, and short to offer access to all of the students:

- Rate your understanding of the material covered today on a scale of 1 to 5 (1 = low, 5 = high). What makes sense? What does not make sense?

- Can you connect what we have done in class today to other lessons or material? Explain your thinking.

- Explain the procedure or concept covered in class today to a student who was absent.

- What were two important ideas discussed today? Why are they important?

- Define _____ and _____. How are they the same? How are they different?

- Summarize today's lesson in twenty-five or fewer words. Choose your words carefully!

Much can be gained from a short write. Your observations while working the room as students write are as valuable as what is written! Who has difficulty self-starting? Who writes . . . and says nothing? Who breezes through the task with coherence and confidence?

My students are aware that short writes are not corrected. They write short writes in their math notebooks, and after I read them I mark the short writes with a checkmark. From prior conversations, they are aware that I need to know where they are at the moment. Nick, who claimed to hate to write, would often ask for a short write. "You need to know something!" he would often offer in his moments of frustration. I quickly learned that Nick was a very good mathematical barometer—as he went, so did many others who were not so vocal. Imagine my surprise when I asked students to complete a short write and Nick was completely flummoxed. "I get this . . . so why should I write about it?" Much to his dismay, Nick still had to write!

Quizzes

Quizzes can have a myriad of purposes. They can become a classroom routine. They can be a warm-up to a lesson. They can conclude a lesson.

You can construct the quiz ahead of time based on your mathematical objectives. You can ask a student to construct the quiz based on their understanding of the lesson. My suggestion is that quizzes be short (mine are ten points), frequent, and corrected as students complete them. The feedback is immediate—for you and for them! I would also suggest that some fun be woven into the process while keeping the focus on the mathematics. Construct a quiz in which the answers follow a numerical pattern. Construct a quiz in which the last item is ridiculously easy or just plain ridiculous. Construct a quiz with a class context. Soon your students will be *asking* to take math quizzes!

Summative Assessments

Summative assessments *sum up* the learning at the end of a unit of study. Ideally, summative assessments should be aligned with the mathematical objectives and experiences of the unit. Many researchers and educators suggest a "planning backward" approach to instruction. If we begin our unit planning with the construction of the summative assessment, we can start with where we're going (Wormeli 2006). In other words, if we start with our stated goals and objectives and what we want our students to know and be able to do, we can construct learning experiences to support those goals and objectives.

The depth and flexibility of conceptual understanding and procedural proficiency are important in all areas of mathematics. I stay very true to the convictions and format of a unit exam (see the "Assessment" section of Chapter 2), keeping in mind that students are that much further into the school year and that much more sophisticated in their mathematical thinking, reasoning, and communicating. Although the focus of the exam may be similar from year to year, it is one that I rethink and rework from year to year based on the strengths and needs of students as well as on my instructional goals and objectives, making sure that every test question is important enough to ask and clear enough to question.

Mixing traditional and not-so-traditional questions and prompts makes for a balanced assessment, especially if that is how you present the material in class. I include required calculation items as well as constructed response questions from which the students can choose. (See Figure 4–23, pages 205–206.)

The idea of offering choice on a unit test may be foreign to many and may cause a few raised eyebrows among colleagues and parents alike. But take a minute to think about the power of choice. When they choose what problem to do or not to do, students need to be able to:

- *Assess the mathematics of the question:* What am I being asked to know and do? Do I understand the material?

- *Assess the language requirements of the question:* Do I comprehend what is being asked? Do I have the vocabulary and mathematical language to express my ideas clearly? Are there words, phrases, or symbols that I need help in translating?

- *Assess their ability to apply the applicable mathematics:* Can I apply what I understand to what I am being asked to do?

- *Assess their ability to represent the mathematics:* Can I make my understanding visible? Will the teacher know what I know by reading or seeing my work?

- *Assess their ability to communicate their answer:* Can I justify my reasoning and solution? Will a diagram or chart help me make my position clear? Will a paragraph be a better representation of my thinking? Will a generalization support my thinking?

The process of choosing test items takes time. Students need to read each question and make decisions based on those test items and an awareness of their own understanding. Some students may need support with this process because of their learning needs and the newness of this approach. Others may need the questions read to them. Some students may need to read the question out loud, while others may need to think out loud. Some students may need extra time.

Being offered choice implies the need for self-reflection, self-understanding, and self-direction. Some students may be better at this than others. Choice provides instructional opportunities for differentiation that is student centered and student directed. The authors of *Math for All: Differentiating Instruction, Grades 3–5* (Dacey and Lynch 2007) acknowledge that offering choice may require more preparation than other instructional practices for both the students and the teachers. (See the "Assessment" section of Chapter 5 for a discussion of scaffolding study habits for tests containing choice items.) The gains are well worth it: Choice provides our students with powerful opportunities for differentiated learning that can have a positive impact on their learning and self-esteem (163).

TEACHER-TO-TEACHER TALK ■ About Choice ■ I know what you're thinking: "Now you are suggesting that I differentiate my assessment practices in addition to everything else the school year requires of me." Yes, I am. I can honestly say that offering choice items on tests has been one of the very best practices I have put into place in the past five years. I offer choice items on partner quizzes as well as on unit exams. Watching students move through choice items, starring questions or crossing them out, is an amazing experience. You can *see* them thinking! You can *see* them assessing each question. You can *see* them smiling as they answer a question that they know they know. After reading *Fair Isn't Always Equal: Assessing and Grading in the Differentiated Classroom* (Wormeli 2006), I also began to ask two stock questions on every assessment: What did you think would be asked on this test but was not? How would you answer that question? (85). I love those two questions—and so do my students.

FIGURE 4-23
Justin's Multiplication Unit Exam.

Multiplication Procedural Exam

I. Basic Fact Fluency

$\times\frac{0}{7}$	$\times\frac{8}{8}$	$\times\frac{2}{9}$	$\times\frac{9}{8}$	$\times\frac{6}{9}$	$\times\frac{3}{6}$	$\times\frac{2}{8}$	$\times\frac{9}{7}$
0	64	18	72	54	18	16	63

$\times\frac{7}{8}$	$\times\frac{6}{6}$	$\times\frac{4}{6}$	$\times\frac{1}{6}$	$\times\frac{5}{7}$	$\times\frac{3}{9}$	$\times\frac{4}{7}$	$\times\frac{5}{8}$
56	36	24	6	35	27	28	40

$\times\frac{6}{7}$	$\times\frac{6}{8}$	$\times\frac{7}{9}$	$\times\frac{0}{6}$	$\times\frac{5}{6}$	$\times\frac{7}{7}$	$\times\frac{4}{9}$	$\times\frac{4}{8}$
42	48	63	0	30	49	36	32

+24
(24 pts)

II. Compute: Traditional Algorithm

524 × 78 = 4192 + 36680 = 40,872

804 × 8 = 6,432

326 × 58 = 2608 + 16300 = 18,908

64 × 48 = 512 + 2560 = 3,072

35 × 46 = 210 + 1400 = 1,610

6,406 × 4 = 25,624

+18   (18 pts)

III. Choose 8 of the following problems and solve.

Lattice

3 2 7 ×
6
4
3

Foil

58 × 43

Chunking

4,5 × 7 = 12000 + 1600 + 2100 + 280 + 50 + 30 = 6150

400 + 70 + 5
30: 12000 2100 150
+4: 1600 280 20

Traditional Algorithm

674 × 35 = 3370 + 20220 = 23,590   +3

Traditional Algorithm

364 × 503 = 1092 + 9000 + 187000 = 183,092   +3

Foil

74 × 96

Lattice

8 9 4 ×
7
6
47944

Traditional Algorithm

804 × 59 = 7286 + 40200 = 47,436   +3

Foil

83 × 65

Chunking

324 × 16 = 1800 + 3000 + ...

300 + 20 + 4
10: 3000 200 40
+6: 1800 120 24
+3

Lattice

4 7 6 ×
8
7

Chunking

475 × 53 = 20000 + 1200 + 3500 + 250 + 210 = 25,185

400 + 70 + 5
50: 20000 3500 250
+3: 1200 210 15
+3

Foil

58 × 38

Traditional Algorithm

645 × 24 = 2580 + 12900 = 15,480   +3   +24
(24 pts)

(Continued)

IV. Explain **how** and **why** chunking, **FOIL**, or the traditional algorithm of multiplication are all examples of **partial products** procedures. What do you *do* with those partial products in order to find your solution? Support your thinking with number models *and* words.   (15 points)

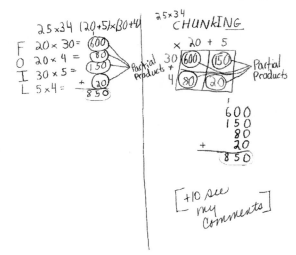

V. Bonus
- Solve the multiplication problem using your preferred method of multiplication.
- Write a story problem to "fit" the problem. Do not forget to include the question!

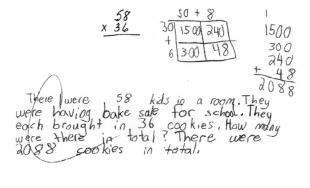

There were 58 kids in a room. They were having bake sale for school. They each brought in 36 cookies. How many were there in total? There were 2088 cookies in total.

+5

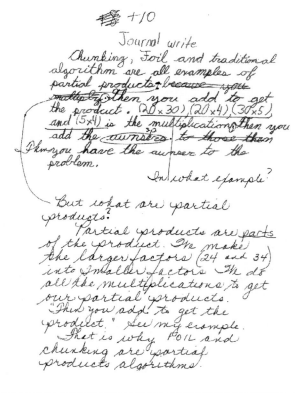

FIGURE 4–23 (Continued)

Home and School Connections

More home-school communication transpires during our study of multiplication than in any other unit. In addition to the Parent Information and Involvement Form, I send home a rather involved parent newsletter at the beginning of the unit. (See Figures 4–24 and 4–25.) This newsletter encompasses an overview as well as the mathematical and philosophical grounding of both the multiplication and division units (middle of the school year). Each year I tweak and revise the letter, but the message remains the same: I want parents to be aware of my focus on the conceptual understanding of

FIGURE 4–24
Parent Information and Involvement Form: December.

▶ REPRODUCIBLE 2.16
Parent Information
and Involvement
Form

Parent Information and Involvement Form

From: Lainie Schuster
Re: Mathematics Curriculum
Unit: Multiplication

During the next unit, the major topics we will be studying are:
- Various classifications/structures of story problems within multiplicative contexts
- Various multiplication algorithms

My goal in studying these topics is for the students to be able to:
- Multiply efficiently using an algorithm that makes "sense" to each student
- Apply knowledge of multiplication and division to solving and writing of story problems
- Classify story problems according to context: that is, *Grouping, Area/Array, Combination, Rate, Comparison*
- Compose and solve multiplication/division story problems to be published in a class collection

Parents can help at home by:
- Listening to your children as they explain different algorithms and how they "work"
- Encouraging your children to assess the reasonableness of their answers and of the calculation procedure that they chose to use
- Encouraging children to share and proofread their story problems at home.
- Reviewing the multiplication tables with your children—orally and with flashcards and computer games.

both operations as well as the connections between the two and I ask for their support. Each year I include articles from NCTM journals that I find interesting, helpful, and in support of what we are doing in class. (See the "Resources" section at the end of this chapter for sample articles.) I also make sure to send a copy of the newsletter to my principal; if she is going to receive phone calls about my teaching, this is usually the time of year and the unit in which she receives them! I want her on board and to understand my thinking and reasoning for teaching this unit as I do.

FIGURE 4–25
Parent Newsletter for Multiplication and Division Units.

Dear Parents of Grade 5 Students,

The study of multiplication and division is important—really important—but it also may look a little different today than it did even as little as ten years ago. We know more about how children think and learn. We know more about the importance of conceptual understanding and its relationship to understanding and executing mathematical procedures efficiently and accurately. We know more about the importance of problem solving and preparing our children for a world that will require skills beyond what our classroom instruction may provide. So what to do with the study of multiplication and division?

Although we spend a significant amount of time discussing what multiplication and division are, when we use them, and when and how they can help us to solve problems, we devote an equal amount of time to calculation instruction and practice. You may see calculations and procedures that may not be familiar to you such as chunking and partial products in our study of multiplication. However, you may recognize the FOIL calculations from those days spent in Algebra I. Your children will explore the partial quotients procedure for long division and may actually prefer it to the traditional algorithm for long division. The traditional algorithms for both multiplication and division are discussed, explored, and practiced. We create and solve story problems in order to assess understanding of the procedures and concepts required by both operations. Engage your children in conversations about these procedures and activities. Allow them to teach you!

I want our children

- to be flexible in their thinking;
- to understand how and why procedures work so that their execution relies on understanding rather than on rote memorization;
- to be efficient and accurate in their thinking and calculation;
- to choose procedures that make sense to them and that make sense within the problem; and
- to be articulate as they explain solutions, concepts, and procedures.

(Continued)

To be quite honest, those are huge wants! And patience, practice, and per-severance are required on all fronts! I think your children will amaze you as we move through this unit. Multiplication and division become problem-solving tools and ideas rather than just isolated procedures. I think you will be impressed.

Attached are two articles that may help to explain this shift in teaching and learning. One article explores the partial quotients algorithm for long division ("Marilyn Burns Demystifies Long Division"). The other explores computational fluency ("Developing Computational Fluency with Whole Numbers").

Please feel free to contact me at any time. I am always up for a good mathematical discussion!

Computationally yours,

Lainie Schuster

Lainie Schuster

FIGURE 4–25 (Continued)

Resources

About Teaching Mathematics: A K–8 Resource, Third Edition (Burns 2007)

The "Number and Operations" and "Extending Multiplication and Division" chapters offer activities rich in multiplicative reasoning and prob-lem-solving. Activities can be completed independently, in a whole-class format, or as menu or independent choice tasks. Burns's introduction to the Teaching Arithmetic section is exceptional and important.

Math Matters: Understanding the Math You Teach, Grades K–8, Second Edition (Chapin and Johnson 2006)

Chapter 2: Computation
This chapter provides excellent descriptions of the mathematical proper-ties and how they relate to multiplication.

Chapter 4: Multiplication and Division
This chapter has exceptional descriptions of story-problem classifications and structures.

Teaching Arithmetic: Lessons for Extending Multiplication, Grades 4–5 (Wickett and Burns 2001)

Activities, student vignettes, assessment recommendations, and superb narration make this a must-have resource.

Young Mathematicians at Work: Constructing Multiplication and Division (Fosnot and Dolk 2001)

This book provides an overview of how students construct meaning and understanding within the contexts of multiplication and division. Student vignettes and excellent narration of topics such as the big ideas of multiplication, algorithms, mathematical models, and assessment make the book stand out.

Groundworks: Reasoning with Numbers, Grade 5 (Greenes et al. 2005)

This book is part of the Grade 5 Groundworks series. The reproducibles provide students with an awareness of how numbers and operations are related. Challenging problems address representation, number sense, ratio and proportion, number theory, and computation.

Fair Isn't Always Equal: Assessing and Grading in the Differentiated Classroom (Wormeli 2006)

This is one of the best resources I have come across on grading and assessment. Wormeli explores what is "fair" and when, why, and how assessment and grading can lead to real student learning.

Articles Sent Home in the Parent Newsletter

"Marilyn Burns Demystifies Long Division" (Burns 2003a)

This one-page article discusses, explains, and supports the application and use of the partial quotients strategy for long division.

"Families Ask: Rules or Understanding?" (Martinie 2005)

This one-page article addresses a question many parents ask: Isn't it more efficient for students just to learn rules and have the understanding come later when they are more mature? The author's response focuses on students' need to understand *why* as much as *how* when it comes to mathematical procedures.

"Developing Computational Fluency with Whole Numbers" (Russell 2000)

This is an exceptional article that defines and discusses computational fluency: what it is, what it looks like, and how it can be assessed.

You may find other applicable articles from both the NCTM *Teaching Children Mathematics* and *Teaching Mathematics in the Middle School* journals. Keeping a file of hard copies of those articles may be of great help for communication with parents in future years.

Chapter 5

Division

Alice had seated herself on the bank of a little brook, with the great dish on her knees, and was sawing away diligently with the knife. "It's very provoking!" she said, in reply to the Lion (she was getting quite used to being called "the Monster"). "I've cut several slices already, but they always join on again!"

"You don't know how to manage Looking-glass cakes," the Unicorn remarked. "Hand it round first, and cut it afterwards."

This sounded nonsense, but Alice very obediently got up, and carried the dish round, and the cake divided itself into three parts as she did so. "Now cut it up," said the Lion, as she returned to her place with the empty dish.
"I say this isn't fair!" cried the Unicorn, as Alice sat with her the knife in her hand, very much puzzled how to begin. "The Monster has given the Lion twice as much as me!"

Through the Looking-Glass and What Alice Found There
Carroll 1986, 88

The Learning Environment

Make Connections Visible and Meaningful

Making sense is all about making connections: between what we know and what we do not know (yet!); between what you know and what I know; between what we think and what the investigation or numbers prove; and between the mathematics we do in school and the mathematics we do outside of school. When we carefully structure lessons and mathematical tasks, we are offering opportunities for students to make those important connections, keeping in mind that we are stewards of those connections. Our questions and conversations can help to make tasks meaningful and the collective knowledge of the class explicit. As a result, our students are better able to make powerful mathematical observations, conjectures, and connections.

Support and Provide Opportunities for Reflection

Effective learning can be associated with and attributed to a learner's ability to access knowledge, and to regulate, monitor, and take responsibility for his or her own learning (Wilson and Jan 1993, 7). When we ask students to reflect on their learning, we are asking them to

- make connections between ideas and understandings
- question and self-question
- assess self and situation

Yes, we are working with ten- and eleven-year-olds, but they are not too young to begin to take responsibility for their own learning. As we offer opportunities for our students to assess what they know, what they do not know, and make judgments about their progress and performance, we are providing them with lifelong learning tools not only for the study of mathematics, but for all disciplines and learning experiences.

The Mathematics and Its Language

Children Continue to Develop Conceptual Knowledge of Division and How It Relates to Multiplication

Traditionally, instruction in division has focused on computational fluency. This is an important goal. However, reaching it requires that our students have a firm understanding of the concept of what it means to divide and how division relates to other operations. Continued attention to place value and the application and manipulation of properties of operations can deepen students' conceptual and procedural understandings of what it means to divide. Spending time investigating, searching for, and learning from patterns as the students build conceptual understanding is crucial to proficiency with division. Students should be able to compute mentally as well as with paper and pencil. They should also be able to explain their thinking and how and why it makes sense. Instructional decisions need be made to support students' growth toward proficiency, efficiency, and accuracy in division computation based on understanding.

Children Recognize Two Types of Division Problems That Involve Equal Groupings

Division-problem situations represent part-whole relationships just as multiplicative situations do. Either the *number of groups* is unknown (quotative) or *the number in each group* is unknown (partitive). When teaching division, we often choose *partitive* division examples to highlight equal sharing. For example:

Kathleen goes apple picking and picks 18 apples. She has 3 baskets. How many apples can she pack in each basket if she wants the same number of apples in each basket?

In *quotative* division, the number of objects in each group is known, but the number of groups is not. For example:

Kathleen goes home with 18 apples packed in baskets. There are 6 apples in each basket. How many baskets of apples does Kathleen have?

The fact family is the same for each problem. Students can choose from the following facts to solve each problem depending on their thinking:

$$3 \times 6 = 18$$
$$6 \times 3 = 18$$
$$18 \div 6 = 3$$
$$18 \div 3 = 6$$

If partitive division is used exclusively, students will have difficulty making sense of the quotative problem structures. Students benefit from exposure to both types of division structures as they work to make sense of division and the procedures that they can apply.

Children Choose, Construct, and Carry Out Efficient and Accurate Computational Strategies Based on the Task and the Particular Numbers Involved

It is helpful for children to have several options for completing division computations accurately and efficiently, keeping in mind that not all students will use the same procedure for all problems. It is important for students to use logical reasoning, their understanding of number, and mathematical properties to construct and apply procedures as they solve division problems. To do so, students also need to become proficient at dividing and multiplying by ten and multiples of ten as well as manipulating their basic multiplication and division facts. See the "Calculation Routines and Practices" section of this chapter for a discussion of division algorithms.

Children Explore Remainders: What They Represent, How They Are Represented, and How They Can Influence the Final Solution Within a Given Context

When we divide within a given context, how we interpret, report, and use the remainder can affect our solution. When students solve problems grounded in a meaningful context, they will treat the remainders sensibly. Students need to solve problems in which

- the remainder causes the quotient to be rounded up to the next whole number;
- the remainder is ignored;

- the remainder is the solution to the problem; and
- the remainder is reported as a fraction or a decimal.

Children Create and Solve Story Problems Based on Division Models

Working with story problems and problem situations helps children to develop familiarity with the language and process of division. Not only will students apply their procedural understandings and proficiencies but they will have the opportunity to apply their conceptual knowledge as well.

Lesson Planning

- Become familiar and compute with the partial quotients procedure for long division (see the "Calculation Routines and Practices" section of this chapter). Because the dividend's place value is preserved in this procedure, making sense of what it means to divide is more accessible to more students. Ultimately, what we want students to do is to choose procedures based on the context and the numbers presented in that context. I frequently use the partial quotients procedure for problems with double-digit divisors because I find the traditional algorithm too time-consuming, and to be quite honest, I always make too many mistakes with the traditional algorithm!

- Remember that we can multiply to divide (and divide to multiply!), and some students will do just that without being able to articulate why it works. This flexibility in thinking actually demonstrates an understanding of the reversibility of the operations and one that will serve students well as they move on mathematically. Take the opportunity to discuss these solutions as they present themselves, and follow up with discussions of how and why this can be done. The connection between division and multiplication needs to be discussed and revisited often.

- Divisibility rules (see Reproducible 5.1) are extremely useful when you apply them in a meaningful context. Learning divisibility rules in isolation or without a context within which to apply them does little to promote their accessibility and use. When you choose tasks or make instructional decisions, pose questions that will move students to apply those rules. A question such as, "What

▶ REPRODUCIBLE 5.1
Divisibility Rules

do we know about divisibility rules that can help us assess the reasonableness of this quotient or solution?" can call their application into play.

- The symbolic representations of division are varied. The following are all symbolic representations of division:

$$126 \div 9 = 14 \qquad 9\overline{)126}^{\,14} \qquad \frac{126}{9} = 14 \qquad 126/9 = 14$$

If you present written calculations in only one representation, students will find it difficult to move flexibly from one representation to another. The fraction notation of division seems to be the most elusive for fifth graders simply because they have not yet had the experiences that will support the connections that can be made between their work and understandings about division to those of fractions and proportions.

Possible Difficulties or Misconceptions

Many students want or try to avoid division—just as they do with subtraction. There is something uncomfortable about division for some, if not many—something that just does not make sense. Over the years, I have witnessed many students choosing to multiply in order to divide. This practice, in reality, is not a bad strategy and one that certainly demonstrates an understanding of how the two operations are related. A fragile, partial, or misunderstanding of what division is and how and why the operation works is at the root of this division phobia. Many students can master the traditional algorithm's "divide-multiply-subtract-compare-bring down" mantra with little or no understanding of what is being divided by what and whether their quotient is reasonable or even makes sense given the numbers or the context of the problem. The principal investigators and authors of *Number Puzzles and Multiple Towers: Multiplication and Division 1* of the Investigations in Number, Data, and Space, Grade 5 curriculum (2008) offer the following guidelines for helping our fifth graders refine their strategies and thinking about division:

- Provide time to work with different strategies.
- Encourage students to think about ways to start a problem.
- Emphasize representations and story contexts.
- Work with students to develop clear and concise notation.
- Help students to think about why and when certain strategies are easy to use. (171–73)

Watch, listen, and question carefully as your students solve computation problems. Find out what makes sense to them—or does not. Do not assume that what seems easy and efficient to you necessarily makes sense to your students. In order for students to solve division problems efficiently and accurately, students need to understand the meaning of division, be able to think about the relationships of the numbers in the problem, and choose an approach they can carry out efficiently and accurately. See the "Calculation Routines and Practices" section of this chapter for a discussion of alternative division algorithms.

Investigations, Games, and Literature-Based Activities

Esio Trot

Duration: 2–3 Class Periods

A literature investigation requiring the use and application of division can offer mathematical accessibility to all students as well as offer initial assessment opportunities on which you can base instructional decisions. The following lesson is adapted from *Math and Literature, Grades 4–6* (Bresser 2004). This lesson offers students opportunities to

- investigate and represent combinations of 10 and/or 15 that total 140 within a division and/or multiplication context;
- identify and articulate the patterns found in those combinations; and
- continue to explore the relationship between multiplication and division.

> **NCTM Connection**
>
> **Strand:** Number and Operations
> **Focus:** Explore the relationship between multiplication and division in a literature context.
> **Context:** *Esio Trot* by Roald Dahl

Materials

- *Esio Trot* (Dahl 1990)
- newsprint

Esio Trot is the delightful tale of Mr. Hoppy, who is hopelessly in love with Mrs. Silver—but she does not even know he is alive! She only has eyes for her pet tortoise, Alfie. Mr. Hoppy devises an ingenious, albeit a bit devious, plan to win the heart of Mrs. Silver. An ancient spell and one hundred and forty pet store tortoises are just the tools he needs.

Longer than a picture book, *Esio Trot* can be read over several days. As I read the book, I share the illustrations with my document camera. Then I present the following problem to my students:

Mr. Hoppy decides to purchase 140 tortoises from his local pet store in his attempt to win the heart of Mrs. Silver. He brings the tortoises home in baskets of 10 and/or 14. How many baskets of tortoises in combinations of 10 and/or 14 could Mr. Hoppy make to bring home 140 tortoises?

I must admit that this is one of my favorite activities of the school year. By this time in my career, I should not be surprised at how quickly the students become engaged in the problem as they scurry for their math notebooks or loose graph paper to begin their thinking and representation. I ask students to work quietly and independently for about five to fifteen minutes. Then I instruct them to work as a table group to investigate the possible combinations of tortoises in baskets, to look for patterns within those combinations, and then to represent their findings in poster form on newsprint. "Can we draw tortoises on our posters?" I knew this question would be coming from Vinay. He was such a talented artist—but quite a talented mathematician as well. I reminded students that their initial focus needed to be on the mathematics and its representation; however, they could take artistic license with their presentation on the newsprint. Vinay was beside himself!

I made an instructional decision not to discuss the prompt or the investigation in a whole-class format before the table groups began to work. I was curious about how students would solve the task. Some groups immediately went to a T-chart representation and manipulated the numbers and combinations within the T-chart. Others chose a more random approach with some pictures and some calculations. Some asked if they could multiply. Others asked if they could divide, but many admitted that they couldn't remember how! Pooja's group fell into this conundrum. "But I think we can multiply in order to divide," Pooja triumphantly reported to her group. Her group thought she was brilliant! So did I!

I called the class back together before the end of that first period to process and debrief the task until this point. I opened up the discussion with "What have you noticed so far?" Most tables groups were still in the thinking and planning stages. No group had started their poster, but the students were sharing many ideas and conjectures around the room. Stopping to process information at this point in an investigation gives students the opportunity to have their thinking validated. It also gives those groups having some difficulty moving forward additional accessibility to the language and mathematics of the task.

Joseph shared his observations of several patterns with the class. (See Figure 5–1.) He noticed that as the number of baskets of ten increased by three, the number of baskets of fifteen decreased by two. As Joseph shared his T-chart under the document camera, Ian offered his conjectures about the number of baskets of fifteen. The number of baskets of fifteen would always be an even number. The total number of tortoises (140) had a zero in the ones place, so the total number of tortoises in the baskets of fifteen had to be a multiple of ten. The mathematical language of this discussion was as rich as the connections made between the patterns in the T-chart and previously covered concepts and procedures.

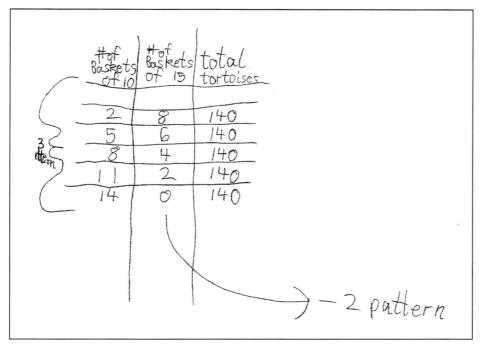

# of Baskets of 10	# of Baskets of 15	total tortoises
2	8	140
5	6	140
8	4	140
11	2	140
14	0	140

→ — 2 pattern

FIGURE 5–1
Joseph's T-chart.

Students created and presented the posters on the following day. As they were presenting the posters and T-charts, we took the time to represent the mathematics with number models on the board. (See Figure 5–2 on page 223.) Because most of the students' thinking and representations were multiplicative, we needed to follow this with a discussion about how to think of these representations within a division model. Vinay, my resident artist, produced diagrams to represent each combination of baskets within a division context. "It is so much easier to see with pictures," Vinay reported to the class. Once again, I was humbled by my class. As teachers, we jump to number models and numerical representations so quickly when a diagram or picture is just as effective—or in the case of Mr. Hoppy's tortoises, even more so!

When students were satisfied with their representations and drawings and I was equally satisfied with our discussions and the connections they made between multiplication and division, we settled in to finish reading *Esio Trot*. Students were delighted with the marriage of Mr. Hoppy and Mrs. Silver and the adoption of Alfie by Roberta Squibb.

Leftovers

Duration: 2 Class Periods

Leftovers is a division game that is played by two students. The game provides calculation practice with division and offers them experience

---

NCTM Connection

Strand: Number and Operations
Focus: Practice division computation in a game context; reason about the significance and relationship of dividends, divisors, and resulting remainders.
Context: *Leftovers*

thinking about the significance of remainders. This lesson is an adaptation of lessons found in several Math Solutions publications (Wicket and Burns 2003; Burns 2007). This lesson offers students opportunities to

- practice division computation;
- apply an understanding of divisibility rules;
- reason about the significance and relationship of dividends, divisors, and resulting remainders; and
- continue to develop number sense and problem-solving skills.

Materials

REPRODUCIBLE 5.2
Leftovers with 50 ◄

- *Leftovers with 50* directions (see Reproducible 5.2)
- math notebooks or paper for recording

Vocabulary

dividend, divisible by, divisor, factor, quotient, remainder

Please note that exposure to divisibility rules prior to playing *Leftovers* will allow students greater access to the mathematics explored by this game. *Leftovers with 100* provides an excellent context for exploring and applying their skills with divisibility rules. See the "Calculation Routines and Practices" section of this chapter for further discussion on the exploration and application of divisibility rules.

Remainders happen! And more often than not, division problems do not always result in whole numbers. Remainders become significant and meaningful when the relationships and patterns between the remainder and the other numbers in a division problem are explored. Because the game of *Leftovers* focuses on the sum of the remainders of chosen division problems, students can begin to predict and understand the magnitude of the remainder based on the dividend and the divisor. The relationships drive the exploration, not merely the calculations.

Starting with a smaller, more manageable game of *Leftovers with 50* can allow greater accessibility to the mathematics of the game. By this time in the year, your students should be able to articulate the importance of starting with a smaller problem. I always let the game board elicit this proposition from students. Looking at the recording sheet can be daunting for some; every year, some wise young mathematician in my class will suggest starting with a smaller problem, accompanied by cheers of relief from many!

REPRODUCIBLE 5.2
Leftovers with 50 ◄

I begin by introducing the rules and object of the game (see Reproducible 5.2). In this particular game, we will play for the largest sum. Then, I show the class a recording sheet for a game of *Leftovers with 50* and divisors of one through twenty:

► REPRODUCIBLE 5.2
Leftovers with 50

Leftovers with 50									
1	2	3	4	5	6	7	8	9	10
11	12	13	14	15	16	17	18	19	20

Start number:

50

This may also be a good time to review division vocabulary. Because the use and understanding of language helps to support the mathematics of this game, a word bank of division words such as the following will be helpful. Modeling the use and clarity of these division words as the game is played with the class will encourage your students to do so as well.

Word Bank
    dividend
    divisible by
    divisor
    factor
    quotient
    remainder

Implementing a *think-aloud* approach while modeling *Leftovers with 50* will offer your students a window into your thinking and the language used to frame your thoughts and mathematical decisions. Think alouds give students the opportunity to witness our thinking as we solve a problem, make connections, ask questions, make inferences, and formulate predictions (Harvey and Goudvis 2000, 33).

By this time in the year, my students know that I always take the first move in a class game. Taking that first move allows me to set up the thinking required by a particular game. By this time in the year, students also realize that after they learn how to play the game, my chances of winning become slim to none as they become more mathematically savvy. My first move might be accompanied by a think aloud such as the following:

Now let's see, I want the largest remainder possible—because I need to have the largest sum to win this game. Let me think about 50 and what I know about it. It is divisible by 1, 2, 5, and 10, so I need to stay away from those numbers because my remainder would be 0. I also know that my largest remainder can legally be 49 because that is one less than my dividend. Can I possibly get a remainder of

49 with these divisors? Hmm . . . I don't think so. So let's start with the largest possible divisor on the board: what is 50 divided by 20? Let's see . . . I can do this in my head. Two 20s are 40, so that would give me a remainder of 10. Not too bad. Can I do better than that? What happens if I use 19—since that is 1 less than 20, will my remainder be 1 less (or maybe 1 more?) since 19 is 1 less than 20? Interesting thought . . . let's try it. Two 19s are 38, so my remainder is now 12 . . . which is 2 more than my original remainder of 10. I think I'm on to something! If I keep choosing smaller divisors, will my remainders keep getting larger? And when does that turn around? I know it will at some point—it always does! Let's try 18. Two 18s are 36 with a remainder of 14. I like that choice more! How about 17? Two 17s are 34 with a remainder of 16. Two 16s are 32 with a remainder of 18. But I can take another 16 out of 18, which leaves me with a quotient of 3 and a remainder of 2. Not so good. So I am going to choose 17 as my divisor. Two 17s give me a remainder of 16, and I cannot take any more 17s out of 16. There it is!

I cross off 17 (my divisor) and circle 16 (my remainder) and write my initials next to it. We both subtract 16 from 50 to get our new start number, which will be 34. With much discussion, the class then chooses a divisor and the game continues. Once the class game is completed and scored, I introduce a *Leftovers with 100* game with divisors of one to twenty.

REPRODUCIBLE 5.2
Leftovers with 50 ◀

Leftovers with 100									
1	2	3	4	5	6	7	8	9	10
11	12	13	14	15	16	17	18	19	20

Start number:

100

I instruct the class to play a game of *Leftovers with 100* with a partner, applying what they know about *Leftovers with 50* to a game with one hundred as the start number. You may need to make an instructional decision at this point about differentiating the task. The beauty of this activity is that the concepts and relationships explored with a game of fifty will be similar to the concepts explored with a game of one hundred.

As with all meaningful games, a processing session following two or three rounds of play of *Leftovers with 100* can help to uncover, identify, and articulate the mathematics of the activity. Because this game is about relationships, pose questions that guide and support the thinking about those relationships. Useful questions for such a discussion may include the following:

- How did you decide which divisors were good to choose?
- How did you choose a divisor for the first move?

- How did the start numbers affect your choice of divisors?
- What was hard about the game?
- How would your strategies change if the starting number changed—say from fifty to forty-nine—or fifty to fifty-one?
- What would happen in a game of *Leftovers with 50* if the divisor list was limited to one through fifteen? How would your strategies need to change?
- The new start number each time is the previous divisor times the quotient without the remainder—why does that make sense?
- At the end of the game, why does it make sense for the sum of both partners' scores, plus the last starting number that remains, if it is more than zero, add up to the original starting number of fifty (or one hundred)?

It may be helpful and instructional to play around with the last two discussion questions listed above before you pose them to your class. Using what we know about multiplication can help us make sense of these assertions. (See Figure 5–2.)

FIGURE 5–2
A Recording Sheet for *Leftovers with 100*.

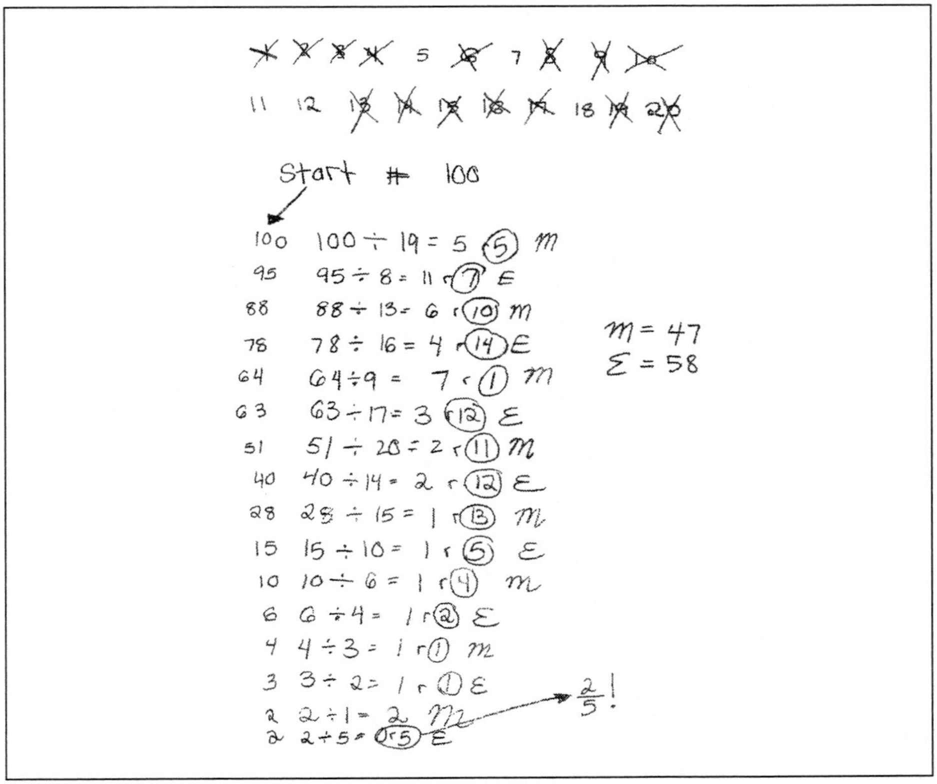

Playing games of *Leftovers* offers important opportunities to explore the relational thinking required of understanding division. Because units of division study have focused almost exclusively on calculation in the past, students have not been given the opportunities or the time to explore the operation and how the numbers of either the divisor or the dividend affect the quotient or the remainder. Discussions during or following games can also provide forums to explore the inherent relationships between division and multiplication. What does an *inverse operation* imply? How does one operation *undo* the other? Why and how can we solve division problems with multiplication? Understanding the connection between multiplication and division is critical to understanding the part/whole relationships found in multiplicative structures (Fosnot and Dolk 2001, 51). As students explore these part/whole relationships, articulating what it is they know—and what it is that they are trying to find out—becomes increasingly important for them.

REPRODUCIBLE 5.3   ◄
Seth's Game

Seth's Game

Duration: 1 Class Period, Followed by Shorter Explorations Several Times During the Unit of Study or for the Remainder of the Year

Seth's Game has morphed from several similar activities that can be found in a myriad of math resources. However, Seth perfected it, after having been intrigued with the endless possibilities the structure of the game offered. This lesson offers students the opportunities to

- continue to explore the relationships between divisors, dividends, quotients, and remainders;
- explore the impact of place value within a division context;
- think flexibly about division and multiplication as divisors and dividends are built; and
- practice division calculations.

Materials

- *Seth's Game* directions (see Reproducible 5.3)
- a set of 0–9 digit cards, 2 of each card
- graph-paper notebooks or paper

According to Seth, there is something very cool about deciding on a winning rule, building divisors and dividends, and then calculating with a partner. We all knew how much Seth loved this game, but he and his partner still managed to lose almost every round of every game! That caused even more amusement in math class! Some days we even agreed as a class to rig the rules a bit for Seth . . . but he and his partner would still manage to lose. There was a class culture, if you will, around this game that made it even more meaningful for students. However, the mathematics and the strategic thinking required for it became more apparent and interesting as games were won and lost.

I instruct students to create the following recording sheet in their math notebooks:

· Six cards will be turned. Students decide which digits to place where with their partner based on the agreed-on winning rule: largest quotient, smallest quotient, largest remainder, or smallest remainder. The rule is decided and written on the whiteboard and in their graph-paper notebooks. Once a number is placed on their recording sheets, it cannot be changed or moved. Students are encouraged (actually, it is more like required in my class) to discuss possible placements of the digits with their partners. Attention to place value and the role of the divisor and dividend will help students to make informed choices. You will certainly be able to tell when students truly understand what types and magnitudes of numbers they need for whatever positions they have to fill on their game boards. You will hear groans from around the room when you announce the unneeded numbers, and cheers when you announce the desired numbers! Both partners keep recording sheets and both calculate with their chosen algorithm once all the numbers have been agreed on and posted. They check solutions with each other for accuracy. Many students take turns talking through their chosen procedures as the calculations are completed to check for accuracy and efficiency. (See Figure 5–3.)

As the game continues, offer other recording sheets, such as:

A.

Discard

or

B.

Discard

Option B can offer an interesting and mathematically significant investigation and discussion that is rooted in context and meaning for students. Although I do not formally introduce division that results in decimals or fractions in my year-long curriculum, exposing students to these types of calculations and what they represent conceptually is always a possibility and well worth the time. Many fifth graders are still convinced that either

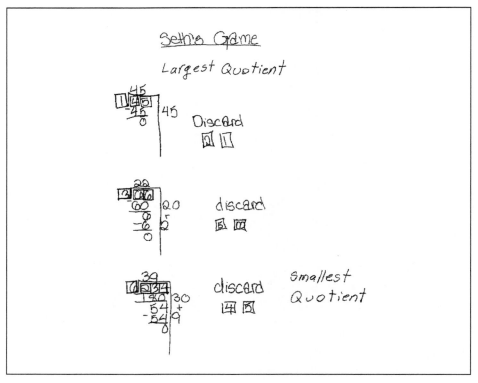

FIGURE 5–3
A Recording Sheet for *Seth's Game*.

- you cannot divide a smaller number by a bigger number; or
- when you do divide a smaller number by a bigger number, you get a negative number.

So what happens when you divide fifty-two by seventy-six? When that problem appeared in one of our games, I asked them to think about that question. Some of their responses included:

- You can't take any seventy-sixes out of fifty-two, so your quotient will be zero with a remainder of seventy-six.
- You can't do it!
- The quotient will be less than one.
- Can you have a quotient of zero?

Not one student asked or referred to a decimal or fraction as a possible solution to the problem. I always find this interesting because we do spend time throughout the unit discussing that division problems can be expressed as fractions. In this case:

$$52 \div 76 = \frac{52}{76}$$

I present this equivalency on the board and ask the class if this is a true or false number sentence. That question certainly gives them pause! At this point in their mathematical careers, I do want students to be able to identify this number sentence as true and that division number models can be written as fractions. Without calculation, students can quickly reason about the quotient; it will be less than 1 because $\frac{52}{76} < 1$. Some of your students may be able to generalize even further that the quotient will be greater than $\frac{1}{2}$ because half of 76 is 38, and 52 > 38. As students offer ideas and conjectures, document their thinking in number models on the board. It is helpful for them to see how their ideas can be translated into mathematical symbols and number models including equalities as well as inequalities.

Once the class has played several rounds of *Seth's Game*, you can have a guided discussion about strategies using some of the following questions as prompts:

- How do we build divisors and dividends to get small quotients? Large quotients? Small remainders? Large remainders?

- Are there any digits that are good in any situation?

- Are there any digits that are hideous in given situations? (My class loves the word *hideous*.)

- Do odd or even digits or numbers play into winning strategies?

- What would be the difference in playing a game with a decahedron die with faces of 0–9 and a card deck with two of each card, 0–9? Which number generator would you rather use? (You might want to play games using each one to test out the class's conjectures.)

Once again, I must give credit where credit is due, and Seth was responsible for the plethora of extensions that this game can offer. We have played this game with addition, subtraction, multiplication, and even open-number sentences that require the application of the order of operations. Playing this game with subtraction opens up conversations about and exposure to integers and how we manipulate positive and negative numbers when calculating.

TEACHER-TO-TEACHER TALK ■ About Mathematical Curiosity and Integrity
■ Those of us who have taught fifth grade for centuries grasp the betwixt and between nature of this year in mathematics education. Our fifth graders are at the upper end of the elementary years, but not quite ready for a middle school mathematics curriculum. We have students who continue to be rooted in *concrete* operational thinking and others who have entered the world of *formal*, more abstract, operational thinking. And then there all those other fifth graders who fall somewhere in-between the two

(Continued)

Piagetian stages. And as teachers, we all come to the mathematical table with differing mathematical experiences as well as strengths and weaknesses. Some of us feel comfortable having those out-of-the-box mathematical conversations and others not so much. Just as we encourage our students to self-reflect, we need to do the same. Accessing resources continues to be an important skill that we, as teachers, need to pursue. My next-door teaching neighbor is a recent graduate of Boston University, teaches sixth-and seventh-grade math, and has impeccable mathematics. I find myself wandering into Diana's room whenever I have a mathematical quandary or query. My copy of *Math Matters* (Chapin and Johnson 2006) is never far from my reach. (I actually have two copies of *Math Matters*—one at home and one at school.) But perhaps my best resource tool is being willing and able to say to my students, "That is a great idea (or question or conjecture). I really don't have a response (or answer) to that right now. That is something I have not thought of. Give me a day or two and I will get back to you on that." When you establish and nurture a culture of mathematical curiosity and integrity, every member of the community is engaged and responsible for posing and answering conjectures and questions. Our students become better mathematical thinkers because of it—just as we do!

NCTM Connection

Strand: Number and Operations

Focus: Interpret and represent remainders in story problem and problem-solving contexts.

Context: Remainder Explorations: Story Problems

REPRODUCIBLE 5.4
Remainders Happen
Recording Sheet ◄

Remainder Explorations: Story Problems

Duration: 3–4 Class Periods

When students' understanding of division is grounded in context and they have the opportunity to manipulate problems realistically, they treat remainders sensibly (Fosnot and Dolk 2001, 63). Division instruction that offers such instruction can deepen students' understanding of the operation and the interpretation of remainders. These lessons offer students the opportunities to

- interpret and represent remainders in story-problem and problem-solving contexts;
- apply divisibility rules;
- apply conceptual and procedural understandings of division;
- continue to develop understandings about connections between division and multiplication; and
- apply the language of division.

Materials

- *Remainders Happen* recording sheet, 1 per student (see Reproducible 5.4)
- story-problem sequence, one that follows or one that you have created, 1 per student

- newsprint, 4 pieces, each labeled with an interpretation of remainder generalization
- math notebooks or paper

The reading, writing, and solving of story problems can be particularly useful in supporting students' understanding of the meaning of remainders in division contexts. The solutions of those problems can depend on the remainder and how it is interpreted. Examine the following scenarios and how the remainder influences the solution:

A. Twenty-five fifth graders are going to the Red Sox game. Four fifth graders can be seated in one car. How many cars will be needed to get the fifth graders to Fenway Park?

Howard, a baseball-a-holic, has $25.00 in his pocket. Red Sox pennants cost $4.00 each. How many pennants can Howard buy?

Remember Howard? He still has $25.00 in his pocket. And he still wants to buy pennants that cost $4.00 each. How much money will he have to put toward a Fenway Frank (hot dog) if he buys 6 pennants?

Howard decided not to buy the pennants. Who needs 6 pennants, anyway? And he still has that $25.00. Howard realizes he can buy 4 baseballs, instead. How much does each baseball cost? (Schuster and Anderson 2005, 37–38)

The number model for all four scenarios is $25 \div 4 = 6r1$, and we certainly do not respond with a solution of needing *6r1 cars* to take the fifth graders to Fenway Park, or that we can buy *6r1 pennants*. The remainder influences the solution of the problem in each related story problem. Also, note that the solution to each problem is different, although all are represented by the same symbolic representation.

So what do we do with remainders? In a given context, remainders can

- "tell" us to round up the quotient to the next whole number (as referenced in story problem A);
- be ignored (as referenced in story problem B);
- be the solution (as referenced in story problem C); or
- be written as a fraction or decimal (as referenced in story problem D).

Offering students a set of related story problems that can be represented by the same number model will push them to interpret the remainders differently based on the context of the problem. Although I am not a native New Englander, I certainly sound like one when the opportunity to talk baseball rolls around! It is hard not to get swept up in the Red Sox ups and downs of each season. And nothing appeals more to my fifth graders than story problems about our beloved Sox. Creating a sequence of problems within a meaningful context for your students will offer an opportunity for them to identify and articulate the influence of the remainder on a solution of the division problem. You may wish to use these same problems but change the city and the team, or you might create another set of problems with a more relevant context for your students. Just remember to keep the number model the same and simple—the focus is on interpreting the remainder, not necessarily on a complex calculation. Although the mathematical objective is the interpretation of remainders, we also want students to be aware that all four scenarios have the same symbolic representation. If no one offers that observation in the initial class discussion, a question such as "What do you notice about the number models of each story problem?" will help them make the connection. You can print out the sequenced story problems for students or post them on the board. Because I like to give students a chance to read and solve the problems individually prior to any small-group or whole-class interaction or instruction, making individual copies for each student works best in my classroom.

As with any task requiring reading in a content area, attention to comprehension is important. And in this lesson, such attention is crucial because the comprehension of the context influences the interpretation of the remainder. By now, you are well aware of who struggles with comprehension. As you circulate around while students are reading, you may wish to support your struggling readers by asking questions, such as the ones below, to ensure that they understand what is being asked by the story problem.

- Can you tell me what you know about the problem?
- Can you tell me what is being asked in your own words?
- What have you already done to solve the problem?
- Have you seen or solved a problem like this before?

Once students have had time to work independently, have a whole-class discussion about each story problem and how to interpret the remainder in each context. As students discuss each story problem and formulate generalizations about how to treat the remainder, ask them to record the generalizations in their math notebooks while you capture them on the board or on chart paper. (See Figure 5–4.)

Introduce the class to *Remainders Happen*. Ask them to work in groups of two or three to complete the *Remainders Happen* recording sheet (see Reproducible 5.4). Once this is completed, each group compares their answers with another group's. While students are working, four pieces of newsprint labeled with each of the four generalizations are posted on the board. Each pair of students will

REPRODUCIBLE 5.4 ◄
Remainders Happen
Recording Sheet

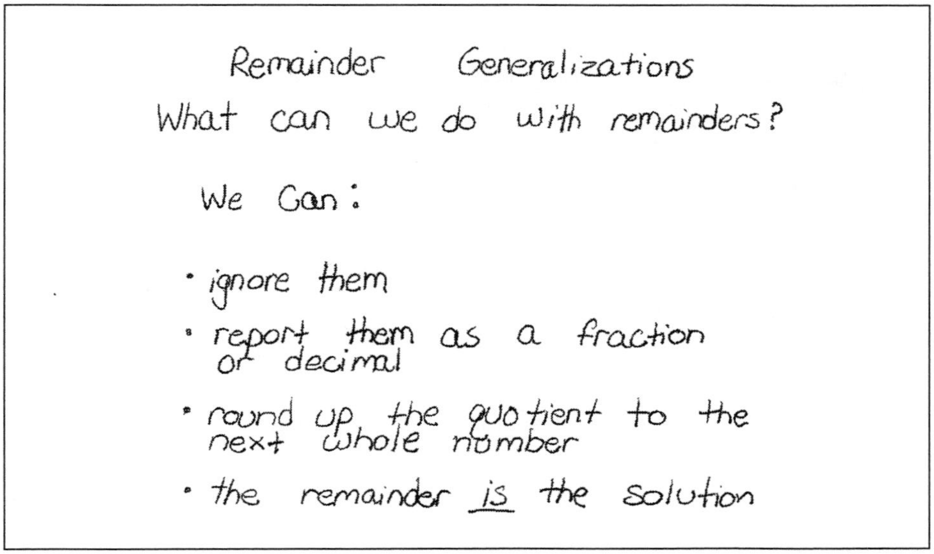

Remainder   Generalizations
What can we do with remainders?

We Can:

- ignore them
- report them as a fraction or decimal
- round up the quotient to the next whole number
- the remainder _is_ the solution

FIGURE 5–4
Pooja's Notes About Remainders.

then post each problem number on the appropriate chart. (See Figure 5–5.)

Posting the solutions allows students to self-correct and self-reflect. You can spend minimal time processing the task in a whole-group discussion because students have already discussed and agreed on their solutions with each other. Rather than processing each story problem, you might consider opening up the discussion by asking students which problems were the most difficult to solve—and why, of course!

Writing Story Problems

Writing story problems may be standard fare on your mathematical menu by this time, and your students will be stronger mathematical thinkers and doers if this is the case. This task offers students the opportunity to think about contexts and situations that could be represented by the following number model: $33 \div 6 = \square$. The question asked and the applicable interpretation of the remainder will determine the varied solutions of 5, $5\frac{1}{2}$, 6, and 3.

To introduce the task, write the above equation and its four possible solutions on the board. Inform students that they will be working in pairs to construct a sequence of story problems that fit the posted equation following the format of the Fenway Park stories. (See Figure 5–6.) They do not have to write the story problems in the same order that the solutions are presented. As the authors share their story problems with the class under the document camera, the rest of the class will identify the solution and remainder generalization. The pairs of students write the

FIGURE 5–5
The Class Made Recording Sheets for the Story Problem.

The remainder tells us to round up the quotient.	The remainder is ignored.
The remainder is the solution.	The remainder is reported as a fraction or decimal.

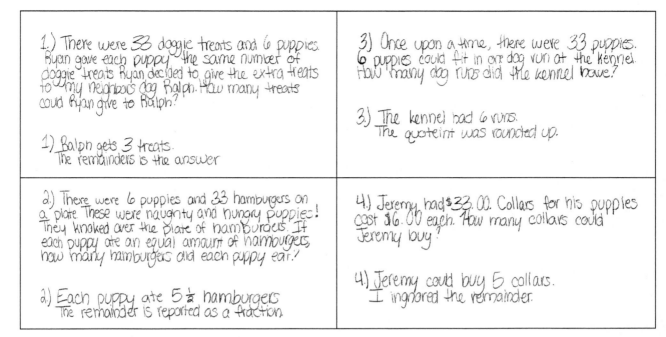

1.) There were 33 doggie treats and 6 puppies. Ryan gave each puppy the same number of doggie treats. Ryan decided to give the extra treats to my neighbor's dog Ralph. How many treats could Ryan give to Ralph?

1) Ralph gets 3 treats.
   The remainders is the answer

2.) There were 6 puppies and 33 hamburgers on a plate. These were naughty and hungry puppies! They knoked over the plate of hamburgers. If each puppy ate an equal amount of hamburgers how many hamburgers did each puppy eat?

2.) Each puppy ate 5½ hamburgers
    The remainder is reported as a fraction.

3) Once upon a time, there were 33 puppies. 6 puppies could fit in one dog run at the kennel. How many dog runs did the kennel have?

3.) The kennel had 6 runs.
    The quoteint was rounded up.

4.) Jeremy had $33.00. Collars for his puppies cost $6.00 each. How many collars could Jeremy buy?

4.) Jeremy could buy 5 collars.
    I ingnored the remainder.

FIGURE 5–6
Sequence of Story Problems with Remainders and Their Solutions.

problems in one of the partner's math notebooks with the understanding that they may be shared under the document camera. It is amazing how much neater and more creative the problems become with pending public sharing! Students must document the solutions to the accompanying story problem as well as the generalization about the remainder in complete sentences.

This task is not as easy as students assume it will be! For example, one context may work well for three of the equations, but a fourth story that fits the context and uses the remainder as the solution may be elusive. Encouraging students to write from the solution can be a successful reworking strategy. If your solution is three turtles, for example, what could the story problem be? In what context would the remainder *be* the answer? That conversation may be all students need to gain access to the task.

Reviewing the qualities of a good story problem with your class may be necessary before students start creating and writing. Referring students to their work in the previous month when they classified and wrote story problems according to multiplication story-problem structures (see Chapter 4) will help them make connections between their prior work and what they are now being asked to do. Capturing this list of expectations on a piece of chart paper will offer a quick and easy reference for them. Experience and research informs us that when students are aware of the parameters and expectations of a writing task, they are more willing and able to meet those objectives. A class list brainstorming the qualities of a good story problem may look like the following:

The Qualities of a Good Story Problem

The story makes sense.

The story fits the number model.

The story is simple: not too complicated and easy to follow.

The story has been proofed or revised by both partners.

A "thinking page" is made for each problem with number models, ideas, scenarios, and cool words to use.

The story problem is legible.

The solution accompanies the story problem and is written in a complete sentence.

Once you have made a list of qualities, you can save the list for future reference and revision as students continue to develop their skill of writing (and understanding) story problems.

I continue to be amazed and humbled by the importance of mathematical conversation, whether it is a discussion between two students, among a table group, or between a teacher and a student. In *Classroom Discussions: Using Math Talk to Help Students Learn* (Chapin, O'Connor, and Anderson 2009), the authors write that mathematical thinking is supported and developed by hearing what others think. When students are asked to put thoughts into words, they are pushed to clarify their thinking. Teachers can identify student misunderstandings much more easily when they are revealed in a conversation instead of remaining unspoken (5). As students create story problems, I find it extremely important to circulate around the room having walk-by discussions with partners about their stories, choice of numbers, choice of context, and the representation of that context within their number models. Let's say the number model from which students are writing is the same as previously proposed: $33 \div 6 = \square$. As the students are writing, ask the following questions to clarify the understanding and purpose of the task:

- Where is the thirty-three in your representation? Where is the six?
- How does your representation show the solution? What *is* the solution? What are you going to do with the remainder? How does it affect your solution?
- How do you know that your context and solution make sense?

Posing questions to your students and engaging them in conversations about their thinking and writing can help them focus on the thinking and reasoning required of this, or any other, task rather than on the mere completion of it. Natalie and Caroline were incensed one morning when I failed to engage them in a conversation about their story problems. These two young ladies were so competent that I often bypassed them as I made my rounds. Not a good thing to do! "You never talk with us!" they cried out with outrage that particular morning. I was caught off guard—which, as you well know, can often happen when working with fifth graders. I realized how right they were and sat down to have a discussion about snowmen, buttons, and the ill effects of global warming!

Remainder Explorations: Riddles

Materials

- *Remainder Riddles* directions, 1 per student or pair of students (see Reproducible 5.5)
- *Remainder Riddles 1, 2,* and *3* reproduced on chart paper or on overheads (see Reproducibles 5.6, 5.7, and 5.8)
- math notebooks and paper

I use the riddle format frequently throughout the year. Riddles immediately engage students as well as invite thinking, reasoning, and conversation. I have a spiral notebook on my bookshelf at school that is filled with riddles created for just about every topic, strand, and operation. That spiral notebook is twenty-something years old and has accompanied me to many meetings and on many airplane rides. My goal in creating a good riddle is to start with clues that are rather open-ended, but begin to eliminate possible solutions clue by clue. Sometimes I start out with the solution and work backward. Sometimes I just begin writing because I am intrigued by a certain classification of number or mathematical idea and just see where it takes me. For this particular batch of riddles, the following constraints would be necessary:

- The mystery number would fall between (and including) one and twenty-five for each set of clues.
- Known divisors would be identified in the clues.
- Known remainders of an unknown dividend (mystery number) would be identified in the clues.

Prior to the lesson, have *Remainder Riddles 1, 2,* and *3* (see Reproducibles 5.6, 5.7, and 5.8) reproduced for public viewing by your class. The riddle is not presented in its entirety initially, but clue by clue. Sliding an opaque piece of paper on the clues as they are presented on an overhead or folding up a piece of chart paper from the bottom to expose only one clue at a time works well. Also make students aware that each riddle presents solutions with divisors of one through seven.

NCTM Connection

Strand: Number and Operations

Focus: Interpret and represent remainders in story problem and problem-solving contexts.

Context: Remainder Explorations: Riddles

▶ REPRODUCIBLE 5.5 Remainder Riddles Directions

▶ REPRODUCIBLES 5.6, 5.7, AND 5.8 Remainder Riddles 1, 2, and 3

▶ REPRODUCIBLES 5.6, 5.7, AND 5.8 Remainder Riddles 1, 2, and 3

Remainder Riddle 1 is presented in a whole-class format. Read each clue out loud and follow it up with a "What do you know about the mystery number so far?" discussion.

Because the first clue of every riddle starts with divisors of one, you can have an important mathematical discussion about why zero is not offered as a possible divisor. The idea that a calculation or procedure is impossible or undefined in mathematics is intriguing to fifth graders. By this time, they are mathematically savvy enough to realize that if something is undefined, it can never happen and it applies to all situations and classifications of numbers. "That's a lot of never!" Seth, our resident division aficionado, informed the class.

Understanding that multiplication is the inverse of division can open up a rich mathematical discussion and epiphany about any number divided by zero. I write the following open-number sentence on the board:

$$6 \div 0 = \square$$

When students are asked for a solution, they will invariably respond with zero. I follow up the offer of such a solution with an "if, then" number sentence:

$$\textit{If } 6 \div 0 = 0, \textit{ then } 0 \times 0 = 6$$

The students will immediately respond that this is a false statement. Some students will quickly assume that the quotient of $6 \div 0$ would have to be 6 if it is not 0, and some students will be flummoxed realizing that you cannot create a true inverse multiplication fact out of any division fact with a divisor of zero. The beauty of mathematical disequilibrium! So we agree that division *by* zero is undefined for all classifications of numbers.

So what about using zero as a dividend? Can that work? Students quickly start working with paper and pencil to create division equations and their related multiplication facts. They have much discussion, head nodding, and pointing at the written number models represented in math notebooks. There is something truly magical about observing ten-year-olds discovering something for the first time! They are delighted with themselves and impressed with the logic and reasoning they can apply to prove that zero can, in fact, be used as a dividend—but not as a divisor. They are thinking and behaving as mathematicians!

When we return to investigating *Remainder Riddle 1*, we are satisfied knowing that each remainder riddle could begin with a divisor of one. Posing questions about generalizations that one can make from the clues will support the logical and algebraic thinking embedded in riddle investigations. "What do you know about remainders with divisors of one?" The class quickly responds that every number is divisible by one, so all clues asking about a divisor of one will result in a remainder of zero. A question such as "What do we know about our mystery number so far?" can offer an opportunity to slow down the discussion and focus on the generalizations that the class can make about the mystery number after each clue or collective clues.

Once again, you can apply and manipulate divisibility rules to make sense of the clues. When solving any remainder riddle, if a number has a remainder of 0 when its divisor is 2, we know that the number is even. If a number has a remainder of 0 when its divisor is 3, we know that the number is divisible by 3 and its digits will sum up to a multiple of 3. The real beauty of each series of riddles, however, is the manipulation of multiple (as in *many* . . . no pun intended) divisibility rules and understandings that the task requires.

As the class generates generalizations about the mystery number, keep a running list on the board. As you read additional clues, you can refine and adjust the generalizations. By the time the class processes the fifth clue ("When you divide my number by 5 . . . ") of *Remainder Riddle 1*, a class list of generalizations may look like the following:

The number is even.

It is not divisible by 3 . . . so the mystery number could be:

$$2, \cancel{4}, \cancel{8}, 10, \cancel{14}, \cancel{16}, 20, \cancel{22}$$

It *is* divisible by 5.

As the class reads and processes each clue, it continues to eliminate numbers and the mystery number starts to become apparent. Going back and reviewing earlier clues can help eliminate additional possibilities. In this particular riddle, returning to Clue 3 can eliminate 20 because $20 \div 3 = 6r2$, not 6r1! So now we are left with a possible mystery number of 10. The class reads and applies the remaining clues. Now we are fairly certain that the mystery number is 10. The class reads all the clues and checks them against a mystery number of 10 as mathematical proof for the agreed-on solution. The class agrees that we have solved the first riddle.

Because of the rich discussion than can ensue from riddles, I ask students to solve *Remainder Riddle 2* and *Remainder Riddle 3* with partners. Afterward, we come together as a class to discuss the process of solving both riddles. Students are then ready to set off with a partner and the *Remainder Riddles* student worksheet and create their own series of remainder riddles. Because we have already modeled solving three riddles, students are aware of the format of the riddles they are being asked to write. They can write completed riddles on composition paper with the solution written on the back. I also ask them to offer mathematical proof as part of their solution, which is supported by number models and accompanying labels of *true* or *false* following each number model.

Lastly, each pair signs their names at the bottom of their riddles. You can then copy the completed riddles, number them, add an answer key, and create a class riddle book. If you don't want to compile a book, or don't have time, have students swap riddles with one another during designated class or free-choice time. If you choose to create a class riddle book, check for duplicate riddles and make sure that each student has at least one riddle in the class collection.

Good Questions to Ask

For more good questions, see *Good Questions for Math Teaching: Why Ask Them and What to Ask, Grades 5–8* by Lainie Schuster and Nancy Anderson (Math Solutions 2005).

- *Without calculating,* identify these number sentences as *true* or *false*. Include an explanation of why your label of true of false makes sense for each problem.

  $35 \times 127 = 4448$ *true or false*   *How do you know?*

  Teacher note: Two odd factors will not result in an even product because odd × odd = even)

  $392 \div 15 = 29$ *true or false*   *How do you know?*

  Teacher note: If we know that multiplication is the inverse of division, then we know that two odd factors will not result in an even product. Estimating the magnitude of the quotient is also an option with which to solve the problem. If I know that twenty 15s are in 300 and six 15s are in 90, then a quotient of 29 is too large.

  $657 \div 6 = 108$ *true or false*   *How do you know?*

  Teacher note: Since we know that in order to be divisible by 6, a number must be divisible by 2 and 3, 657 is not divisible by 2 because it is not even. Therefore, 657 cannot be divisible by 6.

- Are the quotients below correct? If you think a quotient is incorrect, tell whether the quotient is too large or too small. How do you know? Then calculate to see if you were correct!

  $$\frac{696}{8} = 87 \qquad\qquad \frac{2,428}{4} = 670$$

  $$\frac{6,785}{5} = 1,357 \qquad\qquad \frac{338}{2} = 194$$

  $$\frac{2,016}{12} = 168 \qquad\qquad \frac{2,026}{13} = 159$$

- What three- (or four- or five-) digit number is divisible by two, three, five, and six? How do you know? Explain your thinking.

- Three is a factor of nine. Is every number that is divisible by three also divisible by nine? Why or why not? Use number models to support your thinking.

- Create a story problem represented by a division number model with a solution of 12r5. How will the remainder affect your solution within the context of your problem?

- Study this progression of division number models. How does each equation or open-number sentence build on the equation or open-number sentence that precedes it? What generalizations can you make from these patterns?

A.

$$4 \div 4 = \triangle$$
$$40 \div 4 = \triangle$$
$$400 \div 4 = \triangle$$
$$4,000 \div 4 = \triangle$$
$$4,000 \div 40 = \triangle$$
$$4,000 \div 400 = \triangle$$
$$4,000 \div 4,000 = \triangle$$

B.

$$48 \div 8 = \square$$
$$480 \div 8 = \square$$
$$480 \div 16 = \square$$
$$480 \div 32 = \square$$
$$480 \div 64 = \square$$

Calculation Routines and Practices

Divisibility Rules

Years ago, exploring and applying divisibility rules were lessons rarely seen in a fifth-grade curriculum. I like to think that our hard work of teaching for understanding has invited students to think about the structure of numbers. Divisibility rules were covered in September and October (see the "Calculation Routines and Practices" sections of Chapters 2 and 3), but are well worth revisiting at this time of year.

> **TEACHER-TO-TEACHER TALK** ■ **About Accessible Resources** ■ As the year progresses, my students' math notebooks become as much reference books as they do a documentation of a particular unit's work and progress. All those painful years I endured as a middle school math student taught me something very important: knowing where to go for help is as important as knowing the answer to any given problem. I created a handout notating the divisibility rules (see Reproducible 5.1) that is distributed to students and placed in a plastic sleeve in their math notebooks among the other sleeves they have collected throughout the year. At this point in the year, a completed *Sieve of Eratosthenes* (see Chapter 2) and this divisibility rules handout seem to be the favorite go-to references. Although I do not require students to memorize the rules, the more the rules are accessed and applied, the more fluent students become with them. My students can access their divisibility rules at any time throughout the year—for class work, homework, and even formal assessments. Yes, I want them to know and apply these helpful rules, but I also want them to realize that knowing where to find and how to use a resource is as applicable to doing mathematics as it is to researching social studies.

NCTM Connection

Strand: Number and Operations

Focus: Explore, practice, and apply alternative as well as standard division algorithms.

Context: Division Algorithms

▶ REPRODUCIBLE 5.1 Divisibility Rules

Our charge becomes one of helping to make divisibility rules accessible, applicable, and relevant to the problems our fifth graders are solving. We need to make the connections between the problems we solve and the use of these rules deliberate and explicit:

- You are solving 238 ÷ 5. Will there be a remainder?
- If we need to divide cookies into six batches with no leftovers, how many dozen cookies could we bake?
- What is wrong with this problem and its solution: 4380 ÷ 6 = 724r4? How do you know?
- What four-digit number is divisible by 2, 5, and 10?
- What three-digit number is divisible by 3?
- What three-digit number is divisible by 2, 3, 6, and 10?

Maryann Wickett and Marilyn Burns offer three well-scaffolded lessons that explore divisibility rules in *Lessons for Extending Division: Grades 4–5* (Wickett and Burns 2003). Student vignettes, author commentary, and a discussion of the mathematics involved are well worth the read.

Procedural Routines

According to the NCTM *Curriculum Focal Points and Connections for Grade 5* (National Council of Teachers of Mathematics 2006), our fifth graders need to "apply their understanding of models for division . . . as they develop, discuss, and use efficient, accurate, and generalizable procedures to find quotients involving multi-digit dividends" (17). Students are also expected to "develop fluency with efficient procedures, including the standard algorithm, for dividing whole numbers, understand why the procedures work (on the basis of place value and properties of operations), and use them to solve problems" (17).

It is mathematically sound and important for students to solve computation problems by building on numbers, relationships, and procedures they know and can make sense of. By the end of fifth grade, students should have computation strategies that they can justify and carry out easily for addition, subtraction, multiplication, and division of whole numbers. Although many students will prefer one algorithm or procedure over another, they should also be familiar with, understand, and be able to explain more than one procedure for each operation, including long division (Russell, Economopoulos, et al. 2008, 171).

Partial Quotients Algorithm

I have found that working through the partial quotients algorithm with my class prior to introducing the standard algorithm works well. This algorithm is a tad different from the "divide, multiply, subtract, compare, bring down" procedure that is referred to as the traditional algorithm. This alternative procedure builds on and makes use of students' number sense, their knowledge of multiplying by ten and multiples of ten, and the conservation of place value. The better a student can estimate, the more efficient his multiplication and subsequent division will be.

Beginning with single-digit divisors can give better access to the mathematics, reasoning, and logic that one applies while working through the partial quotients procedure:

$$7\overline{)674}$$

Employing a think-aloud strategy as you introduce the procedure presents students with a model of the thinking and reasoning required by this procedure. I prefer not to introduce a procedure without a context, so I offer a context in my think aloud and then move on to the mathematics.

I have 675 marshmallows. Let's see, each cup of hot chocolate can hold 7 marshmallows each. So how many cups of hot chocolate can I serve with these 675 marshmallows? In other words, how many groups of 7 can I take out of 675? I like to multiply by 10s and multiples of 10 because it is easy for me to do that in my head. Let's see, I cannot take out 100 7s because that is too much; 100 7s is 700 and I only have 675 marshmallows. But 675 is only 25 away from 700, so why don't I start with 50? Or maybe 60? Or even 70? Let's see. $70 \times 7 = 490$. That's close, but how about even more? $80 \times 7 = 560$. OK, that's a start.

$$
\begin{array}{r|l}
7\overline{)\;674} & \\
-560 & 80 \\
\hline
114 &
\end{array}
$$

Now I have 114 marshmallows. Let's go back to the original problem. I can use 7 marshmallows per cup of hot chocolate. I have already used up enough marshmallows for 80 cups, so how many more cups can I make with the remaining 114 marshmallows?

I love multiplying by 10s, so let's do that. 10×7 would give me 70. 20×7 gives me 140, which is more than I have left. So I am going to make 10 more cups of hot chocolate.

$$
\begin{array}{r|l}
7\overline{)\;674} & \\
-560 & 80 \\
\hline
114 & \\
-70 & 10 \\
\hline
44 &
\end{array}
$$

Now I am getting somewhere. I can do this in one final step because I know that $6 \times 7 = 42$, and I will have only 2 marshmallows left. Can't make a cup of hot chocolate with only 2 marshmallows . . . so I will just eat them myself!

$$
\begin{array}{r|l}
7)\,674 & \\
-560 & 80 \\
\hline
114 & \\
-70 & 10 \\
\hline
44 & \\
-42 & 6 \\
\hline
2 & \\
\end{array}
$$

Let's see, where is the quotient that I built? Here it is: first I took out 80 7s, then 10 7s, then 6 7s. $80 + 10 + 6 = 96$—with 2 extra marshmallows! That was cool.

$$
\begin{array}{r|l}
\multicolumn{2}{c}{96r2} \\
7)\,674 & \\
-560 & 80 \\
\hline
114 & + \\
-70 & 10 \\
\hline
44 & + \\
-42 & 6 \\
\hline
2 & \\
\end{array}
$$

When working through the partial quotients algorithm, students are always considering the dividend as a whole rather than focusing on individual digits as is the practice when working through the traditional algorithm. Most students can learn this procedure quickly and use it accurately because it relies on their ability to apply what they know about multiplication and estimation. This procedure also allows students to differentiate the factors chosen given their facility and fluency with the multiplications. In this example, I could have started with ninety as my first factor, which would have brought me very close to the dividend. However, I made a deliberate instructional decision not to do so. This procedure would work with ninety as the first factor as well as it works with eighty—or with sixty or even fifty. As students explore and complete problems, I am always reminding them of the need for efficiency. Yes, we could start with a factor of ten . . . but we would be taking out ten sevens until the cows come home! And when we take out groups of ten repeatedly, we are also apt to make more errors in subtraction.

Once students have applied the partial quotients algorithm with problems requiring one-digit divisors, you can introduce two-digit divisors. Because this procedure is based on making sense of the numbers presented in the problem and a particular student's choice of factors or divisors by which to decrease the dividend, you will be absolutely amazed at how quickly students learn to manipulate two-digit divisors. Although many of the students work through their calculations with personal think alouds, I ask that they do not work with a partner on the initial calculation. Once they have completed the calculations, I ask students to share their strategies and chosen factors or divisors with a neighbor to compare solutions and procedures.

$$
\begin{array}{r}
32r14 \\
26{\overline{\smash{\big)}\,786}} \\
-720 \quad\;\; 30 \\
\hline
66 \quad\;\; + \\
-52 \quad\;\; 2 \\
\hline
14
\end{array}
$$

Pooja started the "How close can I get?" game with her twin brother, Vinay. Both students were becoming proficient estimators with this division procedure. Pooja liked to see how close she could get to her dividend with her first multiplication. Her facility with multiplications by multiples of ten became more efficient and more accurate with each problem solved. Not to be outdone by his sister, Vinay joined her game. Soon the entire class was working harder to get closer to their dividends! They quickly realized that the closer one could get to the dividend in the initial multiplication, the less work one had to put into continued multiplications, the greater the efficiency and accuracy of the procedure became, and the fewer the mistakes that were being made with the subsequent subtractions.

The partial quotients procedure and the conversations that it generates keep the focus on the process of division and what it means to divide. I have yet to be convinced that the traditional algorithm offers such opportunities to connect the conceptual understandings of division with the procedural, which is why my procedural instruction always begins with the introduction of this algorithm. You can now move the instruction to the traditional algorithm, which should be accompanied by continued conversations about efficiency and pushing students to think about choosing procedures based on the context and numbers of a problem.

TEACHER-TO-TEACHER TALK ■ **About Alternative Algorithms** ■ Making the instructional decision to explore alternative algorithms with your class may very well be viewed as an act of civil disobedience! Many parents and colleagues may be unfamiliar with the partial quotients algorithm for long division—and I can guarantee that you will meet with some resistance! However, the resistance will not be from students—they love it! Sean was new to my class and new to our school. Alternative algorithms were not on his radar—and neither was achievement in mathematics. "Holy cow!" he exclaimed one day, after taking the time to figure out how the partial quotients

(Continued)

algorithm worked. But it was his comment that followed that stopped me in my tracks and caused me to once again take notice of the power of students' thinking and success. Sean looked up at me with a huge smile. "So *this* is what it means to divide!" The entire class broke out in laughter and started cheering! Parents and colleagues who question your implementation of alternative algorithms will not see these interchanges in your class. They will not hear the cheers of success or see the fist pumps as kids solve long division problems efficiently and accurately. But you will! Just a few days ago, a small group of students in my class were struggling with a multidigit calculation. They were applying the traditional algorithm and kept omitting the zeros in the partial products. Their number sense was strong enough that they knew their answers were incorrect, but they couldn't seem to identify their errors. Caroline had had enough. She threw up her hands and huffed, "Let's just chunk it. We *know* how to do that!" So they began constructing "chunkers" (see the "Calculation Routines and Practices" section in Chapter 4 for a description of chunking) and multiplying with a procedure that made sense to all of them. Needless to say, they arrived at the correct answer! I keep copies of a wonderful NCTM article "Alternative Algorithms: Increasing Options and Reducing Errors" (Randolph and Sherman 2001), close at hand when I am working through my division unit. Even though you may not convert those that question your choice to explore and encourage alternative algorithms, you will raise awareness. But your greatest advocates and those that gain the most from this decision will be your students. And isn't that the way it should be?

Traditional Algorithm

Once students have made sense of the partial quotients algorithm, they have little trouble understanding the traditional long division algorithm. Because they have scaffolded the division in ways that make sense both mathematically and personally, they can begin to understand and explain why the "divide-multiply-subtract-compare-bring-down" method works. Research and classroom teaching experience remind us time and time again that students become more proficient (and efficient!) at long division when they understand why and how it works.

When I introduce the standard algorithm, students often recognize it as the one their parents have tried to teach them. "I just don't get it!" Caroline remarked. "It makes no sense. Why are we taking apart the numbers in ways that don't make sense?" Although I was absolutely delighted with Caroline's remarks, unbeknownst to her, she had been set up by my curriculum and classroom policies over the years. I had taught both of her brothers in the past, and both had become proficient in long division thanks to the exploration of the partial quotients procedures before tackling the traditional algorithm. I had support from home as well as from Caroline's brothers.

What I want students to see is that the decomposition of the dividend in the traditional algorithm appears to be contradictory to our understanding and use of place value when calculating whether in multiplication or division. The class is aghast—or at least pretends to be to humor me! Seth did notice that we really are conserving place value in the traditional algorithm, but not in the way we are accustomed to seeing it. Now I was aghast! Seth's insight was based on his understanding of place value and his ability to make it all make sense in this context and with this algorithm.

$$
\begin{array}{r}
x72r4 \\
6\overline{)436} \\
\underline{42} \\
16 \\
\underline{12} \\
4
\end{array}
$$

According to Seth, we cannot take any 6s out of 4, hence the *x* in the quotient. But we *can* take seven 6s out of 43. But what that really means is seventy 6s out of 430; we are just eliminating the zeros to move the process along quickly. Max was a bit perturbed by this method and my instructional decisions. "When we were doing the traditional algorithm for multiplication, you told us *not* to ignore the zeros [in the partial products] . . . and now you are telling us to do just that here!" This complaint led us into a rich class discussion about the need to choose procedures that make sense to the mathematician doing the calculation. I told student that I flip-flopped between long division procedures depending on the numbers used or the context, and that I wanted them to be comfortable doing so as well. I still use the partial quotients algorithm with two-digit divisors and revert to the traditional algorithm for single-digit divisors.

Although every year most of my students are more comfortable with the partial quotients algorithm, I spend time practicing and applying the traditional algorithm in order to meet parental and administrative expectations. As the students become more proficient at the traditional algorithm and are encouraged to compare and contrast division strategies and preferences, they begin to make calculation choices based on number sense, contexts, and the numbers involved. Once again, they are thinking and behaving as mathematicians think and behave—and I repeatedly remind them of that!

Calculation practice becomes an important component of instructional routines when students are learning new procedures. However, pages and pages of calculation practice do not have to be standard fare. Annette Raphel, author of *Math Homework That Counts* (2000), writes of the need to rethink worksheets as a form of computational practice. According to Raphel, there are "good worksheets and not-so-good ones" (7). Good worksheets should

- be mathematically rich;
- be interesting;

- stimulate connections;
- be rooted in problem formation, problem solving, and mathematical reasoning; and
- advance student understanding.

You may find that you can easily rethink the format of worksheets from your prescribed text or those you have used in years past just by changing the directions. Rather than simply presenting student with a page of twenty-five long division problems (which would make just about anyone shudder, let alone a ten-year-old working to understand the process!), try presenting those same problems with one of the following sets of directions:

Only solve those problems that have even (or odd) quotients and no remainders.

or

Only solve those problems that have remainders.

or

Only solve the problems with two-digit quotients.

or

Only solve the problems with remainders larger than the quotient.

or

Only solve the problems whose quotient is divisible by six (or nine or even twelve). (This is a great one!)

Even though students may only be solving five or six of the twenty-five given problems within this format, think about the mathematical reasoning, estimating, and conversation they will be carrying out as they work hard to do as few problems as possible. They will have to analyze each problem in order to decide which problems actually fit the constraints of the directions. The mathematical generalizations and calculations that students make in the process of completing only five of six problems are meaningful and just plain interesting—within this routine, we are asking our students to problem solve, think, and reason as well as to calculate.

Games to Support Division Practice

Paper-and-pencil routines are not the only way to support the conceptual and procedural understandings required by division. The following games—*Leftovers with 50*, *Remainders Race*, and *Division Dash* (see Reproducibles 5.2, 5.9, 5.10, 5.11, and 5.12)—offer additional

REPRODUCIBLE 5.2
Leftovers with 50

REPRODUCIBLES 5.9
AND 5.10
Remainders Race
Directions and
Game Board

REPRODUCIBLE 5.11
AND 5.12
Division Dash
Directions and Score
Sheet

computational practice, continued opportunities to talk about division, and a context within which to apply number sense and mental computational skills. These games are three of my favorites—easy to play and easy to organize.

Leftovers with 50

The game of *Leftovers with 50* has already been discussed in the "Investigations, Games, and Literature-Based Activities" section of this chapter. Because students are already familiar with the format of the game, they can easily carry out the following extensions with little or no preparation:

- For an easier (and quicker) game, use fifty for the start number and divisors of one to fifteen.
- For a harder game, use two hundred for the start number and divisors of five to thirty.
- Change the goal of the game so that the player with the smaller sum of remainders wins.

Remainders Race

This game contains game boards that teachers can reproduce and laminate for future years' use. Students move around a game board (retired game board markers work well) by mentally calculating remainders of division problems with single-digit divisors. The game ends when one player reaches or goes beyond the finish line. (Refer to the original write-up of this game for more details [Childs and Choate 1998].)

Division Dash

In this game, students use calculators as random number generators and perform mental single-digit divisor mental calculations as they keep running totals of quotients. The game ends when one player reaches a sum of one hundred. (Refer to the original write-up of this game for more details [Everyday Learning Corporation 2002a].)

Reading, Writing, and Vocabulary

When writing about mathematical ideas, students are engaged in the learning process as they communicate their conjectures and positions instead of waiting for the teacher, or another student, to explain, discuss, summarize, generalize, or evaluate. If one of our instructional goals in this month of study is to make the connections between division and multiplication explicit, then we need to ask our students to be equally explicit in their thinking about and articulation of those connections.

Writing to a prompt is a valuable task in any fifth-grade mathematics classroom. Writing not only benefits students by supporting and contributing to their learning, it benefits teachers by helping them assess what their students are learning and understanding—what they know, what they do not know, and what they do not know . . . yet! Writing to a prompt that targets a big idea or salient understanding provides valuable insights into how our students think and reason.

My students are quite accustomed to journal writes and mathematical writing in general. After a rich class discussion, I will often forewarn student, muttering, "I feel a journal write coming on. . . ." They groan, but they are also well aware that this means the mathematics covered in that particular discussion was important and worthy of deeper thinking and reasoning.

I offer two journal prompts *prior* to the end-of-unit exam, including the following journal writes presented in their study sheets:

IV. Writing Piece

Two possible journal writes:

1. How does $6 \times 7 = 42$ help you to understand $42/7 = 6$?

2. $a \times b = b \times a$

    Is this number sentence true or false? Is it *always* true or false?

    How do you know?

    $a \div b = b \div a$

    Is this number sentence true or false? Is it *always* true or false?

    How do you know?

What students do *not* know is that *both* prompts will be presented as options on the exam and they can choose which one they wish to complete. How the commutative property applies (or does not apply) to multiplication and division and the understanding that division and multiplication are inverse operations are crucial understandings. Many fifth graders know these principles intuitively by this point in their mathematical careers, but equally as many will have some difficulty in the articulation of these understandings because they have not been asked to do so formally. Making the prompts available prior to the exam allows students the opportunity and time to dig deeper into the mathematics that will be required by their responses.

Although working through revisions is not routine in the mathematical writing we do in class, there are times when the *process* becomes as important to learning as the product, and this is one of those times. Offering students the time to write, rethink, and revise supports the writing process. I encourage them to work up an initial draft of either or both prompts; however, I do not permit students to bring along their drafts on the day of the exam. I inform them of this when I distribute and discuss the study sheets. This preparation task is about process; I find time to conference with each student individually about their piece if they wish to do so. The focus of the initial read-through is on content, style, and word choice.

By this time in the year, fifth graders should be aware of the qualities of good mathematical writing. They know that

- word choice and concise language are critical and required;
- number models can help support mathematical reasoning and can serve as necessary mathematical proofs;
- examples need to accompany and support positions;
- introductory sentences state the main idea of the response or restate the prompt in some way; and
- concluding sentences give closure to and summarize the response.

We do need to be mindful of the reality that students do not always represent their thinking in ways that match adult forms! We can certainly offer guidance and help them to identify and recognize the traits of good mathematical writing, but we still need to be willing to navigate through their mathematical understandings and knowledge as demonstrated through their writing. Writing is a process, and participating in that process as either teacher or student takes time, patience, and practice.

We spend time in class front-loading the thinking and writing that students are being asked to do as they organize their ideas and prepare drafts. First I ask them to web each prompt in their math notebooks. They do this activity independently and quietly. Because students are accustomed to webbing and brainstorming in other subjects, all are familiar with this task. Once I call "time," students work in their table groups to compare webs and ideas that respond to each prompt. These initial conversations offer a forum for students to rehearse and work through their ideas. I encourage them to keep personal word lists as they share ideas and thoughts, which they can refer to as they construct their own responses. (See Figure 5–7.)

Sim had a difficult time with both prompts although she was one of my better students. "I know this stuff, but I can't get it on paper!" she said. Sim worked through multiple drafts and spent some time at home working with her dad as well. As we conferenced, I realized that she was having difficulty with the concepts of *reversibility* and *inverse*, which I then addressed. We also found that writing from number models and counterexamples was extremely helpful to Sim as she crafted and recrafted her responses.

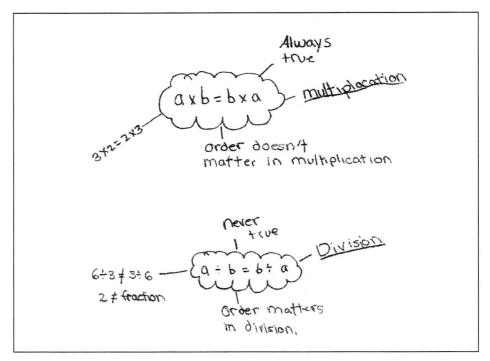

FIGURE 5–7
Web and Word List.

Writing to prompts provides opportunities to access and assess the mathematical understandings of our students as they organize their thinking and create a written record of their knowledge (Thompson et al. 2008, 17). When students are required to describe, explain, and support their thinking, they are able to make visible what they know and understand.

Assessment

As in all of my formal teacher-generated assessments, I offer choice items on the end-of-unit division exam. (See Figure 5–8.) You may wish to refer to the "Assessment" section in Chapter 4 for an overview of the instructional opportunities that offering choice items can provide on a formal, and in this particular case, summative assessment. If we believe in the mathematical power of alternative algorithms and support reasoning based on number sense and context, then those same beliefs must be supported by our assessments.

That being said, we should also recognize that offering choice items does require more preparation for both teachers and students than more traditional exam routines.

FIGURE 5–8
Division Unit Exam.

Division Procedural Test

I. Basic Fact Fluency

7 ×4 = 28	4 ×3 = 12	2 ×9 = 18	0 ×7 = 0	3 ×3 = 9	9 ×2 = 18
5 ×8 = 40	3 ×6 = 18	8 ×9 = 72	9 ×1 = 9	4 ×8 = 32	6 ×6 = 36
3 ×7 = 21	6 ×9 = 54	7 ×8 = 56	2 ×6 = 12	9 ×5 = 45	3 ×9 = 27
1 ×8 = 8	6 ×0 = 0	7 ×7 = 49	6 ×4 = 24	4 ×5 = 20	7 ×3 = 21
5 ×6 = 30	2 ×7 = 14	6 ×8 = 48	9 ×7 = 63	8 ×3 = 24	4 ×7 = 28

+30
(30 pts)

II. Compute: Traditional algorithm

8 r5
6)527
−48↓
  47
  42
   5

1 r13
43)486
   43↓
   56
   43
   13

905
8)7240
  72↓↓
  040
   40
    0

31 r6
18)564
   54↓
   24
   18
    6

+12
(12 pts)

III. Choose 6 out of the following 10 problems. You may use EITHER the **partial-quotients** algorithm or the **traditional algorithm.**

65 r6
8)526
  48↓
  46
  40
   6

52)701

43)926

837 r5
7)5864
  56↓
  26
  21
   54
   49
    5

58 r4
12)640
   60↓
   40
   56
    4

25 r12
15)387
   30↓
   87
   75
   12

14)527
   42↓
   07
   98
    9

37 r9

428 r4
7)3000
  2800   400
   200   +
   140   20
    60   +
    56   8

+18 (18 pts)

IV. Writing Piece

Choose **ONE** of these two possible short-answer questions. Remember to support your thinking with number models.

1. How does $6 \times 7 = 42$ help you to understand $\frac{42}{7} = 6$?

OR

2. $a \times b = b \times a$

Is this number sentence true or false? Is it *always* true or false? How do you know?

$a \div b = b \div a$

Is this number sentence true or false? Is it *always* true or false? How do you know?

(15 points)

V. The quotient is 4 with a remainder of 12. What could the problem be?

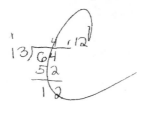

$+5$

(5 pts.)

Bonus

Solve (using either algorithm) and write a story problem to "fit" this division model. Make sure your story makes sense!

$$\frac{328}{55} = \square$$

$$35\overline{)328} \quad 9 \, r \, 13$$
$$\underline{3\,1\,5}$$
$$1\,3$$

$+5$

There were 328 flowers and 35 baskets. How many flowers went in each basket?

Journal Write

$6 \times 7 = 42$ helps me understand $42/7 = 6$ because if I look at the fact family I can see that it is basicly "backwards". If I had 6 groups of 7 there would be 42 in all and if I started with 42 and divided it into 6 groups, there would be 7 in each group. That is how a fact

family helps me understand each problem.

Fact Family

$6 \times 7 = 42$
$7 \times 6 = 42$
$42 \div 6 = 7$
$42 \div 7 = 6$

$+5$

FIGURE 5–8 (Continued)

For the Teacher

- *Prior to constructing the exam, identify those procedures or big ideas for which every student will be responsible.* In my school, fifth grade is the first year in which we formally introduce students to the traditional long division algorithm. (Our fourth grade is introduced to the partial quotients algorithm exclusively.) Therefore, I expect all my students to demonstrate fluency with the procedure. I offer *four* problems, and I ask students to complete *all four*.

- *Choose numbers within problems mindfully.* Some numbers may be more suited to specific algorithms. You may already have an idea of which students will choose which algorithms given the numbers of the problem, which will be of great help as you construct the test items. Being mindful of the number of problems with one- and two-digit divisors is important. Make sure that the option to choose those problems with single-digit divisors does not outweigh those with double-digit divisors!

- *Determine how many problems are enough to demonstrate fluency and understanding.* I often offer *ten* straight calculation problems and ask students to choose *six*. They can apply whatever algorithm they choose to each problem based on the numbers presented. I also ask students to write and solve story problems and to solve a problem or two requiring conceptual and procedural understanding of division as well as comprehension of the task—reading and mathematical comprehension.

- *Craft your journal writes keeping in mind the big ideas of division.* We must hold ourselves to high standards when crafting journal prompts, making sure prompts are clear, age-appropriate, interesting, and compelling. I offer *two* prompts and ask students to complete *one*.

- *Keep the length of the test manageable.* You will need to work within your time schedule. My tests are not timed; students who need more time after the scheduled period are permitted more time. I have learned to schedule tests on the days that my students have library or what we call study periods. Then there are those days when I have to beg, borrow, and steal from my colleagues to get a little extra time for those students who need it. Nothing can deplete a child more than not finishing an exam, and I am not willing to do that in the fifth grade.

- *Take the test yourself!* I have been known to ask my husband or younger son to look over a test—or to even take it! Neither of these men have the same opinion that I do of mathematics, so their opinions are often insightful and extremely helpful. We need to make sure the directions are clear and the language accessible. I do expect that by the fifth grade, the majority of students can move through their exam independently by calling on their reading and comprehension skills.

For the Student

- *Use the study sheet.* I distribute study sheets four to five days prior to the exam. There are no surprises on my exams: If it is on the study sheet, it may be on the exam. If it is not on the study sheet, it will not be on the exam. Once again students need to read through the study sheet and make strategic decisions about which pages to complete thoroughly or partially. They need to self-assess as they move through the study sheet.

- *Plan out study time.* My fifth graders keep homework planners. When I schedule an exam, I ask that they get out their planners and commit their study schedule to writing. If the exam is on Friday, they may plan to work on the study sheet on Monday and Wednesday. They can work up their journal write on Tuesday and have me look it over on Wednesday. That leaves Thursday night for revisions and final preparation.

- *Draft the journal writes.* Again, students need to be willing and able to self-assess. They need to determine what type of feedback they need from you—if any. I encourage students to come to me with a plan and questions in mind: Can you help me with my introduction? Does this number model prove what I need it to prove? Can we look at my word choice? Is it too long? Too short? It seems to ramble, can you help me tighten it up?

The bottom line in all of this is to make sure we assess what we want to assess! As we design assessments, we constantly need to refer to the essential understandings required by the unit of study. We also need to ensure that our assessment is authentic to the instruction. The test questions should be reliable and valid indicators of what students know (or do not know) and what they have experienced in class.

Home and School Connections

As with previous units of study, you can create a Parent Information and Involvement Form and distribute it to parents to help them support their children at home. (See Figure 5–9.) If this already has become part of your teaching repertoire, you may find parents waiting or even asking for this information. This is a good thing! When parents are interested and engaged in what is going on in math class, everyone benefits.

January seems to be a routine check-in month for many parents. I get more phone calls requesting conferences at this time of year than any other. Some conferences are in response to curricular issues: Sarah continues to struggle with long division or Michael still does not know

Parent Information and Involvement Form

From: Lainie Schuster
Re: Mathematics Curriculum
Unit: Division

During the next unit, the major topics we will be studying are:
■ division: partial quotients algorithm *and* traditional algorithm

My goal in studying these topics is for the students to be able to:
■ divide efficiently using an algorithm that makes "sense" to each student
■ apply knowledge of division and multiplication to solving and writing story problems

Parents can help at home by:
■ listening to their children as they explain different algorithms and how they "work"
■ learning the partial quotients algorithm*
■ encouraging their children to assess the reasonableness of their answers and of the calculation procedure that they chose to use
■ reviewing the multiplication tables with their children orally, with flashcards, and with computer games

*Many children may prefer this method because the division makes more sense to them. This stresses efficiency, as well as proficiency. Moving toward increased use of the traditional algorithm (when the numbers of the problem make sense to do so) can help to develop greater efficiency. I myself move back and forth between division algorithms depending on the context of the problem and the numbers used.

FIGURE 5–9
Parent Information and Involvement Form: January.

his multiplication tables. Some conferences are focused on the future: What mathematics will the middle grades require? Will Cole be prepared? When parents call or email to request a conference, I routinely ask about the reason for their request. Letting parents know that you are asking in order to meet their informational needs puts them at ease. I often ask if their child knows that they are requesting a conference. The answer to this question offers additional insight into the nature of the request.

The reason for a conference will determine the type of preparation required. If parents schedule a conference because of academic issues, collected student work can be of great help to both you and the parents. Samples of student work can offer a focus and talking points as you move through the conversation. I often have the student's math notebook available as well, since it is a record of the year's mathematical growth and progress. Be mindful that parents may not be aware of what their child's thinking and work are lacking. Providing anonymous examples of strong student work from others in the class can be helpful if parents are unsure of class expectations.

Less is often more in a conference setting. Review the pieces of work that you have selected to share at the conference and make some notes to yourself about the student's progress, strengths, and needs. You might also want to mention behavior or attitude if these have influenced the student's progress and participation in class. I do not present a laundry list of issues, however. Depending on the student, the parents, and the circumstances, presenting one or two major concerns can be enough. You can address additional concerns in follow-up conversations.

The writing component of the study of mathematics often comes up in conferences. Many parents are confused about the purpose and benefit of mathematical writing. Be aware of your audience when addressing this topic with parents. Some parents are intrigued with the idea that writing makes thinking visible. Others may be concerned that you are focusing too little on calculation and too much on communication. Reminding those parents that one cannot exist without the other can help broaden their perspective on the teaching and learning of mathematics. It is difficult to talk and write about what we do not understand. Parents become easily frustrated when trying to help their children with writing tasks at home, which also can explain their concern. An available handout can support parents as they work with their children. I gently remind the parents that this is not about teaching by telling, but rather learning by listening! This can be the same handout provided at the fall parent conferences (see Chapter 2, page 87). Whether parents are familiar with this handout or not, take the time to model good questioning and how to facilitate deeper thinking with additional questions.

In any conference and for whatever reason it is scheduled, link the expectations of the math curriculum with the student's actual work and performance. Parents need to realize that you know and respect their child. It is equally important for teachers to present themselves as professionals and to show they have command of the curriculum and grade-level expectations. Nancy Litton, in *Getting Your Math Message Out to Parents* (1998), writes of parent conferences:

> Holding conferences with parents has a deserved reputation for being time-consuming and emotionally demanding. The high-stakes quality of conferences is inherent to the situation: both teacher and parents care deeply about the child they are discussing and feel a high degree of responsibility for that child's success as a student and person. Finding a way to tap into this high degree of caring in a relaxed and positive way is important because conferences are a rare commodity—a time and place to focus on the needs and abilities of each child as an individual. (49)

Resources

About Teaching Mathematics: A K–8 Resource, Second Edition (Burns 2007)

The Number and Operations and Extending Multiplication and Division chapters offer activities rich in multiplicative reasoning and problem-solving. Activities can be completed independently, in a whole-class format, or offered as menu or independent-choice tasks. Burns's introduction to the Teaching Arithmetic section is exceptional and important.

Math Matters: Understanding the Math You Teach, Grades K–8, Second Edition (Chapin and Johnson 2006)

Chapter 2: Computation
This book provides an excellent description of mathematical properties and how they relate to division, as well as a description of the partial quotients procedure of long division.

Chapter 4: Multiplication and Division
This chapter discusses divisibility rules and the interpretation of remainders.

Teaching Arithmetic: Lessons for Extending Division, Grades 4–5 (Wickett and Burns 2003)

Activities, student vignettes, assessment recommendations, and outstanding narration make this a must-have resource.

Nimble with Numbers: Grades 4 and 5 (Childs and Choate 1998)

Nimble with Numbers: Grades 5 and 6 (Childs and Choate 2000)

This collection of math activities and games provides meaningful practice with the high-priority skills necessary for number sense, operation sense, and number competence.

"Alternative Algorithms: Increasing Options, Reducing Errors" (Randolph and Sherman 2001)

This outstanding article in NCTM's journal *Teaching Children Mathematics* explores the benefits of teaching and applying alternative algorithms.

Chapter 6

Fractions, Decimals, and Percents

SUGGESTED MONTHS:
FEBRUARY/MARCH

"We dig them and polish them right here," volunteered the Dodecahedron, pointing to a group of workers busily employed at the buffing wheels; "and then we send them all over the world. Marvelous, aren't they?"
"They are exceptional," said Tock, who had a special fondness for numbers.
"So that's where they come from," said Milo, looking in awe at the glittering collection of numbers. He returned them to

the Dodecahedron as carefully as possible but, as he did, one dropped to the floor with a smash and broke in two. The Humbug winced and Milo looked terribly concerned. "Oh, don't worry about that," said the Mathemagician as he scooped up the pieces. "We use the broken ones for fractions."

The Phantom Tollbooth
Juster 1961, 180

The Learning Environment

Listen to Ideas Rather Than Listen for Responses

As our fifth graders work hard (and it is hard work, indeed!) to make sense of fractions and construct understandings of fractional concepts and procedures, we need to listen to our students as *they* make sense of ideas rather than impose or even insist on *our* ways of thinking or doing. When we ask questions or pose problems, we may often look for specific responses— responses that make sense to *us* and are aligned with *our* expectations. However, there is a difference between our expectations and the mathematical objectives of the lesson or conversation. One of the mathematical objectives of any lesson should be for students to make sense of the material given their own understandings, skills, and experiences. We want them to understand that $\frac{1}{2}$ is greater than $\frac{1}{6}$, but not because we expect them to create common denominators and then compare numerators. Some students may compare both fractions to benchmark fractions, or identify how far each one is from one whole, or ignore the numerator since they are the same and focus on the size of the pieces given the magnitude of the denominator. Manipulating and talking about fractions is hard, really hard. That said, we need to listen really hard as well. We need to support our students with what is needed (models, symbols, language) as they articulate their ideas rather than give them the procedure or reasoning that we expect to see or hear.

Choose Meaningful Mathematical Tasks

Meaningful mathematical tasks provide the foundation that is critical to instruction that supports thinking, reasoning, problem solving, communication, and reflection. These tasks require no memorized rules and are open-ended whether in answer or approach. Tasks become opportunities to explore important mathematics and to construct reasonable methods for solution. The authors of *Making Sense: Teaching and Learning Mathematics with Understanding* (Hiebert et al. 1997) propose three features of meaningful tasks:

1. *The tasks are problematic.* Students view the problem as interesting. There is something to find out as a result of solving the problem, something to make sense of.

2. *Tasks must connect where the students are.* Students must be able to apply the knowledge and skill they already have to begin developing a method for completing the task or solving the problem.

3. *Tasks must engage the students in thinking about important mathematics.* Students must have the opportunity to reflect on important mathematical ideas and to take something of mathematical value away from the experience(8).

The tasks they are asked to complete determines how students spend their time and what they explore and subsequently understand. If your classroom culture is one that promotes understanding and communication, then your choice of tasks will need to support the same.

Slow Down!

Students need time to accomplish learning. Our fast-paced world does not often value time spent exploring, thinking, and talking. And if done well, all of this takes a great deal of time! Careful planning and identification of the goals and mathematics of a lesson will help to justify doing less rather than more. Instead of tackling ten or fifteen problems in a class period, investigating just one or two in greater depth will offer increased opportunities to slow down the pace of the class and allow more time for exploring, talking, and thinking hard about the mathematics.

The Mathematics and Its Language

Children Build an Understanding of Fractions, Decimals, and Percents and the Relationships Between and Among These Concepts and Representations

Traditionally, fractions, decimals, and percents have been presented as separate units and separate concepts, each with its own set of rules and procedures. For too many children, the world of fractions and the world of decimals are distinct (Van de Walle 2004, 280). Instruction should focus on the relationships among numbers and quantities across and within notational systems. When you make the connection between rational numbers deliberate and visible (literally and figuratively!), students will begin to move flexibly between them.

Children Explore and Represent Fractions and Decimals with Various Models and Symbolic Representations

Rational numbers can be represented by different visual models. Fractions, for example, can be represented by area models, linear models, and set models. Decimals and percents can be represented with base ten blocks and hundreds-grid models. In order to develop and support the flexibility of thinking that work with rational numbers requires, students need to investigate various models. As students become more willing and able to move flexibly between one representation and another, one model and another, or between a model and its notation as they explain ideas, present conjectures, and solve problems, they develop a deeper understanding about fractional relationships. Too often decimal concepts are presented to students solely with symbols. Physical models that can represent the quantities and the multiplicative relationships between place values can support our fifth graders as they work to make sense of these important ideas. Using physical models also allows students to apply their understandings of fractional concepts to those of decimals without the limitations of symbolic representation.

Children Explore Equivalent Representations of Rational Numbers as Well as Compare and Order Them

Equivalence is one of the most important mathematical ideas for students to understand as they work to make sense of rational number concepts and procedures. Equivalent representations are those that represent the same value but with different notations. Equivalent fractions are used when comparing fractions, ordering fractions, and adding and subtracting fractions. Encountering a variety of instructional models and applications can support students as they begin to generalize some big ideas about equivalent fractions (Chapin and Johnson 2006, 114–15). Exploring how the application of multiplication and division can be used to form equivalent fractions is one of those big ideas. Exploring equivalent representations between and among decimals builds on an understanding of place value and its multiplicative relationships as values move to the left or right of the decimal point. It is useful for students to become familiar with common fraction, decimal, and percent equivalents and to learn how to move flexibly back and forth between them. Making sense of *why* as well as *how* to convert one to the other will support students' conceptual as well as procedural understanding. Students may find that they prefer one representation over the other when solving problems. Being able to "equivalate" representations allows students to think about and solve problems with greater proficiency, efficiency, and confidence. The understanding of equivalence and the ability to apply that understanding to problem-solving situations take time, patience, and much conversation.

Children Use Benchmarks to Make Comparisons and Reasonable Estimates When Problem Solving

Benchmarks, such as 0, $\frac{1}{2}$ (0.5, 50 percent), and 1 (1.0, 100 percent), are referents that can be used for comparison purposes. Familiarity with benchmark fractions, decimals, and percents can support students as they manipulate rational numbers, articulate their understanding about those quantities, and solve problems applying their understanding of rational numbers.

Children Compute with Fractions and Decimals

Learning to add and subtract fractions and mixed numbers requires that students understand, articulate, and represent the idea of equivalence and equivalent fractions. As students explore problems that require the addition and subtraction of fractions, they also need to construct and explore strategies that make sense to them and to the context of the problem rather than applying specific recording systems or algorithms.

> When children are given the chance to compute in their own ways, to play with relationships and operations, they see themselves as mathematicians and their understanding deepens. Such playing with numbers forms the basis for algebra and will take children a long way in being able to compute not only efficiently but elegantly. (Fosnot and Dolk 2002, 125)

When students can make sense of decimal concepts, they will then be able to build meaning and construct strategies for the addition and subtraction of decimal numbers. Estimating sums and differences of both fractions and decimals can set the stage for procedural proficiency based on number sense and meaning.

Children Apply Their Understanding of Fractions, Decimals, and Percents to Problem-Solving Situations

When applying newly explored concepts and procedures in problem-solving situations, students have the opportunity to refine and revise their thinking and understanding about rational numbers. They can test conjectures and apply strategies. When students solve meaningful and interesting problems, thinking, reasoning, and calculating are made visible. We can then make informed instructional decisions based on the understandings or misunderstandings demonstrated by students as they problem solve.

Lesson Planning

- Many of the understandings required of students as they work to make sense of fractional concepts and procedures are difficult and complex. According to Marilyn Burns, learning about fractions in the upper-elementary grades is hard, really hard. Fractional concepts and procedures are hard not only for students to learn but also for teachers to teach (Burns 2001, ix). Our fifth graders are beginning to recognize the mathematical power of making and applying generalizations about what they know to be true about whole-number concepts, operations, and procedures. Much of the work with fractions is counterintuitive to what students expect when compared with previous experiences with whole numbers. Because of that, students have to work hard and think hard to make sense of fractions. Taking the time to listen to explanations, ask good questions, and identify fragile understandings will help direct instructional decisions that will support student learning and understanding.

- Keep in mind that our students will not leave the fifth grade with mastery of rational-number concepts and procedures—nor should we expect them to. Students need to come back to these concepts and procedures frequently over time. Some curricula refer to this process as *spiraling*. I am well aware that this can be a dangerous disclaimer to make to administrators, parents, and even sixth-grade teachers! Our fifth graders will undoubtedly deepen their understanding of fractions, decimals, and percents, but these new concepts and procedures will need to be revisited, rethought, and refined as they move through their middle school years. The study of mathematics is a developmental process, not merely a set of hurdles to be jumped once and only once (Corwin, Russell, and Tierney 1990). However, the concepts and procedures explored in later years do build and rely on those understandings that students explore and acquire in fifth grade. For this reason, I have found that my fifth grade's study of fractions, decimals, and percents covers a six- to eight-week timespan that is longer than my prescribed curriculum's pacing guide recommendations.

- It will help to consult your state, district, or school curricular expectations before you begin to plan lessons and investigations. Becoming familiar with the rational-number concepts and procedures that will be addressed on the standardized test that your students will be taking will also help to direct instruction. Keeping in mind mathematical objectives and expectations will help you choose and develop meaningful tasks that not only will support the learning of your fifth graders but also will keep your instruction aligned with prescribed expectations.

- Do not hesitate to confront misunderstandings head on—there will be many! An activity such as *Put in Order* (see "Investigations, Games, and Literature-Based Activities") can present many partial understandings, which is one of the beauties of the task! An initial series of eight to ten fractions for students to put in order can take an entire class period because of the accompanied discussion and misunderstandings that the discussion may make apparent. You may find that one particular task uncovers more fragile understandings than others. If so, revisit that task with different fractions. Be deliberate in your instruction. Remind students that they have had experience with this task and that you would like to see them extend and apply the thinking that was done in the previous experience.

- Fifth graders still need the support that physical models can give. Fraction kits or fraction strips (see "Investigations, Games, and Literature-Based Activities") can offer the visual mathematical proof that scaffolds the construction and application of strategies and procedures as students learn to manipulate fractions.

- The same can be said of decimal instruction. Decimal cards (Bennett 1992) and tenths and hundredths grids can visually support the learning about decimal numbers and the quantities they represent. Too often we jump to the symbolic level before perceptual grounding is achieved and understood.

- Minilessons, or problem strings, are a structured set of tasks that are related in such a way as to develop and highlight number operations and relationships (Fosnot and Dolk 2002, 112). When comparing fractions, for example, having a set of related problems such as the following for students to solve and discuss can offer opportunities to choose, assess, and rethink strategies.

$$<, >, or =$$

$$\frac{1}{8} \ \square \ \frac{3}{4}$$

$$\frac{1}{8} \ \square \ \frac{1}{3}$$

$$\frac{3}{8} \ \square \ \frac{3}{21}$$

$$\frac{7}{8} \ \square \ \frac{12}{13}$$

$$\frac{9}{8} \ \square \ \frac{6}{5}$$

As students move through the following string, they can be encouraged to articulate

- the similarities between the fractions;
- how the numerators or denominators inform their comparing strategies;
- when they can reason through the process;
- when a calculation is necessary; and
- when benchmarks can be applied.

Designing strings requires an understanding of purpose as well as number and operation; the choice of numbers and contexts is not random. You may find that some of your developed strings may be better than others. Make note of those to use for instruction in future years.

■ Most real-life applications using rational numbers require estimation. Being able to estimate that one-half of something and two-thirds of something else is going to be greater than one of something can be important to know: I have one-half of this gallon of paint left and two-thirds of another gallon. Will I have enough if I need one gallon of paint to finish the project? A sweater costing $49.00 is on sale for 25 percent off. Do I have enough money in my pocket to buy it? Dustin Pedroia, second baseman for the Red Sox, hit four for five last night. What was his batting average for the night? Was it better than Kevin Youkilis's, who hit five for seven? Offering opportunities and encouraging students to estimate solutions prior to digging into the problem will support continued development of number sense. Having students return to and reflect on their original estimates can offer important insights and help to direct instruction as well.

Possible Difficulties or Misconceptions

The whole matters . . . a lot! As students begin to interpret and identify fractional parts of a whole, they can overlook the magnitude of the whole. Winning one-third of Robert's twenty-four marbles is quite different from winning one-third of Max's nine! Interpreting a fractional part depends on the child's ability to make a comparison of the number of parts to the size of the whole. Offering activities that require the partitioning of different-sized wholes will help to develop and support the proportional thinking that such tasks require.

You may find that some students think of a fraction as simply a pair of numbers rather than as a *relationship* between those two numbers. We can make assumptions about the background knowledge of our students that can impact our instructional decisions and influence students' mathematical progress and understanding. In a given fraction model, our students should be able to identify the numerator, as well as articulate the information that the numerator gives us about that particular fraction. The same holds true for the denominator. Knowing that the denominator is the "bottom" number of a fraction is not enough. Understanding what the denominator (or numerator) represents in a particular fraction or fraction model helps our students give meaning and purpose to the language of fractions.

Visual models are important when teaching and learning about fractions, but you will need to vary those models. A whole can be represented by a circle, rectangle, strip, number line, or set of objects. Relying on one model will limit students' thinking, understanding, and flexibility. As students explain strategies and solutions to the problems, support the use of differing models by asking students just that: "Who used a different model to think about or solve this problem?"

Students may not seek out connections that can be made from one unit of study to another. We need to be mindful of those times when the previous lessons can deepen understanding and help to move learning along. We then need to encourage our students to seek out and make those connections. Applying understandings developed from previous work with factors and multiples can help support the thinking and reasoning that you need to manipulate fractions. Seth's vocabulary and wit often caught me off guard. He announced to the class one day that I "really wasn't daft" after all when I pushed them so hard to make generalizations about LCMs and GCFs earlier in the year because here they were again!

Some students assume that decimal numbers are negative because they can represent values less than *one*. You can move students forward from that thinking with conversations supported by number-line models. Negative numbers are those values less than *zero*!

TEACHER-TO-TEACHER TALK ■ **About Classifications of Numbers** ■ Although we do not formally classify numbers by sets with our fifth graders, it is important for us, as teachers, to be aware of those sets and how they intersect with one another—or not! We work with sets of numbers in the upper-elementary grades: counting numbers, whole numbers, integers, and rational numbers. The authors of *Math Matters: Understanding the Math You Teach* (Chapin and Johnson 2006) offer an in-depth discussion of these number classifications (4–6). For length's sake, here are some truncated definitions of each:

- *Counting numbers:* a set of whole, positive numbers without zero (1, 2, 3, 4, 5 . . .)

- *Whole numbers:* a set of numbers that includes zero and the set of counting numbers (0, 1, 2, 3, 4 . . .)

- *Integers:* a set of numbers that includes zero, the counting numbers, and their opposites (. . . −5, −4, −3, −2, −1, 0, 1, 2, 3, 4, 5 . . .)

- *Rational numbers:* a set of numbers that can be expressed as a ratio of two integers and that includes the set of whole numbers and negative numbers. The rational number set also includes all fractions and those decimals that can be represented as a fraction. Decimal numbers that have expansions that do not terminate or become periodic are known as *irrational numbers*, such as π.

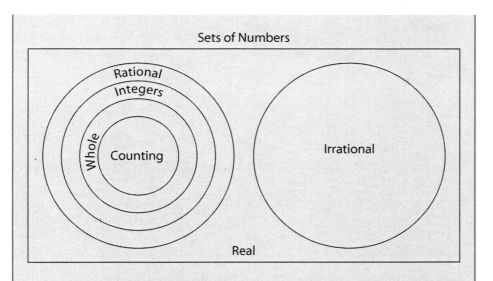

Many times students will ask about classifications—and that is always a good thing! When studying fractions, I often use the classifications of *whole numbers* and *rational numbers*. I want students to be continually exposed to the language of mathematics and also to the properties of such classifications. Many of us, children and adults alike, continue to be amazed at the hugeness of mathematics—and how all that we learn and do builds on an understanding of what we know! There is something very cool about a ten-year-old (or a fifty-three-year-old, for that matter!) explaining that zero is a *whole number* but not a *counting number*, and that any *whole number* can be reported as a *rational number*. Very cool, indeed.

Investigations, Games, and Literature-Based Activities

Fraction Kit Investigations

Duration: 2–3 Class Periods

When using manipulatives or physical models to explore part-whole relationships, teachers can directly observe how students make sense of those relationships. In order for students to attach meaning to fractions and the relationships they represent, teachers should introduce and make available a variety of physical models during instruction. Experience has repeatedly shown that as problems and tasks become more challenging and complex, students who can use materials to build models with which to think and solve problems are in a much better situation than those who merely manipulate numbers (Corwin, Russell, and Tierney 1990, 8). Although

NCTM Connection

Strand: Number and Operations

Focus: Represent and compare fractions with a linear model.

Context: Fraction Kit

many curricula promote the use of fraction strips, the initial write-up of this lesson focuses on fraction kit investigations from *About Teaching Mathematics: A K–8 Resource* (Burns 2007). These lessons provide students with opportunities to

- construct and label equal-size parts of a whole;
- explore how the whole determines the size and name of its parts;
- represent and compare fractions;
- explore equivalence of fractions with like and unlike denominators; and
- explore and articulate the relationships between the numerator and denominator.

Materials

- rules for the game of *Cover Up* (see Reproducible 6.1)
- rules for the game of *Uncover, Version 1* (see Reproducible 6.2)
- rules for the game of *Uncover, Version 2* (see Reproducible 6.3)
- fraction spinners, for homework and if dice are unavailable
- 5 colors of 12-by-18-inch construction paper cut into 3-by-18-inch strips. Arrange the 12-by-18-inch construction paper in alternating colors, then cut five sheets at the same time with a paper cutter to have sets of five-color 3-by-18-inch strips. (See the "Resources" section of this chapter for information on ordering ready-made fraction kits.)
- fraction dice, labeled with $\frac{1}{2}$, $\frac{1}{4}$, $\frac{1}{8}$, $\frac{1}{8}$, $\frac{1}{16}$, and $\frac{1}{16}$ on each of the six faces (also available with the ready-made fraction kits)
- quart-size zip-top food storage bags

Vocabulary

denominator, equal, equivalent, numerator, unit fraction

A Note About Fraction Kits

The teaching directions for making your own fraction kits can be found in several Math Solutions publications, including *About Teaching Mathematics: A K–8 Resource* (Burns 2007) and *Teaching Arithmetic: Lessons for Introducing Fractions, Grades 4–5* (Burns 2001).

If the financial resources are available, ordering the ready-made fraction kit is well worth the convenience and investment. The kit contains the following elements:

- precut fraction strips of varying colors, including strips for thirds, sixths, and twelfths. Students fold and cut the strips just as they would with teacher-made strips.

REPRODUCIBLE 6.1
Cover Up

REPRODUCIBLE 6.2
Uncover, Version 1

REPRODUCIBLE 6.3
Uncover, Version 2

- plastic zip-top storage bags for storing the kit
- 2 sets of fraction dice (one set labeled $\frac{1}{2}, \frac{1}{4}, \frac{1}{8}, \frac{1}{8}, \frac{1}{16}, \frac{1}{16}$, and the other set labeled $\frac{1}{2}, \frac{1}{3}, \frac{1}{4}, \frac{1}{6}, \frac{1}{12}, \frac{1}{12}$)
- magnetic fraction kit display for the board, which is absolutely wonderful to have
- *Fraction Kit Guide* handbook

Please note that creating fraction kits from construction paper without the aid of the ready-made kit is equally effective. If you are creating your own kits, be mindful that you will also need to create multiple sets of fraction dice. You can purchase blank dice from school specialty suppliers and mark the faces with the appropriate fractions listed in the "Materials" section of this activity.

A completed and labeled kit will look like the following:

1															
$\frac{1}{2}$								$\frac{1}{2}$							
$\frac{1}{3}$					$\frac{1}{3}$					$\frac{1}{3}$					
$\frac{1}{4}$				$\frac{1}{4}$				$\frac{1}{4}$				$\frac{1}{4}$			
$\frac{1}{6}$			$\frac{1}{6}$			$\frac{1}{6}$			$\frac{1}{6}$			$\frac{1}{6}$			$\frac{1}{6}$
$\frac{1}{8}$		$\frac{1}{8}$		$\frac{1}{8}$		$\frac{1}{8}$		$\frac{1}{8}$		$\frac{1}{8}$		$\frac{1}{8}$		$\frac{1}{8}$	
$\frac{1}{12}$	$\frac{1}{12}$	$\frac{1}{12}$	$\frac{1}{12}$	$\frac{1}{12}$	$\frac{1}{12}$	$\frac{1}{12}$	$\frac{1}{12}$	$\frac{1}{12}$	$\frac{1}{12}$	$\frac{1}{12}$	$\frac{1}{12}$				
$\frac{1}{16}$	$\frac{1}{16}$	$\frac{1}{16}$	$\frac{1}{16}$	$\frac{1}{16}$	$\frac{1}{16}$	$\frac{1}{16}$	$\frac{1}{16}$	$\frac{1}{16}$	$\frac{1}{16}$	$\frac{1}{16}$	$\frac{1}{16}$	$\frac{1}{16}$	$\frac{1}{16}$	$\frac{1}{16}$	$\frac{1}{16}$

There will be (and should be!) much conversation as students complete the fraction kits. What is so engaging about the construction and use of this kit is that fractional relationships can be seen and touched. Encourage your students to talk to each other about the relationships they are seeing as they cut and construct their kits. Questions such as the following will help students focus on the relationships between the actual pieces of the kit as well as the numbers:

- What do you notice about halves and fourths? How are they related? Fourths and eighths? Eighths and sixteenths?
- How are two, four, eight, and sixteen related?

- Where do we see that relationship in the fraction strips?
- How can you make sixteenths from fourths?
- How can you make eighths from halves?
- How can you make sixteenths from halves?

Ask students to show and tell when they offer observations as mathematical proof. The numbers need to work—but so do the physical models!

Cover Up

REPRODUCIBLE 6.1
Cover Up

With their newly constructed fraction kits, students can now play the game of *Cover Up* (see Reproducible 6.1). Playing this game will help students to connect the use of fraction strips to representing and comparing fractions. Model the game with two students as a whole-group lesson. Allow plenty of time for students to play multiple games. The more students play, the more opportunity they will have to talk about the relationships that are made visible by the fractional pieces and will quickly move to discussions about equivalence.

Uncover, Version 1

REPRODUCIBLE 6.2
Uncover, Version 1

Have two students model the game of *Uncover, Version 1* (see Reproducible 6.2) in much the same way that you did for *Cover Up*. Have the students play in pairs. I often ask that students choose partners other than those chosen for *Cover Up*. Allow yourself about fifteen minutes at the end of the period to process the game and to share experiences and strategies.

Uncover, Version 2

REPRODUCIBLE 6.3
Uncover, Version 2

Because of seeing the visual representation of these unit-fraction strips, students are well aware of equivalence and how some fractions can be traded in for others. *Uncover, Version 2* (see Reproducible 6.3) offers students the opportunity to do just that. You can pull the class together to introduce the adjusted rules for *Uncover, Version 2*. More often than not, I prefer to have the rules available for pairs of students when they are ready for a new challenge after playing a few rounds of *Uncover*. I ask students to read over the new rules with their partners and then proceed to play *Uncover, Version 2*.

Uncover, Version 2 gives students the opportunities to manipulate equivalent fractions: to see them, model them, and exchange for them. Strategies become more important when playing *Uncover* than with *Cover Up*. The mathematics of the game becomes richer when those strategies are discussed and analyzed.

Cover the Whole

Students create addition fraction strings when I ask them to cover their whole in five different ways. I ask students to record number sentences for each string of fractions used to cover one whole. Once the strings are recorded, the class can have discussions about how to shorten the sentence by combining fractions with like denominators. A covered whole and its symbolic representation might look like the following:

$\frac{1}{4}$	$\frac{1}{4}$	$\frac{1}{8}$	$\frac{1}{8}$	$\frac{1}{8}$	$\frac{1}{16}$	$\frac{1}{16}$

Asking the class if there is a more efficient way to record this string will help move the class to thinking about combining fractions with like denominators. Once they combine like fractions, this string becomes more efficient and shorter:

$$\tfrac{2}{4} + \tfrac{3}{8} + \tfrac{2}{16} = 1$$

I have no difficulty leaving $\frac{2}{4}$ as $\frac{2}{4}$ because the objective of this lesson is one of comparing and combining fractions, not one of simplifying fractions. However, some students may ask if they can change $\frac{2}{4}$ into $\frac{1}{2}$. Once again, the objective of your lesson will help direct your instruction and focus if this question is asked. Each year someone asks this question. I want students to represent what they are *seeing* covering the whole. Yes, two-fourths is equivalent to one-half, but there are two-fourths covering this whole and I ask that we stick to that representation for the time being. I tell students that their sentence needs to represent their particular model. It is also important to realize that as students move into more complex manipulations of fractions, keeping a fraction such as two-fourths in this unsimplified form might be preferable when completing computational and probability tasks.

Next I ask students to work independently to cover the whole in at least five ways. I ask them to cover their whole, represent their fraction string with a number sentence, and then combine fractions with like denominators as they make their sentences shorter and more efficient. I remind them that their number sentences need to model the visual representation of their string of fractional pieces. I suggest that they ask themselves, "Am I recording what I am seeing?" as they construct their number sentences.

Equivalence is one of the most important mathematical concepts for students to explore and understand (Chapin and Johnson 2006, 114). Conversations that elicit prior knowledge about equality and equivalence (see the "Calculation Routines and Practices" section of Chapter 3 on

NCTM Connection

Strand: Number and Operations

Focus: Explore, identify, and articulate parts of a whole in a game (fraction kit activity) context.

Context: *Cover the Whole* and *Cover the Whole: The Sequel*

algebraic thinking for prior instruction on equivalence in regard to number sentences) can move students to access prior knowledge and apply what they already know about equivalence to their work with fractions (and decimals). Encountering multiple models and applications will support students as they generalize concepts and strategies for creating equivalent fractions. The fraction kit is one model that they can access and manipulate when they are thinking about equivalence. Other models may include number lines (see the following *Put in Order* task) or area models. When they are represented on a number line, equivalent fractions represent the same distance. Area models are useful and helpful because they require the equality of area, not congruence of the compared shapes (see the "Resources" section of this chapter for further references on additional activities for area models).

Some curricula devote little, if any, time to exploring the concept of equivalence. Instead, the focus remains solely on the symbolic manipulation of denominators and numerators. Instructional activities that use models and drawings, as well as discussion that offers opportunities for students to reflect on why two or more fractions are or are not equivalent, are necessary if our instructional goals are to teach and learn with understanding.

Cover the Whole: The Sequel

Once students have had experiences covering the whole and recording their representations that are equivalent to one, they can move on to representing other equivalent strings.

I ask students to construct a string, as follows:

$$\tfrac{1}{4} + \tfrac{1}{8} + \tfrac{1}{8} + \tfrac{1}{8}$$

I then ask them to find another string that is equivalent to the one above. Once students have found equivalent strings, I ask them to explain to their neighbor how they know that the two strings are equivalent. If the strings are equivalent, they must be of the same length: One can be stacked above the other and be of equal length. This visual representation of equivalence (equal length) is powerful for many students.

$\dfrac{1}{4}$		$\dfrac{1}{8}$	$\dfrac{1}{8}$	$\dfrac{1}{8}$
$\dfrac{1}{2}$				$\dfrac{1}{8}$

Playing devil's advocate is great fun at this point in the year—and my students are anticipating that I will do so with an activity like this in which they are asked to defend their thinking! "I can see the equivalence

$$\frac{1}{4} + \frac{1}{8} + \frac{1}{8} + \frac{1}{8} = \frac{1}{2} + \frac{1}{8}$$

FIGURE 6–1
Joseph's Symbolic Representation.

with the model, but I still don't get it," I begin. "It might help if I could see it with symbols. How might that look? Prove what you are seeing with symbols!"

As students work to represent this model on paper, I ask them to represent it as an equation. (See Figure 6–1.) Having a visual model available as they notate equivalent expressions can be extremely valuable and helpful as students make sense of equivalency. Expressing representations as an equation offers students additional opportunities to make sense of the equal sign as a relational symbol representing the equivalence of both sides of the equation.

Questions such as "What do you notice about all of the fractions?" can elicit generalizations about this particular grouping of fractions. Such responses as "They all have one as a numerator . . ." can move the class to a conversation about the importance of *unit fractions*. Paying attention to the denominators will support students as they work to make sense of the relationship among factors, multiples, and denominators.

Feigning uncertainty about the equality of these two expressions can continue the classroom conversation about equivalence and the benefit of creating equivalent fractions that can be easily combined to prove equality. If all of the given denominators are factors of eight, can we then think of all these fractions as eighths? How and why could we do that and what would that *look* like?

$$\text{If } \tfrac{1}{4} = \tfrac{2}{8}, \text{ then } \tfrac{2}{8} + \tfrac{1}{8} + \tfrac{1}{8} + \tfrac{1}{8} = \tfrac{5}{8}$$
$$\text{If } \tfrac{1}{2} = \tfrac{4}{8}, \text{ then } \tfrac{4}{8} + \tfrac{1}{8} = \tfrac{5}{8}$$
$$\tfrac{5}{8} = \tfrac{5}{8}$$

Some students may be able to manipulate this task mentally. The availability of the fraction kit provides access to this task for those students who have not yet made sense of this routine. If Max claims that one-fourth is equivalent to two-eighths, you can pose a "How do you know?" question to elicit proof of such a claim. Max may be able to explain his reasoning arithmatically (see the "Calculation Routines and Practices" section for further discussion about the use of multiplication to calculate equivalent fractions), or he may choose to align two-eighths with one-fourth with his fraction kit pieces. If this task is one of the initial lessons in your unit of study, you will undoubtedly find that many students are at different places in their understanding of fractions and equivalence. Such information can be extremely helpful to you as the instruction moves forward.

When you are working with the fraction kit, do not offer formal instruction on arithmatic manipulation of fractions. Not only can the use of this visual model support the thinking and defending of ideas about fractions, it can also inform and direct instruction. Taking note of who can manipulate fractions with meaning, who prefers the support of the fraction kit, who needs the support of the kit, and who has little idea of how they can use and apply the pieces to solve problems can help you to construct a better understanding of your students as learners. This understanding can inform your instruction as you plan and carry out the lessons. (See the "Assessment" section for further discussion about the need for formative as well as summative assessment as instruction unfolds.)

TEACHER-TO-TEACHER TALK ■ **About Visual Models** ■ Each and every year, I am amazed and delighted at the mathematical power of the fraction kit. After completing the fraction kit and playing a few games of *Cover Up* and *Uncover*, Sean announced to the class, "So *that* is what one-fourth looks like! Who knew?"

Sean was new to our school and told us that he had studied fractions in the third and fourth grades having no idea what one-fourth even looked like. He was beside himself—and so was I. How many Seans have we had in our classrooms who go through the motions and manipulations without any visual and conceptual grounding of what it is we are trying teach and that they are trying to learn? It is a scary realization, but one that we need to remember when we begin our unit on rational numbers. Fractions become meaningful to students as the fraction kits are created and utilized. The relationships are right there: they can see them, they can touch them, they can talk about them.

NCTM Connection

Strand: Number and Operations

Focus: Explore equivalence and compare magnitudes of fractions in a game context.

Context: *The Comparing Game*

The Comparing Game

Duration: 1– 2 Class Periods and Can Be Revisited Throughout the Unit of Study

This activity, adapted from *Teaching Arithmetic: Lessons for Extending Fractions, Grade 5* (Burns 2003b, 53–61), provides a game context within which students can represent and compare fractions. (The original write-up of this activity contains student vignettes and author commentary.) This game offers students the opportunity to

- represent and compare fractions symbolically and pictorially;
- articulate and demonstrate understanding about equivalence;
- apply logical reasoning to the placement of numbers within the fractions; and
- think about fractions greater than one.

Materials

- *The Comparing Game* rules (see Reproducible 6.4)
- a die, a 1–10 spinner, or a deck of cards numbered 1–10, 1 per pair of students
- paper for constructing game boards

► REPRODUCIBLE 6.4
The Comparing
Game

Vocabulary

denominator, equal, equivalent, improper fraction, mixed number, numerator

It remains important to provide students practice with reading, writing, and comparing fractions, which is much more enjoyable in a game format! You may also find that students spend more time writing, thinking, and even arguing about fractions within a game than they do completing worksheets and sets of written exercises.

Each player creates the following game board:

As players place their numbers in their chosen places, they create fractions. Once they choose and place the numbers, they cannot change them. As my students say, "Once it's down, it's in cement!" Once the fractions are created, both players represent the fractions in a number sentence and with a drawing. (See Figure 6–2.) Many students will opt for the fraction kit model if the fraction kit has been used in class. I ask students to use at least two models in their games—and one can be the fraction kit model. After my request, we discuss the use of circle models, number lines, and even set models. Being able to move flexibly between models demonstrates a deeper understanding than the use of one.

Students may create improper fractions as they work through their games. You will need to make an instructional decision about whether the appearance of such a fraction warrants a whole-class discussion. Sitting with a pair of students and drawing and talking about fractions greater than one offers some valuable one-on-one instruction time that our daily schedule does not often allow. Several years ago, Paul and Rachel were playing a game when an improper fraction made an appearance. "Hey, you can't do that! That fraction is inappropriate!" yelled Paul. That comment caught the attention of the class! From that day forward with that particular class, improper fractions were affectionately referred to as "inappropriate fractions."

The importance of the whole becomes apparent as students draw and compare fractions. The partners need to agree on the fraction model that they are using—and on the shape of the whole. Students need to realize that in order to compare fractions, they need to compare like models. This

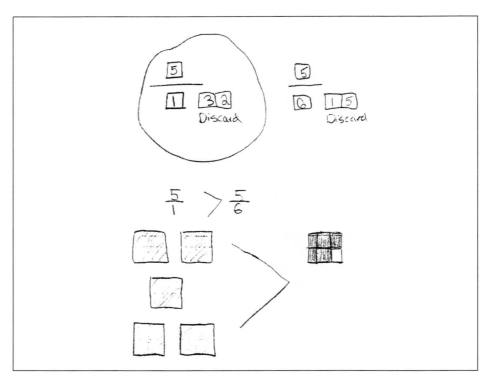

FIGURE 6–2
Marissa's Representation of a Greater Fraction Wins the Game.

idea of utilizing like models can set the stage for thinking about adding and subtracting fractions. As you circulate through the class, you may find that some students are trying to compare unlike models, which can make for valuable class discussion. I often ask the pair if they would be willing to address the class about their dilemma. Students are more than willing to share confusion or frustration with the class when a culture has been established that supports making sense of mathematics. More often than not, responses of "Me, too!" or "I know what you mean!" can be heard from the class as classmates present their concerns. These discussions also give students the chance to problem solve without teacher interference. Posing questions that can guide the discussion and offer entry points for thinking about the issue becomes our charge. The instructional goals of the lesson need to structure the discussion as well as guide the conversation. The constant questions of "What do students know?", "What do they not know?", and "What do they need to know?" will help to keep you grounded in what is important.

Knowing who your students are as mathematicians will help you differentiate your instruction. You can offer various extensions for *The Comparing Game*, such as the following:

The larger fraction wins.

The smaller fraction wins.

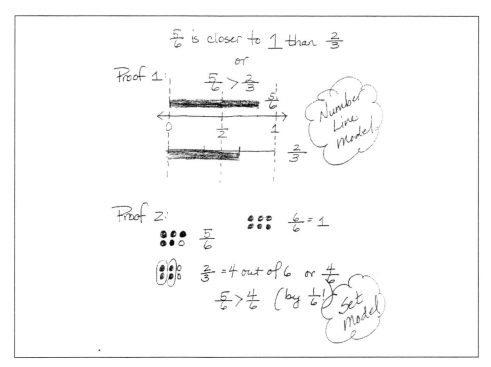

FIGURE 6–3
Class-Generated Proof that $\frac{5}{6}$ Is Closer to 1 Than $\frac{2}{3}$.

The fraction closer to one-half wins.

The fraction closer to zero wins.

The fraction closer to one wins.

Once the games are won, students ready for the challenge can figure out how much larger or smaller one player's fraction is than the other or how far their fraction is from zero, one-half, or one. Once again, they need to offer proof on paper. (See Figure 6–3.) Modeling these challenges with students can give them a framework from which to work. Ian harumphed when I presented my proof. "This is one of those 'How do you know' questions, right?" It does not take too long for fifth graders to see right through you!

How Much Is Blue?

Duration: 2–3 Class Periods

This activity, adapted from *Teaching Arithmetic: Lessons for Introducing Fractions, Grades 4–5* (Burns 2001, 97–104) offers a context within which students investigate fractional parts of a design made with thirteen pattern blocks. (The original write-up of this activity contains student

NCTM Connection

Strand: Number and Operations

Focus: Investigate fractional parts and how they relate to the area of a given shape; explore the area model of fractions.

Context: *How Much Is Blue?*

vignettes and author commentary.) This game offers students the opportunity to

- investigate fractional parts and how they relate to the area of a given shape;
- explore the area model of fractions;
- apply the fractional relationships found between and among pattern block shapes; and
- articulate and provide written support for their thinking.

Materials

- Pattern Block Design (see Reproducible 6.5)
- Pattern Block Triangle Paper (see Reproducible 6.6)
- pattern blocks, enough so that each student or pair of students can build the design and have extra blocks as well. The design requires
    3 green triangles
    6 blue parallelograms
    3 red trapezoids
    1 yellow hexagon
- paper or graph paper notebook

Vocabulary

congruent, contiguous, hexagon, parallelogram, trapezoid, triangle

As with all manipulative materials, students need to be familiar and comfortable with the materials, and I have yet to meet a fifth-grade class who does not delight in pattern blocks! Allowing a specified amount of free exploration with the blocks prior to the introduction of the lesson will appease everyone. As students are building and creating, encourage them to be aware of the relationships between and among the various blocks.

The following activity can be used as a quick introduction to the fractional relationships found between the blocks. I like to use the actual blocks when modeling work with pattern blocks. I still reach for my overhead set of pattern blocks even though the kids tease me endlessly. I like the size of the projected images and their ease of manipulation. I still use my overhead projector and am the only teacher in our lower school who does so from time to time. The following diagrams work just as well on chart paper or with the blocks and use of a document camera.

Present the following image:

$$\triangle = \frac{1}{4}$$

If the triangle is worth one-fourth, then I ask students to create a design worth two-fourths. The design needs to be contiguous, with side meeting side. Then I ask students to share shapes with their neighbor and a few to share their shapes with the class on the overhead. My fifth graders come to me with pattern block experience and quickly begin to substitute blocks with equivalent values. Once again, the opportunity arises to continue conversations about equivalence and what it means in this context of pattern blocks. For example:

A. = 1

B. = 1

C. = 1

As the class shares different representations, I pose a "How do you know?" question to each mathematician creating the shape. Not only will students break down their shapes into the smallest fractional part (the triangle, in this case) to prove that each shape is worth four-fourths or one, but also many will label or write an equation for each shape:

A. $\frac{1}{4} + \frac{1}{4} + \frac{1}{4} + \frac{1}{4} = 1$

B. $\frac{3}{4} + \frac{1}{4} = 1$

C. $\frac{1}{2} + \frac{1}{2} = 1$

Some students may recognize this practice from their previous work with the fraction kit. This is a good thing! If no one offers this recognition, a question such as "Have we seen this notation somewhere before?" can move students to access prior knowledge and experiences.

Changing the values of the pattern blocks and asking for shapes of different values can take up an entire class period, but this can be very valuable and offer yet another model that students can access when thinking about and solving problems with fractions. Perhaps one of the greatest mathematical benefits of this type of activity is one that supports the flexibility of thinking about fractional parts and their relative wholes. As the fractional part values change, so too does the value of the whole. We all too often assume that our fifth graders "get" this when, in fact, their understanding of part-whole relationships may continue to be fragile. Although formal fraction instruction often begins in the third grade, I often wonder how deep their understanding really is about these fundamental fractional concepts. Offering a paper-and-pencil prompt such as the following after this activity as a check for understanding can give you valuable information and help you make informed instructional decisions.

You can now present the *How Much Is Blue?* pattern block design to students:

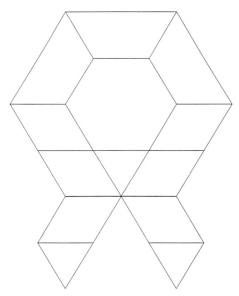

REPRODUCIBLE 6.5
How Much Is Blue?
Pattern Block Design

Present the design to each student as a handout (see Reproducible 6.5) and have pattern blocks available. Although I ask students to work with a partner on this task, I also ask that they initially think alone and quietly about the problem and the question. The beauty of this problem is that there are many entry points for solving it, and it also offers an opportunity for misconceptions to make themselves known. Keep in mind that while thirteen of the blocks are blue, the rest of the blocks are in different colors and sizes, and students must account for those differing sizes. Some students may jump to the conclusion that six-thirteenths of the design is blue . . . which is an incorrect response. It is increasingly important for students to make the realization on their own—with guidance offered by your good questions—that this response is not the correct one. But perhaps more important, *why* six-thirteenths of the design is *not* blue!

Once you have called the independent thinking time, ask students to write the following question: What fractional part of this design is blue? Ask them to work with a partner to discuss and then represent on paper what fractional part of the design is blue, with an explanation consisting of words, fractional notation, and pictures to support their reasoning. (See Figure 6–4.) Although students are working together, ask each to complete his or her own paper. I have found over the years that encouraging students to use colored pencils can further support and demonstrate their thinking and reasoning.

Although there is only one correct solution to this problem, solving it offers a myriad of approaches and strategies. Students present their solutions under the document camera, often opting to move back and forth between their paper and the initial pattern block design with the support of pattern blocks to explain their reasoning. The language demands of an

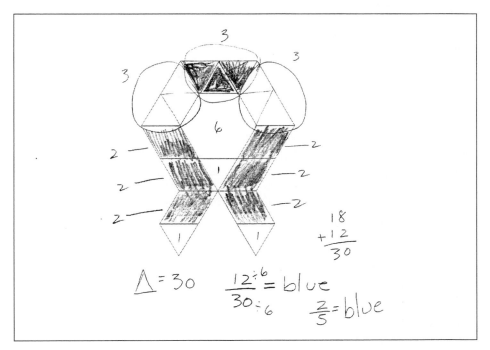

FIGURE 6–4
Hannah's Solution.

explanation can be tricky for some students. Whenever possible, offer word-choice guidance. The words *whole*, *denominator*, *numerator*, and *equivalent* become extremely helpful as students explain their thinking. Reminding them to refer to the word wall of fractional terms while presenting their solutions sets the stage for a continued focus on word choice and mathematical acuity.

Extension

Students can make pattern block designs of their own using the Pattern Block Triangle Paper (see Reproducible 6.6) with two constraints:

▶ REPRODUCIBLE 6.6
Pattern Block
Triangle Paper

- They can use only *green*, *blue*, *red*, and *yellow* blocks. (You can pose a question such as "Why am I asking you to only use these blocks?" to again focus attention on the fractional relationships between and among these particular blocks.)
- The design must fit on the pattern block paper so that it can be reproduced.

The following question should be written at the top of each student's design:

What fractional part of the design is _____?

Students create designs on the pattern block paper and carefully color them. When they have colored the designs, the triangle outlines are more difficult to see and require the student solving the problem to work a little harder to convert the blocks to equal-sized shapes or pieces.

Students not only create designs, but must also solve their own problems and represent their reasoning on a separate piece of paper, just as they did with the initial designs that will be used as answer keys. Once again, the whole changes from design to design—an important concept for students to recognize, internalize, and articulate. Once you have had the opportunity to check over the designs and solutions for accuracy, offer them as free-choice activities. Designs can be labeled 1, 2, 3 or A, B, C and their solutions labeled the same. The designs can be placed in one folder and the solutions in another for others to check their solutions against. Each year I choose a few designs to laminate to keep for following years' use.

NCTM Connection

Strand: Number and Operations

Focus: Compare and order fractions with like and unlike denominators.

Context: *Put in Order*

Put in Order

Duration: 1 Class Period and Can Be Revisited Throughout the Remainder of the School Year

This activity, adapted from *Teaching Arithmetic: Lessons for Introducing Fractions, Grades 4–5* (Burns 2001), provides students with experience comparing and ordering fractions with a number-line model. You can add decimals and percents in later lessons. (The original write-up of this activity contains student vignettes and author commentary; teaching directions can also be found in *About Teaching Mathematics: A K–8 Resource* [Burns 2007].) This game offers students the opportunity to

- compare and order fractions with like and unlike denominators;
- establish the use of benchmarks such as zero, one-half, and one when comparing fractions;
- apply and articulate mathematical and fractional reasoning;
- develop and articulate strategies for comparing and ordering fractions based on the fractions being considered; and
- develop and articulate strategies for comparing and ordering fractions, decimals, and percents by applying what they know and understand about fractions to decimals and percents.

Materials

- 4-by-6-inch index cards with a fraction written on each card large enough for all the students in the class to see, several sets; sample sets include:

  Set 1: $\frac{1}{8}, \frac{3}{8}, \frac{5}{8}, \frac{1}{4}, \frac{2}{4}, \frac{1}{2}, \frac{3}{4}, \frac{7}{8}, \frac{1}{1}$

  Set 2: $\frac{1}{16}, \frac{3}{16}, \frac{1}{4}, \frac{1}{2}, \frac{7}{16}, \frac{8}{16}, \frac{6}{8}, \frac{3}{4}, \frac{5}{8}, \frac{15}{16}, \frac{1}{1}, \frac{9}{8}$

Set 3: $\frac{1}{8}, \frac{1}{6}, \frac{1}{4}, \frac{1}{3}, \frac{1}{2}, \frac{2}{3}, \frac{3}{4}, \frac{15}{16}, \frac{8}{8}, \frac{17}{16}, \frac{4}{3}$

Set 4: $\frac{1}{11}, \frac{1}{4}, \frac{3}{8}, \frac{2}{6}, \frac{2}{4}, \frac{7}{12}, \frac{2}{3}, \frac{6}{8}, \frac{9}{10}, \frac{10}{11}$

Set 5: Add in the following decimals and percents to any of the previous sets: 0.03456, 0.255, 0.5, 0.74, 1.01, 1 percent, 50 percent, 25 percent, 60 percent, 75 percent, 99 percent

■ optional: fraction kits

Vocabulary

denominator, equal, equivalent, improper fraction, mixed number, numerator, whole number

Number lines are very, very cool. Number lines represent the magnitude of numbers as points on a line. This visual representation encourages the use of benchmarks such as zero, one-half, and one when ordering and comparing fractions. Although *Put in Order* is played on a chalk tray, the linear image of the placement of the fractions can be easily compared to the placement of numbers on a number line. The use of number lines early in the unit can also set the stage for their later use when adding and subtracting fractions (see "Calculation Routines and Practices" section of this chapter).

I walk around the room with the cards face down and fanned in my hand from which students can choose. Students volunteer to take a card. As they each take a card, they walk to the chalk tray (which we've cleared off for this purpose) and place the card in the appropriate spot based on its magnitude. I have to remind students that placing the card in the appropriate spot is not enough—they need to explain their reasoning for doing so. They may also make adjustments in the placement of other cards if some need to be moved in order to fit in their card.

As with so many good math activities, the beauty of this activity is the simplicity of its presentation and the opportunity it offers for all of us to practice talk moves. Because this lesson relies heavily on oral communication, you may once again need to establish expectations for talking and listening behavior. You may want to quickly discuss how students can respectfully disagree with placements and also stress the importance of wait time as students who have made an error rethink their placement while they are at the board.

Several times over the years my class has completed placing a set of cards with one in an incorrect spot—and no one has caught the mistake. I tell the class that I am troubled by the order of the fractions, and that I think something is amiss. (The kids love that word!) I ask them to talk with a neighbor about where the misplacement has occurred and how they can correct it. As students offer suggestions and solutions, I expect them to justify their thinking with reasoning or visual representations, or both. Some students may reach for their fraction kits, which can offer visual grounding as students defend their placements. Sets 1 and 2 contain fractions found in the fraction kit and denominators that are all multiples or

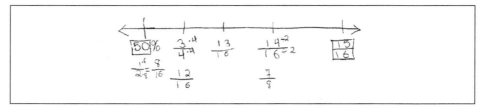

FIGURE 6–5
Caroline's Number Line Representation of Her In-between Fractions.

factors of each other. Sets 3, 4, and 5 contain a few of the fraction kit pieces but move beyond them. The fraction kit is still a valuable tool, but students quickly realize that their understanding needs to extend beyond sixteenths, eighths, fourths, and halves!

Using the cards of Set 4 can elicit fragile understandings or strategies as students post and explain placements. The fractions are not so friendly and require a deeper understanding of the relationships between numerators and their respective denominators or between one fraction and another (*inter*-fractional relationships versus *intra*-fractional relationships, if you will!). Although I do not formally teach common denominator conversions, conversations about creating equivalent fractions can help students compare fractions with greater ease and confidence. I much prefer having students think in terms of equivalence rather than in terms of finding common denominators. There is little difference *procedurally* between the two strategies. The difference and importance lie in the ability to *interpret* and *understand* equivalence. Keep in mind that you are scaffolding the understanding necessary for students to add and subtract fractions.

As you move into decimal and percent instruction, introduce Set 5. I do not inform my students that decimals and percents are in this particular set. They are a little surprised when they draw a decimal, but quickly rise to the challenge! Again, defending placement is crucial to this task.

Extensions

- Present five cards to the class. Ask students to order the cards and to defend their placements.

- Present two cards to the class. Ask students to identify and justify three fractions (or decimals or percents) that could fall in between the two cards. (See Figure 6–5.)

Decimal Gardens

Duration: 2 Class Periods

Decimals allow us to represent fractional quantities using our base ten number system. Instruction in many classrooms focuses on developing

NCTM Connection

Strand: Number and Operations
Focus: Explore and identify decimal representations of fractions.
Context: *Decimal Gardens*

computational skills rather than on helping students develop a conceptual and visual understanding of quantity, order, and equivalence related to decimal quantities (Chapin and Johnson 2006, 133). This activity, adapted from *Bits and Pieces I* (Lappan et al. 1998), offers students the opportunity to

- explore and identify decimal representations of fractions;
- explore tenths and hundredths with a grid-area model;
- explore and articulate the connection between fractions and decimals; and
- explore and discuss the place value and notation of decimal numbers less than one.

Materials
- Decimal Garden Problem (see Reproducible 6.7)
- sheets of 1-inch grid paper with a 10-by-10-inch square outlined for the garden at the top of the paper. Cutting off strips from a roll of 1-inch grid paper that can be purchased through a school specialty store is very useful for this task. Students will need white space below their gardens to notate the items that they will grow in their gardens. (See Figure 6–6.)

Vocabulary
constraints, equivalent, hundredths, tenths

Many years ago, we read *Seedfolks* (Fleischman 1997) as a faculty summer read. To be quite honest, I cannot remember under what context we were asked to read the book, but I loved it nevertheless. It is a charming and poignant collection of short stories about the members of a neighborhood garden co-op. When I first came across this garden math activity, I immediately thought of *Seedfolks*, and I choose a story or two from it to read to my class before we begin the investigation each year.

To begin the investigation, I post a garden template on the whiteboard. Then I pose a "What do you notice?" question as students view the 10-by-10-inch outlined grid. Because my students are so accustomed to working with arrays, they often immediately notice that this is a ten-by-ten array. "So there are one hundred little squares in the big square," announced Marissa. Joey observed that each small square was one hundredth of the large square. Bingo! Right where I wanted the class to go!

Once the class agrees that this ten-by-ten grid can represent one whole, you can introduce the problem (see also Reproducible 6.7).

▶ REPRODUCIBLE 6.7
Decimal Garden
Problem

▶ REPRODUCIBLE 6.7
Decimal Garden
Problem

FIGURE 6–6
Decimal Garden Template.

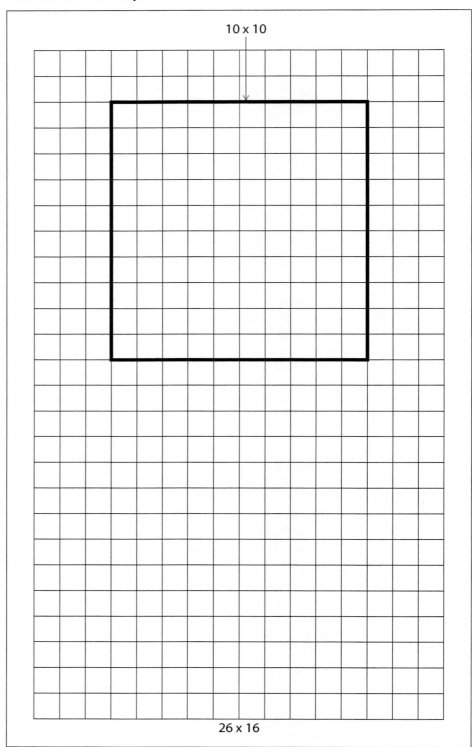

Decimal Garden Problem

Jacob wants to plant a family garden. He first draws a grid with 100 squares to represent his 100-square-meter plot. Here are his family's requests for the plantings:

- Jacob's brother Jason wants to be sure that potatoes, beets, corn, and tomatoes are in the garden. Jason wants twice as much of the garden to be planted in corn as potatoes. He wants three times as much of the garden planted in potatoes as tomatoes.

- Jacob's father, Jonathan, wants cucumbers in the garden.

- Jacob's mother, Lainie, wants carrots in the garden.

- Jacob's two other brothers, Max and Wayne, want eggplant and zucchini in the garden.

1. Use your grid to make a suitable plan for Jacob's garden. Create a key to designate each crop.

2. Write a description of the garden that you plan, keeping in mind the family's requests.

3. Create a T-chart on the bottom of your plan. Name the *fraction* of the garden space that will be allotted for each vegetable.

Vegetable	Fraction	Decimal	Percent

(Adapted from *Bits and Pieces I: Understanding Fractions, Decimals, and Percents (Connected Mathematics 2)* [Lappan et al. 1998].)

▶ REPRODUCIBLE 6.7
Decimal Garden
Problem

Although open-ended in both solution and approach, the Decimal Garden investigation has several constraints of which students need to be mindful. The term *constraint* can and should be used with the students. Initially, I only ask students to represent each vegetable with a fraction. Although the investigation will eventually move to completing the T-chart with decimal and percent equivalencies, some students may be ready to identify or at least attempt to identify the decimal and percent representations based on what they already know and understand. If a group is representing their vegetable amounts with decimals and percents, I do ask them to write these numbers in pencil so that they can be adjusted if need be. I also ask students to plan their gardens out on the bottom of their handout before they set off to "plant"!

TEACHER-TO-TEACHER TALK ■ **About Simplifying** ■ I always seem to get caught up in the faculty room argument about when to simplify fractions—or not. And there always seems to be one going on at this time of year! Why or when is six-eighths the "wrong" answer? And are there situations when it is the "right" answer? When and why is using four-eighths just as effective as using one-half? Is it as simple as the solution needs to fit the context, or the ease of making sense of the fractions being used? We need to be careful with this argument as fifth-grade teachers because in my opinion (and I have many as you can probably tell!), it *is* all about making sense and it *is* all about the context. We want our fifth graders to be flexible in their thinking. We want them to be able to visualize and to articulate that yes, six-eighths is equivalent to three-fourths but when I am talking about eight fresh-out-of-the-oven peanut butter cookies, and my brother ate six of them, having six-eighths of the cookies disappear makes perfect sense to me! A follow-up question could certainly move the thinking and response to three-fourths, and those follow-up questions do need to happen in fifth grade. It is also important to realize that as students move down that mathematical road, solving equations or manipulating proportions with simplified fractions does not always make sense!

Although the *relationship* between square meters for vegetables chosen by Jacob's father will remain the same for all groups and all gardens, the vegetable arrangements and the number of square meters allotted to corn, potatoes, and tomatoes will vary, as will the amounts of the other vegetables. Students may (and hopefully will) recognize a familiar multiplication structure: that of multiplicative comparison (twice as many, three times as much). The class wrote and solved comparison story problems back in November.

I have yet to have a class not totally engaged by this task! There are jobs for all within the group: for the artist, the thinker, the number cruncher, and the writer. Every year an argument breaks out about the difference between the color of a radish and an eggplant. And how and where do eggplants grow? And do radishes have "hair" like carrots do? Just another confirmation that our students are products of their environments . . . and their curiosities!

Once the class completes the posters and names the vegetable fractions, each group shares their garden with the class. Posting all the vegetable amounts on a class T-chart such as the one that follows can be very informative and helpful. If students have not yet realized that there are many solutions to this task, they will after they post the data and review the constraints for each posting. For this first go-round, we post the data in fractions.

Table Group	Potatoes	Beans	Corn	Tomatoes	Cucumbers	Carrots	Eggplant	Radishes
1								
2								
3								
4								
5								
6								

A question such as "How do I know my solution is correct if there are so many possibilities?" can move the class to thinking about the whole. All the fractional parts must add up to one. Once we post each table group's data, we quickly combine the fractions to make sure that they sum up to one. As the class reviews the postings, they should continue their conversations about equivalent fractions. The teacher should also continue to pose questions asking students to justify their reasoning. "How do you know that?" or "Why do you think that?" can help students to deepen their understanding and to make fragile understandings visible. Remember that you can view each and every conversation as a form of formative assessment. If these conversations are to direct our instruction as formative assessments have the power to do, then we must listen carefully and adjust our instruction to what we are hearing.

You will need to decide when and how to post the plantings in decimals and percents. In some years my class has made that leap easily and with understanding. The hundreds grid helps to keep those groups grounded in hundredths and percentages. Mistakes will more than likely make themselves known as students represent three radishes or seven eggplants as 0.3 or 0.7, rather than 0.03 or 0.07. This misconception and misrepresentation lends itself nicely to instruction pertaining to place value. In other years we put the gardens aside. Then we devote several class sessions to place value, place-value charts, and reading, writing, and modeling decimal numbers (see the following *Place-Value Round Robin* activity). Then we pull out the gardens once again and notate the equivalent decimal and percent representations.

Once completed, these gardens make a lovely bulletin board. My class's posters are displayed outside of my classroom. I love hearing students from previous years walking by and commenting on the posters—and how much fun they had with this activity—and still wondering why eggplants are purple!

NCTM Connection

Strand: Number and Operations

Focus: Construct, visualize, and represent decimal numbers with a physical model.

Context: *Place-Value Round Robin*

Place-Value Round Robin

Duration: 2 Class Periods

The concepts and multiplicative relationships that support our place-value system support both whole *and* decimal numbers. Too often we present place-value concepts as they apply to decimal numbers to students using only symbols. The use of base ten blocks offers a structure and context that can help students extend their understanding of what they already know about whole numbers to what they need to know about decimal numbers. This activity offers students the opportunity to

- construct, visualize, and represent decimal numbers with a physical model;
- investigate how the value of a unit, long, flat, or cube can change according to the whole;
- identify and articulate the difference between face value and place value; and
- articulate and represent the relationship and connections between fractions and decimals.

Materials

REPRODUCIBLE 6.8
Place-Value Round Robin Recording Sheet

REPRODUCIBLE 6.9
Place-Value Mat

- Place-Value Round Robin Recording Sheet, 1 per student (see Reproducible 6.8)
- Place-Value Mat, 1 per student (see Figure 6–7; see also Reproducible 6.9)
- place-value charts, 1 reproduced as a poster or on chart paper for class reference and 1 per student
- base ten blocks (flats, longs, and cubes):

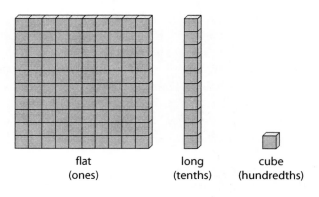

flat
(ones)

long
(tenths)

cube
(hundredths)

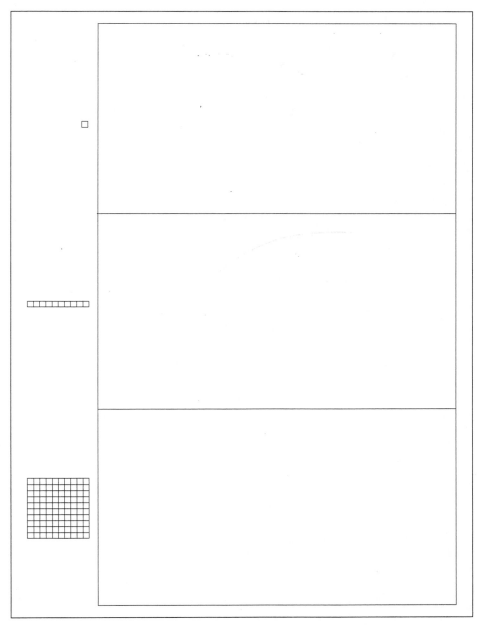

REPRODUCIBLE 6.9
Place-Value Mat

FIGURE 6–7
Example of a Place-Value Mat.

- containers to hold blocks, such as those for frozen dinners with no compartments, 1 per student
- overhead marking pens or (less recommended) dry-erase markers, several per group of students
- optional: overhead base ten blocks

Vocabulary

equivalent, face value, hundredths, multiplicative relationship, place value, tenths, thousandths

What can make the conceptual understanding of what decimals are and what they represent initially elusive to many fifth graders is their connection to both whole numbers *and* fractions. Established understandings of whole-number place value extend to decimals. Decimals are also equivalent representations of fractional relationships. When students can create models of decimal numbers, represent them with both fractions and decimals, and talk about how the digits to the right of the decimal point represent fractional parts and to the left, the whole, we have done our jobs well (or have exhausted ourselves trying)! As you well know, this is not an easy charge. Realistically and developmentally, we cannot expect our fifth graders to *completely* understand these dichotomies when we present them in a relatively brief time span. Students need to revisit these ideas and topics frequently over time and in varied contexts. And they will!

The beauty of this lesson is that you can adjust and revise it to meet the needs of your students. But because of that, you will need to determine what parts of the lesson you choose to deliver and what materials you will need to do so. If you do not have place-value mats (usually found in large 18-by-24-inch tablets through school supply companies), you can easily make them by cutting and pasting base ten models from other reproducible materials onto 12-by-18-inch white construction paper, partitioning the columns with black marker, and then laminating each mat. You will need the place-value mats for a number of reasons. First, they give structure to the chaos of the blocks! Keeping the base ten blocks organized in front of students helps them to keep the groups of blocks organized mentally. Second, the mats support the understanding of the ten-ness of our base ten system as we move to the left or right on the place-value chart. Third, the mat presents a physical model that the place-value chart does not. If it sounds as if I am trying to talk you into using this model and the place-value mats, I am! Each year I am astounded at how many students refer to this model when comparing decimals with decimals, converting decimals to fractions, or comparing decimals to fractions.

There are also two different organizational systems for the base ten blocks. When you use the place-value mats, you can house the blocks in bins on tables. When you work through the round-robin task, you will need to organize the blocks in individual pans according to the number being represented. Because of the organizational needs of the blocks, it makes sense to spend one day building decimal numbers on the mats, and the next day representing them on the student worksheets. You must also establish an agreed-upon language to identify the blocks. Throughout the lessons, I have a mat posted on my whiteboard with labels. (See Figure 6–8.)

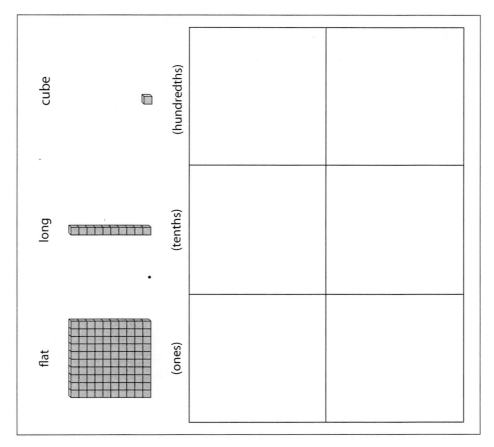

REPRODUCIBLE 6.9
Place-Value Mat

FIGURE 6–8
Example of a Place-Value Mat with Labels.

Building Decimals

With the place-value mats in front of the students, you can commence the lesson with a discussion of the mat and how it can be used to represent numbers. Many students will remember using base ten blocks in first and second grade. They will also remember using the blocks with whole numbers. These connections are important and should be drawn out of students. Questions such as "How did you use the blocks?" and "What did they help you to understand?" will help to facilitate the conversation.

Talking about the ten-ness of our base ten system is important. Fifth graders are old enough and mathematically sophisticated enough to understand and articulate that each place value to the left of a given place is *ten times greater* than that given place. The *multiplicative* nature of our place-value system is what they need to understand and articulate. That is why we can trade in ten cubes for one long, or ten longs for one flat—or trade in one flat for ten longs, or one long for ten cubes.

Ask students to build several whole numbers on their mats, such as 47 or 349. You can present a model to students with the overhead blocks or blocks under a document camera and ask what number is represented. You can introduce the terms *face value* and *place value* as students compose and decompose numbers. *Face value* refers to the digit alone—such as the three or the four or the seven in 347 with no place value attached. *Place value* refers to the value that digit holds in a specified number. In 347, the three (face value) represents three hundred (place value). In other words, a three is not always a three!

As students compose and decompose whole numbers, additional conversations can be had about operating on these numbers. What happens when you add two whole numbers together—and you end up with sixteen cubes? Is that "legal"? What do we do with those sixteen cubes? What happens when we try to subtract eighteen cubes from thirty-two cubes? How can we take eight cubes away from two cubes? What can we do to make that happen? You may be wondering why these conversations are necessary with fifth graders. The underlying mathematics and understanding necessary to answer these questions is huge and powerful. Even though decimal numbers may look different, the concept of ten-ness and how to manipulate that ten-ness remains the same whether working with whole numbers or decimal numbers. The awareness of the consistency (and beauty) of our base ten system can prepare our students to manipulate decimal numbers with greater ease and understanding.

Now you can begin discussion about the decimal point: What it is and how it helps us to represent numbers less than one whole but greater than zero. Post the enlarged place-value chart on the whiteboard. (See Figure 6–9.)

My place-value chart is laminated so that we can write on it and reference it throughout the unit. I have to replace it every year because it is so worn, but it is well worth the effort.

Keep in mind that we are still working with young students—sometimes I forget that by this time in the year! Students have come so far in their mathematical thinking, writing, and articulation that I sometimes forget

FIGURE 6–9
Class Place-Value Chart.

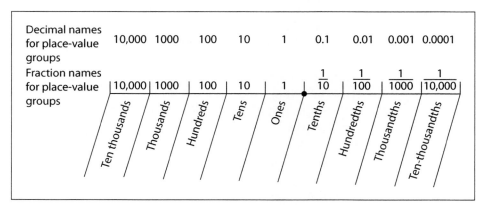

their ten-ness! The base ten blocks can become a helpful model as we introduce, discuss, and manipulate decimal numbers.

I distribute place-value mats to each student. Some students may quickly notice that the place values of the blocks have been shifted. If they do not notice this, ask about it!

- What do you notice about this place-value chart?
- How is the place value of these blocks different (and the same) from other work you have done with the blocks?
- How does this change how we talk about place value within this model?
- Do we need new labels? What could they be? Why do the new labels of tenths and hundredths make sense?
- What would thousandths look like? Ten thousandths?

I have made the conscious decision only to explore tenths and hundredths with the blocks. Students feel (and are!) mathematically empowered when they can make generalizations and apply what they already know to what is new. Students will realize that thousandths follow all the same rules, but are just ten times smaller than the hundredths.

I have also made a conscious decision to have students represent decimal numbers with the blocks as well as in equation form with expanded notation. We can "tell" students about the connections between fractions and decimals till the cows come home, but until they *see* those decimals in fractional notation, the connections can elude them. (See Figure 6–10.)

You can take an entire class period to build, discuss, and notate decimal numbers. You can begin some construction with the blocks and then move to the notation. Some students can begin with the notation and move to the blocks. We want our students to be flexible not only in their thinking, but also in their choice of models and language.

Place-Value Round Robin

This is an activity that allows students to build and represent decimal numbers. Each year I am somewhat surprised at how meaningful this exercise is for some students because of the simplicity of presentation. For some individuals, the physical models of decimal numbers offer a visual anchor that is not only meaningful, but necessary for their understanding.

You will need the same number of pans of base ten blocks as you have students. Label each pan with a number that corresponds with the same number on their Place-Value Round Robin Recording Sheet (see Reproducible 6.8). Each pan contains combinations of blocks with which students will construct a decimal number. Many pans will have quantities of

► REPRODUCIBLE 6.8
Place-Value Round
Robin Recording
Sheet

	ones	"and"	tenths	hundredths	Expanded Notation
1	3	•	8	5	$3 + \frac{8}{10} + \frac{5}{100}$
2	7	•	0	6	$7 + \frac{0}{10} + \frac{6}{100}$
3	4	•	8		$4 + \frac{8}{10}$
4	0	•	0	6	$0 + \frac{0}{10} + \frac{6}{100}$
5	0	•	1	1	$0 + \frac{1}{10} + \frac{1}{100}$
6	6	•	6	6	$6 + \frac{6}{10} + \frac{6}{100}$
7	8	•	1	0	$8 + \frac{1}{10} + \frac{0}{100}$
8	1	•	9		$1 + \frac{9}{10}$
9	0	•	2	1	$0 + \frac{2}{10} + \frac{1}{100}$
10	1	•	1	1	$1 + \frac{1}{10} + \frac{1}{100}$

REPRODUCIBLE 6.8
Place-Value Round
Robin Recording
Sheet

◀   **FIGURE 6–10**
Marissa's Place-Value Chart with Expanded Notation.

longs (tenths) or cubes (hundredths) that will need to be regrouped. This particular pan requires the student to regroup the twelve longs and seventeen unit cubes into one flat plus three longs plus seven units, which is equivalent to 1.37. (See Figure 6–11.)

Place numbered pans at each student's seat. Students circle the number of the pan placed at their seat on their recording sheets (see Reproducible 6.8). This will be their beginning decimal number. In this activity, *students* move from seat to seat, the pans do not. After a pan or two, students become accustomed to the routine and move through the numbers with ease. Remind students to keep their blocks confined to their space and pan. Sometimes a block or two can make their way to another pan, which will obviously affect the represented numbers!

The following suggestions may help you to create the pans of numbers to be represented:

- Include some whole numbers so that students will become familiar with the placement of the decimal point in whole numbers.
- Include some numbers that require zeros; a pan with eight unit cubes would require a zero in the tenths place.
- Include some that require regrouping over the decimal point; fifteen longs would be represented by the decimal number 1.5.

FIGURE 6–11
A Pan of Blocks Equalling 1.37 Once Regrouped.

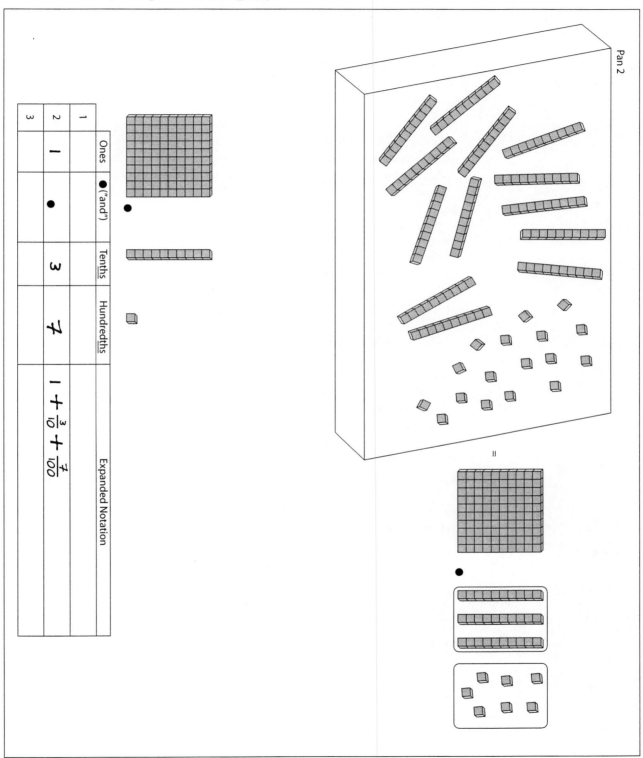

Once students have moved around the room, you can carry out a whole-class discussion as each number is identified and discussed. As you identify each number, ask students to use place-value terminology rather than that of face value. The decimal 1.38 is read as "one and thirty-eight hundredths" rather than as "one point thirty-eight." Questions such as "What would adding two more hundredths do to this number?" or "How many hundredths would I have to add to this number to get to 2.0?" will move students to regroup mentally with the aid of this visual model.

TEACHER-TO-TEACHER TALK ■ **About Visual Models** ■ Harriet never seemed to miss a *greater than, less than,* or *equal to* exercise with decimals. She struggled somewhat with fractions, but she obviously had a greater understanding of decimals. I questioned her about that in class one day, commenting on her competency with decimals and my awareness that she preferred decimal representations over fractional ones. Harriet shared her thinking and strategies with the class, and all were based on the base ten blocks. "I see longs or unit cubes—or even flats—and I know where the decimal point needs to be. I think better in pictures. I don't have to go very far in a decimal number to compare it, either. I just start with the flats: are there more in one number than the other? Then I move to the longs. I just stop when one number has more in one place value than the other." Now this conversation was not reported verbatim—even though it happened just recently, which made writing this piece extremely relevant—but Harriet was so articulate in her understanding and in her comparing strategies that it took me by surprise. She was a quiet student who had some difficulty finding the words to explain her thinking. Her animation and excitement about something being so clear and visible captivated the entire class. We even had some fun with some visualization routines similar to those that we do in reading. "Close your eyes. Visualize a place-value mat in front of you. What does four and sixty-three hundredths look like? Take away four longs—or four tenths. What does the number look like now? What do you see?" For Harriet and no doubt others, this picture was worth a thousand words—important ones!

Percent Designs

NCTM Connection

Strand: Number and Operations

Focus: Construct and estimate percentages created on a hundreds grid.

Context: *Percent Designs*

Duration: 2–3 Class Periods

Percent Designs provides a visual grounding for the concept of percent and its connection to fractional and decimal representations. This activity, adapted from *Teaching Arithmetic: Lessons for Decimals and Percents, Grades 5–6* (De Francisco and Burns 2002), offers students the opportunity to

- estimate percentages created on a hundreds grid;
- check estimates with a physical model;
- represent the designs of a color in percents as well as fractions and decimals; and
- challenge themselves with the designs they choose to make.

Materials

- T-Design, copied onto a transparency or used under a document camera (color the T red and the rest blue for class demonstration) (see Reproducible 6.10)
- Percent Designs Worksheet, 2 per student (see Reproducible 6.11)
- Percent Designs Recording Sheet, 1 per student (see Reproducible 6.12)
- 10-by-10 Percent Grids, copied onto transparencies and cut apart, 1 grid per student (see Reproducible 6.13)
- large 10-by-10 Grid copied on a transparency, for class demonstration (see Reproducible 6.14)
- blue and red pencils; additional colors for the extension

► REPRODUCIBLE 6.10
T-Design

REPRODUCIBLE 6.11
Percent Designs
Worksheet

REPRODUCIBLE 6.12
Percent Designs
Recording Sheet

REPRODUCIBLE 6.13
10-by-10 Percent
Grids

REPRODUCIBLE 6.14
10-by-10 Grid

Vocabulary

percent

Spending some time deconstructing the word *percent* makes this simple but powerful lesson even more meaningful. *Per cent*—and I visually divide the word as such—means just that, *per hundred*. Fifth graders are certainly familiar with the root word *cent*, and they also have used and applied the word *per* in their mathematical and everyday lives. Students are often quite surprised at the simplicity of the word. Keep in mind that percents greater than 100 percent can easily cause some disequilibrium! If you carefully make reference to percent being *per* hundred rather than *out of* one hundred, students will be better able to visualize 175 percent as being (100 percent plus 75 percent) greater than the whole, or one and three-fourths greater than the whole.

Although the study of percents is more than representing fractional quantities (45 percent = $\frac{45}{100}$) or comparing magnitudes (45 percent > 6 percent), it is extremely important to build and develop concepts of percent based on students' prior knowledge of fractions and decimals. Expressing percents as fractions and decimals can help to make those connections visible and accessible.

Prior to the lesson, color in the T-Design (see Reproducible 6.10), with the T red and the rest of the sheet blue. You will use this grid for whole-class instruction, so prepare it on a transparency or for use under a document camera. As the discussion erupts, as it usually does by this time of the year when a model of just about anything is presented, you will want to keep a marker in hand to script students' analysis of the design. Symbolic representations (T $\approx \frac{1}{3}$ or T $\approx$ 0.33) or language ("the T is less than one-half of the grid but more than one-fourth") describing the design can initiate a discussion of the task and the concept of percent.

Focusing on the whole—the hundreds grid—can help to anchor students' thinking and conversation about percent. Estimating the percent of

► REPRODUCIBLE 6.10
T-Design

the grid in red and blue is an important part of the lesson. Once again, benchmarks become helpful: Is the T more than one-fourth of the grid? Greater than one-half? Less than one-half?

You can ask students about a strategy for determining how much of the design is red and how much is blue. If percent means *per hundred*, and we are using a hundreds grid, how can we figure out what percent of this design is red? Can we report this percent as a fraction? As a decimal? Which representation makes more sense given the question being asked?

As students count squares, ask volunteers to come up to the board and represent the amounts in percents, fractions, and decimals. This task offers yet another opportunity to revisit equivalence—what it means and how it can help us report our solutions.

REPRODUCIBLE 6.11 ◀ Percent Designs Worksheet

Distribute the Percent Designs Worksheet (see Reproducible 6.11). Ask each student to create a design in red and blue in each of the six squares. They should not leave any squares uncolored. After the children create and color each design, ask them to record their estimates on their Percent Designs Recording Sheet (see Reproducible 6.12).

When several students have completed their designs and estimates, interrupt the class for the next set of instructions. Each student will pair up with someone else who is finished with his or her designs. Students will exchange designs and record estimates of those designs on their recording sheets. They can exchange their designs with another student if time permits.

REPRODUCIBLE 6.13 ◀ 10-by-10 Percent Grids

Begin the second lesson by distributing one transparent 10-by-10 Percent Grid to each student (see Reproducible 6.13). A question such as "What is helpful about this grid?" can move students to think in terms of one hundred and of the whole. Elicit representations of the whole: $\frac{100}{100}$, 1.0, and 100 percent. Because the mathematical objective of this task is focused on introducing the concept of percent, ask students to focus on that representation: What it means and how it is useful in this context.

REPRODUCIBLE 6.14 ◀ 10-by-10 Grid

Using a transparency of the large 10-by-10 Grid (see Reproducible 6.14) and the T-Design that you posted in the prior lesson, model for the students how to use the grid to identify the percent of the design that is red and the percent that is blue. Compare the calculated percentage with the prior lesson's estimates.

The students can now check their designs with the grids, record the percentages, and compare their estimates. Designs with curved lines are always interesting—and certainly a bit more challenging and fun! When students have completed their own designs, they can exchange papers and calculate percentages for each other's designs. (See Figure 6–12.)

Good Questions to Ask

- I have a pile of pattern blocks. Two-thirds of the blocks are trapezoids. There are one-fourth as many triangles as trapezoids. The remaining shapes are hexagons. How many total shapes are there?

For more good questions, see *Good Questions for Math Teaching: Why Ask Them and What to Ask, Grades 5–8* by Lainie Schuster and Nancy Anderson (Math Solutions 2005).

	My Estimate (%)	Classmate's Estimate (%)	Measured (%)
Design A	45%	45%	55.5%
Design B	49%	50%	47.5%
Design C	50%	32%	50%
Design D	36%	34%	42.75%
Design E	70%	70%	67%
Design F	49%	24%	30.4%

FIGURE 6–12
Maisie's Designs and Recording Sheet.

► REPRODUCIBLE 6.11
Percent Designs
Worksheet

REPRODUCIBLE 6.12
Percent Designs
Recording Sheet

How many of each shape could there be in this pile? Could there be other solutions? How do you know? **Note:** Have the pattern blocks available for each student to manipulate.

■ Marissa is getting a snack for herself and her brother. There are two brownies on the counter. Marissa takes half of one brownie for herself and half of the other brownie for her brother. Marissa's brother complains that Marissa got more. Marissa argues that her brother is nuts! Marissa says that she got one-half and that her brother got one-half. What might the problem be?

■ When pitching the ball, Ryan struck out seven of eighteen batters. Ryan thought about his performance that day on the mound. He thought it would be more accurate to say that he struck out about one-third of the batters than to say he struck out about one-half. Do you agree with Ryan's thinking? Explain your reasoning.

■ Decide whether each decimal number is closest to 0, 0.5, or 1.0. Explain your reasoning.

$$0.6 \qquad 0.15 \qquad 0.976523 \qquad 0.33$$

■ Solve this riddle:

☐   ☐   •   ☐

The mystery number's tens digit is less than its ones digit.
Its tens digit is less than its tenths digit.
Its tenths digit is even.
Its ones digit divided by its tens digit is seven.
The product of the two of its digits is eight.
It only has one even digit.
One of its digits is the sum of the other two digits.
One of its digits is seven.

■ I have twenty-four coins in my pocket.

One-half of the coins are quarters.
One-fourth of the coins are dimes.
One-eighth of the coins are nickels.
One-eighth of the coins are pennies.
How much money do I have in my pocket? How do you know?

■ Annie is a great babysitter. She makes $6.50 an hour. Dava is an even better babysitter. She makes two and a half times more than Annie per hour.

How much does Dava make per hour?
How much more does Dava make than Annie per hour?
How many hours does Annie need to babysit before she can equal Dava's pay for two hours of babysitting?

■ California has twelve letters in its name.

What fraction of the state's name is made up of vowels?
Write the above fraction as a decimal.
What percent of the state's name is made up of consonants?
What fraction of the state's name is made up of the letter a?
What percent of the state's name is made up of the letter c?
Write the above percentage as a decimal.

■ Mrs. Dunne posed a challenge to each fifth-grade class. If the students in a class read a projected number of books, they would receive a week with no homework! Maddie said that her class had reached three-eighths of its goal—the students had read ninety books! Joey was convinced that *his* class had also reached three-eighths of its goal—the students had read one hundred and fifty books! What's the deal? How can both students be convinced that their classes have both reached three-eighths of their book goals when the numbers of books read are different?

Calculation Routines and Practices

Too often students perform operational procedures with fractions and decimals by applying memorized algorithms or expected routines with limited conceptual understanding. When they apply *rule-driven* algorithms, they pay little attention to the meaning of the operation or to the meaning of the quantities involved. Without conceptual understanding, students can easily become inflexible about applying rules and algorithms. They become more focused on following the steps rather than on the reasonableness of their procedures and solutions. When our instruction offers opportunities for students to add and subtract fractions and decimals in meaningful problem-solving contexts, they will explore, develop, test, and apply strategies. Keeping in mind that efficient computational methods are important, you can implement instructional decisions that support and develop both conceptual and procedural understanding.

> **TEACHER-TO-TEACHER TALK** ■ **About Instructional Decisions** ■ Standardized testing looms large before all of us, no matter what state, district, or school (see the "Assessment" section of this chapter for continued discussion of high-stakes testing). As you consider problems and tasks that require calculation and symbolic manipulation, be mindful of your national and state standards as well as district guidelines. For example, the NCTM Focal Points suggest an emphasis on "...developing an understanding of and fluency with addition and subtraction of fractions and decimals" in their grade 5 recommendations. Because we use a standards-based prescribed curriculum in my school, fortunately I can and do use the Focal Points as a point of reference. Each year I have a few parents who feel that multiplication and division of fractions and decimals should also be on our mathematical menu. I often refer these well-intentioned but overzealous parents to the NCTM website. I also refer them to the scope and sequence of our text, which makes no mention of the multiplication and division of rational numbers. The study of fractions, decimals, and percents needs to be revisited over several years, which is the goal of almost every middle grades math curriculum. I also remind parents that my goal is to encourage and support their students as they add and subtract with number sense. I want students to assess the problem first and then determine how and why to proceed with a strategy—and those strategies may not look like the ones used by their parents, but can be equally efficient and accurate. Calculating and generalizing about calculations with number sense and understanding is not asking students to learn less, but asking them to learn more (Fosnot and Dolk 2002, 106).

Equivalence

Learning to add and subtract rational numbers requires that students understand the idea of equivalence and how fractions and decimals can be represented as equivalent forms. Moving flexibly from fraction to fraction, decimal to decimal, fraction to decimal, or decimal to fraction requires repeated experiences within which to apply, practice, and discuss understandings and strategies. Minilessons on common factors and common multiples as students manipulate equivalent fractions or move from fractions to equivalent representations of decimals may be helpful and necessary to support the connections between new expectations and previously covered material. It never hurts to remind students of the interrelatedness of mathematics—and how and why to use and apply what they already know and understand to what they do not!

Importance of Models

As students work to make sense of concepts and procedures while exploring problems with fractions, decimals, and percents, models continue to be increasingly important. Our students must develop representational fluency that makes sense to them within the contexts of problems and investigations. When used effectively, models can move from those *of* thinking to those *for* thinking (Fosnot and Dolk 2002, 74).

Models for Addition and Subtraction

Early experiences with the addition and subtraction of fractions should be linked to models and their related symbolic representations. Initial explorations can be problem based and require an informal manipulation of fractional concepts and procedures. The teacher should make models such as the fraction kit accessible and available during these initial investigations. Various models can offer visual grounding and support as students manipulate fractions and solve problems. Keep in mind that it is extremely important for students to choose and use models that make sense to them within the context of the problems. (See Figure 6–13.)

The following problem, or something similar, offers a context for students to apply what they already know about fractions as they create a model of the problem and its solution:

> *Marissa and Caroline ordered a pizza. They agreed to order the following toppings: cheese, pepperoni, onions, and mushrooms. The girls asked that $\frac{1}{4}$ of the pizza be cheese, $\frac{3}{16}$ of the pizza be pepperoni, and $\frac{3}{8}$ of the pizza be onions. How much of the pizza will be mushrooms?*

After you pose and discuss the problem, ask students to work with a partner to determine how much of the pizza will be mushrooms. Ask each student to represent the problem with a model and an equation. Because my students are very comfortable with the fraction kit model, I choose fractions that are available in their kits. Common denominators are not necessary when working with models, which is one of the many benefits

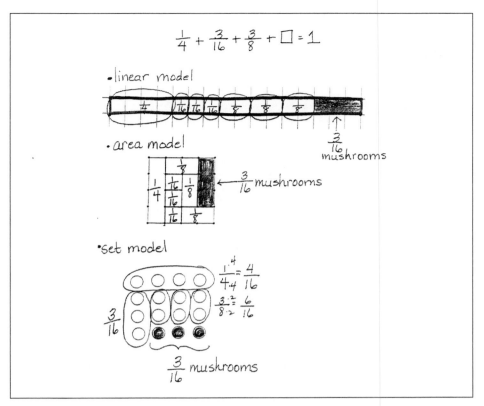

FIGURE 6–13
Solutions Applying Various Models.

of working with them. You can also represent these particular fractions with other models that can be shared in a whole-class discussion following the completion of the task.

This particular problem can be represented with addition or subtraction—another deliberate instructional decision. When we present problems as either *addition* or *subtraction*, we limit our students' awareness and understanding of the relationships between the two operations. This particular problem can be modeled as both:

$$\frac{1}{4} + \frac{3}{16} + \frac{3}{8} + \square = 1$$

$$1 - \left(\frac{1}{4} + \frac{3}{16} + \frac{3}{8}\right) = \square$$

Caroline loved the open number-line model and developed a strategy to help her subtract fractions. What impressed me the most about Caroline's strategy was her ability to apply what she already knew about whole-number subtraction to our work with fractions. Caroline was also aware that regrouping was required in a problem such as this, and she preferred to manipulate equivalent forms and add rather than regroup and subtract.

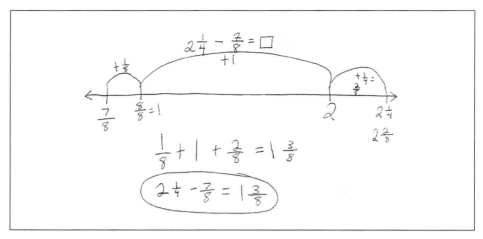

FIGURE 6–14
Caroline's Representation of $2\frac{1}{4} - \frac{7}{8} = 1\frac{3}{8}$.

This strategy demonstrated a deep understanding of addition and subtraction, equivalence, and the ability to move flexibly between equivalent forms. (See Figure 6–14.)

Models for the addition and subtraction of decimals should be equally available and accessible. If students have built decimal numbers with base ten blocks, you will find that many will quickly apply this model when exploring the addition and subtraction of decimals. When models are applied and discussed, the "line up the decimal points then add or subtract" rule becomes a generalization grounded in their understanding of why and how equivalence and regrouping works with the addition and subtraction of decimals. (See Figure 6–15.)

Standard Notation

As students solve and make physical and mental models of problems involving rational numbers, the symbolic representation of their thinking, their generalizations, and their strategies need to be available and explicit. The ability to model a problem with standard notation is yet another aspect of representational fluency—and an important one! Recording the number models on the board as students discuss solutions and share strategies will offer them accessibility to the symbolic representation of the mathematics as well as access to others' thinking. I vary my recording—sometimes I present the problem vertically—sometimes horizontally. Many textbooks present fraction and decimal addition and subtraction vertically. I have found that vertically presented problems encourage a more traditional approach to calculation, whereas a horizontal approach appears to open up the thinking and approach to a problem.

FIGURE 6–15
Addition and Subtraction Models with Base Ten Blocks.

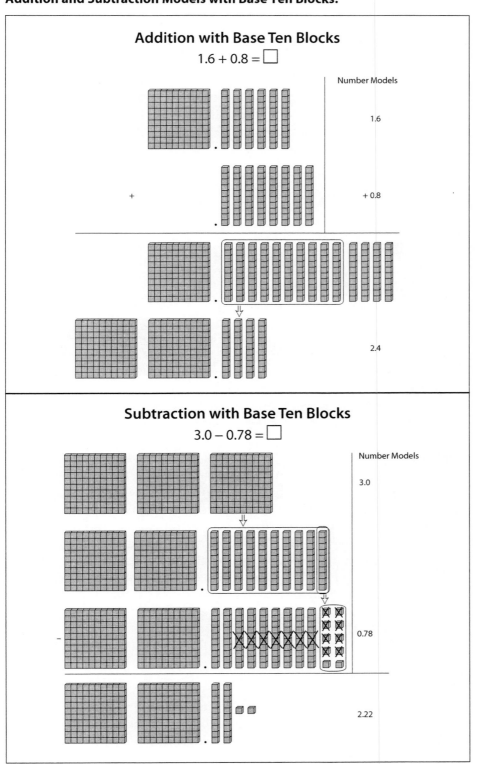

$$3\tfrac{3}{5}$$
$$-1\tfrac{5}{6}$$
$$\implies \qquad 3\tfrac{3}{5} - 1\tfrac{5}{6} = \square$$

$$5.3$$
$$-0.76$$
$$\implies \qquad 5.3 - 0.76 = \square$$

Presenting notation horizontally also promotes the use and understanding of place value, particularly with decimal notation. I also ask my students to place a zero in the ones place for all decimals less than one when recording decimal numbers. Such a simple request can move students to a deeper understanding of the value of zero—both figuratively and literally!

Reading, Writing, and Vocabulary

Reading is the process of constructing meaning from written language. Reading is thinking. Furthermore, readers interact with what they read. They do not passively *receive* its meaning, they *construct* it (Hyde 2006, 5). When fifth graders read, they make meaning personal. When fifth graders *mathematize*, they need to do the same—make meaning personal.

So what has reading research taught us about mathematics? A lot. Research and classroom experience continually remind us that mathematics texts are dense. They contain more concepts per sentence and paragraph than any other type of text (Kenney 2005, 11). Each sentence contains a great deal of information with little redundancy. The text can contain words as well as numeric and nonnumerical symbols to decode. It may also contain graphics that need to be understood for the text to make sense.

Because of the requirements and expectations of mathematical reading, comprehending multipart questions can be difficult for some students. And as students move up through the grades, there may be less mathematical reading instruction, if any, because of the content and pacing demands of the yearly curriculum. If students are expected to interact with mathematical text as they read, answer questions, and solve problems, then it is to all of our benefit to have the strategies and scaffolding available to support and develop these necessary skills.

Tagging

As students read multistep questions, have them *tag* important words and phrases. Underlining or light circling will do the trick. Several years ago, the father of one of my students was working with his daughter at home. He encouraged her to tag the parts of the question (see below) with circled numbers so that she would not miss any parts of it. This worked well for Sophie, who was, by the way, an exceptional mathematical thinker. I realized that this strategy not only helped those who needed help in decoding and comprehending a multistep question, but also helped the stronger students align their thinking with what was asked in the question.

> Jacob and Jason went fishing in the Swift River. They each caught one fish. Jacob's fish was $\frac{5}{8}$ of a foot long and Jason's was $\frac{2}{3}$ of a foot long. Who caught the <u>longer</u> fish?① How do you know?②

KWC Charts

In his book *Comprehending Math: Adapting Reading Strategies to Teach Mathematics, K–6* (2006), Arthur Hyde presents a graphic organizer he has labeled a KWC chart for solving story problems. The KWC chart is similar to the KWL chart used in reading, which can activate schema to make sure students have the necessary knowledge they need *before* they read.

What do I know? (K)	What do we want to know? (W)	What have we learned after reading? (L)

Hyde's KWC chart does the same. It presents a structure for students to front-load information prior to solving a problem. It allows them to identify what they know for sure (K), what they are being asked to find out (W), and the constraints or special conditions of the problem (C).

What do I *know* for sure? (K)	*What* am I trying to find out? (W)	Are there any special *conditions*? (Special rules? Constraints? Things to remember?) (C)

Having KWC charts available (see Reproducible 6.15) or asking students to construct them in their math notebooks prior to solving a problem can offer significant support to all students of all mathematical abilities as they begin to solve a problem. This process can help our students distinguish between the *literal information* and *inferential meaning* of a story problem. Identifying which is which is critical in the comprehension of a story problem. Some students do not read much of the text of a story problem,

▶ REPRODUCIBLE 6.15
KWC Chart for
Problem Solving

KWC Chart for Problem Solving		
What do I *know* for sure?	*What* am I trying to find out?	Are there any special *conditions*? (Special rules? Constraints? Things to remember?)
Jacob's fish → $\frac{5}{8}$ of a foot Jason's fish → $\frac{2}{3}$ of a foot	who caught the longer fish? $\frac{5}{8}$ ◯ $\frac{2}{3}$	denominators are not the same LCM of 8 & 3 → 24

FIGURE 6–16
Brett's KWC Chart for the Tagged Problem on Page 309.

while others read selectively and make inferences without realizing that they are doing so. The KWC chart grounds the student in the literal information presented by the problem—an entry point for all students. (See Figure 6–16.)

The KWC chart also gives students a framework with which to define the task—understanding exactly what it is that you are being asked to do. Spending the initial time to define the task and front-load information is time well spent. There is always a danger in assuming one knows what the problem is and offering what could be a correct answer but to the wrong question!

Modeling these two strategies in whole-class formats is extremely helpful. Using a document camera to illustrate your tagging as well as thinking out loud as you prepare to answer a question will allow your students to *see* your thinking and preparation. Observing you complete a KWC chart as you think aloud through the process does the same.

When good structures are in place for comprehending and solving story problems, the content and context become meaningful. Our students then become more motivated to pay attention, reason, and persevere as they read, comprehend, and work through mathematical text.

Assessment

The assessment of proficiency with rational numbers on standardized tests looms large for fifth graders . . . and their teachers! Because of this, early in the school year you need to familiarize yourself with the standardized test that your students will be taking. Taking the time to review the concepts being tested and the format in which those questions may be presented will help you coordinate your instruction to fit the needs of teaching mathematics with meaning and preparing your students to test well.

In *This Is Only a Test: Teaching for Mathematical Understanding in an Age of Standardized Testing*, Nancy Litton and Maryann Wickett (2009) write about computation proficiency and expectations on standardized tests. They remind us that to do well on these tests, students must know much more than computational procedures and memorized basic facts and rules (Litton and Wickett 2009, 29). It is also interesting to notice that most state tests do not require traditional algorithms. What they do require is making sense of a problem and identifying or constructing a solution. The good mathematics instruction that you offer throughout the year is going to enable and empower your students to think through and model many of the test items and problems.

The Massachusetts Comprehensive Assessment System (MCAS 2009), for example, offers multiple-choice as well as open-response questions—an important piece of information to know about your particular state test as you think about and prepare for instruction. The following open-response question was presented in the release of sample test questions for grade 5 (MCAS 2009):

Question 13 is an open-response question.

- *Be sure to answer and label all the parts of the question.*
- Show all your work (diagrams, tables, or computations) in your Student Answer Booklet.
- If you do the work in your head, explain in writing how you did the work.

Ms. Hendricks asked her students how they get to school each day. She collected their answers and determined the following results.

- *Half of her students take the bus.*
- $\frac{1}{5}$ *of her students walk.*
- *The rest of her students ride with their parents.*

A. *What percent of the students take the bus?*

B. *What percent of the students walk? Explain how you know your answer is correct.*

C. *What percent of the students ride with their parents? Show or explain how you got your answer.*

This particular question poses some interesting instructional and conversational opportunities. Comprehending what is being asked by the question is paramount. Students may jump to identifying possible class sizes by number. Is this a class of thirty students, or forty? However, the more important question here is *what is being asked* of students by the problem. Are we *really* being asked how many students are in the class? This is a question that asks students to connect concepts and to be flexible in their thinking about all three forms of rational numbers: fractions, decimals, and percents. This is actually a very good question— and in reality, one to which many fifth graders should have access. That said, the understanding of the language and vocabulary of the question is crucial. Those students who struggle with the language of mathematics will find this question difficult. Knowing who those students are and intervening with problems such as this prior to the test may be necessary.

The following question is a released sample multiple-choice question (MCAS 2009):

Which point on the number line below best represents the location of 10.2?

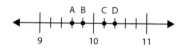

A. *point A*
B. *point B*
C. *point C*
D. *point D*

Again, the ability to connect and be flexible with various forms of rational numbers is what is being assessed in this question, not just the ability to calculate. If you provide your students with the opportunities to think about problems in ways that make sense to them throughout the year, they can apply their own methods for solving problems on their respective state tests (Litton and Wickett 2009, 18).

Home and School Connections

Once again, I create a Parent Information and Involvement Form and distribute it to parents prior to beginning our study of rational numbers to help parents support their children at home. (See Figure 6–17.)

As standardized testing dates draw near, you may also want to consider an additional piece of parent communication that can be attached to the Parent Information and Involvement Form or sent home in a separate delivery. Crafting a letter to parents offering specific information

FIGURE 6–17
Parent Information and Involvement Form: February/March.

▶ REPRODUCIBLE 2.16
Parent Information
and Involvement
Form

Parent Information and Involvement Form

From: Lainie Schuster
Re: Mathematical Curriculum
Unit: Fractions, Decimals, and Percents

During the next unit, the major topics we will be studying are:

- rational numbers: fractions, decimals, and percents

My goal in studying these topics is for the students to be able to:

- interpret various models relating to the representation of fractions, decimals, and percents
- develop strategies and "ways of thinking" when dealing with fractions, decimals, and percents
- develop meaning through problem-solving situations and meaningful contexts
- interpret fractions as parts of a whole:
  - fractions as measures or quantities
  - fractions as indicated division
  - fractions as decimals
  - fractions as percents

Please note: "Formal" procedural manipulations (such as adding, subtracting, multiplying, and dividing) *will not* be addressed in this unit.

Parents can help at home by:

- talking about rational numbers in everyday use: measurement, cooking, effort, grade reporting, and so on
- encouraging students to use what they learned in class to work through homework questions and tasks
- checking out the fraction kit; students can use these throughout the unit at any time
- not teaching your children tricks to find common denominators and equivalent fractions, please; what worked for us may not work for them! It is very important that your children develop their *own* understandings and even their own "tricks," if you will!
- being supportive: this is a long and important unit; it may take us eight to ten weeks to cover the unit

about the test and testing period can help them to better understand and support your efforts in the classroom. (See Figure 6–18.) When we enlist the help and support of parents in creating a positive attitude and approach toward the upcoming testing, everyone benefits. My yearly letter is based on the parent letter presented in *This Is Only a Test: Teaching for Mathematical Understanding in an Age of Standardized*

FIGURE 6–18
Parent Letter About Testing in the Classroom.

Dear Grade 5 Parent(s),

On Monday of next week we will begin standardized testing. The testing will be held in the first two periods of each day and will continue for the week. Testing will continue the Monday and Tuesday of the following week as well. Please help us out by making sure your child comes to school rested and having had a nutritious breakfast each morning. Expect your child to be tired at the end of the school day, and please consider cutting back on extracurricular activities during the testing period.

Throughout the school year, we have addressed test-taking skills. We have had discussions about using reasoning and estimation skills to eliminate possible answers in a multiple-choice format. We have also had conversations about using generalizations and what we know about classes of numbers to further eliminate incorrect answers. For example, if a problem such as $36 \times 88 = \square$ is posed, you can eliminate all odd possible products because we know that an even number times an even number will result in an even product. I have also encouraged students to use their scratch paper to diagram or chart problems so that a visual representation of the problem is available to them.

A lot has been done in class and in homeroom discussions to make this a positive experience. I have encouraged students to think deeply and support their ideas in oral and written form. In these past few weeks, the emphasis has been on how much students have learned throughout the year and on assuring them that this testing process will allow them to show at least some of their growth over these past months.

We do take the time to review questions of interest after each section. You might wish to ask your child about those questions or those class discussions. There have been those times when none of us agree about the "correct" answer . . . and that tells you something right there about the nature of standardized tests!

Remember that a test score is only a snapshot of your child's success, proficiency, and growth. Multiple-choice tests do not allow students to explain their thinking or why they have made a particular choice. A standardized test cannot measure many kinds of intelligences. Please feel free to contact me if you have any questions when you receive your child's scores.

Thank you for your continued support and understanding.

Assessingly yours,

Lainie Schuster

Lainie Schuster

Testing (Litton and Wickett 2009, 121–22). Keep in mind that only you can decide how best to communicate with your parents. You may find it necessary to tweak your correspondence a bit from year to year given the culture of your class. By this time in the year, you know and understand them well. That knowledge and understanding can and should be apparent in your message.

Resources

About Teaching Mathematics: A K–8 Resource, Third Edition (Burns 2007)

The "Fractions" chapter offers rich activities and whole-class lessons. The creation of the fraction kit is presented in detail.

Math Matters: Understanding the Math You Teach, Grades K–8, Second Edition (Chapin and Johnson 2006)

Chapter 5: Fractions
This chapter provides excellent descriptions of the multiple meanings of fractions, with emphasis on conceptual development of the part/whole interpretation of fractions and equivalence in elementary school instruction. It also offers discussion on models of the addition and subtraction of fractions.

Chapter 6: Decimals
This chapter offers excellent descriptions of the concepts and procedures required in understanding and manipulating decimals.

Chapter 7: Percents
This chapter provides excellent narration on the meaning of percent and how to scaffold beginning understandings.

Beyond Pizzas and Pies, Grades 3–5 (McNamara and Shaughnessy 2010)
This valuable resource addresses common misunderstandings children have about fractions. The authors offer classroom strategies and activities to address each misconception.

Teaching Arithmetic: Lessons for Extending Fractions, Grade 5 (Burns 2003b)

Marilyn Burns offers games, investigations, problem-solving activities, classroom anecdotes, narration, and insights in this must-have resource. This set of lessons focuses on the continued development of naming, ordering, and comparing fractions, but it also offers activities supporting the addition and subtraction of fractions with meaning. Every time I open this book, I continue to be amazed at the density of all it has to offer!

Teaching Arithmetic: Lessons for Decimals and Percents, Grades 5–6 (De Francisco and Burns 2002)

The authors offer games, investigations, problem-solving activities, classroom anecdotes, narration, and insights that are designed to help students make sense of decimal and percent application in math and science. This resource provides lessons that will support students as they learn to relate decimals to fractions and percents.

Young Mathematicians at Work: Constructing Fractions, Decimals, and Percents (Fosnot and Dolk 2002)

This book is an overview of how children construct meaning and understanding within the contexts of fractions, decimals, and percents. It presents student vignettes and excellent narration of topics such as the big ideas of rational numbers, mathematical models, and assessment.

This Is Only a Test: Teaching for Mathematical Understanding in an Age of Standardized Testing (Litton and Wickett 2009)

This superb resource offers guidance in planning instruction that takes testing into account while focusing on understanding, meaning, and a love of mathematics. One of the very best resources on standardized testing I have come across.

Comprehending Math: Adapting Reading Strategies to Teach Mathematics, K–6 (Hyde 2006)

This resource shows how to adapt some of the most effective reading comprehension strategies to the study of mathematics. It explains the KWC chart and discusses many examples of its use. This is an unusual and important resource because it is as well researched and supported by best practice in the reading field as it is applicable to the work we do in mathematics.

Chapter 7

Geometry and Measurement

Then they start on turns. First, a ninety-degree turn. Left, then right. Then forty-five-degree turns. Then about face turns. Zinkoff cannot seem to get the hang of it. He's okay with either one: He can march without playing, or play without marching. But when he tries to put them together he marches into parked cars, the bike rack, his fellow marchers. It's like bumper cars at the fair. On his worst day he runs into the tuba and bloodies his nose and is told to go home. But he doesn't give up, and nobody tells him not to come back.

Loser
Spinelli 2002, 167

The Learning Environment

Acknowledge and Celebrate Effort

Putting forth effort in and out of class is a habit of mind that every child can develop. Our students need to realize the importance of this approach to thinking and learning. By speaking openly and directly about necessity of the "three Ps"—practice, patience, and persistence—we can help to make our expectations explicit through in-class discussions. It is equally important to be aware of the difference between effort and achievement. One does not necessarily beget the other! Assessing effort relies on our understanding of our students as learners. In these times of high-stakes testing and, at times, questionable external expectations, the student who consistently puts forth his very best in class day in and day out can often be overlooked. We cannot afford for that to happen.

Provide Opportunities for Children to Identify and Articulate Connections between Concepts, Skills, and Procedures

Arthur Hyde, primary author of *Understanding Middle School Math: Cool Problems to Get Students Thinking and Connecting* (Hyde, Friedlander, Heck, and Pittner 2009), reminds us of the need to aggressively promote connections between concepts and procedures in mathematics because few curricular programs do (61). We need to be deliberate with our instruction and in our mathematical conversations as we help our fifth graders make connections between concepts, skills, and procedures. When mathematics is viewed as a coherent whole, we all seek out those connections that make the study and subsequent understanding of new material meaningful. Questions such as the following can help students connect what they already know to that which they are learning:

- How is this like . . . ?
- Where have you seen this before?
- How can you compare this with . . . ?
- How can knowing this help you to understand . . . ?

The Mathematics and Its Language

Children Develop Meaningful Strategies and Skills for Measurement

Learning to measure is crucial. To measure, a student needs to

- select an attribute of something to be measured (the area of a kitchen, the length of a line, or the volume of a cube);
- choose an appropriate unit of measure (square feet for the kitchen, centimeters for the line, or cubic centimeters for the cube); and
- determine the number of units (120 square feet for the kitchen, 5.5 centimeters for the line, or 125 cubic centimeters for the cube).

Because the measurement process is elusive to so many students, estimating measurements is equally elusive. You need to design the instruction to give students the opportunity to measure! As students become more familiar with and engaged in the process, the more able they will be to estimate measurements and especially those related to our everyday lives.

Children Develop Personal Benchmark Measurements

Benchmarks can help students develop a working familiarity with various units of measure (Chapin and Johnson 2006, 274). Some students may identify the length of a meter as being the distance from the floor to a doorknob, or the weight of a pound as four sticks of butter, or the length of an inch as the distance between two knuckles of a finger. Benchmarks can also help students make sense of how our customary units of measure relate to those of the metric system, such as the following:

A liter is slightly larger than a quart.
An inch is a bit longer than two centimeters.
A meter is a hand width larger than a yard.
A kilogram is a little more than two pounds.
A kilometer is about two-thirds of a mile.

Conversion benchmarks such as the above can temporarily eliminate the need for more formal conversion formulas as students estimate and make sense of customary and metric measurements based on their own real-world experiences.

Children Investigate the Relationship Between Three-Dimensional Shapes and Surface Area

As students identify three-dimensional shapes as those whose faces are composed of two-dimensional shapes, they will develop an understanding of geometric decomposition: the taking apart of a shape, analyzing it piece by piece, and putting the analysis together to draw a conclusion (NCTM 2009, 66). This reasoning connects the geometry of the shape with the eventual algebra of the area or volume formula.

Children Explore the Concept of and Strategies for Calculating Area

When you explore area as a measure of *covering*, rather than as a rule or formula, students are better able to estimate, measure, and generalize about area. This idea of covering also helps students make sense of the square units used to measure area. The conservation of area is a difficult concept for many young students, and our fifth graders are no exception! What happens to the area of a shape when it is decomposed or rearranged into a different *looking* shape? Many fifth (and sixth and even seventh) graders will be convinced that the area will change once the shape is rearranged. Using color tiles or grid paper as measuring units helps move students to a greater understanding of the conservation of area. As students manipulate tiles, shapes, and numbers, they will begin to develop strategies for calculating area based on their understanding of the concept of area rather than on an applied rule or formula. Even though these formulas are helpful, it is preferable to introduce and apply them as students discover them.

Children Explore the Difference Between Area and Perimeter

Our students need to understand the distinction between length (perimeter) and area. Investigations involving fixed areas or perimeters can help students make sense of how one may or may not affect the other. Because fifth graders have had some experience with perimeter and area in earlier grades, they can now explore and generalize about how the two measurements are related. These investigations can be a source of disequilibrium for students as they work to make generalizations about the effects of one measurement on the other. Concrete manipulations, models, organizing collected data, and meaningful class discussions can help them to think beyond assumed generalizations.

Children Explore the Concept of and Strategies for Calculating Volume

When the class explores volume as a measure of *filling*, rather than as a rule of formula, students are better able to estimate, measure, and generalize about volume. Using unit cubes as they fill containers can help students mentally organize the measurement as a model of layers rather than a model of outside faces. As students manipulate containers, cubes, and numbers, they will begin to develop strategies for calculating volume based on their understanding of the concept rather than on an applied rule or formula. As in the study of area, these formulas are certainly helpful, but are better introduced and applied as they are discovered.

Children Develop Proficiency in Manipulating Both the English and Metric Systems of Measurement

Our students must become proficient in using both the English system, also known as the U.S. Customary system, and the metric system of measurement. They will use English units in their daily measurement tasks and the metric system units in science. Unfortunately, the relationships between units are quite different between systems, but important to understand nevertheless. In order to prepare our students for the demands of future mathematics and science, we must offer opportunities that require our students to measure with and manipulate both systems of measurement.

Children Solve Problems Requiring Them to Measure and to Collect, Analyze, and Interpret Measurement Data

Our students need many and varied experiences with length, area, perimeter, and volume in order to make sense of these measurements. Measurement tasks should require students to estimate, make comparisons and generalizations, do mental math, and use number sense. There is no substitution for hands-on measurement tasks. Our students need to measure. They can then organize, analyze, and interpret the collected data to solve posed problems.

TEACHER-TO-TEACHER TALK ■ **About Standards and Expectations** ■ NCTM's *Focal Points* and the *Common Core State Standards* have quickly become a reference for my curriculum planning, instructional decisions, and discussions with administrators and parents. The *Focal Points* are not presented as discrete topics to be taught and checked off, but rather as a cluster of related knowledge, skills, and concepts (NCTM 2009, 2). The *Focal Points* recommend the following for Geometry, Measurement, and Algebra:

(Continued)

> Describing three-dimensional shapes and analyzing their properties, including volume and surface area.
>
> The Common Core State Standards (2010) also offer a set of focused standards that aim for clarity, coherence, and specificity. They, too, suggest a focus on volume. The Common Core State Standards recommend instruction in which students explore and understand the concept of volume. These standards also suggest instruction that supports students in understanding how the measurement of volume relates to multiplication and addition.
>
> This is the reason that I focus my instruction during this month primarily on surface area and volume. As with every unit we teach, it is crucial that we are aware of our state and district standards and expectations. The arithmetic and mathematical reasoning involved in exploring area and volume is rich. Students are able to access prior knowledge and understandings as they make sense of new concepts and procedures. They then work on activities that encourage solving problems, constructing generalizations, and developing strategies that make sense to them. Being aware of standards and expectations, as well as the mathematics embedded in tasks and topics, will help you to make decisions that not only will support the needs of your students, but also the administrative needs of your school, district, and state.

Lesson Planning

- Collecting, developing, and archiving a plethora of meaningful measurement lessons will become an invaluable resource. As you speak with colleagues and peruse through math and science journals, be on the lookout for those tasks that are rich in both measurement and number opportunities. Finding tasks that rely on a student's ability to relate and apply number and operational sense to measuring and collected measurement data can be beneficial for everyone. Once you have identified your state and district standards for measurement and geometry, you may find other activities in sources outside of your prescribed text that better fit your needs and the needs of your students. *Sizing Up Measurement: Activities for Grades 3–4 Classrooms* (Confer 2007; see also the "Resources" section of this chapter) is an excellent place to start.

- Do you remember learning stations? Learning stations or centers are a wonderful venue for small groups of students to become experts on a specific measurement topic. Because measurement is so often ignored in elementary math classrooms, you may have fifth graders who are not aware of the nuances, units, and tools used in measuring length, weight, capacity, volume, and time. Having small groups of students assigned to one measurement station to complete a series of tasks, and then to organize, present, and share collected data with the class can raise awareness and understanding of specific measures. Although creating stations initially can be time intensive for you, the implementation of such an undertaking will take up fewer class periods, giving you more time to focus on the big ideas of area and volume. See *A Month-to-Month Guide: Fourth Grade Math* (Schuster 2008; see also the "Resources" section of this chapter) for a write-up of possible learning stations.

- Please require students to use measurement labels in oral and written communication and representation. When speaking about area, are we speaking of square inches, square centimeters, or square yards? When speaking about volume, are we speaking of square or cubic units? When speaking about length, does *sixty-seven* refer to inches, meters, or miles? I love the word *aardvark* (I think it is the double *a* that does it for me), so the running joke in my class is that if no unit is identified, then we must be measuring in aardvarks!

- Be aware of measurement in the world around you. Measurement is directly related to and visible in the world in which we live. Engage and challenge your students to look for measurement in all that they (or their parents) do in a day or on a weekend. Creating a bulletin board or running list on chart paper to keep posting to throughout the month can keep us all aware of the important work that we are doing.

- Have measurement references available at all times. Many textbooks will have measurement conversion tables available on the front or back cover. You may find one in another resource that you like better. Reproduce it, laminate it, and have students place it in their math notebooks or folders for reference.

Possible Difficulties or Misconceptions

Many students will struggle with articulating and identifying the difference between area and perimeter. These are two very big concepts in measurement and ones that take time to develop. Be patient. Having a visual model posted in the classroom may give those students a necessary visual reference. (See Figure 7–1.)

The language of measurement is tricky—and important! What is the difference between a centimeter, a square centimeter, and a cubic centimeter? A show-and-tell approach works well as you define and discuss terminology. What does it look like? How is it labeled? And what does it measure? Using a language arts class to discuss the root words and prefixes of metric measurement can be time well spent. Too bad our customary system was not as well thought out!

Many students will struggle with the tools of measurement: rulers, scales, measuring cups, even analog clock faces. In order to investigate measurement, students need to know *how* to measure! A learning stations model (see the "Lesson Planning" section of this chapter) can offer

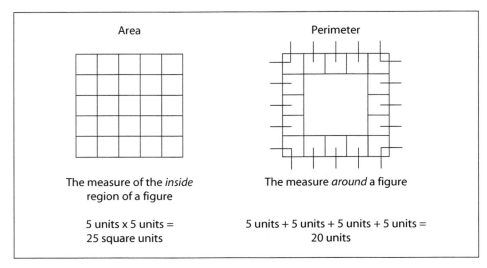

FIGURE 7–1
Class Reference Chart for Area and Perimeter.

measuring opportunities for your students. This may be a time to integrate science instruction into math class if these skills are part of your science curriculum.

Investigations, Games, and Literature-Based Activities

TEACHER-TO-TEACHER TALK ■ **About Area and Perimeter** ■ The relationship between area and perimeter is a tenuous one for adults and children alike. Does knowing one help us to determine the other? If I know that the area of a dog yard is sixty-four square feet, can I determine its perimeter? Interesting question.... And what if my sixty-four-square-foot dog yard starts as a *regular polygon* and then I reconfigure it into an *irregular polygon*: Is the area of that dog yard still sixty-four square feet? Does the perimeter of that new dog yard stay the same as the previous one? Or does it change? I still have to think about these questions...and I know what I am supposed to think! The following two activities, *Area Stays the Same* and *Perimeter Stays the Same*, are important and helpful as our students work to understand the difference and relationship between the two measures. However, be aware that these two activities may not be enough to solidify these ideas for all students. If you present one activity, please present the other. The reality of it is that once you present one, the students are apt to pose the other themselves! The discussions, confusion, and generalizations that develop during and following these two tasks are mathematically rich and significant. Now about that dog yard . . . can a dog yard with an area of sixty-four square feet have several different perimeters? Or just one?

Perimeter and Area Explorations

Duration: 3–5 Class Periods

The following two activities continue to build on students' developing understanding of area and perimeter: what they measure, how they are measured, and how both measures relate to each other. These activities, adapted from *Math by All Means: Area and Perimeter, Grades 5–6* (Rectanus 1997), offer students the opportunities to

- investigate area;
- investigate perimeter;
- investigate fixed area and how it is related to perimeter; for example, shapes with the same area can have perimeters of different lengths;
- investigate fixed perimeter and how it is related to area; for example, shapes with the same length perimeter can have different areas; and
- investigate areas and perimeters of irregular shapes.

Materials: Area Stays the Same

- 1-inch grid paper
- 5-by-5-cm square cut from an index card, several per student
- 36-inch pieces of string, several per pair of students
- 12-by-18-inch piece of white construction paper, 1 per pair of students

Materials: Perimeter Stays the Same

- centimeter grid paper
- chart paper

Vocabulary

area, area measurement, contiguous, linear measurement, perimeter, square units

Area Stays the Same

Prior to the lesson, cut 5-by-5-centimeter squares from index cards, several for each student. You will also need to cut thirty-six-inch lengths of string, several for each pair of students. Students will work in pairs as they investigate shapes with the same area (twenty-five square centimeters) but different perimeters.

Holding up the 5-by-5-centimeter square, ask, "What is the *area* of this shape? How do you know?" The multiplication is accessible (five times five) as is counting the centimeters on the square. If students share only one strategy, push them to think of another way to find the area of the square. Then move to, "What is the *perimeter* of this shape? How do you know?"

NCTM Connection

Strand: Geometry, Measurement

Focus: Investigate fixed area and how it is related to perimeter; for example, shapes with the same area can have different-length perimeters.

Context: *Area Stays the Same*

Some fifth graders may not have had prior experience manipulating these two concepts within the same task. Their previous work with area and perimeter may have taken place in isolated lessons, if at all. You may find that some students substitute one word for the other or confuse the two procedures. Referring to a chart that identifies the difference between area and perimeter measurements (as in Figure 7–1) can help those who need the visual support as they identify the area and perimeter measurements of the 5-by-5 square. If you can post the chart in the room as a visual model throughout the unit of study, students can access the information easily if they become confused in the process of cutting, measuring, or writing.

Inform the students that they will be working with a partner as they make two or three cuts of the square. They will then tape the pieces together to make a new shape different from the square. Ask the class for suggestions about how the square could be cut. The cuts may be straight or curved, but *they are not to discard any pieces of the square*. Model how to cut the shape into parts, and then tape the pieces together again to make a new shape. (See Figure 7–2.)

Compare the new shape to another 5-by-5 square. When you ask them about the area of the new shape, most students will agree that it continues to be twenty-five square units. When you ask them about the perimeter, however, students may have differing opinions. Some may assume that the perimeter has stayed the same because the area has stayed the same. Some may argue that the perimeter "looks" longer or shorter than the original square's perimeter.

Asking students how to resolve the question of the perimeter of the new shape will move the discussion to one of measurement and how best to measure this new shape. Once students have had a chance to offer some suggestions, hold up a piece of string and ask, "How could this help me?" They quickly see how the string can be shaped to fit the perimeter. The objective here is to establish which shapes have the longest—or shortest—perimeters. You do not need the actual measurement, which is an interesting concept to some students in itself! I often ask students when estimates of length—or knowing when something is longer or shorter than something else—is enough in everyday life.

On each table, place white construction paper, scissors, tape, a tub of 5-by-5 squares, and a tub of strings. With the help of a volunteer, I model how to cut a shape and then cut a piece of string to the length of the perimeter. By this time, students are used to representing their work in some way. Asking students how they can best compare the perimeters of our shapes can initiate some interesting conversations about the need for standard representation so that we can all look at the same thing. We often agree rather quickly that we need to draw a margin at the top of the construction paper. You can tape the shape in the top margin and then tape the string on the line of the margin. When you post it, the string will hang down the paper (and sometimes off) to identify the length of the perimeter. Students are ready to cut, tape, and compare.

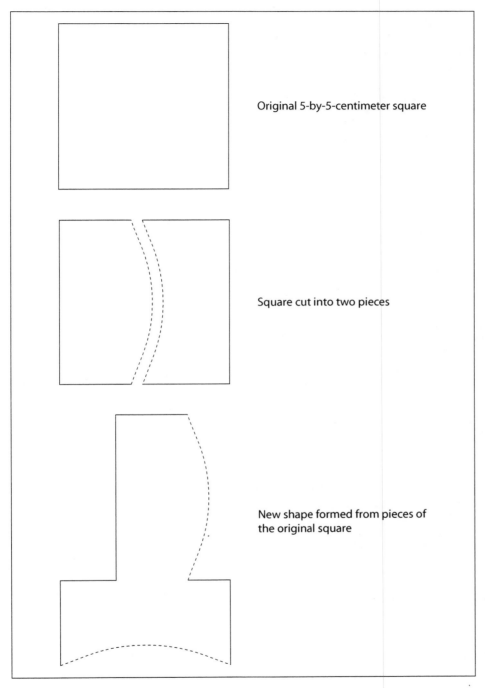

Original 5-by-5-centimeter square

Square cut into two pieces

New shape formed from pieces of the original square

FIGURE 7–2
Cut a Square and Tape the Pieces into a New Shape.

When each pair of students has completed at least three shapes, I ask them to post their papers on the board. Opening up a class discussion with the ever-popular, "What do you notice about our shapes and perimeters?" helps direct the conversation. Many students will initially be surprised that shapes with the same area (twenty-five square centimeters) can have so many different perimeters. And to be honest, at first I was surprised by the variance in perimeters, too! Most likely, students will focus on the shapes with the longest and shortest perimeters. Do you notice anything about these shapes that can help us to make generalizations and predictions about shapes with long or short perimeters?

Making generalizations about why different shapes with the same area could have differing perimeters may be difficult for some. The results of reconfiguring the initial 5-by-5-centimeter square and then predicting and measuring the perimeter of the new shape often contradict students' original expectations. I have learned to be pleased with the generalization that a "longer" or "skinnier" shape will have a longer perimeter and that a "fatter" shape will have a shorter one. This exploration truly opens up the world of mathematical wonder for some students. Most fifth graders begin this investigation with the belief that a defined area will dictate one defined perimeter. What they thought to be true about the relationship between area and perimeter just isn't! As I move around the room watching the students work and listening to the surprise in their observations, I respond, "Makes you wonder, doesn't it?"

You can extend this exploration with the use of color tiles. Ask students to create a rectangular array with a specified number of tiles, say twelve, sixteen, or twenty-four tiles. (Choosing an area with many factor pairs offers greater shape variations.) Ask students to create polygons with differing perimeters but with this same area. Before you calculate the perimeters, ask students to predict whether the perimeter will be a "long" one or a "short" one. Students can re-create their shapes on one-inch grid paper and post them with their perimeters on a class poster entitled, "The Area Stays the Same." You can also mount the original rectangular array and its area measurement at the top of the poster. Using color tiles also helps students further visualize and manipulate the square units used to measure area.

NCTM Connection

Strand: Geometry, Measurement

Focus: Investigate fixed perimeter and how it is related to area; for example, shapes with the same-length perimeter can have different areas.

Context: *Perimeter Stays the Same*

Perimeter Stays the Same

This activity explores the areas of shapes with the same perimeters but differing areas, which is a natural follow-up to the preceding activity in which students explored shapes with the same areas but differing perimeters. Instruct students that they will draw at least three shapes with perimeters of thirty centimeters. Students will use centimeter grid paper to create their shapes. As students construct their shapes, they will need to be reminded to

- stay on the lines of the grid paper; and
- create shapes that are *contiguous* and will remain in one piece when cut out (only corners touching is not allowed).

It will be helpful to model this task for students. Create a shape of your own, labeling its perimeter and area in the center of the shape. The use of slash marks to designate counted sides will help students keep count of their perimeter units. (See Figure 7–3.)

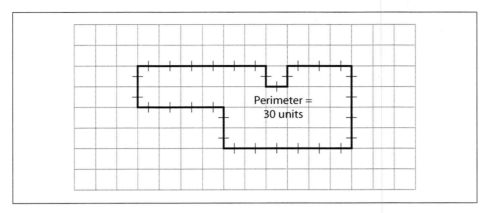

FIGURE 7–3
Model of Shape with a Perimeter of Thirty Centimeters.

Students then work in table groupings as they create their own shapes on centimeter grid paper. Students may do much erasing and redrawing as they use a trial-and-error approach to constructing their shapes. Encourage them to count frequently! The accuracy of the perimeters is necessary for the success of the lesson. Post two charts on the board, one labeled *Greatest Area* and the other labeled *Least Area* while students are working.

When students are ready to process, call them together for the next phase of the exploration. Inform them that they will exchange papers with each other in their table groupings. Ask each student to check another table mate's shapes to be sure that each shape has a perimeter of thirty centimeters. Also ask students to check each other's area measurements. Within their groups, instruct students to examine their shapes and what they notice about the shapes with the same and different areas. Each table group is to cut out the shape with the greatest area and the shape with the least area and post them on the appropriate chart.

Once students have posted the shapes with the greatest and least areas, you can begin a class discussion by asking, "What generalizations can you make about the posted shapes?" Asking students to share their observations with a neighbor before they share as a whole class will offer them opportunities to practice wording their responses. Students will notice that the shorter, fatter shapes have greater areas while the longer, thinner shapes have lesser areas. I often end the discussion with a question about when this generalization would be important to know in everyday life. Gardens and skating ponds tend to come up in my class: I like to garden and my students like to skate!

The relationship between area and perimeter is an interesting one, and one that is more important to explore than to master at this point in a student's mathematical career. These topics and concepts will continue to be explored in greater depth as our students move into their middle school years. At this point, we can expect our fifth graders to generalize that the "fatter" a shape, the smaller its perimeter will be. The "skinnier" the shape, the larger the shape's perimeter will be. If the truth be known, I still have to stop, explore, and think about these relationships each time I present these lessons. And when planning new garden beds, I snicker as I realize that I am once again investigating area and perimeter and what works best for doing what I want or need to do.

REPRODUCIBLE 2.5 ◄
Centimeter Grid
Paper

Dog Yards

Duration: 2–3 Class Periods

Similar to the *Perimeter Stays the Same* task, in this exercise students explore and design different rectangular dog yards using a specified number of feet of fencing. The task offers students writing opportunities as they defend their choice of dog yard. This exploration, adapted from *Sizing Up Measurement: Activities for Grades 3–5 Classrooms* (Confer 2007), offers students opportunities to

- continue to explore area and perimeter and the relationship of one to the other;
- connect previously studied concepts and procedures for identifying and manipulating rectangular arrays and their dimensions (factor pairs) to the study of area and perimeter; and
- defend mathematical positions and decisions in writing.

Materials

- centimeter grid paper, 2 sheets per student and 1 transparency for the class (see Reproducible 2.5)
- *The Dog Who Belonged to No One* (Hest 2008)

Vocabulary

area, constraints, dimensions, length, perimeter, square units, width

An oral reading of *The Dog Who Belonged to No One* (Hest 2008) can set the stage for a lesson asking students to create dog yards for the small dog with crooked ears who belonged to no one.

This activity gives students the opportunity to again bump up against the big idea explored in the *Perimeter Stays the Same*. In this task, students are asked to design different *rectangular* dog yards using exactly thirty-six feet of fencing. Having a grid paper transparency or chart paper can help you make the constraints of the problem clear as you design a few dog yards—some that are OK, and some that are not OK. Modeling rectangular dog beds will also allow you to use hash marks along the perimeter to designate and count each linear unit—in this scenario, feet:

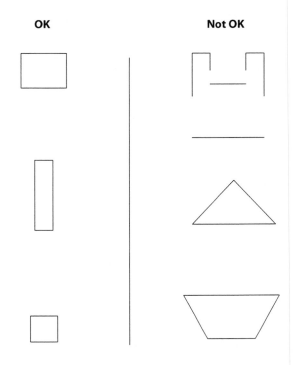

Students can do this task with partners, but each student is required to represent his or her own collection of dog yards. Ask each student to design on grid paper all the possible dog yards that can be made with thirty-six feet of fencing with the following constraints and directives:

- Each dog yard must be a rectangle.
- The dimensions of each dog yard must be labeled.
- Each dog yard must be represented with an equation to prove that each has a perimeter of thirty-six feet.
- Students will choose a dog yard that would be best suited for their dog and explain why. (See Figure 7–4.)

As students begin work on their dog yards, posing questions to small groups of students about the patterns they are seeing or exploring can help to support the representation that a T-chart can offer as students process the task in a whole-group discussion.

It's helpful to have an overhead transparency of centimeter grid paper (see Reproducible 2.5) available to overlay on top of dog yards so that you can prove the areas and perimeters for those students who might want or need the visual.

▶  REPRODUCIBLE 2.5 Centimeter Grid Paper

REPRODUCIBLE 2.5
Centimeter Grid
Paper ◀

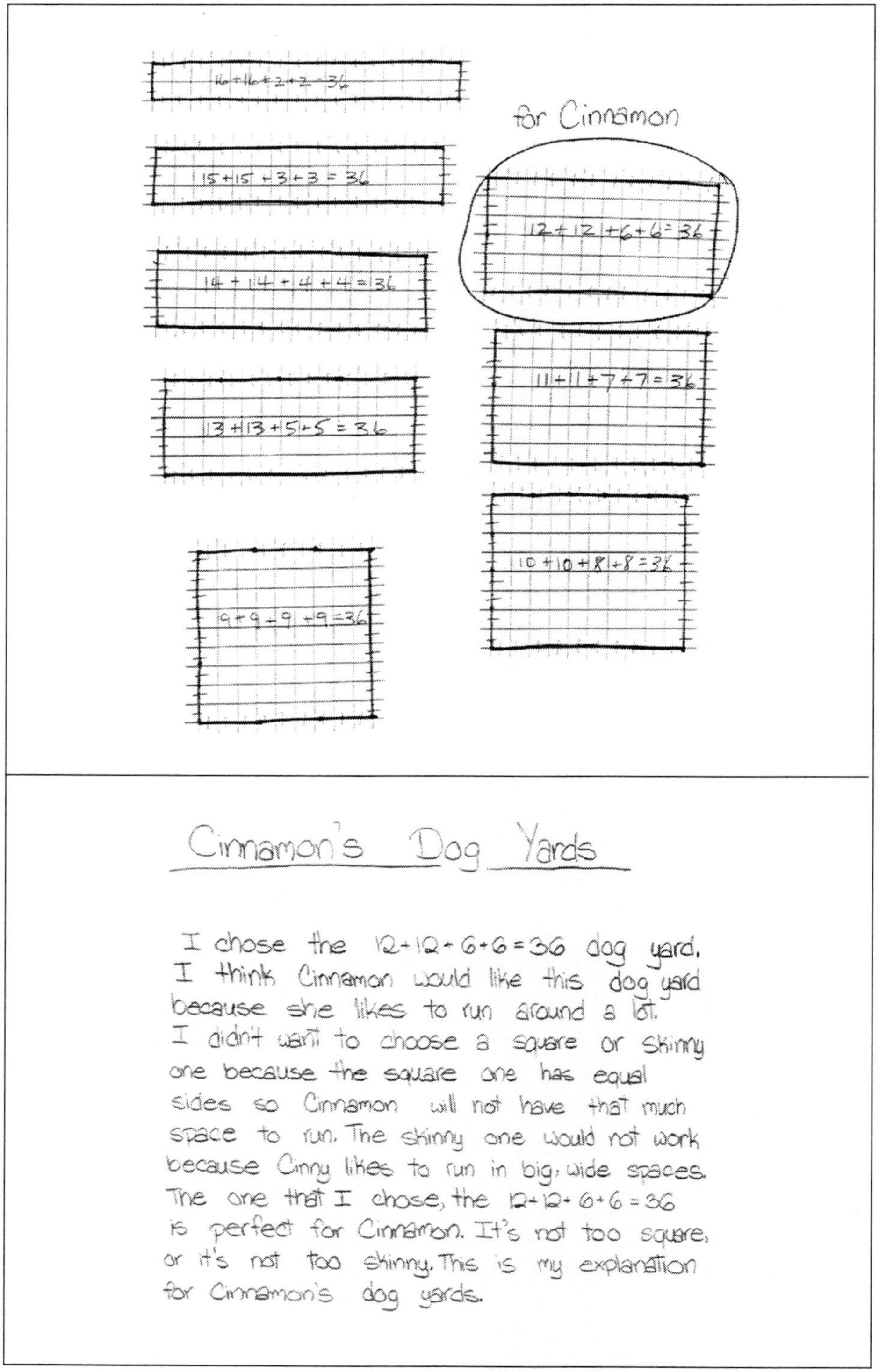

16 + 16 + 2 + 2 = 36

15 + 15 + 3 + 3 = 36

for Cinnamon

12 + 12 + 6 + 6 = 36

14 + 14 + 4 + 4 = 36

11 + 11 + 7 + 7 = 36

13 + 13 + 5 + 5 = 36

10 + 10 + 8 + 8 = 36

9 + 9 + 9 + 9 = 36

Cinnamon's Dog Yards

I chose the 12+12+6+6=36 dog yard.
I think Cinnamon would like this dog yard
because she likes to run around a lot.
I didn't want to choose a square or skinny
one because the square one has equal
sides so Cinnamon will not have that much
space to run. The skinny one would not work
because Cinny likes to run in big, wide spaces.
The one that I chose, the 12+12+6+6=36
is perfect for Cinnamon. It's not too square,
or it's not too skinny. This is my explanation
for Cinnamon's dog yards.

FIGURE 7–4
Lea's Completed Dog Yards and Response.

Width in feet	Length in feet	Total square feet
1	17	17
2	16	32
3	15	45
4	14	56
5	13	65
6	12	72
7	11	77
8	10	80
9	9	81

Posing a question such as, "How can all these dog yards have the same perimeters, but different areas?" can help the students access prior experiences with shapes with the same perimeter but differing areas. I hesitate to suggest that they can access prior knowledge, because this knowledge may be fragile at best. It is confusing! However, it continues to be important for students to use what they learned from those prior experiences to explain what is happening in the T-chart. Asking for a generalization to explain the mathematics in the T-chart can move students to articulating and better understanding that the closer the arrangements are to a square, the larger the area—an important idea that architects and contractors apply to maximize room space for the fewest materials and least cost!

Although most students may choose the 9-by-9-foot dog yard, in order to give a different perspective I share my experiences with my Siberian husky, Maxx, who is a pacer, as most huskies are: A square yard does him no good! My husband and I constructed a dog yard for Maxx that is long and skinny enough to give him more length to pace, but wide enough for a dog house. This year my class decided that with thirty-six feet of fencing, a 5-by-13-foot or 6-by-12-foot yard would be the best for Maxx. He would have plenty of linear feet to pace as well as plenty of room in the middle of the pen for his dog house—*under* which he sleeps!

Covering Polygons: Investigations of Area

Duration: 3–5 Class Periods

Too often, students encounter area through rules and formulas for rectangles and other "friendly" shapes. They may become facile at substituting numbers in formulas, but miss developing a deeper understanding of the concept of area—how it is measured, what the measure means, and how the measure can be used. These activities offer students the opportunities to

- construct and articulate predictions and generalizations about shapes and their areas;
- construct, test, and apply strategies for calculating areas of irregular polygons; and
- represent, organize, compare, and interpret data.

Materials

- Paving Patios, Bear Paw Borders, Criss-Cross, and the Banquet Table Problem directions and recording sheets (see Reproducibles 7.1 through 7.8) (**Note:** Taking the time to reproduce and laminate the directions on larger paper [18-by-24-inch tag board or card stock works well] can save time for use in future years.)
- Menu Exit Slip (see Reproducible 7.9)
- centimeter grid paper, several sheets per student or a stack at each station (see Reproducible 2.5)

Vocabulary

area, irregular polygons, regular polygons, vertex

You can present the following activities in a menu format or as stand-alone lessons. Offering some or all of the tasks in a menu format allows students multiple opportunities to revise, rethink, and apply what they know about area. The menu approach, in which students work independently, has many benefits, including

- solving the problem of what some students do when they finish activities more quickly than others;
- facilitating differentiated instruction by allowing students to work at their own pace;
- allowing students to dig deeper into the mathematics of a particular task; and
- freeing up your time to work with individuals, pairs, and small groups of students who may need your attention.

Because menu items may or may not relate to previous instruction, they need to be introduced carefully so that students understand what is expected of them and are more able to function as independent learners. Reviewing the directions and focus of each menu item will help the students choose tasks carefully. Depending on the group of students, some items can be required and others optional. Posting laminated labels of *Partner* and *Individual* at each station can advise students of the working constraints. (See Figure 7–5; see Reproducibles for directions and materials for each menu item listed.)

NCTM Connection

Strand: Geometry, Measurement
Focus: Calculate areas of irregular polygons.
Context: *Paving Patios*

Paving Patios

This menu item focuses on calculating areas of irregular polygons using grid paper:

> *Patios-R-Us specializes in creating unusual patios for unusual gardens. If each patio tile costs $25.00, what would be the cost of each completed patio design? How would the shape of a patio influence its use?*

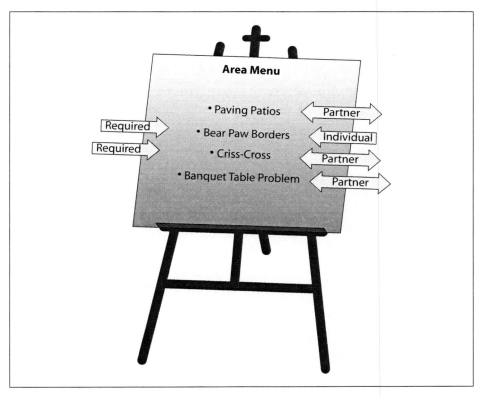

FIGURE 7–5
Master Listing of Menu Items.

Bear Paw Borders

This menu item focuses on calculating and generalizing about the areas of triangles and squares within squares. "The Bear Paw" is a popular quilt pattern, easy to construct because of the simplicity of its shapes.

Study the design of the bear paw quilt block, especially its border. [See Figure 7–6, page 336.] *Identify the polygons in the pattern. If we only have patterns for pieces C and D, how can you make pieces A and B? How do you know that your cuts will be accurate? How are all of the pieces related in area? Construct a bear paw block from cut paper. Label it and describe how you found the area of each piece.*

Criss-Cross

This menu item focuses on predicting, measuring, calculating, and generalizing about the areas of triangles resulting from the partitioning of a rectangle.

Construct two intersecting lines from vertex to vertex on a sheet of white paper. Label the triangles A, B, C, and D. Color A and C one color. Color B and D a different color.

NCTM Connection

Strand: Geometry, Measurement
Focus: Calculate and generalize about the areas of triangles and squares within squares.
Context: *Bear Paw Borders*

NCTM Connection

Strand: Geometry, Measurement
Focus: Predict, measure, calculate, and generalize about the areas of triangles resulting from the partitioning of a rectangle.
Context: *Criss-Cross*

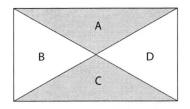

Make a prediction about the areas of the resulting four triangles. Identify the areas of triangles. How do the triangles relate to each other? How do you know? Describe the strategy you used to make your comparisons. What do

FIGURE 7–6
Example from the *Bear Paw Borders* Menu Item.

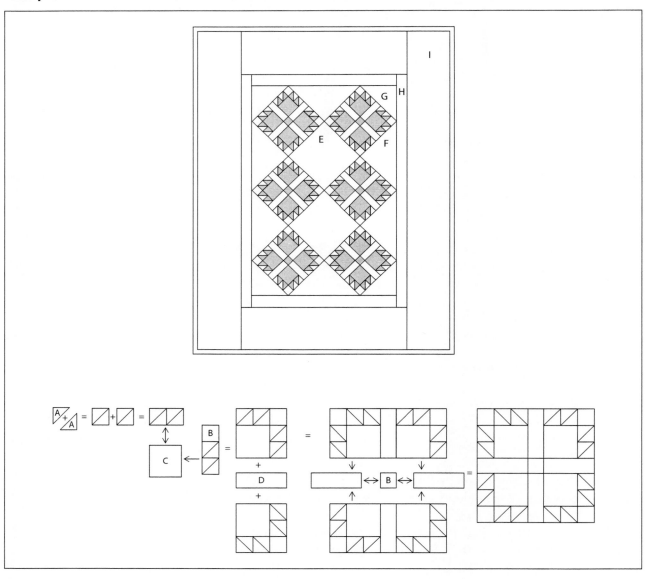

you notice about the sum of the areas of triangles A, B, C, and D and the area of the original rectangular piece of paper?

What will happen and what relationships can you predict about the areas of the resulting triangles if you begin with an 8-by 8-inch square? Try it. What do you notice?

Banquet Table Problem

· This menu item focuses on predicting, calculating, and generalizing about perimeters of growing areas of linear banquet tables.

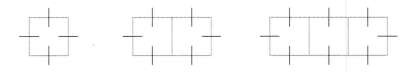

How many people can be seated around one banquet table? How many people can be seated around two tables pushed together? How many people can be seated around three tables pushed together? Four tables? Five tables? Ten tables? Can you predict how many people could be seated around thirty-seven tables? How about one hundred? Represent your thinking in pictures and a T-chart. Can you construct a rule so that we can determine how many people will sit around a banquet table made up of any number of tables pushed end to end? Write your rule in words and symbols.

Giving clear directions by itself will not help students learn to work independently. Devoting time and attention will help to develop and support this desired behavior, especially if it is new to students. You may need to remind students of their responsibilities from time to time as you circulate throughout the room. You may also find it necessary to remind students to refer to the menu directions for additional information about the task.

Students complete Menu Exit Slips (see Reproducible 7.9) once they finish a menu item. These quick-writes give students the opportunity to reflect and assess—and for you to do the same! (See Figure 7–7.)

Processing what students discovered and learned from these particular menu items in a whole-class discussion following the investigations is especially important. Sharing false starts, successes, and insights will deepen students' understanding of calculating and interpreting area measurements. As you pose questions that will help and support students in uncovering the mathematics involved in specific tasks, ask them to share their thinking and opinions with a neighbor before opening up the discussion to the entire class. This practice will give every student the opportunity to articulate and refine their thinking, observations, and generalizations.

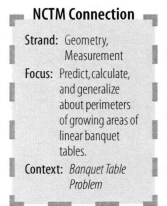

NCTM Connection

Strand: Geometry, Measurement

Focus: Predict, calculate, and generalize about perimeters of growing areas of linear banquet tables.

Context: *Banquet Table Problem*

▶ REPRODUCIBLE 7.9
Menu Exit Slip

REPRODUCIBLE 7.9
Menu Exit Slip ◄

Menu Exit Slip

Name: Nick

Partner: Caroline

Date: April 6

Menu: Area

Activity/Task: Banquet Table Problem

What did you like about the task?
I liked using color tiles and building tables. T-charts are fun—you can get a lot of information from them.

What did you learn from the task?
You can figure out a rule from the T-chart. My rule was $(2 \times \square) + 2 = \triangle$

FIGURE 7–7
Isabelle's Exit Slip for the Banquet Table Problem Menu Item.

Once students have had the opportunity and time to investigate the area measurements of polygons, you can follow this with more formal instruction that will help and support students as they construct rules (formulas) for calculating area from generalizations based on their menu explorations. When rules (formulas) are grounded in understanding and experience, they are easily re-created if forgotten. (See the "Calculation Routines and Practices" section of this chapter for further discussion on area formulas.)

TEACHER-TO-TEACHER TALK ■ **About Orchestrating Menus** ■ My students adore menu time. They relish having a choice of what to do when and how best to proceed. They greatly enjoy working through the tasks with a partner and having the time to talk, compare ideas, and even argue—respectfully, of course! But don't kid yourself, implementing and orchestrating a menu is hard work, as is the implementation and orchestration of any strong instructional tool or task. The preparation for a block period or periods of menu time is done in advance. You cut the paper, create handouts for each station, and prepare menu exit slips. The real work comes as students are working and you are circulating through the room. Your vigilant commitment to helping students make sense of the mathematics of a particular task is what will make menu a worthwhile and meaningful experience. Area formulas will not magically appear (as I thought they did when I was a fifth grader!), but observations and generalizations about calculating area will. It is from these observations and generalizations that formulas will develop. It is our charge to help our students see those connections—to think about those comparisons—and to articulate those generalizations. This *making sense* business is the hard part, but it is the part that moves our students to think like mathematicians and to ground their understanding in what they have explored, discovered, and made their own.

Filling Boxes: Investigations of Volume

Duration: 3–5 Class Periods

While length is one-dimensional and area is two-dimensional, volume describes the space or region of a three-dimensional object or region. These lessons offer students the opportunities to

- construct and articulate predictions and generalizations about objects (boxes) and their volumes;
- explore and generalize how dimensions of a three-dimensional shape can be used to estimate and calculate volume; and
- develop strategies for thinking about and calculating the volume of rectangular and nonrectangular containers.

Vocabulary

cube, cubic units, dimensions, height, layer, length, net, prism, pyramid, width

Whereas the *Covering Polygons* lessons could be offered in a menu format, these two lessons warrant whole-class instruction. The concept of volume—what it is, how is it measured and reported, and how to use it to solve problems—may be new to students. Manipulating three dimensions can be a new challenge for many. Piaget's research reminds us that conservation of volume is the last of the conservation hierarchy (Wadsworth 1971, 83). The ability to conserve volume implies the ability to conserve weight, area, substance (mass), and number. Teaching and learning about volume with meaning requires developmentally appropriate tasks that allow the students to concretely investigate, manipulate, and internalize the concepts presented. Whole-class discussion is necessary to ground these new ideas in the class's collective experience.

Filling Boxes

In order to understand volume, students need to measure volume. In this initial investigation, adapted from *Containers and Cubes: 3-D Geometry: Volume, Grade 5* (Battista and Berle-Carman 1998), pairs of students look at pictures or written descriptions of rectangular boxes (prisms) and predict how many unit cubes will fit inside the boxes. They will then check their predictions by building open-topped boxes and filling them with cubes. Students describe their method for making predictions and determine whether their strategy will always work. (**Note:** You will need many materials that will need to be housed and easily accessible. Each year I borrow plastic bins from a first-grade classroom to keep the materials organized and labeled for each table group. You will need to spend class time reviewing the materials, how and where they are housed, and the guidelines for their use.)

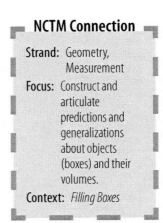

NCTM Connection

Strand: Geometry, Measurement

Focus: Construct and articulate predictions and generalizations about objects (boxes) and their volumes.

Context: *Filling Boxes*

NCTM Connection

Strand: Geometry,
          Measurement
Focus: Explore and
          calculate volume of
          irregular solids.
Context: *The Painted Cube
            Problem*

Materials

- *Nets for Boxes* (see Reproducible 7.10)
- *How Many Cubes?* recording sheet (see Reproducible 7.11)
- *More Boxes to Fill* recording sheet (see Reproducible 7.12)
- *The Painted Cube Problem* (see Reproducible 7.13)
- three-quarter-inch grid paper (see Reproducible 7.14)
- centimeter grid paper (see Reproducible 2.5)
- Snap Cubes, 80 per pair of students (**Note:** It will be necessary to "snap" the cubes together so that the ends are flush.)
- centimeter cubes, 1 tub of 1,000
- container to house completed open-topped boxes, 1 per table group

Open this lesson with a story about a packaging factory, which offers the context for building and filling boxes. This packaging factory makes cardboard boxes of differing sizes for shipping glass ornaments. Each ornament is shipped in its own cube. It is important for students to understand the meaning of *cube*—a prism in which all the faces are congruent squares. This packaging company makes and ships boxes of different shapes and sizes to accommodate the number of ordered ornaments.

Present the first task in a whole-class format with pairs of students working to solve the problem together. The class's first job at the factory is to solve the following problem:

How can you accurately predict how many cubes [hold up one linking cube] will fit in a shipping box of a particular shape and size? Describe your strategy in writing.

Display and discuss the following box-pattern diagrams (see also Reproducible 7.10).

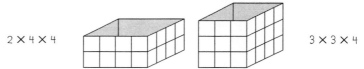

$2 \times 4 \times 4$ $3 \times 3 \times 4$

"Seeing" three-dimensionally may be a challenge for some students. It may take a little time to talk about the two completed box pictures. Asking students to identify the sides of the box, the bottom of the box, and the open top will help to open up this type of visualization.

You can then post the following box pattern:

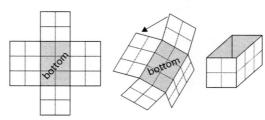

Asking students to identify the bottom of the box and its sides can help to ground their visualization of the model. Cut out and construct the box for the class to observe. Some students may find it helpful to shade or label the bottom of the box. Personally, I find it much easier to reconstruct a pattern by outlining the bottom of the box first, then the sides. I offer this strategy to students, reminding them that this is how *I* see it, which may not be the same way that *they* see it! I encourage students to talk to their partners as they construct their boxes on paper and to identify the bottom of the box and its dimensions as well as the sides.

Once the children have created their boxes, I ask them how many packaged ornaments they think will fit into one box. At this point, students are not permitted to hold their boxes or to count the dimensions of the bottom or side arrays. As they ask to hold the boxes, you can pose the following question: "Why would holding the box help?" Students will quickly agree that they want to identify the dimensions of the bottom or sides. Some students will add that they want to fill the box with ornaments (cubes) and then count them. Strategies for identifying the volume of this given box are already making themselves visible.

Distribute the *How Many Cubes?* recording sheet (see Reproducible 7.11), three-quarter-inch grid paper (see Reproducible 7.14), linking cubes, and tape to each table group. Even though students are working in pairs, each student is responsible for his or her own paper. First students predict how many ornaments can be packaged in each of the given boxes, then they construct and fill boxes of various dimensions as they begin to make sense of this measurement we call volume.

You will notice from the recording sheet that patterns and pictures are offered for the initial boxes. As students work through the boxes, first the picture is omitted, then the pattern. The final two boxes are given in dimensions with no pattern or picture. Do not assume that students can make that cognitive leap from one or two pictures and patterns straight to the numerical representation of the box. Our fifth graders need time and hands-on experience constructing *nets* (open-box patterns) and then filling them. Some students may only need to construct one or two, but others may need to construct all seven. Allow them the time to do so. Having an additional recording sheet available for those who finish early can give others necessary additional time. (See Figure 7–8; see also Reproducible 7.12.)

Once students have completed their recording sheets and put away their materials, you can begin more formal instruction about *volume*— what it is and how it is measured. Be sure to make the distinctions among one-dimensional, two-dimensional, and three-dimensional measurement. Such a discussion will support students in developing the understanding of the units of measure of volume—*cubic* units. Making the connections between the earlier study of exponents and their use in this discussion will help the students to connect this new knowledge to previously covered material. Continue to remind students to support and defend their thinking with conjectures and generalizations made from their experiences

► REPRODUCIBLE 7.11
How Many Cubes?

REPRODUCIBLE 7.14
Three-Quarter-Inch
Grid Paper

► REPRODUCIBLE 7.12
More Boxes to Fill

REPRODUCIBLE 7.12
More Boxes to Fill

◄

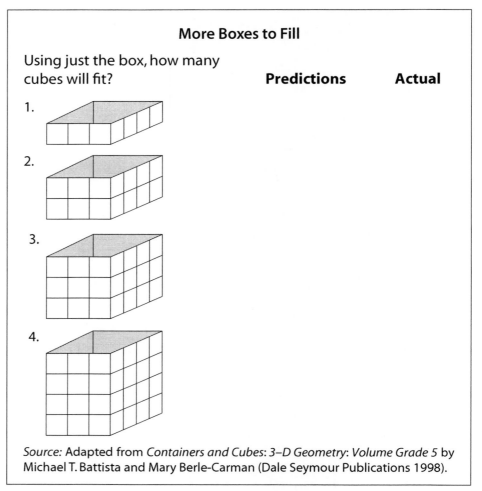

More Boxes to Fill

Using just the box, how many cubes will fit?   **Predictions**   **Actual**

1.

2.

3.

4.

Source: Adapted from *Containers and Cubes: 3–D Geometry: Volume Grade 5* by Michael T. Battista and Mary Berle-Carman (Dale Seymour Publications 1998).

FIGURE 7–8
Example of *More Boxes to Fill* Recording Sheet.

with filling boxes. A question as simple as "How do you know?" can help students offer mathematical proof. Because our ultimate goal is for students to develop efficient and meaningful strategies and generalizations for calculating volume, questions such as the following will help students think about and assess applied strategies:

- How did you predict the number of cubes that fit in each box?
- Were your predictions correct?
- Will your method always work? How do you know?
- Did anybody try methods that did not work? What were they? Why didn't they work?

As students share generalizations, script them in words on the board. Moving from words to a symbolic representation of a rule (formula) allows conceptual understanding to drive the procedure. (See Figure 7–9.)

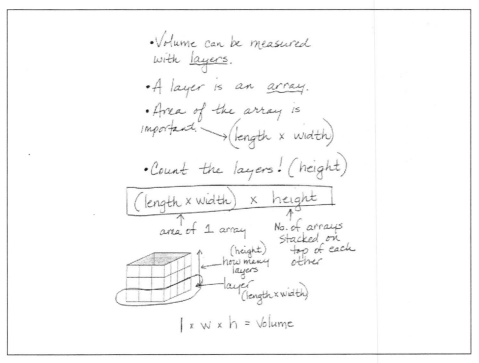

FIGURE 7–9
Showing Students How to Move from Words to Symbols.

As the discussion unfolds and you fill the board with words and symbols, you will need to take time to discuss and model the standard notation of dimensions of two- and three-dimensional shapes:

12 ft. × 10 ft. is read 12 by 10

The × symbol does, in fact, represent multiplication, but we read the × as *by* in the language of measurement.

3 cm × 4 cm × 5 cm is read 3 by 4 by 5

You can give the dimensions in various orders depending on the context of the measurement. Making catalogs available with items and their given dimensions can offer everyday applications of length, width, and height measurements.

TEACHER-TO-TEACHER TALK ■ **About Initial Understandings of Volume** ■ So what are we really looking and listening for in class discussions about volume? My hope is that students will *eventually* focus on the dimensions of any box as they describe strategies to find its volume. Some students will connect the cubes together to make layers of arrays to fill the box. This method helps to illustrate the dimension of *height*—the

(Continued)

number of layers. Such a visual model is mathematically powerful and effective. Initially, not all students will focus on dimensions. Pushing those who are not ready to do so will force them to adopt numerical procedures that they do not own and to abandon procedures that make sense to them visually. The language of volume may also be new to many students, and we cannot assume they understand terms and phrases. We need to ground the understanding of this language in experience and constructed knowledge. I also want to hear students progress to more articulate and efficient ways of conceptualizing cube configurations as they make predictions, build boxes, fill them with cubes, enumerate the cubes, and defend their thinking with others. Right now, I am more concerned with how students make sense of and visualize the concept of volume as well as how willing, able, and proficient they are at defending their thinking and strategies.

NCTM Connection

Strand: Geometry, Measurement
Focus: Explore and calculate the dimensions of a solid when the volume is doubled.
Context: *Doubling the Number of Cubes*

REPRODUCIBLE 7.15 ◀
Doubling the Number of Cubes Preinvestigation Prompt

REPRODUCIBLE 7.16 Doubling the Number of Cubes Postinvestigation Prompt

REPRODUCIBLE 7.14 Three-Quarter-Inch Grid Paper

Doubling the Number of Cubes

Duration: 1–2 Class Periods

Materials

- Doubling the Number of Cubes Preinvestigation Prompt (see Reproducible 7.15)
- Doubling the Number of Cubes Postinvestigation Prompt (see Reproducible 7.16)
- three-quarter-inch grid paper (see Reproducible 7.14)
- linking cubes

Once students have had time to investigate volume by predicting, building, and counting or calculating, you can pose a problem such as the following:

You have a box that is 2 units by 3 units by 5 units. The factory wants you to build a box that will hold twice as many cubes. *What could the dimensions of this new box be? Why do your dimensions make sense?*

This problem can be offered as a whole-class investigation, preceded by a preinvestigation write and followed by a postinvestigation write. (See Figure 7–10.) I often ask students to work independently on this task; many will want to test their strategies, others may try out strategies from classmates that they have decided make more sense to them than their own methods.

As students begin testing their predictions of the volume of this new box, they will undoubtedly chatter. Many students may feel unsettled about the outcomes of their building, filling, and calculating. Many will double all the dimensions in order to double the number of cubes. Those students who think about volume in terms of layers or arrays are less apt to make this mistake. But making this mistake creates a wonderful opportunity to once again discuss volume in terms of layers and the dimensions of those layers. As students discuss their right or wrong predictions and share strategies and thinking, keep physical models available and ask that they be used.

FIGURE 7–10
Karina's Pre- and Postinvestigation Write.

Preinvestigation Prompt

You have a box that is 2 units by 3 units by 5 units. The factory wants you to build a box that will hold *twice as many cubes*. What are the dimensions of a box that holds twice as many cubes as a box that is 2 by 3 by 5? *Why do your dimensions make sense?*

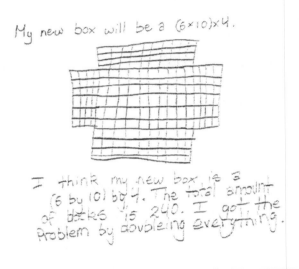

My new box will be a (6×10)×4.

I think my new box is a (6 by 10) by 4. The total amount of cubes is 240. I got the problem by doubleing everything.

▶ REPRODUCIBLE 7.15
Doubling the
Number of Cubes
Preinvestigation
Prompt

Postinvestigation Prompt

You have a box that is 2 units by 3 units by 5 units. The factory wants you to build a box that will hold *twice as many cubes*. What are the dimensions of a box that holds twice as many cubes as a box that is 2 by 3 by 5? *Why do your dimensions make sense?*

If you made a miscalculation in the preinvestigation, please address it in this entry!

1. My new box will be a (5×3)×4. All I did was double the 2 at the end 2nd made it 4. Then I did the math and got my answer which is 60.

$$(5×3)×2=30 \sim (5×3)×4=60$$
Before   After

2. At the begining of this investigation I made a miscalculation. My mistake was that I doubled all the numbers. Since I doubled the answers I ended up timesing 30 by 8.

▶ REPRODUCIBLE 7.16
Doubling the
Number of Cubes
Postinvestigation
Prompt

NCTM Connection

Strand: Geometry, Measurement

Focus: Estimate and compare magnitudes of volume of containers of varying sizes and volumes.

Context: *Put in Order*

REPRODUCIBLE 7.17 ◀
Put in Order

Put in Order

Duration: 1–2 Class Periods

Materials

- *Put in Order* recording sheet (see Reproducible 7.17)
- 7 sets of containers, various shapes that are not easily compared visually (paper cup; half-pint milk carton; rectangular storage container; tall, narrow jar; toothpaste box; short, wide jar; cottage cheese container; shallow rectangular storage container). Label each container A, B, C, D, E, F, G in random order (not in order of their volume), 1 set per table group
- 2 cards with each set of containers, 1 labeled *Least Volume*, the other *Greatest Volume*
- tubs of rice with more than enough to fill the two larger containers, 1 per table group
- quarter-cup measuring scoops or nonstandard measuring scoops, 1 per table group
- newsprint

This activity, adapted from *Sizing Up Measurement: Activities for Grades 3–5 Classrooms* (Confer 2007), can be a tad messy and takes some before-class organization, but is well worth the mess and work. You may wish to spread newsprint on the tabletops to keep the rice somewhat contained. I prefer to prepare for this lesson when students are out of the classroom. When they return, containers, labels, and student worksheets are on the tabletops ready to go. The tubs of rice and scoops are on my counter ready for distribution.

I instruct students to take the *Least Volume* and *Greatest Volume* cards and place them on their tables, with "least" on the left and "greatest" on the right. Then I ask them to *visually* organize their containers from those that have the least volume to those that have the greatest. Once students have organized the containers and recorded them on the "Prediction" section of their recording sheets, we can have a whole-group discussion about the order of the containers and why a particular group's ordering makes sense to them. Push for the specifics of their explanations. Why does this container look as if it holds more? What are the attributes of this container that make you think that it holds less?

The next part of this activity focuses on *transitive reasoning*. Transitivity allows students to compare two objects using a third. When students can reason with transitivity, they know that if the marker is shorter than the pencil and the pencil is shorter than the stick, they can then reason that the marker is shorter than the stick. An understanding of transitivity allows students to measure objects in relationship to one another. Most researchers agree that transitivity is one of the four components of measuring (Chapin and Johnson 2006, 271) with the other components being *conservation* (objects maintain their same size and shape when measured), *units* (the type of unit used to measure an object depends on the attribute being measured), and *unit iteration* (the units must be repeated, or iterated, in order to determine the measure of an object).

Now for the messy (and fun) part of the lesson! As you distribute the tubs of rice, tell students that they can now compare measures with rice—but *no* measuring devices! This will encourage students to pour rice from one container to another to organize the containers according to their volume. Some students may struggle because of the transitivity required by this task. Once again, discussion among the members of the table group is necessary as students make sense of the ordering. Have students record this order on their recording sheet in the "Comparing with Rice" section and then compare this order with their original predictions.

Once students have returned the rice to the tubs, introduce the final stage of the lesson: measuring with scoops. As you place scoops at each table, tell students that now they will be able to use a scoop to identify the actual measure of each container. Ask them to record these measures on their recording sheet in the "Measuring with Scoops" section and then compare this order to the previous ones. As you circulate through the room, keep careful watch over the measuring techniques. Students need to understand that the unit of measure (scoop) must be consistent. They should scoop the rice evenly with the top of each scoop every time.

Once the class has completed the task, made their recordings, and cleaned up, have a class discussion about what students noticed, discovered, and learned from all of the measuring tasks. It is also important to discuss what was difficult or challenging for them to do or to understand as well.

Both *Doubling the Number of Cubes* and *Put in Order* require students to reevaluate their predictions and assumptions about volume with the understanding that sometimes what we *see* is not always what we get!

Good Questions to Ask

- A pentomino is a shape made up of five square units that are connected along straight sides.

Pentomino   Not a pentomino

Flipping or turning a pentomino does *not* make a different pentomino.

$\neq$

For more good questions, see *Good Questions for Math Teaching: Why Ask Them and What to Ask, Grades 5–8* by Lainie Schuster and Nancy Anderson (Math Solutions 2005).

REPRODUCIBLE 7.18 ◀
One-Inch Grid Paper

- Using one-inch grid paper (see Reproducible 7.18), find all the possible pentominoes. Cut them out and label each pentomino with letters or numbers (A, B, C or 1, 2, 3).

- Order the pentominoes according to their perimeters *without* measuring, from shortest to longest, using what you have discovered about shapes with the same area but differing perimeters. Record the order.

- Now you can measure. Record this order.

- How accurate was your original order? Describe the shape with the shortest perimeter. Describe the shape with the longest perimeter.

■ The following two tiles can be used to tile a room. When measured with the larger tile, the area of the rectangular room is twelve square units and the perimeter is sixteen square units.

- What would the area and perimeter of the room be (in tile units) if it were measured in small tiles? How do you know?

- How do the measures of the room using the large tiles compare to the measures of the room using the small tiles? Support your reasoning with diagrams, words, and number models.

■ What happens to the area of a circle when you double its circumference? When the circumference of a pizza doubles, should the price double? Explain your reasoning.

- Trace a circular object onto centimeter grid paper. Calculate the area in square units and record it in the middle of the circle.

- Use string to measure the circumference of the traced circle. Cut another piece of string that is double the circumference and use it to form a new circle. Tape it in place. What is the area of the new circle? What is the relationship between the circumferences and the areas of the two circles?

■ What could be the dimensions of a rectangle with an area of twenty square units and whole-number side lengths that has the longest perimeter? The shortest perimeter? Explain your thinking for each.

■ What could be the dimensions of a rectangle with a perimeter of sixteen units and whole-number side lengths that has the largest area? The smallest area? Explain your reasoning for each.

■ Gracie says her rectangle has a perimeter of thirty units and an area of fifty square units. Jack says his rectangle also has a perimeter of thirty units but an area of fifty-six square units. Can they both be correct? Explain. Use drawings to support your thinking.

- Can you always determine the perimeter of a figure if you know its area? Can you determine the area of a figure if you know its perimeter? Are area and perimeter related? If so, how?

- Use two methods to find the area of the figure below. Explain why both of your methods make sense.

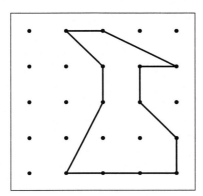

Calculation Routines and Practices

Students are expected to recall many area formulas by the end of their middle school years. Many students, including our fifth graders, try to commit these formulas to memory and then apply them when needed (Chapin and Johnson 2006, 286). When formulas are simply committed to memory, they are easily forgotten because the concepts of area have not been explored or understood. Students are far better served when they discover, test, and revise formulas as they solve problems and build models. Knowing a formula for area such as length times width without conceptual understanding does little to help you find the area of the following figures:

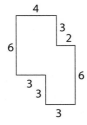
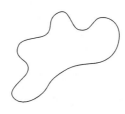

Most students first encounter the formula for the area of a rectangle when studying arrays. The picture below illustrates a three-by-four array:

The dimensions offer the length and width, but which side is given to the length and which to the width is totally arbitrary. Arrays support the idea of area in that the area of any rectangular array is the product of its dimensions.

What can muddy the waters in making sense of area (and volume) measurements and subsequent formulas is the introduction of the mathematical terms *height* and *base*. The dimensions of a rectangle can be labeled as height and base as well as length and width. Any side can serve as a base, *but the height is always perpendicular to the side chosen as the base*. When we label the sides of parallelograms, the base and height labels are used because the sides of parallelograms are not always perpendicular to each other:

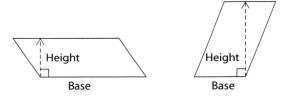

The area formulas for various quadrilaterals can, therefore, be explored and constructed from a student's understanding of the area formula of a rectangle. Moving eventually to an area formula of base times height for a rectangle will help students generalize more readily to other figures:

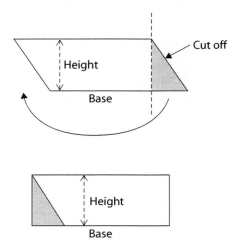

The parallelogram and the rectangle have the same area. We can therefore use the same formula to find the area of both: $A = b \times h$.

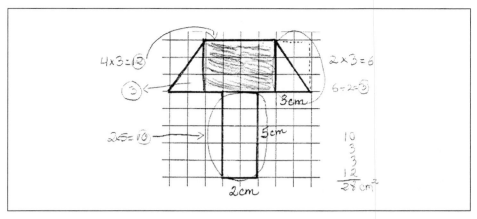

FIGURE 7–11
Maisie's Area Calculations.

Decomposing shapes can greatly support the understanding and calculation of area concepts and formulas. Once students are able to understand and conserve area (the *Area Stays the Same* activity is of great support), their ability and willingness to decompose shapes into more manageable "chunks" can help them to calculate the areas of irregular shapes. (See Figure 7–11.)

Reading, Writing, and Vocabulary

The language of measurement and geometry are crucial to the exploration of these concepts with meaning. However, keep in mind that it takes more than definitional knowledge to really *know* a word. We have to know words to identify them in multiple reading and listening contexts and to use them in our speaking and writing (Allen 1999).

As we plan instruction, we need to be cognizant of those words that are critical to the understanding of the targeted concepts and procedures. We need to decide which of these critical words can be connected to students' prior knowledge and learned through context and which will have to be approached with direct instruction. The following is a list of ideas to help support and develop word knowledge adapted from *Words, Words, Words: Teaching Vocabulary in Grades 4–12* (Allen 1999, 10–11). When applicable, I have offered sample questions for each idea based on the lessons in this chapter.

Repeat words in varied contexts.

- What are the *dimensions* of your dog yard?
- Why are the *dimensions* of this array (base) important as we calculate its volume?

Describe or define words.

■ What makes a *rectangle* a rectangle?

■ What do you mean by *volume*?

Supporting words with visuals.

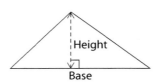 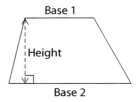

Connecting words to everyday usage.

■ How does knowing the *perimeter* of a room help us to calculate the length of the baseboards that we need to purchase?

■ How many *cubic feet* of mulch will I need to fill this garden bed?

Extending words with anecdotes.

■ Sharing stories about

• finding volume; and

• mistakes that we have made in buying paint . . . and not having enough and why that happened!

Making associations.

■ How does knowing the *dimensions* of a polygon help us to find its *area*? Its *perimeter*?

Give definitions.

■ What is a *polygon*?

■ What is a *regular polygon*?

■ What is an *irregular polygon*?

Comparing and contrasting.

■ How are *area* and *perimeter* the same?

■ How are they different?

Rephrasing definitions.

■ Can someone give me another way to define or think about *volume*?

Give examples of correct and incorrect usage.

■ The area of this polygon is sixteen *square centimeters*, not sixteen *centimeters*.

- When we fill a pond in a garden, we are concerned about its *volume*, not its *area*. But when we buy a liner for a pond, we are often concerned about both!

If our ultimate goal is to offer opportunities for our fifth graders to integrate words and concepts meaningfully, we need to plan and implement our language instruction accordingly, even in math class!

Assessment

Partner quizzes are just that: quizzes taken with a partner, as so much of our daily work is completed in class. I assign partners to students at the beginning of the quiz. My purpose in making partner assignments is to make pairs of like thinkers. I try to pair visual thinkers with other visual thinkers, those who are fluid with the language of others of similar ability, and those who need to talk more with others who also need the discussion. And I do pair the weaker student with another of similar abilities and needs. No two students are paired up again during the remainder of the year, which can be a little tricky, but doable nonetheless. I also inform students that I am pairing up like thinkers, and you would be astounded at how accurate students are at guessing the pairs! They are learning to know who they are as mathematicians—what they need—and how they learn best. I must admit that I was hesitant to pair students up in this manner. But somewhere along the line, I became convinced that like thinkers would be able to approach the quiz with greater confidence, poise, and competence, and each year I find my convictions to be well founded. Ironically, students who fare the worst each year are those pairs who choose not to communicate or collaborate with each other. And I have a few each year! I give students eight or so problems and ask them to choose five to complete. Reading is involved, and students have to make decisions about which problems to solve. That is a process in itself. Then come solving the problems and reaching consensus about how best to represent the solutions. Each student completes his or her own paper, which may or may not be identical to their partner's. It is up to the partners to decide how to proceed with the representation of their thinking and work.

The pairs are scattered about the room. There is a low hum of young voices and even some giggling from time to time! Students are focused, engaged, and amazingly productive. They do ask me questions, but those questions are few because students have each other to ask. And ask each other they do! Some pairs discuss the question and solution in its entirety before they put their thoughts on paper. Some discuss the question, work the problem independently, and then compare and revise final solutions.

Because this is such a new process for students of this age, we process the process after all the quizzes have been turned in. I ask questions that encourage students to reflect on the successes or difficulties they encountered, and this discussion can help to guide others when they take the next partner quiz. My students take three partner quizzes a year . . . but they ask to take them all year long!

TEACHER-TO-TEACHER TALK ■ **About Taking Risks** ■ When I first came across the idea of partner quizzes, I was skeptical at best. Would fifth graders really be able to take advantage of the communication and cooperation opportunities that partner quizzes offer? Would the written work truly be a collaboration of two fifth-grade mathematical minds, or would one student lead the other? How would students and parents react when they heard I was pairing up "like thinkers"? What would the reaction of the parents be to assessments on which their children could share ideas and answers and talk as they formulated and revised them? Initially, this all seemed to be risky business. And more important, was I willing to take that risk? I have never been one to shy away from a challenge, but there seemed to be many contingents to please with this one: students, parents, and even my principal because this might all eventually end up in her office! When I gave my first partner quiz years ago, I was honest and open with my class about my reservations. I needed their help and feedback, but I also wanted to know if this assessment process could work. Students were absolutely wonderful! Once the quiz was finished, I offered my observations—and they offered theirs with some very good suggestions. One of the best suggestions was to allow groups that needed more quiet to work in the hallway. Another was to have the quiz right before the library or PE period so that if the students needed more time, they could work into the next period. Another astounding observation was that students actually proofread their quizzes before they turned them in! Partners read their answers to each other out loud, making necessary additions or revisions. Who saw that one coming? So if this practice interests you, take that risk!

Home and School Connections

As with previous units of study, I create and distribute a Parent Information and Involvement Form prior to the beginning of our study of measurement and geometry to help parents support their children at home. (See Figure 7–12.)

As the school year draws to a close, identifying those students who may need additional support over the summer in preparation for sixth grade may be necessary.

In order to keep this request and practice from being punitive, I suggest that all students continue with math practice over the summer. Some do and some do not. This tends to be a decision that is ultimately made by the

▶ REPRODUCIBLE 2.16
Parent Information
and Involvement
Form

Parent Information and Involvement Form

From: Lainie Schuster
Re: Mathematical Curriculum
Unit: Geometry and Measurement

During the next unit, the major topics we will be studying are:

- measurement
- area and perimeter
- volume

My goal in studying these topics is for the students to be able to:

- explore measurements of area and perimeter
- explore measurements of volume
- calculate measurements of area, perimeter, and volume that are grounded in personal understanding
- estimate and generalize about measurements based on previous explorations and understandings

Parents can help at home by:

- discussing and identifying the use of geometry and measurement in everyday life, especially area, perimeter, and volume
- identifying units of measure appropriate to that which is being measured
- engaging your child in tasks around the house or yard that require measurement
- estimating measurements, and then measuring
- asking how a measurement was determined or calculated

FIGURE 7–12
Parent Information and Involvement Form: April.

family, but my request is there and actually documented with one sentence in each child's end-of-year report card:

It is recommended that Joey work through the Summer Skills Sharpener math review (http://summerskills.com) for grade 5 or 6 in preparation for that which lies ahead in the sixth grade.

For those students who need the additional work more than others, I make a phone call or send an email to their parents. My request is gentle, but the message is clear that middle school is fast approaching and their child has some mathematical areas that need additional work. If we have carried out positive and ongoing school-home communication throughout the year, these parents may be more accommodating than you would expect.

I also address the class about my summer expectations. I am clear that this is their choice, but one that will be of great benefit to them when September rolls around. I try to set them up with a framework or a routine: Complete two pages every Monday and Thursday morning right after breakfast, and work with your friend across the street for an hour every Wednesday afternoon. I also suggest that they take some time off in mid-summer—everyone needs a break—and set these routines in place in late summer.

Because I have been implementing this summer work practice for the past five years or so, it is expected—students and parents who are in my class know that I will make this request. I make no apologies about the importance of the study of mathematics. By this time, students are well aware of my interest and concern about their future mathematical success. This is just one more chapter in that book!

Resources

About Teaching Mathematics: A K–8 Resource, Third Edition (Burns 2007)

The chapters on geometry and spatial sense offer lessons and author discussion about geometric thinking and meaningful activities.

Math Matters: Understanding the Math You Teach, Grades K–8, Second Edition (Chapin and Johnson 2006)

> Chapter 10: Geometry
>
> Chapter 11: Spatial Sense
>
> Chapter 12: Measurement

Chapter 12, "Measurement," offers an excellent discussion of area formulas and their teaching and learning implications. The authors explain how various formulas are connected to one another, which can be of great help to teachers as they support the exploration and learning of area formulas with meaning.

Sizing Up Measurement: Activities for Grades 3–5 Classrooms (Confer 2007)

This is an outstanding resource for measurement activities and discussion about the teaching and learning of measurement procedures and concepts, and offers excellent support for both math and science classrooms.

Containers and Cubes: Investigations in Number, Data, and Space (Battista and Berle-Carman 1998)

This is an excellent collection of investigations about 3-D geometry and volume. The explorations are well organized and carefully designed to engage students as they visualize and describe geometric relationships.

Summer Skills Sharpener for math (http://summerskills.com)

You can order workbooks of a variety of disciplines for summer study at this website. Although the exercises tend to be of more of a skill-and-drill nature, the practice is valuable to keep skills current.

Chapter 8

Data Analysis

Hogwarts School of Witchcraft and Wizardry

UNIFORM
First-year students will require:

1. *Three sets of plain work robes (black)*
2. *One plain pointed hat (black) for day wear*
3. *One pair of protective gloves (dragon hide or similar)*
4. *One winter cloak (black, silver fastenings)*

Please note that all pupils' clothing should carry name tags

COURSE BOOKS
All students should have a copy of each of the following:

The Standard Book of Spells (Grade 1) *by Miranda Goshawk*
A History of Magic *by Bathilda Bagshot*

Magical Theory *by Adalbert Waffling*

A Beginners' Guide to Transfiguration *by Emeric Switch*

One Thousand Magical Herbs and Fungi *by Phyllida Spore*

Magical Drafts and Potions *by Arsenius Jigger*

Fantastic Beasts and Where to Find Them *by Newt Scamander*

The Dark Forces: A Guide to Self-Protection *by Quentin Trimble*

OTHER EQUIPMENT

1 wand

1 cauldron (pewter, standard size 2)

1 set glass or crystal phials

1 telescope

1 set of brass scales

Students may also bring an owl OR a cat OR a toad

PARENTS ARE REMINDED THAT FIRST YEARS ARE NOT ALLOWED THEIR OWN BROOMSTICKS.

Harry Potter and the Sorcerer's Stone
Rowling 1997, 66–67

The Learning Environment

Support and Celebrate the Having of Wonderful Ideas

According to Eleanor Duckworth (1987), the having of wonderful ideas is the essence of intellectual development. Our willingness to accept students' ideas and provide an environment that can initiate such ideas gives our students reason and occasion for having them! It is *by* thinking that students get better *at* thinking. Our students have now spent the better part of a school year thinking, investigating, collaborating, and creating in many areas of mathematics. As students collect, represent, interpret, and discuss data, your charge as their teacher is to elicit, support, and act on their wonderful ideas. Allow their questions and insights to drive the instruction whenever you can. Then take the time to be amazed and delighted with their wonderful ideas.

Continue to Develop and Enjoy Your Classroom Culture

When tasks are treated as genuine mathematical problems and our students are treated as genuine mathematicians, meaningful teaching and learning occur. An environment that focuses on reflection and communication about mathematical activities and ideas stimulates and supports all those who are a part of it. By this time in the year, our students are thinking and writing with greater clarity and are more willing and able to dig deeper into the mathematics. Celebrate and enjoy the competence, confidence, and playfulness that a productive and successful culture can provide.

The Mathematics and Its Language

Children Pose, Formulate, and Refine Questions They Wish to Explore

Offering students the opportunity to formulate their own questions in order to collect, represent, analyze, and interpret data gives meaning and purpose to statistical tasks. Not only can the questions posed by students be interesting and engaging but they can also empower students as they apply the process of data investigation to those topics and questions that are of interest to them.

Children Collect, Represent, Analyze, and Interpret Data

Data can be gathered, organized, and examined in order to answer questions about the populations or topics from which the data comes. How best to do this depends, however, on the question being asked. Statistical landmarks such as sample size, range, mode, median, and mean can help our students describe and make sense of data, as can their developing proficiency with graphing and generalizing.

Children Identify, Interpret, and Analyze Data Sets as *Numerical* or *Categorical*

Real-world questions and surveys often result in responses that involve two general kinds of data: *numerical data* or *categorical data*. Understanding the type of data helps students determine how best to represent the data and the most appropriate measure of center (average) with which to interpret and analyze the data set.

Children Explore Measures of Center

The *mean*, *median*, and *mode* are measures used to describe a typical item in a data set. Note that these three measures of central tendency can be quite different from or similar to one another within the same data set. Also note that some data sets are best represented by only one of these "averages," depending on whether the collected data is numerical or categorical. Many fifth graders will have had some experiences with identifying and interpreting medians and modes of various data sets, but the mean may be a relatively new concept.

Children Explore, Interpret, and Analyze Graphical Displays of Data

Our world is inundated with graphical displays of data. Newspapers, magazines, television, and websites all commonly use graphical displays of data to convey what they believe to be important information. How we interpret those displays is based on our understanding (or misunderstanding!) of the visual representation of the data.

Pictographs, circle graphs (pie charts), line plots, bar graphs, and stem-and-leaf plots are examples of *one-variable graphs*. *Two-variable graphs*, such as scatter plots and line graphs, display two different variables on the same graph.

Lesson Planning

- Representing the same data in different ways can be interesting and mathematically powerful. Our fifth graders are used to pictographs and bar graphs, but what does that same data look like in a line plot? Or a stem-and-leaf plot? Or in a chart or table? Does one representation skew the meaning of the actual data? Why would someone prefer to represent data using one form over another? Varying the representation of data is important as our fifth graders enter this world of media and data overload.

- Students should construct the graphs themselves rather than exclusively working on prepared graphs. How to scale the intervals on the x- and y-axes becomes a point of conversation and instruction as well as interpretation.

- Your prescribed text may offer some meaningful tasks, but the data used in the text may not be applicable or interesting to your particular class. It may be worth the time and effort to customize the data for the class. Collecting class data or sharing collected data from a local newspaper or magazine can deepen the meaning of the targeted mathematics of the lesson.

- Too often elementary school lessons in statistics are based on mere interpretation of the data. Encourage your students to think beyond the data. Ask them to make predictions and generalizations based on the data presented.

- Many times we focus on the creation of graphs with little time spent on their interpretation. Once students have created the graphs, take the time to process the represented data with questions such as the following:
  - What do you notice?
  - What "story" is this data telling us?
  - What do the "lumps, bumps, and holes" of the data tell us?
  - Is this representation easy to read? Why?
  - Would another representation be as effective? Why or why not?

Possible Difficulties or Misconceptions

Not all graphs are created equal! Deliberate misrepresentation of data can cause misunderstanding. Both of the following graphs display the same data. Because the intervals on the x and y axes are different on the two graphs, one appears to show more rapid growth. Graphs can be deceiving and improperly scaled to prove to consumers what producers want to prove.

If our goal is to develop savvy fifth-grade consumers, then we need to offer opportunities for them to analyze graphs for misinformation!

Increase in Sales per Month

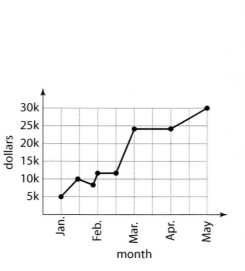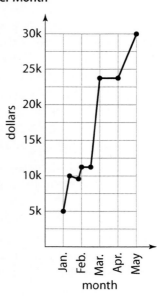

Investigations, Games, and Literature-Based Activities

What Do You Mean?

Duration: 2–4 Class Periods

As students collect, represent, interpret, and analyze data identifying the length of classmates' names, have a conversation and instruction about the *measures of central tendency* of a data set. These activities are adapted from lessons referenced in *Data About Us* (Lappan et al. 2006a). These lessons offer students the opportunities to

- collect data;
- describe the distribution of data;
- explore and use tables, line plots, and bar graphs to represent data distributions;
- identify statistical landmarks; and
- explore and identify the measures of central tendency of a given data set: *mode, median,* and *mean;* what they are and how they are measured.

Materials

- *What Do You Mean?* recording sheet (see Reproducible 8.1)
- centimeter grid paper (see Reproducible 2.5)
- chart grid paper
- 3-by-5-inch note cards, 1 set of 16 cards (or a few more than the class sample size) per pair of students
- linking cubes, about 16 per student (one cube per letter of their first name)

Vocabulary

average, data set, distribution, frequency, line plot, maximum, mean, median, minimum, mode, organized list, outlier, range, sample size

My guess is that most parents spend little time worrying over the number of letters in the names they choose for their children. But there are certainly those times when name length matters. Kevin Henkes's beloved *Chrysanthemum* (see the "Investigations, Games, and Literature-Based Activities" section in Chapter 2) certainly found that out the hard way! It is difficult for long names to fit on a friendship bracelet or on a bubble sheet for a standardized test. This series of lessons explores name lengths and measures of central tendency of the collected data. If you have not read *Chrysanthemum* (Henkes 1991) to your class, this is a wonderful

NCTM Connection

Strand: Data Analysis and Probability

Focus: Explore and identify the measures of central tendency of a given data set: mode, median, and mean.

Context: What Do You Mean?

▶ REPRODUCIBLE 8.1
What Do You Mean?
Recording Sheet

REPRODUCIBLE 2.5
Centimeter Grid
Paper

time to do so. The story is delightful and the watercolor illustrations delicious.

Gathering name-length data at this time of the school year should be orchestrated by students. Posing the task of collecting the name lengths of classmates can open up a discussion about how best to go about the data collection. I had never thought about two data-collection representations until last year when my class agreed (after a rather heated discussion, I might add) that one representation did not offer easily accessed information. They initially decided just to list names and name lengths. As the data were being collected, Jack, Will, and Lea realized that the data were not very well organized and that it would take us too much time to analyze it when there was no order to it. I was flabbergasted—and delighted—with this observation. I quickly realized that they had learned an important lesson about the benefits of efficiency—especially when math class backed up against recess!

The class came to a consensus about the constraints of the data collection:

- First *and* last names would be used.
- No nicknames would be used.
- Mrs. Schuster's name would be included.
- They would use a frequency chart to collect the initial data; then Jack, Will, and Lea would create an organized representation of the data set to use for the later lessons. (See Figure 8–1.)

When I questioned Jack, Will, and Lea about the use of a line plot for the second representation, they all agreed that the individual data points were visually more helpful on a line plot than they were as bars on a bar graph. They also agreed that the same information was presented, but in a format that they thought would be more useful to the class.

I knew from conversations in the faculty room that as fourth graders, this group of students had investigated the following statistical landmarks:

- sample size
- range
- minimum
- maximum
- mode
- median

Being aware of this gave me a better sense of where to start my lessons. Although I would spend time reviewing each term, I was not planning to reteach these landmarks. It was time to move on.

# of letters	Frequency (tallies)
7	
8	|
9	||
10	||
11	||||
12	|||||
13	||||
14	||||
16	|

FIGURE 8–1
Two Representations of Fifth-Grade Name Data: Frequency Chart and Line Plot.

As the class began to identify, explain, and discuss the mode and median, students were confused about which was which. We agreed to use what we knew about the English language to help us out with these landmarks. *Mode* sounds like *most*—which it is, the *most* frequent response of a data set. We also applied what we knew from previous work with geometry prefixes to identify multiple modes. A data set with two modes could be called *bimodal*—three, *trimodal*. Cool! We all agreed what a *median* on a highway was and identified the *median* response as the *middle* response of the data set, an actual or hypothetical value given the odd or even number of the sample size.

The mode was evident on the line plot, but the median not so much. Representing the data points in an organized list is a tool that can be used to identify the median.

Reproducing the organized list on a piece of grid paper offers a strong visual representation of the median. I distribute sheets of centimeter grid paper (see Reproducible 2.5) to each table group. Students cut strips for themselves from the sheet that will accommodate the sample size—one data point per grid. If the strips are longer than the sample size, they will need to cut off the excess grids from each end of the strip.

Folding this strip in half will identify the median. If the sample size is an odd number, the fold (median) will fall on a value; if the sample size is an even number, the fold (median) will fall between two values. Present both scenarios to students. Data is not always neat and tidy, and the median helps us to make sense of messy data: 50 percent of the data will fall above the median and 50 percent below. (See Figure 8–2.)

Students need to be engaged in developing strategies as they identify the median when it falls between two values. For example, many students will misinterpret a median that falls between the values of twelve and twelve.

► REPRODUCIBLE 2.5
Centimeter Grid
Paper

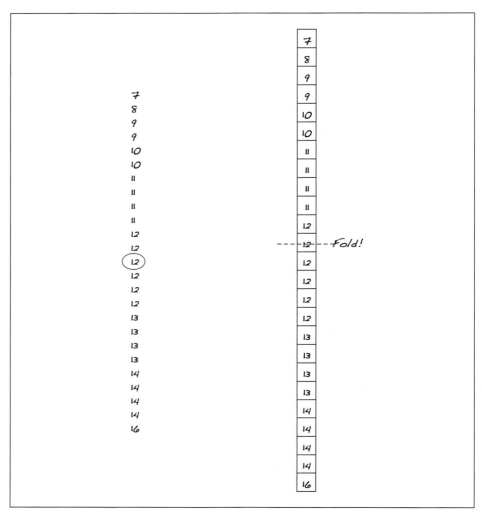

FIGURE 8–2
From Organized List to Median.

They will often incorrectly assume that the median is 12.5 because anything that falls midway between two values has a "point five (*x*.5)" in the measure! And what happens when the median falls between eleven and fourteen? Diagramming such a scenario can offer students a visual model that will work with smaller, more manageable numbers. As students become comfortable with calculating mean values, they can apply that understanding in situations such as this. (See Figures 8–3 and 8–4.)

Identifying the *mode* and *median* are ways to describe what is *typical* about a data set. These are useful landmarks that can help us describe the distribution of data. Quite often, the mode and median will be close in value—and in my class's collection, the same.

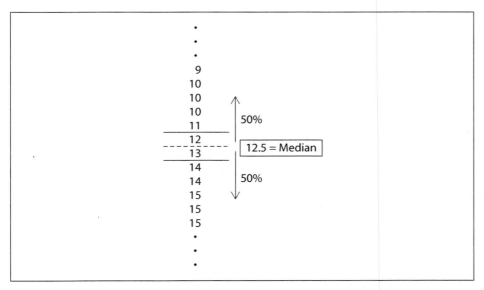

FIGURE 8–3
Median Identified with a Diagram.

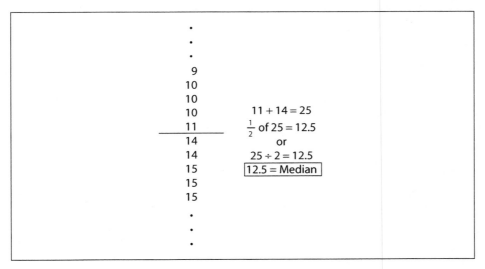

FIGURE 8–4
Median Calculated with a Mean Calculation.

TEACHER-TO-TEACHER TALK ■ **About the Median** ■ I still struggle a bit with the median. I know what it is and how to identify it, but I still am not sure when it is best used. And I am speaking as an adult consumer, not necessarily as a fifth-grade math teacher! I read about median home values in the New England area and wonder what that tells me. From what I know about the median of any data set, it tells me that there are homes valued

(Continued)

above a particular value (50 percent, to be exact) and homes that are valued below that (50 percent). But what does that tell me about *my* house? And who sets these median values? And do they change as the real estate market changes? But I also know that I do not want to use the *mean* to describe a *typical* house price, because a very expensive house will distort the *average* house value. I get that. So here is my question: If I put my house on the market, are my chances of selling better if my asking price is below the median price or above? And are home buyers really interested in these statistics? What makes this all so interesting is that this is important stuff in the real world, and we need to make these real-world connections visible to our fifth graders. When we ask questions and make assumptions based on what we know as we contemplate what we do not know, we are thinking like mathematicians—and good ones, at that. When we let our students in on our world and on our thinking, it can validate their own! Except for Nick. When I posed this personal quagmire to my class a few years ago, Nick decided that it would be far easier just to rent . . . or just to move in with his buddy Patrick!

As students discuss this particular data set, encourage and support the language of data analysis. Terms such as *range* and *sample size* can give immediate focus and reference to the conversation. Isn't it a lot easier (and more efficient?) to use the term *sample size* rather than "the number of students polled in our class"? And isn't it easier (and more efficient!) to use the term *range* rather than "the distribution of values from the lowest to the highest value"? Just as we want to move our students toward more efficient methods and strategies of calculation, we want to do the same with their language. When we speak the same language, conversations are carried out and understood better. We can make better sense of what we see and hear.

Exploring the Median

What happens to the median when you add values to a data set or remove them? This exploration gives students the opportunity to add or subtract values from a data set and make subsequent generalizations about the median. You will need a list of ten of your students' names. List the names on a piece of chart paper for the class to refer to:

Dudley Dursley
Albus Dumbledore
Ron Weasley
Hagrid
Hermione Granger
Draco Malfoy
Harry Potter
Professor Snape
Professor McGonagall
Peeves

Students will work with a partner and this list of names. Give each pair of students a set of sixteen cards, and ask them to write the names of the ten posted classmates on the front of each card with the length of the name on the back.

front   back

There will be six extra cards. Have students place the cards in order from the shortest name to the longest. Using the cards, have students identify the median of the data set. You can post this on the class chart.

Students can now experiment with the cards and the following questions with the focus on the median and how it is affected as the cards (names) are added or subtracted.

Experiment with your cards to perform each task described below. Keep a record of your thinking and the generalizations you can make once a task is performed.

A. *Remove two names from your list without changing the median.*
B. *Remove two names so that the median increases.*
C. *Remove two names so that the median decreases.*
D. *Add two new names so that the median increases.*
E. *Add two new names so that the median decreases.*
F. *Add two new names without changing the median.*

Once students have had a chance to work through the tasks, ask the pairs to present examples that meet the constraints of each task. You want students to realize that the median is a fairly stable value; adding a large value (or a small value) has little effect on the median. In the data set presented, the median would increase to twelve whether we added a name of thirteen letters or fifty-six letters.

Exploring the Mean

It is important for our fifth graders to realize that measures of central tendency can be referred to as an *average*. We can use one of *three* averages to describe what is typical about a set of data. Students have had experiences identifying the *mode* (most frequent response of a data set) and the

NCTM Connection

Strand: Data Analysis and Probability

Focus: Explore and identify the median, mode, and mean of a collected set of data.

Context: Exploring the Mean

median (the middle value of a data set that divides a set of ordered data in half). The mode and median are both averages. The *mean* is a third average and can also be used to describe that which is typical in a data set.

I introduce these lessons with the *Chrysanthemum* activity referenced in the "Investigations, Games, and Literature-Based Activities" section of the Chapter 2. Next, I ask students to build towers of linking cubes that correspond with the lengths of their first names. Students can see from their towers that their name lengths vary in size. Asking a question such as, "What if we wanted to 'even out' the distribution of the number of letters in everyone's first name?" can begin the exploration and can start students thinking about the mean as a *balancing* of values.

Engage students in thinking about how we could redistribute the number of letters of our collective set of data. If everyone had the same number of letters in their first name, how many letters would that be? Some students may suggest that they trade letters (linking cubes) with one another; those students with fewer letters would get a few cubes from those with longer names and more letters. Have students take part in trading until the majority of students have the same number of letters (cubes). Each student needs a tower, but the towers should be of relatively equal height or number of cubes. You have now calculated the mean name length of the class.

The arithmetic calculation of a mean now makes sense: the summing up of all the values and then dividing by the sample size. Too often, calculating a mean is presented without a conceptual grounding of what it means to find a mean. In this context, the sharing of cubes and subsequent distribution of the data offer students a physical and visual experience to ground their conceptual understanding of mean.

Students can now move to representing mean calculations symbolically. Presenting the *What Do You Mean?* recording sheet (see Reproducible 8.1) can offer students additional practice with an already familiar visual of cube towers and line plots.

It is important for students to realize how the distribution and range of data affect the mean, median, or mode. Asking students to create data sets with specified constraints such as the following can help this understanding to develop:

REPRODUCIBLE 8.1
What Do You Mean?
Recording Sheet

◀

The mean number of students in 6 families is 4. How many children might be in each family? Create a line plot to represent your data. Why does your distribution make sense? Will everyone's distribution look the same? Why or why not?

Make a data set representing the ages of students with the following statistical landmarks:

> *sample size: 12 students*
> *range: 8 years*
> *median age: 12.5 years*
> *mode: 10 years*

Make a line plot to represent your data set. Be prepared to explain why your distribution makes sense. Will everyone's distribution look the same? Why or why not?

Implementing activities and investigations that focus on the difference between the mean, median, and mode can support our students as they make sense of these measures and interpret them properly.

Data About Us

Duration: 1 Class Period; Can Also Be Implemented as a Daily Routine

Data generated from class graphs can supply engaging and interesting information to interpret and analyze. This lesson offers students opportunities to

- collect, interpret, and analyze everyday data;
- view and discuss data displayed in various graphs and tables; and
- pose questions and preferred representational formats for future class surveys.

Materials

- chart paper, prepared with the posed question and the data-collection format

Vocabulary

categorical data, distribution, frequency, generalization, numerical data, prediction, sample size, survey population, typical (as in "What is *typical* for this class?" [mean? median? mode?])

NCTM Connection

Strand: Data Analysis and Probability

Focus: Construct and articulate predictions and generalizations about objects (boxes) and their volumes.

Context: *Data About Us*

Everyday data is just plain interesting! Each morning during this unit of study, my students enter homeroom to find a graph or table of some kind posted on the whiteboard. I post a question at the top of the graph to which they respond. I pose the questions for the first few days, and then they quickly begin asking to pose the questions themselves. I ask them to write down their question and the graphical representation with which they would like to collect the class data. Once they have turned in their requests, I take the liberty of deciding what question to post and create a graph or table on chart paper on which we will collect the data the next morning.

Using data collected from class graphs not only encourages the application of the studied statistical concepts and procedures but it also offers the opportunity to apply previously covered concepts and procedures from past years. This type of data collection offers a set model from which to interpret and analyze the data. Because the sample size represents the whole in this model, students can comment on trends and the distribution of data using what they know about fractions, decimals, and percents. It is important for students to realize that the sample size can change daily based on the day's attendance. This data is often represented with "messy" fractions that I also really like! If we notice that thirteen-twenty-sevenths of the class owns a dog, what generalization can we make? About half the class owns a dog. About 50 percent of the class does not own a dog, but they could own a cat or a frog or a turtle. Using rational number benchmarks as we interpret the data becomes meaningful and very helpful.

I posed the following question and collected data for it in my class this year. (See Figure 8–5.) The "scribble-scrabble" surrounding the collected data was scripted from the class discussion as we processed what we collected. You may want to analyze the data quickly yourself before you open up a class discussion. The questions you pose can help the students uncover and apply important mathematics as well as identify and interpret the trends that the data presents. Every picture tells a story—as does each data set!

As you create data-collection charts, keep in mind that presenting varied collection formats will offer your students the opportunity to use graphs and tables other than the ever-popular bar graph. It is important to offer some surveys that collect *numerical* data and others that collect *categorical* data. Collected data that are numbers are classified as *numerical* data, whereas collected data that are words or categories are classified as

FIGURE 8–5
Data Collection from a Class Discussion.

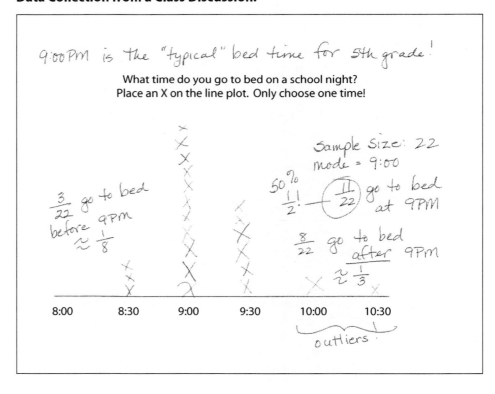

categorical data. Some possible questions and data collection formats are illustrated below.

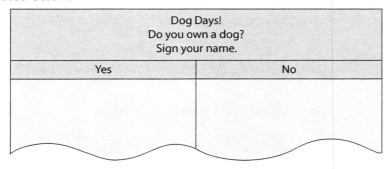

Dog Days! Do you own a dog? Sign your name.		
Yes	No	

What is your favorite lunch? Place a tally next to your choice.		
Pizza		
Hot dogs		
Pasta		
Shepherd's pie		
Tacos		
Other		

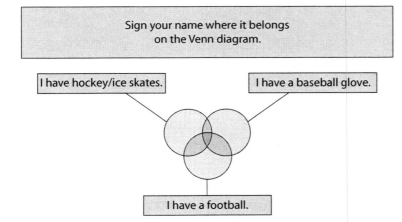

Sign your name where it belongs on the Venn diagram.

I have hockey/ice skates. I have a baseball glove.

I have a football.

Graph Round Robin

Duration: 1–2 Class Periods

Collected data can be presented in a myriad of formats and representations. In order to prepare our students for the onslaught of everyday data that is presented to us as consumers and citizens, we need to expose them to those varied representations. This lesson offers students opportunities to

- read, analyze, and interpret collected data in various formats presented in everyday media.

NCTM Connection

Strand: Data Analysis and Probability

Focus: Read, analyze and interpret collected data in various formats presented in everyday media.

Context: *Graph Round Robin*

REPRODUCIBLE 8.2
Graph Round Robin
Recording Sheet

Materials

- *Graph Round Robin* Recording Sheet (see Reproducible 8.2)
- graphs from newspapers, magazines, or online resources
- graph task cards (see description below), 1 per student
- card stock for graph task cards, 1 piece per card

Vocabulary

consumer, media, propaganda, skew(ed), source

I often worry that our fifth graders do not connect the importance of what we do in math class to their outside-of-school experiences. Exploring graphs, tables, and charts that appear in the media gives us the opportunity to make those connections real, important, and meaningful. As consumers and citizens, we all need to be able to interpret data—and at times, interpret it quickly by knowing what to look for and what questions to ask. Many years ago I began to collect graphs, charts, and tables that I found in magazines and newspapers to use for this particular lesson. I change the graphs as they become outdated—which in today's world can be a daily task!

Prior to the day's lesson, I create the task cards, numbering and laminating them. You can create the task cards by hand, but I have found that technology makes this production process easier; I have a desktop folder that contains stock templates that can be used for various types of graphs, charts, and tables. I can customize each set of questions for the data-collection representation by simply changing the words in each question to fit the pictured data. I can then print out the task card on card stock, mount the graph on the card, laminate it, and be ready to go. For example, task cards with data published in *USA Today* Snapshots® might look like this:

Eco-Friendly Things Not Part of Daily Routine

Adults who "rarely" or "never" do these:

- *compost food and organic waste: 69 percent*
- *carpool/take public transportation: 65 percent*
- *walk/ride bike: 63 percent*
- *purchase organic products: 44 percent*

1. *What is the sample size of this survey?*

2. *What percent of adults do not carpool or take public transportation?*

3. *What percent of adults do carpool or take public transportation?*

4. *44 percent of adults do not do this: _____.*

(*Source:* Carey and Ward, date unknown. Published in *USA Today* Snapshots®.

> **Rolling Fast**
>
> *The fastest roller coaster in the USA is the "Steel Phantom" in West Mifflin, PA. How fast does it go?*
>
> A. 48 mph
> B. 65 mph
> C. 80 mph*
> D. 94 mph
>
> 1. *What is the name of the fastest roller coaster in the United States?*
>
> 2. *How fast does it go? [answer: C, 80 mph]*
>
> 3. *What state is lucky enough to have this roller coaster?*
>
> 4. *Mrs. Schuster grew up ten miles from this park. True or False?*
>
> (*Source:* Throgmorton, date unknown. Published in *USA Today* Snapshots®.

Prior to the lesson, I also make packets of the *Graph Round Robin* recording sheet. (See Figure 8–6; see also Reproducible 8.2.)

Before students come to class, I place the numbered task cards at the tables in numerical order. The *Graph Round Robin* process is similar to *Place-Value Round Robin* in Chapter 6.

After students are seated at their tables, I instruct them to circle the task number at their seat on the recording sheet. This is where they will begin moving from task card to task card in numerical order. When it is time, I call out "switch," and students move to the next card. I remind them that they can return to cards that they have not finished once we have moved through all the cards. The process begins a little slowly, with lots of questions and a little confusion. But by the third or fourth card, students understand how the process works and what is being asked of them—and they really like it!

Once the process is completed, I find it is more worthwhile to open up a discussion about the graphs that interested or surprised students than to process each one of the graphs. It is also important to ask students how they learned to assess the information quickly: What did they look for? How did they find it? Personally, I seem to be drawn to the sample size of polled populations if the information is available on the graph. So what if only fifteen people are polled? Does that make a difference in how one interprets the data?

Encourage your students to be on the lookout for interesting graphs, charts, and tables. You may want to reserve a section of a bulletin board for interesting collections of data, or to begin a class or end a day with a discussion about a graph brought in by one of your students or one that you have found.

▶ REPRODUCIBLE 8.2
Graph Round Robin
Recording Sheet

Graph Round Robin
Recording Sheet

Graph No. _____

1. _____
2. _____
3. _____
4. _____

Graph No. _____

1. _____
2. _____
3. _____
4. _____

Graph No. _____

1. _____
2. _____
3. _____
4. _____

Graph No. _____

1. _____
2. _____
3. _____
4. _____

FIGURE 8–6
Graph Round Robin Recording Sheet.

NCTM Connection

Strand: Data Analysis and Probability

Focus: Make, collect, and record measurements within a literature context; identify, compute, and analyze measurement averages: mean, median, and mode.

Context: *A Giant Among Wizards*

A Giant Among Wizards

Duration: 1–3 Class Periods

The continued popularity of the Harry Potter books (Rowling 1997, 1999, 2000a, 2000b, 2003, 2005, and 2007) provides a wonderful opportunity to connect mathematics to real-world settings—that is, if you believe that the real world is inhabited by muggles and wizards! A wizard named Hagrid offers a context in which to explore his giant-sized height and shoulder width compared to class averages of the same. This lesson offers students opportunities to

- make, collect, and record measurements;
- identify, compute, and analyze measurement averages: mean, median, and mode; and
- solve multiplicative comparison problems based on collected and analyzed data (see Chapter 4).

Materials

- *Harry Potter and the Sorcerer's Stone* (Rowling 1997)
- measuring tape, 1 per pair of students
- chart paper for class data collection, 1 piece labeled *Height*, 1 piece labeled *Shoulder Width*
- optional: newsprint and markers for table posters

Vocabulary

muggle

For the uninitiated, Harry Potter is a young wizard whose story is told in seven novels. *The Sorcerer's Stone* (Rowling 1997) is the first of the series and introduces us to ten-year-old Harry. Chapter 1, "The Boy Who Lived," provides the setting and tone for the reader's introduction to Harry and the wonderful world of Hogwarts, Platform Nine and Three-Quarters, Diagon Alley, and the Leaky Cauldron. In Chapter 1, we are also introduced to several well-seasoned wizards: Dumbledore, Professor McGonagall, and Hagrid—about whom this lesson is constructed. With Hagrid and his newly found wizard friends Ron and Hermione, Harry discovers a hidden world of witches and wizards all living in fear of the return of the Dark Lord, Voldemort.

An oral reading of the first chapter will engage even the most reluctant of believers and mathematicians! It is a brilliantly written chapter, especially if you have taken the time to reread the chapter after reading all seven books of the series. The foreshadowing is flawless, the characters ageless, and the setting is magical, mystical, and mysterious. Your students will adore it!

Hagrid makes his appearance on a huge motorcycle that falls from the air:

> If the motorcycle was huge, it was nothing compared to the man sitting astride it. He was almost twice as tall as a normal man and at least five times as wide. He looked simply too big to be allowed, and so *wild*—long tangles of bushy black hair and beard hid most of his face, he had hands the size of trash can lids, and his feet in their leather boots were like baby dolphins. In his vast muscular arms he was holding a bundle of blankets. (Rowling 1997, 14)

To begin a delightful exploration of data collection, interpretation, and prediction, ask the class, "So, how large is Hagrid—especially when compared to a fifth grader?"

Before data is collected, you will need to establish a few constraints—the class will need to agree on the measurement unit, the measuring tool, and how the data will be collected and represented. My Harry Potter aficionados often request that we measure to the nearest centimeter—Harry is, after all, a good Brit! We also quickly agree that measuring tapes would serve our measurement needs well. My students like collecting class data on chart paper, so we post two pieces, one entitled *Height* and the other *Shoulder Width*. Students work in pairs to measure and post the collected data. (See Figure 8–7.)

Once the data have been collected, have a discussion about identifying the "typical" height and shoulder width of the class. We begin by discussing

FIGURE 8–7
The Students' Collected Data and Agreed-on Averages.

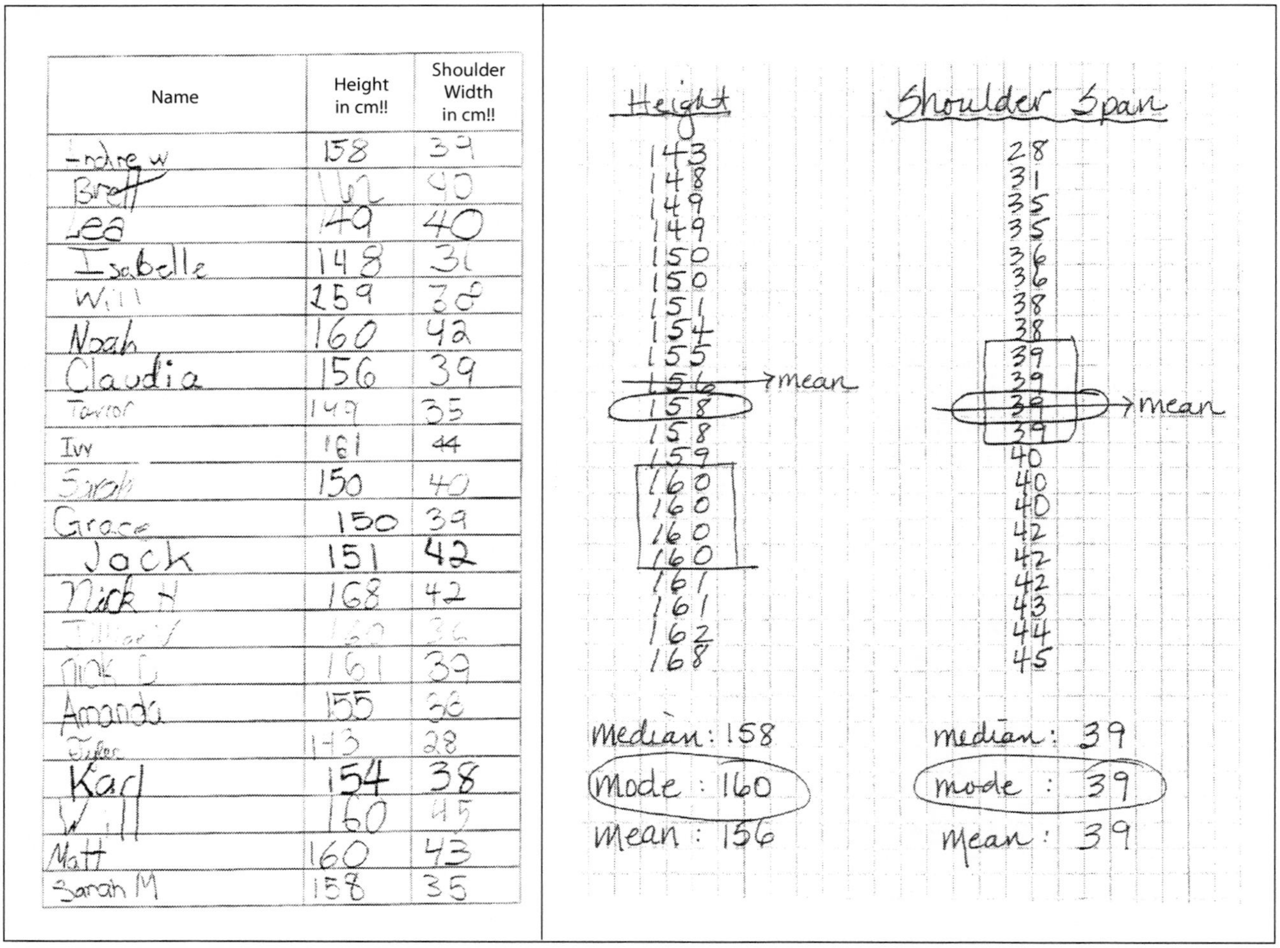

and analyzing the collected data. Statistical landmarks such as *sample size*, *minimum*, *maximum*, and *outliers* can refine and clarify our observations. Each year, the class has a rather animated conversation about what average would serve our needs and purposes the best. And each year, the decision is often between the mode and mean of the data sets. The median is identified, but students prefer to focus on the mode and mean. The class calculates all the measures of central tendency, and class consensus determines the value we want to use to help us calculate Hagrid's size of "twice as tall . . . and five times as wide" (Rowling 1997, 14).

Reference to our work with multiplicative comparison problems back when we discussed the relationship of multiplication to division (see Chapter 4) serves our needs well. When asked how we can calculate Hagrid's height and shoulder width, students quickly and easily identify multiplication as the procedure to help us do so.

Before we calculated, I asked students to create equations with words or symbols that could help us to calculate Hagrid's dimensions. They offered following equations:

Hagrid's height = 2x (class height average: mode)
Hagrid's shoulder width = 5x (class shoulder width average: mode)

$\square$ *= class average height (mode)*
$\triangle$ *= class average shoulder width (mode)*
Hagrid's height = 2 × $\square$
Hagrid's shoulder width = 5 × $\triangle$

x = class average height (mode)
y = class average shoulder width (mode)
Hagrid's height = 2 • x
Hagrid's shoulder width = 5 • y

This particular year, we agreed that Hagrid was 320 cm tall (160×2) and his shoulder width was 195 cm (39×5). This was one big wizard!

Jack wanted to know if Hagrid could fit through the doorway that opens into our hallway. Our investigation took a new twist—Jack and three other boys went out to the hallway and took the measurements of the doorway: It measured 320 cm wide and 250 cm high. No, Hagrid could not visit our math class; that is, if he came lumbering down the hallway . . . ! Comparing Hagrid's measurements to landmarks around the school can offer additional measurement extensions. Could Hagrid fit under the beech tree in front of the gym? Could he fit in the kiosk in the drop-off/pickup area? Could he stand up in the cafeteria? We all laughed when we figured out that he could stand up in ours, but not fit through the doorway!

If time allows, creating table posters to illustrate the posed question and class results can give closure to this investigation. If your students are as well versed in Harry Potter as my students are, they will adorn the posters with Harry Potter trivia; you might find it necessary to remind students that the important part of their presentation is the mathematics!

For more good questions, see *Good Questions for Math Teaching: Why Ask Them and What to Ask, Grades 5–8* by Lainie Schuster and Nancy Anderson (Math Solutions 2005).

Good Questions to Ask

■ The fifth grade is planning a movie night in the theater. Molly is conducting a survey about the movie interests of the fifth grade in order to gather information for possible movie choices. If Molly asks her classmates one question that results in categorical data and another that results in numerical data, what could the two questions be?

■ Ms. Zito gave a math unit test worth 100 points. Following the test, she organized the scores into a stem-and-leaf plot. State five conclusions Ms. Zito could make about her students' performance. Use vocabulary words such as *range, median, mean, mode*, and *sample size* in your conclusions. What do you think the unit of study was? Why?

1	
2	4
3	4 9
4	3 7
5	7 9
6	1 6 8
7	3 5 5 6 8
8	3 6 6 6 7
9	2 5 6

■ Two frogs had a race. Fred the Frog took eight jumps with a mode of twenty-two inches in length. Frank the Frog took five jumps with a median of twenty-two inches in length. Create a *graphical display* to represent the *frequency* and *distribution* of Fred's and Frank's jumps.

■ These are the results of a survey:

Place	Frequency
library	(2) II
playground	(5) ℕ
under the trees	(9) ℕ IIII
on a porch	(7) ℕ II

What might the survey be about? Why does your survey make sense given the data presented?

■ What does it mean to say that a person's arm span *is related* to his height or how the time it takes to travel to school *is related* to the distance traveled? Give other examples of data sets that could have a relationship with each other.

■ Katie conducted a survey of her fifth-grade class. This is what the graph looked like:

```
x
x   x
x   x   x
x   x   x   x
x   x   x   x   x
x   x   x   x   x
_____
1   2   3   4   5
```

What might the survey be about? Why does your survey topic make sense?

Calculation Routines and Practices

Examining our everyday use of mathematics reveals that we most often rely on mental computation when we use arithmetic: getting to school on time, computing taxes and tips, doubling or halving recipes, figuring out how much yarn is needed for a sweater pattern, and so on. Life is not all that different for our fifth graders. They employ their mental calculation skills when they calculate batting averages, price out video games or CDs, determine if they have enough money left for a soda once they pay for the movie ticket, and so on. Our ability to calculate mentally is highly dependent on our number sense—a direct correlation exists, if you will, between the two. We talk about the development of number sense with younger students in the primary grades, but how often do we discuss the importance of this with our fifth graders? Not enough.

Students with good number sense can think and reason flexibly with numbers. They use numbers to solve problems, spot unreasonable answers, understand how numbers can be taken apart and put back together in different ways, see and articulate connections between operations, figure mentally, and make reasonable estimates (Burns 2007, 24).

In contrast, students with poor number sense tend to rely on procedures based on memorized steps rather then reason, often do not notice when answers or estimates are unreasonable, and have limited numerical common sense.

Although we want our students to calculate on paper efficiently and accurately, we also want them to estimate and reason efficiently and accurately, which requires strong number sense. The following teaching strategies may help you to build your students' numerical thinking and reasoning skills.

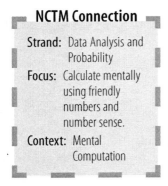

Model Think Alouds as You Estimate or Perform Mental Computation Tasks

Think aloud as you compute mentally so that your students can observe such a routine or practice. My students often ask me what 90 percent would be on an exam. I offer a conversation with myself as I use benchmarks to identify 90 percent of an exam with 86 points. I identify what 50 percent would be (43 points), and then take 50 percent of that (about 22 points) and add that to 43 points (65 points), which would get me to 75 percent on the exam. The difference between the 86 total points on the exam and the estimated 65 points is 23 points. So I halve the 23 points to about 11 or 12 points—12 to be safe to get halfway between 75 percent and 100 percent—and add that to 65. So I want to score 77 out of 86 points on the test.

Demonstrate Different Models for Computing

I move between the partial-quotients procedure for long division and the traditional algorithm for long division based on the divisors. I still find the traditional algorithm more efficient for single-digit divisors, but I almost always use the partial-quotients procedure with double-digit divisors. If I am dividing in front of the class, I make note of what I am doing and why it makes sense to me to make those choices.

Engaging your students in calculating mentally by decomposing factors when multiplying is helpful and very powerful. When multiplying 28 by 6, decompose 28 into 20 plus 8 (just as you do when chunking—see the "Calculation Routines and Practices" section Chapter 4):

$$20 \times 6 = 120$$
$$8 \times 6 = 48$$
$$120 + 48 = 168$$

The product is 168.

Ask Students to Calculate Mentally on a Regular Basis

Encourage your students to mentally calculate everyday needs and tasks. A "How do you know?" follow-up question can push students to evaluate their mental arithmetic strategies.

- How long is it until lunch? How many minutes?
- How much money did we make at the bake sale?
- What percentage of the class is absent today?
- How many more days until summer vacation?

Have Class Discussions About Mental Calculation Strategies

When students report results of arithmetic they have done mentally, ask them about their strategies and reasoning. The other students in the class can benefit greatly from listening to a classmate's strategies. They can compare and contrast their own strategies with those being offered, or abandon less-efficient strategies for those that make more sense to them.

Make Estimation an Integral Part of Computing

I love the word *about*; it is so very useful when estimating! I refer to estimates as *abouts*, and students often begin to do so as well. Asking students to estimate products, quotients, percentages, or fractional amounts can further develop numerical reasoning and number sense. Using benchmarks such as *about one half* or *about 75 percent* can also help students to better estimate as they think about problems and solutions.

Question Students About How They Reason Numerically

Questions such as the following can help students to focus on numerical reasoning skills and routines:

- Why do you think that?
- Why does your answer make sense?
- How do you know when you have an answer?
- Is there only one solution? How do you know?
- Will your strategy work with every number? Every similar situation?
- Did anyone think about this differently?

Pose Open-Ended Numerical Problems

Open-ended problems can be open in their approach or solution. An open-ended problem may have multiple approaches or multiple solutions. Number sense requires the flexibility to reason numerically. The selection of a particular approach often depends on the numbers and the context of a particular problem. Open-ended problems require students not only to apply facts and procedures but also to make connections and generalizations in the process of solving the problem. Solving open-ended problems requires that students make sense of the mathematics. Examples of open-ended questions are offered in the "Good Questions to Ask" section of this chapter and all other chapters throughout this resource.

In the classroom, we need to provide our fifth graders with many opportunities to reason mathematically, talk with others about their ideas, and see different ways of thinking with and about numbers (Burns 2007, 26).

Reading, Writing, and Vocabulary

Students benefit when we provide them with opportunities to explain and support their thinking and reasoning not only with discourse but also with representations of reasoning and proof. Our fifth graders are aware of the need to test and prove conjectures. They are aware of the power of generalization. They know that to disprove a conjecture or generalization, you only need one false result. Our fifth-grade mathematicians also continue to need our feedback and guidance as they refine and strengthen their writing and reasoning skills.

Implementing and continuing effective and supportive instruction for mathematical writing is hard work—really hard work. Mathematical writing is much more than simply writing in response to a prompt. According to the authors of *Content-Area Writing: Every Teacher's Guide* (Daniels, Zemelman, and Steineke 2007):

> Writing helps students *get more actively engaged in subject matter*, understand information and concepts more deeply, make connections and raise questions more fluently, remember ideas longer, and apply learning in new situations. . . . If we say reading helps us *take in* knowledge, with writing, we *make it our own*. (5)

When we ask students to formulate, organize, represent, prove, and refine their thinking, we are asking them to think deeply. But posing a question or posting a prompt is not enough. We need to support our students as they learn to write mathematically. Pose the following questions to help support students (and yourself) as they continue to refine their mathematical writing skills:

- What is the question asking, and asking of you?
- Would a diagram, chart, or number model help to support your thinking?
- Would it help to begin with that diagram, chart, or number model and write from it?
- What mathematical language can help you to clarify your ideas?
- How might the introductory sentence look? Have you taken a stand?
- How might your concluding sentence look? Have you summarized your thinking?

Keeping and reviewing writing samples throughout the year will help you to stay the course. Take a look at a writing sample from the beginning of the year and one from this point in the year—you will be amazed and impressed.

Assessment

Understanding is revealed in performance. If a student understands, then he can transfer the core ideas, knowledge, and skills on a challenging task to a variety of contexts. Therefore, assessment for understanding should be grounded in authentic performance-based tasks (Wiggins and McTighe 2005, 153). The study of data analysis lends itself quite nicely to performance-based assessments. Because students have spent time collecting, representing, and analyzing data throughout the month, why not create a summative assessment that asks them to do the same?

Wiggins and McTighe (2005) outline guidelines for an authentic assessment task. These tasks

- are realistically contextualized;
- require judgment and innovation;
- ask the student to "do" the subject;
- replicate key situations in which adults are "tested" in the real world;
- assess the student's ability to efficiently and effectively apply and use a repertoire of knowledge and skills to negotiate a complex and multistage task; and
- offer opportunities to rehearse, practice, consult resources, get feedback on, and refine a product. (153–54)

An assessment grounded in authentic work calls students to two important understandings: the first being how adults in the larger world really use the knowledge learned in school, and the second being that lessons taught in school are meaningful and can lead to high-quality thinking or performance. An authentic assessment that requires students to pose questions of interest to them, and then to collect, represent, and analyze the data can offer such opportunities.

Introduce a culminating assessment to students early in the month so that they can begin to think about what interests them: the question they will pose, the graphical representation they will use to present their data, or the generalizations that will come from the data interpretation. (See Figure 8–8 on page 386.)

You can create a rubric *with* students prior to start of the project. Eliciting assessment criteria from those being assessed makes good sense in this context. Keep in mind that you will need to have had enough instructional time before a comprehensive rubric can be created that will meet your mathematical objectives as well as students'. When I create rubrics with my class, I remind the when necessary that I continue to be in charge—and that my mathematical objectives for them need to be addressed. The wonderful thing about all of this is that often we do not have to have this conversation. They get it and are well aware of the high expectations for both process and product!

FIGURE 8–8
Sample Questions for Creating an Assessment Rubric.

Meet a Typical Lower Schooler!

What do we know about the students in our lower school?

- *What are their favorite foods?*
- *How many miles do they travel to school every day?*
- *What is their favorite topic in math? (Hey, you knew I was going to get that in there somewhere!)*

Here is your charge:

- *Create a question that interests you about the students in the lower school. If we wanted to describe a typical lower schooler to someone new to our community, what kind of information could we offer them?*
- *Collect data in response to your question.*
- *Study and interpret your data once it is collected.*

    What do you notice?

    Any lumps, bumps, or holes in the data distribution?

    How would your data be best represented?

    What are the statistical landmarks of your data set?

    How do the mode, median, and mean influence the generalizations you can now make about a typical lower schooler?

- *Represent your data in a table and a graph.*
- *Analyze your data in narrative form with words!*
- *Make three generalizations about lower schoolers based on your data.*

Your project will be in poster form. Be interesting and interested. Be creative and thorough. Have fun with this! You are the expert!

REPRODUCIBLE 8.3   ◄
Rubric Template

You can then begin a conversation about what a good project looks like as the rubric develops. Use a template as the criteria are discussed and agreed on. For this particular rubric, I offer a scoring scale that runs from 0 to 4, with specific criteria for each score. (See Figure 8–9, Figure 8–10 on page 388, and see also Reproducible 8.3.)

FIGURE 8–9
A Sample Assessment Rubric and Scoring Scale.

4: Exemplary Response	■ complete, thorough, and coherent ■ shows an understanding of the mathematical concepts and procedures ■ satisfies all the essential conditions of the task ■ goes beyond what is asked for in some unique way
3: Complete Response	■ complete, thorough, and coherent ■ shows an understanding of the mathematical concepts and procedures ■ satisfies all the essential conditions of the task
2: Reasonably Complete Response	■ reasonably complete; may lack some detail ■ shows an understanding of most of the mathematical concepts and procedures ■ satisfies most of the essential conditions of the task
1: Partial Response	■ gives a response; the explanation may be unclear or lack detail ■ shows some understanding of some of the mathematical concepts and procedures ■ satisfies some of the essential conditions of the task
0: Inadequate Response	■ incomplete; the explanation is insufficient or not understandable ■ shows little understanding of the mathematical concepts and procedures ■ fails to address the essential conditions of the problem

Prior to assigning this type of project, you will need to make several instructional decisions: What is the population for the surveys? Grade 5? Grades 4 and 5? Will students work with a partner or with a small group? If small-group work is planned, how will time be allotted in the school day for this work? What materials will you have available for the posters? How will the final projects be processed or shared? Is there space available in the school for posting the finished projects? You may want to inform your principal and colleagues about the project because of the impact it may have outside of your classroom.

This is a wonderful time of the year for such a project. Students have gained mathematical independence and sophistication and enjoy being in charge of their learning—and often take on that ownership willingly and enthusiastically. Keeping sample questions and projects to use as examples for future classes can be a great help in planning.

SCORING SCALE	Criteria	Score (4–0)
4: Exemplary Response ■ complete, thorough, and coherent ■ shows an understanding of the mathematical concepts and procedures ■ satisfies all the essential conditions of the task ■ goes beyond what is asked for in some unique way	I posed a "good" question. It was clear and easy to understand.	
	I collected my data and recorded it in a frequency table. I included my rough draft of the data collection.	
3: Complete Response ■ complete, thorough, and coherent ■ shows an understanding of the concepts and procedures ■ satisfies all the essential conditions of the task	I interpreted the data. I paid attention to statistical landmarks such as sample size, range, minimum, and maximum. I identified the mean, median, and mode.	
	I represented my collected data in a graph. My graph was neat, organized, and well presented on the poster.	
2: Reasonably Complete Response ■ reasonably complete; may lack some detail ■ shows an understanding of most of the mathematical concepts and procedures ■ satisfies most of the essential conditions of the task	I analyzed the data in paragraph form. I paid attention to and discussed important statistical vocabulary and landmarks. My writing was well organized and thorough.	
1: Partial Response ■ gives a response; the explanation may be unclear or lack detail ■ shows some understanding of some of the mathematical concepts and procedures ■ satisfies some of the essential conditions of the task	I constructed three generalizations about a typical lower schooler based on the analysis of my data.	
	My poster is well organized and the information on it is well presented. It is creative and really cool!	
0: Inadequate Response ■ incomplete; the explanation is insufficient or not understandable ■ shows little understanding of the mathematical concepts and procedures ■ fails to address the essential conditions of the problem	Total Score	_____

FIGURE 8–10
Completed Class-Generated Rubric for the Data-Collection Project.

Home and School Connections

As with previous units of study, I create and distribute a Parent Information and Involvement Form prior to the beginning of our study of data analysis to help parents support their children at home. (See Figure 8–11.)

As the end of the school year quickly approaches, thoughts about the future loom large. As our fifth graders move on to become middle schoolers, they will experience new schools, new teachers, and new expectations once again in the fall. Many schools mandate an end-of-year report that can benefit everyone involved. Parents appreciate receiving specific information about their child's strengths and challenges. Remember that effective reporting is far more a challenge in effective communication than simply a process of documenting student achievement (Guskey and Bailey 2001). Parents are most appreciative when information about their children is communicated clearly and is easy to interpret. Whether reporting in the form of letter grades or narrative comments, you will need to decide

FIGURE 8–11
Parent Information and Involvement Form: May.

▶ REPRODUCIBLE 2.16
Parent Information
and Involvement
Form

Parent Information and Involvement Form

From: Lainie Schuster
Re: Mathematical Curriculum
Unit: Data Analysis

During the next unit, the major topics we will be studying are:
- data collection, representation, and analysis
- statistical landmarks

My goal in studying these topics is for the students to be able to:
- collect and represent data using tables, line plots, and graphs
- analyze collected data and formulate opinions based on the collected data
- identify the mean, mode, median, minimum, maximum, sample size, and range of a data set
- make informed decisions about which graphs and which of the measures of central tendency (mean, median, or mode) may be used to describe a distribution of data

---

Parents can help at home by:
- pointing out the use of graphs and statistics in newspapers and magazines
- pointing out misleading statistics—often depending on the message the creators of the statistical data want to send!

whether to include other aspects of a student's learning as well as evidence of mathematical achievement or performance. For example, you may wish to consider effort, work ethic, persistence, and participation when assigning a grade or writing a comment. Practical suggestions about what improvements can be made as their child moves on to the sixth grade are of great importance and help to parents. Many parents want to be involved in their child's mathematical education and are highly dependent on the observations, assessments, and recommendations of the teacher.

Resource

Math Matters: Understanding the Math You Teach, Grades K–8, Second Edition (Chapin and Johnson 2006)

Chapter 13: Statistics
This chapter provides an excellent explanation of the measures of central tendency—why we use which one and when. It also offers a thorough explanation of graphical displays, some that we use in grade 5 and some beyond.

Chapter 9

Multiplication and Division Revisited

SUGGESTED MONTH: JUNE

I had been to school most all the time and could spell and read and write just a little, and could say the multiplication table up to six times seven is thirty-five, and I don't reckon I could ever get any further than that if I was to live forever. I don't take no stock in mathematics, anyway.

The Adventures of Huckleberry Finn
Twain 1994, 17

The Learning Environment

Continue to Understand the Thinking of Your Students and Base Your Instruction on That Understanding

As you move into a unit whose purpose is to extend previous learning, the understanding and knowledge of your students become the guiding forces as you help them build on the knowledge that they have already developed. A unit on extending multiplication and division may look different from year to year given your cast of characters. It is important to offer tasks and facilitate conversations that encourage students to make connections and articulate relationships between new material and previously covered concepts and procedures.

Continue to Emphasize the Need to Make Sense of Mathematics

Nancy Anderson, a Math Solutions colleague and dear friend of mine, reminds everyone from ten-year-olds to college professors that mathematics is not an opinion; it makes sense because it is rooted in logic. Knowing mathematics, *really* knowing it, means understanding it. When we study mathematics, we need to get inside it and see how things work, how things are related to each other, and why they work as they do (Hiebert et al. 1997, 2). Our students are coming to the end of their fifth-grade year of math instruction. They have investigated and applied the concepts and procedures of multiplication and division throughout their time with you and your presented mathematics curriculum. We need to continue to make instructional decisions and choices that help our students explore, discover, and articulate the interrelatedness of their understandings and proficiencies.

The Mathematics and Its Language

Children Continue to Develop and Apply Strategies for Multiplying and Dividing While Solving More Difficult Problems Without the Use of a Calculator or Standard Algorithm

Students often perceive problems with larger numbers as more difficult than those with smaller numbers. Because of this perceived reality, it is important for students to develop strategies with which to approach and solve more difficult problems. The more strategies students come to understand well, the more choices they will have when solving problems.

Children Begin to Informally Explore Proportionality

Proportionality is a complex topic: it is estimated that more than half the adult population does not reason proportionally (Chapin and Johnson 2006, 165). *Proportional reasoning is the ability to make and use multiplicative comparisons among quantities.* The understanding of the concepts and procedures required by proportional reasoning tasks takes years to develop. Because of this, students need to informally explore ideas related to thinking multiplicatively throughout the elementary grades.

Children Are Introduced to Rates and Collect and Compare Rate Data

We use rates every day to make comparisons between quantities, miles per gallon, wages per hour, and points per game. Rate problems involve a *rate,* a special type of ratio in which two quantities are compared (Chapin and Johnson 2006, 79). Many young students have little exposure to and experience with rates. Because of this, they are often unsure how to approach, interpret, represent, and solve problems involving rates. It is important for our fifth graders to informally explore rates in preparation for the significant amount of time that they will spend developing these proportional reasoning concepts in the middle grades. Intuitive solutions based on understandings about multiplication and division need to be accessed and applied as we help students move from additive to multiplicative thinking rather than a reliance on algorithms or formulas.

Children Calculate and Compare Unit Rates

Students can calculate per-unit rates when you give them rate information for a number of measurements and they convert it to an equivalent unit rate. They can then calculate additional equivalent rates from the determined unit rate. A pricing and purchasing context is a familiar and engaging one for fifth graders.

Children Use Rate Tables to Record Rate Information and to Solve Rate Problems

Use rate tables to aid in problem solving. Students may recognize rate tables as a special kind of in-and-out table—and one that is very helpful in solving story problems involving a rate (see "Classification of Multiplication Story Problems" in Chapter 4). Rate tables are often horizontal, but they can also be written vertically. Each has its advantages and offers students opportunities to shift from one representation to the other given the context or purpose of the information.

Lesson Planning

- This time of year is ridiculously busy with end-of-year celebrations, field trips, culminating projects, report cards . . . I get tired just thinking of all that goes on now! As busy as it can be, we cannot forget that we are moving our fifth graders into middle school mathematics programs in a few short months. Now is the time to take an informal inventory of what they know, what they do not, and what they will need to know come the fall. Taking a look at the fall topics of their upcoming year will help you to make instructional decisions this month. A review of the concepts and procedures of multiplication and division is always a good thing. However, I have also found that including topics introducing and requiring proportional reasoning can offer needed multiplication practice as well as push students to think outside of their mathematical comfort zones.

- Pulling out favorite games played throughout the year can easily be incorporated into this month's lesson planning. Refer to "Games to Revisit" in "Investigations, Games, and Literature-Based Activities" in this chapter.

- Although you may not have formally covered the multiplication and division of fractions and decimals this year, do not shy away from them as students solve problems involving proportionality and rates. Strong number sense and conceptual understanding will allow them to construct procedures with which to multiply (and even divide!) rational numbers. When students devise strategies to deal with these bits and pieces, engage the class in a discussion of those strategies and why they work.

- Continue to plan lessons and activities that are engaging and challenging. Mathematics teaching and learning is important—even in these last weeks of school. Students will take our lead.

Possible Difficulties or Misconceptions

A great many students believe that numbers in a rate or ratio only represent specific quantities rather than a *relationship* between those two quantities. I have found that students who have moved through a year of instruction in which numerical relationships have been discovered, explored, identified, and articulated are more apt to recognize the relationships found in ratios. Students' awareness and understanding might be fragile, at best, but the seeds of understanding have been sown and will have time to germinate and blossom through the middle school years and beyond.

As mentioned in the previous section, proportional reasoning is the ability to make and use *multiplicative* comparisons among quantities. Many students have difficulty applying this multiplicative relationship to a set of numbers and will often add to find equivalent proportions. Referring students to their work with multiplicative comparison story problems (see "Classification of Multiplication Story Problems" in Chapter 4) may help to move them from thinking additively to multiplicatively.

Investigations, Games, and Literature-Based Activities

The King's Chessboard

Duration: 2–3 Class Periods

The King's Chessboard offers a literary context in which to explore patterns and the exponential growth of numbers. These lessons are referenced in *Math and Literature, Grades 4–6* (Bresser 2004) and offer students opportunities to

- organize, analyze, and interpret data;
- identify and articulate patterns;
- investigate the power of doubling (literally and figuratively!);
- explore place value and periods beyond the millions; and
- apply problem-solving strategies as well as multiplication and division procedures.

Materials

- The King's Chessboard task (see Reproducible 9.1)
- The King's Chessboard Template (see Reproducible 9.2)
- Three-column T-chart (consider laminating on chart paper for future use) (see Reproducible 9.3)
- Power Counting Chart (consider laminating on chart paper for future use) (see Reproducible 9.4)
- *The King's Chessboard* (Birch 1988)
- quart-sized zip-top bags of rice, 1 per table group
- plastic teaspoons, 1 per pair of students
- half-cup measuring cups, 1 per table group
- optional: *On Beyond a Million: An Amazing Math Journey* (Schwartz 1999)
- optional: newsprint, 1 piece per pair of students

NCTM Connection

Strand: Number and Operations

Focus: Explore the magnitude and representation of numbers beyond one million.

Context: *The King's Chessboard* by David Birch

▶ REPRODUCIBLE 9.1
The King's Chessboard

REPRODUCIBLE 9.2
The King's Chessboard Template

REPRODUCIBLE 9.3
Three-Column T-Chart

REPRODUCIBLE 9.4
Power Counting Chart

Vocabulary

average (mean, median, mode), powers of ten, quadrillion, quintillion

The lesson begins with an oral reading of the first fourteen pages of *The King's Chessboard* (Birch 1988). You can finish reading the book once the activity has been completed. This beautifully illustrated book tells the story of a king who insists on giving a gift to his wise man. The man wants no gift, but suggests that the king give him one grain of rice for the first square of a chessboard. On subsequent days, the king would give the man an amount of rice double that from the day before until all sixty-four squares of the chessboard are covered. Not understanding how much rice would be needed, the king agrees. Silly king! You can stop reading the book on page fourteen when the "Weigher had become worried" (Birch 1988). You do not want to give away the mathematics of the investigation!

Show students an overhead or chart paper diagram of the first row of a chessboard, and they can begin counting. Present the following task (see Reproducible 9.1):

REPRODUCIBLE 9.1
The King's
Chessboard ◀

The King's Chessboard Task

The king agreed to double the amount of rice he gives to his wise man day after day until all sixty-four squares of the chessboard are covered. With your partner:

1. Make an *estimate* of how many grains of rice the wise man will receive on the sixty-fourth day. Write it down! Extend the doubling pattern of the first row of the chessboard. Based on this information:

   ■ About how many grains of rice will the wise man receive on the sixty-fourth day? Write it down! Have you changed your estimate? Why or why not?

   ■ Do you think the amount of rice will reach the millions? If so, on what day will this happen?

2. Continue your thinking and patterns. Discuss with your partner how these grains of rice are growing. What strategies are you using to calculate? How effective and efficient are your strategies? Be prepared to discuss how reasonable your estimates are and why.

As students start counting and calculating, you may hear comments of surprise. Initially, the concept of doubling seems minor to students—not a big deal . . . until they start calculating. Soon their calculators will not be able to hold the numbers and students may not even know how to say them! Jeff became quite interested in what comes after billions as he worked with Joseph. "I never thought about numbers that big!" Who knew? (Square number thirty-one reaches one billion with forty-one squares to go.) (See Figure 9–1.)

1	2	4	8	16	32	64	128
256	512	1024	2048	4096	8192	16,384	32,768
				Sq.#21 reaches 1 million			
						Sq.#31 reaches 1 billion	
Sq.#41 reaches 1 trillion							
		Sq.#51 reaches 1 qua-drillion					
				Sq.#61 reaches 1 quintil-lion			Sq.#64 reaches 9 quintil-lion

FIGURE 9–1
The King's Chessboard Template with Landmark Numbers Noted.

I only let this investigation carry on for about twenty minutes. The numbers quickly get large and unruly, and the last thing we want this time of year is for our students to become the same! Keeping an eye on the class and how focused they are while working will tell you when to call the class together.

Begin a class discussion about the rapid growth of these numbers. Initially, doubling may seem simple and manageable, but in reality, the growth is exponential and the resulting numbers are anything but simple and manageable.

The following list of observations may fall out of a whole-class discussion. If not, pose questions, such as the examples listed after each observation, to start students thinking about these ideas.

► REPRODUCIBLE 9.2
The King's
Chessboard
Template

The first row (the eighth day) ends on 128 grains of rice. Not a big deal.

- Can knowing the eighth day help you to predict the sixteenth day?

The second row (the sixteenth day) ends on 32,768.

- Why is that surprising? What has happened from the eighth day to the sixteenth day?
- Why can't you just multiply 128 times 2 to get the sixteenth day?

You reach one million somewhere in the third row.

- On what square do you reach one million (the twenty-first square)?
- In which row do you think you will reach one billion (the thirty-first square)?

It took twenty-one squares to get to one million and only nine squares to get to one billion. It will probably take fewer than nine squares to get to one trillion. (Actually, it only takes nine more squares: one trillion is reached on the forty-first square.)

- Why would that make sense?

REPRODUCIBLE 9.2
The King's
Chessboard
Template

REPRODUCIBLE 9.3
Three-Column
T-Chart

A display of the chessboard and three-column T-chart can move students to represent the growth of the grains of rice both numerically and exponentially, something that may be of interest to your students. (See Reproducibles 9.2 and 9.3.) A quick review of exponents and how they work may be necessary as you process the T-chart with the class.

You will need to decide how far you wish to go with this task. Thinking aloud as you post the numbers for the first three squares offers a model from which students can work. The "What Do I See" column in the T-chart helps students understand that the number of factors is equivalent to the number of the square. (See Figure 9–2.)

Going through each square is not mathematically significant once the pattern is established. What *is* mathematically significant, however, is that we can predict the exponential representation of the sixty-fourth square, as well as every square on the chessboard, which is shown here. (**Note:** The exponent is one less than the respective number of the square.)

$$2^{63} = 9,223,372,036,854,775,808$$

Nine quintillion, two hundred twenty-three quadrillion, three hundred seventy-two trillion, thirty-six billion, eight hundred fifty-four million, seven hundred seventy-five thousand, eight hundred eight!

REPRODUCIBLE 9.4
Power Counting
Chart

Because students are forever asking me what comes after one billion, I laminate and post a Power Counting Chart (see Reproducible 9.4) in the classroom. I also have *On Beyond a Million: An Amazing Math Journey* (Schwartz 1999) available as a convenient resource. (See Figure 9–3.)

Continue reading *The King's Chessboard* once the class has explored and discussed the pickle in which the king quickly finds himself; take time to discuss the message of the wise man's lesson: "how easy it is for pride to make a fool of anyone, even a king" (Birch 1988, 30).

Square Number	What Do I See?	Number of Grains of Rice
1	1	1
2	1×2	2
3	$1 \times 2 \times 2$	4
4	$1 \times 2 \times 2 \times 2$	8
5	$1 \times 2 \times 2 \times 2 \times 2$	16
6	$1 \times 2 \times 2 \times 2 \times 2 \times 2$	32
7	$1 \times 2 \times 2 \times 2 \times 2 \times 2 \times 2$	64
8	$1 \times 2 \times 2 \times 2 \times 2 \times 2 \times 2 \times 2$	128
.		.
.		.
.		.
16	1×2^{15}	2^{15}
.		.
.		.
32	1×2^{31}	2^{31}
.		.
.		.
.		.
64	1×2^{63}	2^{63}

▶ REPRODUCIBLE 9.3
Three-Column T-Chart

FIGURE 9–2
The King's Chessboard T-chart Helps Students Understand Exponential Number Growth.

TEACHER-TO-TEACHER TALK ■ About Big Numbers ■ Sometimes big numbers are just plain interesting! An activity such as this at the end of the year can encourage students to think beyond the year's curriculum and daily routines. When do we take the time to just talk about counting and big numbers? When you think about it, just about everything we do in mathematics classrooms is based on counting. As we get older and wiser, our counting strategies and notation get more sophisticated and efficient with the application of exponents and scientific notation. And here is a sobering thought: as our national debt grows exponentially, it will be increasingly important for future citizens of the world to understand numbers larger than one million—how they are symbolically represented, their magnitude, and how to read them in words. I shudder to think about the national debt our students will inherit as they move into adulthood. Large numbers can certainly grab our attention—and concern!

Follow-Up Activity

A follow-up to the king's chessboard investigation involving measurement and multiplication can be found in *Math and Literature: Grades 4–6*

Power Counting

Number in Words	Standard Form	Powers of Ten
one	1	10^0
ten	10	10^1
hundred	100	10^2
one thousand	1000	10^3
ten thousand	10,000	10^4
hundred thousand	100,000	10^5
one million	1,000,000	10^6
ten million	10,000,000	10^7
hundred million	100,000,000	10^8
one billion	1,000,000,000	10^9
one trillion	1,000,000,000,000	10^{12}
one quadrillion	1,000,000,000,000,000	10^{15}
one quintillion	1,000,000,000,000,000,000	10^{18}
one sextillion	1,000,000,000,000,000,000,000	10^{21}
one septillion	1,000,000,000,000,000,000,000,000	10^{24}
one octillion	1,000,000,000,000,000,000,000,000,000	10^{27}
one nonillion	1,000,000,000,000,000,000,000,000,000,000	10^{30}
one decillion	1,000,000,000,000,000,000,000,000,000,000,000	10^{33}

undecillion, duodecillion, tredecillion, quattuordecillion, quindecillion, sexdecillion, octodecillion, novemdecillion, vigintillion . . .

googol	10^{100}
googolplex	10^{googol}

FIGURE 9–3
A Power Counting Chart Is Posted in the Classroom for Easy Reference.

REPRODUCIBLE 9.4
Power Counting
Chart

◀   (Bresser 2004), with a more detailed explanation of the lesson, a classroom vignette, and suggestions for ensuing discussions.

Pose a new question to students:

On which square would enough of the king's rice arrive to feed everyone in the class?

Students need to reach consensus about how much rice each person will eat; one-half cup is a standard serving size for rice, so students will quickly agree that it would take forever and a day to count the grains of rice that fill a measure of a half a cup. So what do you do when a problem is too big? Tackle a smaller, related problem.

Use a teaspoon measurement to estimate the number of grains in a half-cup serving. Students scoop teaspoons of rice into a half-cup measuring cup, collect and post the measurements, and agree on an average number of teaspoons in a half-cup measurement. The next step is to determine the number of grains of rice in a teaspoon. Following the same process, students scoop out one teaspoon of rice, count the grains, post, identify, and agree on the average number of grains in a teaspoon.

Students can then discuss how to determine the number of grains of rice in a half-cup serving based on what they already have determined. Multiplying the agreed-on average of how many grains of rice there are in a teaspoon times the agreed-on average of the number of teaspoons in a half-cup measure will result in the number of grains in a half-cup serving.

The question of a possible discrepancy between uncooked rice and cooked rice may come up; if not, talk about it with the class. Generally, rice expands to three times its original uncooked size. Students will need to come to a consensus about whether their average needs to be multiplied by three—or divided by three—in order to identify the amount of rice needed for one serving of cooked rice.

Once students have reached a consensus and completed the calculation, they can then multiply the number of class members by the number of grains needed for a half-cup serving of rice.

You will need to make some instructional decisions about the scope and sequence of this investigation. Will you carry out the investigation in stages, or will the class discuss and process the entire investigation before the actual measurement takes place? Being aware of the strengths and needs of your particular class will be important when you make these decisions. As we all know, the classroom culture greatly affects how you present and carry out the lessons.

Once students have completed the calculations, return to the original question to give closure to the activity. On which square would enough of the king's rice arrive to feed everyone in the class? Refer to the chessboard and to the amounts of rice arriving each day. If the estimated amount is not posted on the chessboard, students will need to make further calculations and estimations in order to identify the chessboard square on which enough rice will be delivered.

If time permits, students may enjoy making posters of their findings on newsprint using guidelines that you have devised.

Rep-Tiles

Duration: 2–3 Class Periods

If congruent copies of a shape can be put together to make a larger, similar shape, the original shape is called a *rep-tile* (Lappan et al. 2009, 38). This lesson investigates similar figures and how their areas and perimeters are proportionately related. This activity is adapted from lessons referenced in

NCTM Connection

Strand: Number and Operations

Focus: Explore and make generalizations about the relationship between the area and perimeter as similar shapes grow.

Context: Rep-Tiles

Stretching and Shrinking (Lappan et al. 2009). This investigation offers students opportunities to

- apply understandings of area and perimeter in a problem-solving context;
- explore the relationship between the perimeter and area of similar polygons;
- informally explore scale factors when comparing side lengths;
- move from concrete models to the symbolic explanations and representations of those models; and
- make generalizations about the relationship between the area and perimeter as similar shapes grow.

REPRODUCIBLE 9.5
What Makes a
Rep-Tile?

REPRODUCIBLE 9.6
Rep-Tile Follow-Up
Recording Sheet

Materials

- *What Makes a Rep-Tile?* (see Reproducible 9.5)
- *Rep-Tile Follow-Up* recording sheet (see Reproducible 9.6)
- pattern blocks, 1 complete set per pair of students (**Note:** Only triangles, squares, trapezoids, and rhombi are rep-tiles.)
- four-column T-chart (consider laminating on chart paper for future use):

Initial Shape	Area	Sketch of Larger Shape	Area

- newsprint, 1 piece per pair of students

Vocabulary

area, congruent, perimeter, rep-tiles, similar

In this activity, we ask students to identify relationships: What happens to an area as the number of rep-tiles increase? We want students eventually to be able to articulate and predict the area of a shape as its perimeter grows proportionately.

In similar figures, corresponding sides increase by the same *scale factor*, the number used to multiply the lengths of a figure to either stretch or shrink it to a similar image. Although I do not use the term *scale factor* with my fifth graders, it is important for us as teachers to understand the mathematics behind *What Makes a Rep-Tile?* It is very cool and exciting when our students can informally identify and explain a scale factor and how it can help predict related areas and perimeters of similar shapes without building them; however, the articulation of the concept of scale factor and its related procedure is not the object of this activity.

As with Chapter 7's "Doubling the Number of Cubes" lesson, students and adults alike can make assumptions about doubling the perimeter and how that doubling (or tripling or quadrupling) affects area. When we offer opportunities for our students to bump up against those assumptions and recognize the error of their ways, learning occurs—or at the very least, questions arise. The disequilibrium that *What Makes a Rep-Tile?* presents sets the stage for significant and important mathematical observations, discussions, and generalizations. It is also important to realize that concepts requiring proportional reasoning are often difficult for young students to grasp because they do not match up with their mathematical expectations and assumptions. Your students' understanding of scale factors and how they operate may be fragile at best by the end of this lesson; however, we have sown the seeds for the continued work that our fifth graders will complete in middle school. I make a point of explaining that to students at the *end* of the lesson. I want them to realize that there is something very interesting and mathematically significant about rep-tiles and how they stretch and shrink.

When I bring out the pattern blocks, my class cheers. It is heartwarming to be reminded that our fifth graders are truly children, and that tubs of blocks still represent all the joy that can be built, created, and explored. Because of that, I encourage free exploration with the pattern blocks for a limited period of time. When I call time, we begin the lesson.

I post chart paper on which I've created a four-column T-chart and ask students to work with a partner for this activity. I distribute a piece of chart paper to each pair of students and ask them to reproduce the T-chart on which they will post their findings.

Then I ask students to select a triangle from the pattern blocks. We have a discussion about the perimeter of that triangle and its area, and we agree that we will refer to the side-length units as "units" without a linear measurement attached and that we will refer to the area as "square units." As we discuss the triangle, we post the data:

Initial Shape	Area	Sketch of Larger Shape	Area
△	1 unit^2		

I ask, "Can you make a larger, *similar* triangle out of other triangles?" Asking students to decode and comprehend the question offers an opportunity to explore the concept of similarity and to agree on an informal definition of *similar*. Each year my class seems to agree on variations of the following definition:

A similar figure has angles that are equal to the original shape, and the side lengths have an equal relationship.

Presenting similar and nonsimilar polygons and asking why they are or are not similar can help to anchor the meaning.

Well-constructed questions carry and scaffold this lesson and the predictions and generalizations that you ask students to make. Keep in mind the mathematical objectives of this lesson to help formulate those questions as you move through the investigation. Again, remember that we want students eventually to be able to articulate and predict the area of a shape as its perimeter grows proportionately.

Once students have agreed on a triangle, post it on the T-chart:

Initial Shape	Area	Sketch of Larger Shape	Area
△	1 unit^2	△ (made of four small triangles)	4 units^2

Once the numbers and sketches are available on the charts, ask the following questions:

- Describe the larger triangle. How is it similar to the initial shape?
- What happens to the area when each side length is doubled? Does that surprise you?
- How did *building* the triangle and *seeing* the shape help you to understand what is happening mathematically?
- Is the triangle a *rep-tile* (a shape you can use to make a larger, similar version of the original shape)?
- What did we start with? How many triangles did you need to make the larger shape? How did the perimeter increase? How did the area increase? How are these increases related?

REPRODUCIBLE 9.5
What Makes a
Rep-Tile? ◄

Now present *What Makes a Rep-Tile?* to the class. (See Figure 9–4; see also Reproducible 9.5.)

Students with more developed spatial skills will find rep-tiles more quickly than others. Other students may soon realize that four rep-tiles will make the next larger, similar shape. The same students may also recognize that the areas of all the larger shapes will be four times the area of the initial shapes. As the side lengths of *similar* shapes double (× 2), the area quadruples (2^2). Offer an additional T-chart for visual grounding as students talk about, compare, and contrast the perimeters and areas of the related shapes. (See Figure 9–5.)

Listening carefully and facilitating the class discussion in such a way that these big ideas of scale factors make themselves known becomes your charge. Implementing talk moves such as *re-voicing* ("So you are saying that as a triangle doubles in its side lengths, its area quadruples?") and

▶ REPRODUCIBLE 9.5
What Makes a
Rep-Tile?

What Makes a Rep-Tile?

You need:

- a partner
- 1 piece of newsprint

Directions

1. Using your set of pattern blocks make two different sets:

2. Once you have agreed on which blocks are rep-tiles, continue to add the initial shapes and sketches of the larger shape to the T-chart.

   Be aware of the following questions as you complete your T-chart:

   - Which blocks are rep-tiles?
   - How does the perimeter of the larger shape relate to the perimeter of the initial shape?
   - How does the area of the larger shape relate to the area of the initial shape?
   - How can you predict the area of a larger shape when you know how much the perimeter of each side of that shape has increased?

FIGURE 9–4
***What Makes a Rep-Tile?* Task.**

adding on ("Would somebody like to add on to Nick's idea about doubling the side lengths and quadrupling the area?") will help to support the listening and reasoning required by the discussion and task. (See "The Learning Environment" in Chapter 2 for more about talk moves.)

Follow-Up Activities

If time permits, you may wish to implement the following follow-up activities:

- What happens when the perimeter triples (having a scale factor of three)? Can you predict the area of the larger shape? How does this

FIGURE 9–5
A T-chart Comparing Related Shapes.

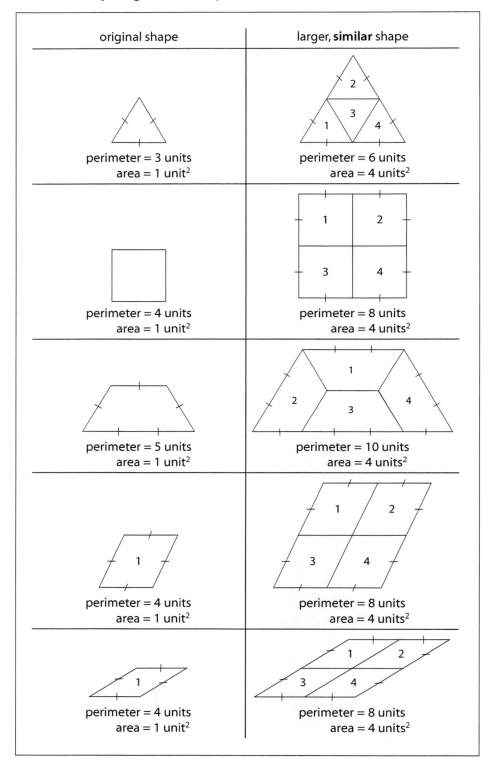

procedure compare to that of doubling the perimeter? Why does that make sense? Have students build models to support their predictions and generalizations.

■ Have students complete the *Rep-Tile Follow-Up* recording sheet (see Reproducible 9.6). Students cut and paste as they work through the questions.

▶ REPRODUCIBLE 9.6
Rep-Tile Follow-Up
Recording Sheet

Note: When working with students on scale factors, keep in mind that each exploration begins with the initial shape, which is then compared to the larger shape. The scale factor identifies how many times each side is increased (perimeter). The (scale factor)^2 identifies the area of the new, similar shape. (See Figure 9–6.)

FIGURE 9–6
Two Shapes with a Sale Factor of 3; x = Original Perimeter (Perimeter = 3x, Area = 3^2).

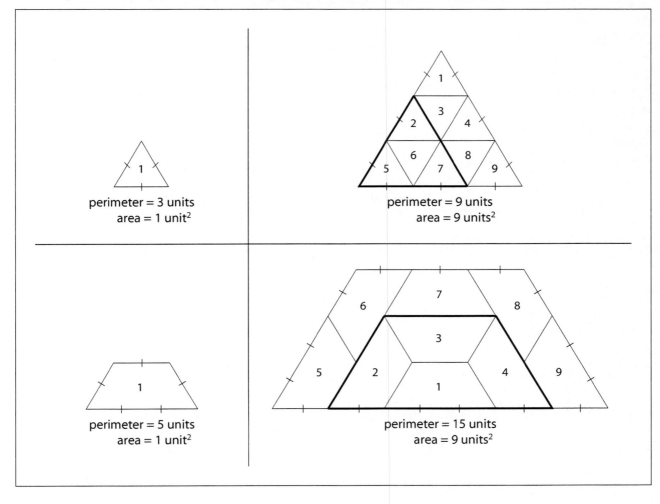

NCTM Connection

Strand: Number and Operations
Focus: Compare, identify, and calculate rates by applying proportional reasoning.
Context: *A Few Good Problems*

REPRODUCIBLE 9.7
Rate Pictures
Recording Sheet

REPRODUCIBLE 9.8
More Rate Pictures
Recording Sheet

REPRODUCIBLE 9.9
A Few Good
Problems Recording
Sheet

A Few Good Problems

Duration: 2–3 Class Periods

Proportional reasoning is not something that you either can or cannot do (Van de Walle 2004, 300). Being able to think proportionately is a process that develops slowly. It represents the ability to understand multiplicative relationships where most arithmetic concepts are additive in nature (Van de Walle 2004, 298). These problems offer students the opportunities to

- rely on multiplicative reasoning rather than on additive comparisons;
- compare and determine rates;
- informally manipulate ratios; and
- solve problems involving proportions in a variety of contexts without depending on rules or formulas.

Materials

- *Rate Pictures* recording sheet (see Reproducible 9.7)
- *More Rate Pictures* recording sheet (see Reproducible 9.8)
- *A Few Good Problems* recording sheet (see Reproducible 9.9)
- paper and manipulatives (such as color tiles) to sketch and model problems

Vocabulary

additive, multiplicative, rate, ratio

A *ratio* is an ordered pair of numbers or measurements that expresses a multiplicative comparison between the numbers or measures. When two different types of measures are being compared, the ratio is usually called a *rate*. Our fifth graders may or may not have had experiences with these terms or the concepts presented in these problems. As students solve and discuss problems that require the comparison of numbers or measures, the idea of ratio will present itself. Take a look at the following problem:

> *Two weeks ago, 2 flowers were measured at 8 inches and 12 inches, respectively. Today they are 11 inches and 15 inches tall. Did the 8-inch or the 12-inch flower grow more?*

One answer that many students may offer, based on *additive* reasoning, is that both flowers grew three inches many students offer. This answer is correct, by the way, but "three inches" does not describe the *rate* of growth.

Another way to look at this problem is based on *multiplicative* reasoning: employing proportional reasoning and comparing the rates of growth to the original height of the flower. For example, the first flower grew three-eighths of its height, while the second flower grew three-twelfths. Applying proportional reasoning skills to this problem helps students understand that the first flower grew at a greater rate because three-eighths is *greater than* three-twelfths—or the first flower grew three-eighths *times* more and the second flower grew three-twelfths *times* more.

TEACHER-TO-TEACHER TALK ■ Importance of Partner Talk ■ For years, I shied away from work with proportional thinking with my fifth graders. I just wasn't sure how to deliver these concepts or how to scaffold the lessons so that students would come away with a better understanding rather than a worse one! Enter the importance of partner talk. Chapin, O'Connor, and Anderson (2009) describe the benefits of partner talk:

> It allows students to practice their ideas—to put them into words—before they face the entire class. It allows students to hear how one other student is thinking about the problem, perhaps giving them confidence that they too have a workable idea . . . of how to proceed if they are stuck. (164)

I am convinced that adults as well as fifth graders are *smarter* collectively. I have learned over and over again that difficult concepts require some level of collective thinking and reasoning. By this time of the year, my fifth graders are really good at talking with one another. They understand how important it is to talk over their ideas, no matter how well-baked they are. They also understand how important it is to listen—and to revoice what their partner is saying and thinking. So when we encounter a difficult concept or procedure, why not allow students to do what they do best? Talk!

Rate Pictures

The *Rate Pictures* recording sheet (see Reproducible 9.7) presents a series of pictures with the *unit rate*—a quantity that is compared with one—posted at the top of the page. (See Figure 9–7.) With this task, ask students to select other pictures that represent the same rate as that presented by the unit rate.

A challenge page, the *More Rate Pictures* recording sheet (see Reproducible 9.8), shows pictures of equal rates but no unit rate. With this task, ask students to identify and describe the unit rate based on the pictures presented.

Sentence frames, which describe the relationship illustrated by a picture such as the one in Figure 9–7, may help to scaffold the relational thinking required by work with ratios:

| _____ _____ *is equivalent to* _____ _____ . |

or

| *For every* _____ , *there is (are)* _____ _____ . |

NCTM Connection

Strand: Number and Operations
Focus: Compare and determine rates; informally manipulate ratios.
Context: Rate Pictures

▶ REPRODUCIBLE 9.7
Rate Pictures
Recording sheet

REPRODUCIBLE 9.8
More Rate Pictures
Recording sheet

REPRODUCIBLE 9.7
Rate Pictures
Recording Sheet

◄

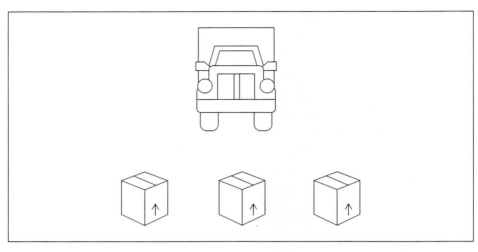

F I G U R E 9 – 7
A Unit Rate of Trucks: Boxes in Pictures.

For the pictures in Figure 9–7, the completed sentence frames would read:

> *1 truck is equivalent to 3 boxes.*

> *or*

> *For every truck, there are 3 boxes.*

There are several conventional notations for this comparison of trucks to boxes:

$$1{:}3 \text{ or } 1/3 \text{ or } \tfrac{1}{3}$$

The fractional notation may be confusing to students. There is no unit whole in such fractions. In our trucks-to-boxes comparison, the whole is not three. We are actually referring to a set of four: one truck and three boxes! However, with fifth graders I prefer the 1:3 notation. Keep in mind that the all notations can be read "one to three."

REPRODUCIBLE 9.7
Rate Pictures
Recording Sheet

◄

The numbers presented on the *Rate Pictures* recording sheet are not complicated or difficult to manipulate, but the concepts they represent can be. Having students work with a partner and asking them to verbalize the presented rates with sentence frames can help to fit the language to the relationship. It is from this dance among the notation, picture, and language that a beginning understanding of rates and ratios can develop.

Creating additional *Rate Pictures* recording sheets can be conveniently with clip art. It helps to focus on the mathematics and identify the unit rate first as you consider pictures to use.

Rate Problems

An understanding of proportional situations includes being able to identify situations in which rates are used to distinguish among the presented rates. *A Few Good Problems* (see Reproducible 9.9) offers students problems with varied contexts in which to apply rates. Allow students to solve the problems with any strategy as long as they can explain why their strategy and solution make sense. Pictures and physical models can help students think through and represent their reasoning as they describe and explain strategies and solutions.

Rate tables, such as the one that follows, offer a mathematical model within which to calculate equivalent rates:

NCTM Connection

Strand: Number and Operations
Focus: Solve problems involving proportions in a variety of contexts without dependence on rules or formulas.
Context: Rate Problems

REPRODUCIBLE 9.9
A Few Good
Problems
Recording Sheet

Trucks	1	2	3	4	5
Boxes	3				

As with T-charts that represent growth patterns, functional relationships exist between horizontal as well as vertical values. Because we have identified a unit rate, a rule to help determine the number of boxes for any given number of trucks may be readily evident. Guiding questions such as the following can help students make sense of the numbers and relationships found in the rate table:

- What do we know?
- What do we need to know?
- Given what we know about the unit rate, how can we keep that same relationship among any number of trucks? Any number of boxes?
- How can we extend this table? What values can we fill in for the boxes? Why do those numbers make sense? Do they fit the established pattern or relationship?
- If we know the number of boxes, how can we determine the number of trucks? What is the relationship between each progressing number of boxes? How do you know?

It will be helpful for you to work through each problem before students tackle this particular task. Being clear on how *you* think through each problem will help you to make better sense of where students are going with their explanations. Be open to out-of-the-box strategies, however! When we give students the opportunity to solve problems such as these in a way that makes sense to them, their solutions are often creative, insightful, and perhaps not what we were expecting—and that is a very good and cool thing!

NCTM Connection

Strand: Number and Operations

Focus: Review and extend multiplication strategies and understandings.

Context: *Multiplication and Division Games to Revisit*

REPRODUCIBLE 2.1 ◀
The Factor Game

REPRODUCIBLE 5.3
Seth's Game

REPRODUCIBLE 5.9
Remainders Race

Multiplication and Division Games to Revisit

Duration: 1–2 Class Periods or Conducted as Shorter Explorations, Class Warm-Ups, or Closers

Replaying and rethinking previously played games offer students the opportunities to

- extend previous understandings; and
- reevaluate previous strategies and develop new ones grounded in deeper understanding.

Materials

- game directions and materials:
  - *The Factor Game* (see Reproducible 2.1)
  - *Silent Multiplication* or *Silent Division* (see Chapter 4, page 178)
  - *Seth's Game* (see Reproducible 5.3)
  - *Remainders Race* (see Reproducible 5.9)

As mentioned throughout this resource, games offer students continued opportunities to practice number and operation skills. Because students are familiar with the rules of each game, revisiting them allows you the opportunity to differentiate their purpose according to the needs of the players. *Factor Game* boards can be chosen or assigned by the players' needs: a *Factor Game* board of thirty or one of forty-nine. The play of *Seth's Game*, including the choice of the operation and the number of digits per operator, can be adjusted according to the needs of your class. Your prescribed curriculum may also offer games that support needed calculation practice.

Good Questions to Ask

For more good questions, see *Good Questions for Math Teaching: Why Ask Them and What to Ask, Grades 5–8* by Lainie Schuster and Nancy Anderson (Math Solutions 2005).

- Green Giant Fertilizer and water are mixed in the ratio of one part fertilizer to two parts water. Complete the chart below:

Fertilizer	100 ml	25 ml	?	?
Water	200 ml	?	250 ml	490 ml

If you have 410 ml of water in your sprayer and 115 ml of Green Giant Fertilizer left in the original container, can you make a full-strength solution? If you cannot, will the solution be weaker or stronger than it needs to be? How much water or fertilizer would you need to make a full-strength solution?

- Mr. and Mrs. Dunne are planting bulbs in their new garden. Mrs. Dunne wants her daffodils to "clump," so she plans to plant the bulbs in bunches in each hole. Consider the following table. How many bulbs will Mrs. Dunne need to buy for twenty-five clumps of daffodils? How many clumps or holes will she need for one hundred seventy-five daffodils? How do you know? Explain your thinking.

Clumps/Holes	1	2	3	4	5
Daffodils	?	?	15	20	?

- In a deck of fifty-two playing cards:
  - What is the ratio of twos to tens? How do you know? Diagram your proof!
  - What is the ratio of hearts to the whole deck? How do you know?
  - What is the ratio of Jacks to Kings and Queens?
- Solve the following pan-balance problem:

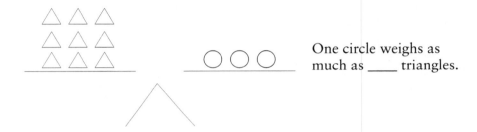

One circle weighs as much as ____ triangles.

How do you know? Use number models to support your thinking.

- Solve the following pan-balance problem:

One square weighs as much as ____ circles.

How do you know? Use number models to support your thinking.

Calculation Routines and Practices

I have yet to meet a fifth grader who did not benefit from the continued practice of multiplication and division skills and procedures. Students are often more willing to carry out this practice in small increments and if it is tailored to their needs and interests. Because so much of the in-class work that we are completing during this month requires classroom discussion, multiplication and division packets have their place. If your students are like mine, and I have no doubt that they are, you may find them more likely to work on practice in the form of logic puzzles or riddles. Over the years I have collected various books and reproducibles of puzzles and riddles that I compile in a packet for students to complete independently over a certain period of days. One such series is the Groundworks series (Greenes, Findell, Irvin, and Spungin 2005, Greenes and Findell 2006). Quality practice work may also be available from your prescribed curriculum by way of reproducibles. As you choose work, continue to be mindful of your instructional objectives as well as the calculation needs of your students.

Minilessons can also be helpful. Perhaps a few students cannot remember how to turn a remainder into a fraction, or other students are not remembering to place that zero in the ones place in their partial products, or yet other students need some additional instruction on multiplication by multiples of ten. Remember that a discussion of the *why* as well as the *how* should accompany minilessons. Rusty Bresser and Caren Holtzman (2006) have published a wonderful set of lessons entitled *Minilessons for Math Practice, Grades 3–5*, which offers a plethora of quick activities and lessons that can be used in various contexts and for various needs.

Reading, Writing, and Vocabulary

For students to learn mathematics with understanding, it must make sense to them. The literacy components of strong mathematical instruction support and allow the learning of mathematics to make sense to students of any age. The more we ask students to read, write, and use mathematical language, the more we are asking them to think harder and deeper about the mathematics presented. In mathematics classrooms in which thinking, reasoning, and communication are valued and practiced, being asked to reason about a mathematical problem, justify or explain their ideas and strategies, represent their mathematical ideas in multiple ways, and build new knowledge as well as apply knowledge through problem solving, become part of students' daily routine.

Taking the time to compare the mathematical writing your students completed at the beginning of the year with the mathematical writing of which they are now capable will likely astound and humble you. The ability to represent one's thinking is a powerful tool in any discipline and in any walk of life.

Each spring, I ask students to review their portfolios and graph-paper notebooks to identify and reflect on their growth and progress. Each student is given a 12-by-18-inch piece of construction paper. I ask them to choose one piece of writing from the beginning of the year and a similar piece from the end. Before they begin the selection process, as a class we brainstorm about the qualities of good mathematical writing and well-proven and supported ideas. This is the list my class generated last year:

Good Mathematical Writing Looks Like:

- strong introductory and concluding statements
- strong mathematical language; good use of vocabulary
- well organized, both in structure and thought
- complete ideas
- strong voice; we are confident in our writing and know what we are talking about
- no-excuse words (or the words on the word wall) must be spelled correctly; the other spelling needs to be as good as we can get it

Well-Proven Mathematical Writing Looks Like:

- words, diagrams, charts, pictures, and number models used to support our thinking
- whenever possible, number models used to explain situations or diagrams
- multiple representations; proving something or an idea in two (or more) ways
- explaining procedures; knowing where the numbers come from and what they represent

I type up the brainstormed list (I love the comment about spelling—it comes up every year) and post it on one side of the construction paper. On the other side, students post their early-in-the-year piece on the left half of the construction paper and the later-in-the-year piece on the right half. Many of my students will choose a journal write from an exam because the prompt and response are conveniently available. (See Figure 9–8.) To be honest, this documentation of mathematical growth is more powerful than any end-of-year comment or report card. Each year, I send this documentation home to parents along with each student's end-of-year self-reflection (see the "Assessment" section of this chapter) as well as a cover letter from me.

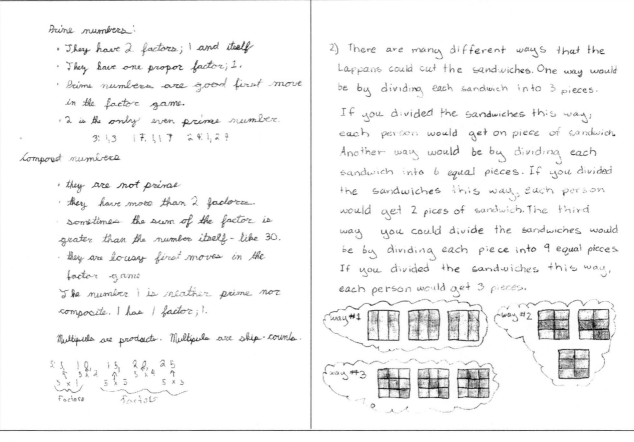

FIGURE 9–8
Kelsey's Documentation of Her Work from Fall to Spring.

Assessment

Although self-assessment has been promoted and supported throughout the year in various formats and contexts, an end-of-year self-assessment allows students the opportunity to review their year's work, thinking, and progress. Wiggins and McTighe (2005) describe self-understanding as the most important facet of understanding for lifelong learning. Central to self-understanding is honest self-assessment based on the clarity of what we do understand and what we do not, what we have accomplished and what remains to be done.

Fifth graders, now soon to be sixth graders, are not too young to develop lifelong self-assessment practices and habits of mind. Our fifth graders have witnessed and experienced considerable cognitive and mathematical growth throughout the year; asking them to identify that growth and the process that supported is a great opportunity for them to assess their own progress rather than relying solely on external assessment indicators such as test scores, report cards, and adult feedback.

Asking students to self-assess requires mindful scaffolding and carefully crafted questions to guide students through the process. As you construct the questions, keep in mind your mathematical goals for the year as well as habits of mind that you and your students value and practice. Although my particular questions may vary from year to year given any curriculum changes, the focus on making sense, effort, commitment, and persistence remains constant from year to year. (See Figure 9–9.)

I give my students a full week to complete this assignment. I ask that they type their responses because they have become accustomed to editing word-processed documents in social studies and science. I also encourage students to return to their initial responses a day or night after they have been written, to reflect on their writing and revise it as they see fit. Because this piece is all about them, their interest in reflecting and revising seems to be greater and more authentic. (See Figure 9–10.)

You may need to give this assignment early in the month; they take a while to read, but they are so worth reading! I do not make any corrections, but I do comment in the margins. This can be a venue for a very special dialogue between you and a student—one that they may not be used to having with a math teacher.

Home and School Connections

I normally do not send out a Parent Information and Involvement Form for this month because this month's schedule is fragmented with end-of-year activities. Instead, I prefer to focus on self-reflection and closure as we move through the end of the school year.

For each student, I collect and collate the portfolio documentation outlined in the "Reading, Writing, and Vocabulary" section of this chapter (see pages 414–16) as well as the self-reflection outlined in the "Assessment" section (see previous page). In a cover letter to parents, I explain the purpose of both pieces. I also encourage both students and parents to engage in a conversation about the collected pieces of work and writing. Prior to sending home the portfolio and self-reflection, I model a parent-child conversation with the class. Students can pair up and share their work with each other as they practice this sharing process. A parent-child conversation about growth and progress can give meaningful closure to a year of hard work. This is also a lovely time to invite your principal into your classroom if you have established such a relationship with him or her. It is a time of closure and celebration.

FIGURE 9–9
Sample End-of-Year Reflection Task.

Grade 5 End-of-Year Mathematical Reflection

GUIDELINES

- This is all about you! Document your feelings and opinions. Make sure to support your positions with examples.
- Take time to think through your answer before you write it. You have had quite a year!
- Be thorough in your responses. Read each question carefully before you answer it.

FOR YOUR REFERENCE

Major units studied this year

- Number Theory: factors and multiples
- Multiplication/Division: different methods of multiplication and division; study of story problem structures; the creation of the multiplication/division storybooks
- Fractions, Decimals, Percents
- Data Collection and Statistics
- Measurement and Volume

QUESTION 1

What kind of mathematician are you?

Are you a number cruncher? Do you prefer table group investigations and poster making? Do you prefer to work alone? Do you like playing around with mathematical ideas? Do you like taking tests? Do you like drawing diagrams to support your thinking? Do you like seatwork? Do you like writing about your ideas? Do you like studying vocabulary?

QUESTION 2

What was your favorite unit of study this year? Why?

Give me *three* supporting details about why this was your favorite unit. What was it that you liked? What we did in class? The "easiness" of the material? The newness of the material? The challenge of the material?

QUESTION 3

In which unit did you complete your best work?

Was it the unit you mentioned in *Question 2*? Why or why not? How do you know this was your best work?

(Continued)

QUESTION 4

In what areas do you need help?

Specific units of study? Writing? Calculating?

QUESTION 5

If you could give five suggestions to next year's fifth graders about surviving fifth-grade math, what would they be?

You can just list or bullet these.

QUESTION 6

What did you think of all the writing we did this year?

How were the open-ended questions? The questions that asked you to summarize investigations or learning? Did the writing help you understand the material better? Did your writing improve? How do you know?

Thank you all for your all your hard work, effort, and progress this year. You all make this job worth it!

Mrs. Schuey

FIGURE 9–9 (Continued)

FIGURE 9–10
Will's End-of-Year Self-Reflection.

End O' Year Reflection

1. I love to do table work and make posters in a group. It is good to have someone to correct you if you're wrong or to give you ideas that you had never thought of. The ideas that are given to you could be used as a strategy for the rest of your life. I don't like taking solo tests as much as partner quizzes. Working in a group or with a partner really helps, as I said before.

   Solo tests are harder because I think it's a lot easier to discuss the problem with a partner. It helps you understand the question better. If I could choose between a partner quiz and a poster, I'd choose to do a poster. I'd choose this because I love to be creative and draw a lot more than working with a partner. Of course, sometimes you get to work on a poster together, like the name length poster. If only there were a partner quiz that you had to make a poster for . . .

2. My favorite unit was the Meet My Number poster. It was so much fun to research the facts for the numbers. I found some pretty funny facts for 16. It was pretty fun to make a poster for one of my favorite numbers

(Continued)

and I also had lots of fun researching everything. The actual project was pretty easy because whenever I have fun with something, it gets really easy. I didn't do as well as I thought I would. I forgot to explain the mathematical facts. Explaining is my main weakness. The project wasn't very new to me. The Meet My Number project was really related to the Piles of Tiles project. It wasn't related to the actual math, but it was a poster that we were supposed to decorate. The titles project was also easy because I had tons of fun with it.

3. I completed my best work in the story problem unit. I was able to write well enough to make the problem understandable. The problems I wrote were not too hard and not too easy, either. I was even able to write three problems related to one another! I also had lots of fun with these stories. They brought out my creative side (that doesn't involve hamsters and tree grinders). One part I would change is the fact that I need to look over my problems. One of them had the completely wrong answer and explanation. This was all because I hadn't checked over my work or confirmed my answers on a calculator. Had I changed this, all my stories would have been my best work.

4. Mostly, I need help in the explanation station. I usually have trouble explaining my opinions or reasons for my answers. This doesn't only happen in math, though. It happens in about all of my classes.

   Another thing I need help in is looking over my work. On most tests, I miss points because I didn't check over my work. One way I could help this is by writing something that reminds me to check over my work. The only problem with that would be that I might not look at the writing and forget to check over my work. I'm probably going to figure out something by next year.

5. ■ Explain all the problems.
   ■ Be specific in your answers.
   ■ Write neatly.
   ■ Don't use backs of pages in your notebook.
   ■ Study thoroughly.

6. The ACE questions really helped me understand math better. The glossary and index really helped me when I forgot what something was.

   The reflections were really helpful. They were like small quizzes. They brought everything of that unit together to test what we remembered. The mathematical reflections also improved my writing. They taught me to be more specific. I used to always start a first sentence with *it* or *they*. Now I explain the question before I answer it.

   My writing helped me to understand the problem better. It's a lot easier to hear words from a kid if you are a kid. Kids usually don't use big words that we have to look up in a dictionary.

   Overall, I thought that math this year was a blast. It was my favorite (real) subject in school. I can't wait until we have math next year!

FIGURE 9–10 (Continued)

Resources

Math Matters: Understanding the Math You Teach, Grades K–8, Second Edition (Chapin and Johnson 2006)

Chapter 8: Ratios
This chapter provides a thorough discussion of proportional reasoning. Working through the problem sets yourself will help you to gain a better understanding of what it means to think "proportionally."

Elementary and Middle School Mathematics: Teaching Developmentally (Van de Walle 2004)

Chapter 18: Developing Concepts of Ratio and Proportion
This chapter gives an excellent and thorough explanation of the big ideas, content connections, and activities supporting the development of proportional reasoning.

Math and Literature, Grades 4–6, Second Edition (Bresser 2004)

This collection of math and literature activities documents a thorough write-up of activities that can accompany *The King's Chessboard*.

The Groundworks Series (Grade 5) (Greenes, Findell, Irvin, and Spungin 2005; Greenes and Findell, 2006)

Algebraic Thinking
Reasoning About Measurement
Reasoning with Data and Probability
Reasoning with Geometry
Reasoning with Numbers

Algebraic Thinking offers two excellent problem sets that explore equivalent ratios and the use of ratio or rate tables. *Reasoning with Numbers* offers excellent problem sets to review and practice computation skills in engaging and challenging problem-solving contexts.

Minilessons for Math Practice, Grades 3–5 (Bresser and Holtzman 2006)

This resource provides wonderful lessons that offer practice and reinforcement for math concepts, skills, and processes. It can also be used for class warm-ups or during transition times throughout the school day.

Afterword
A Year in Review

No matter what school, in what state, or with which cherished colleagues, we share the best of the best stories of the school year during the end-of-year closing faculty meeting:

Jeff demanding that we all be quiet and listen to his moment of brilliance when he described the connection between LCMs and least common denominators because he was convinced that no one had ever made this connection before in the history of mankind.

Or when Elise began a writing task with, "Let me make this perfectly clear. . . ."

Or when Joey wore his "smart" shirt back in February, had an outstanding day in math, and then wore the same shirt (and a wonderful smirk) on every test or quiz day.

Or when Ryan and Justin created the colorful blob on the floor when they used permanent markers to create their decimal garden (unbeknownst to me!) and the marker bled through the paper onto the floor. I still smile every time I catch sight of it!

Or when Joseph wondered out loud in class if chickens laid eggs in arrays, and if they did, how clever it was of them to lay them in multiples of twelves, because twelve had so many factors.

Or when Marissa reported that "poufy" hair can interfere with thinking about mathematics—her own, or anybody else's.

Oh yes, we all have stories to tell each year. Telling those stories is often what sustains us as we maneuver through the long and sometimes grueling year of fifth-grade mathematics. The stories we tell define our lives for those nine or ten months and need to be told. There are stories of wonderful success and growth, of misused language and misunderstood concepts, and of astounding insights and amazing generalizations.

But even as we hear the warm days of summer calling, we still have work to do. However, this work does not have the frenetic pace or urgency of our school year—thank goodness! This work is reflective in nature and can be done in a coffee shop, at the beach, or on the back porch. Take the time to think over the school year while it is still fresh in your mind. What worked? What didn't? What will you do differently next year? What unit needs tweaking? What new resources are you on the lookout for? Putting these ideas on paper will make them binding. Nothing formal is necessary: a simple spiral notebook or journal will do. But do document your thoughts. They are valuable.

NCTM's *Principles and Standards for School Mathematics* (2000) defines our charge as teachers of mathematics as enormous and essential. As mathematics teachers, we are given the daunting responsibility of preparing our students for a future of great and continual change. Mathematical experiences and practices that are rich in content and offer continual opportunities for students to make sense of what they are doing and thinking must be at the forefront of our charge. Even in this educational world of state-mandated testing and prescribed curricula, we do have the opportunity and responsibility to implement change in teaching and learning mathematics. That change may manifest itself in only one lesson or in only one unit in the upcoming year, but the seeds will have been sewn as we engage our fifth graders in thinking like mathematicians.

As Milo contemplates taking another trip courtesy of his Phantom Tollbooth, he realizes that the excitement of the world beyond has been right there in front of him all along.

> And, in the very room in which he sat, there were books that could take you anywhere, and things to invent, and make, and build, and break, and all the puzzle and excitement of everything he didn't know—music to play, songs to sing, and worlds to imagine and then someday make real. His thoughts darted eagerly about as everything looked new—and worth trying. (Juster 1961, 255)

As our fifth graders, who have now become sixth graders, move forward in their mathematical pursuits, we want them to feel the same.

> "Well, I would like to make another trip," he said, jumping to his feet; "but I really don't know when I'll have the time. There's so much to do right here." (Juster 1961, 256)

References

Professional Resources

Allen, Janet. 1999. *Words, Words, Words: Teaching Vocabulary in Grades 4–12.* York, ME: Stenhouse.

Battista, Michael T., and Mary Berle-Carman. 1998. *Containers and Cubes: 3-D Geometry: Volume, Grade 5. Investigations in Number, Data, and Space.* White Plains, NY: Dale Seymour Publications.

Bennett, Albert B. Jr. 1992. *Decimal Squares: Step by Step Teacher's Guide.* Fort Collins, CO: Scott Resources.

Bickmore-Brand, Jennie, ed. 1990. *Language in Mathematics.* Portsmouth, NH: Heinemann.

Bresser, Rusty. 2004. *Math and Literature, Grades 4–6.* 2d ed. Sausalito, CA: Math Solutions.

Bresser, Rusty, and Caren Holtzman. 2006. *Minilessons for Math Practice, Grades 3–5.* Sausalito, CA: Math Solutions.

Burns, Marilyn. 1995. *Writing in Math Class: A Resource for Grades 2–8.* Sausalito, CA: Math Solutions.

———. 2001. *Teaching Arithmetic: Lessons for Introducing Fractions, Grades 4–5.* Sausalito, CA: Math Solutions.

———. 2003a. "Marilyn Burns Demystifies Long Division." *Instructor Magazine.* April: 18.

———. 2003b. *Teaching Arithmetic: Lessons for Extending Fractions, Grade 5.* Sausalito, CA: Math Solutions.

———. 2003c. The Marilyn Burns Fraction Kit®, Grades 4–6. Sausalito, CA: Math Solutions.

———. 2005. Marilyn Burns Classroom Math Library, Grades 4–6. New York: Scholastic.

———. 2007. *About Teaching Mathematics: A K–8 Resource.* 3d ed. Sausalito, CA: Math Solutions.

Carpenter, Thomas P., Megan Loef Franke, and Lenda Levi. 2003. *Thinking Mathematically: Integrating Arithmetic and Algebra in Elementary School.* Portsmouth, NH: Heinemann.

Chapin, Suzanne H., Catherine O'Connor, and Nancy Canavan Anderson. 2009. *Classroom Discussions: Using Math Talk to Help Students Learn, Grades K–6.* 2d ed. Sausalito, CA: Math Solutions.

Chapin, Suzanne H., and Art Johnson. 2006. *Math Matters: Understanding the Math You Teach, Grades K–8.* 2d ed. Sausalito, CA: Math Solutions.

Childs, Leigh, and Laura Choate. 1998. *Nimble with Numbers: Grades 4 and 5.* White Plains, NY: Dale Seymour Publications.

———. 2000. *Nimble with Numbers: Grades 5 and 6.* White Plains, NY: Dale Seymour Publications.

Confer, Chris. 2007. *Sizing Up Measurement: Activities for Grades 3–5 Classrooms.* Sausalito, CA: Math Solutions.

Corwin, Rebecca B., Susan Jo Russell, and Cornelia C. Tierney. 1990. *Seeing Fractions: A Unit for the Upper Elementary Grades.* Sacramento: California Department of Education.

Costa, Arthur L., and Bena Kallik, eds. 2000. *Activating and Engaging Habits of Mind.* Alexandria, VA: Association for Supervision and Curriculum Development.

Dacey, Linda, and Jayne Bamford Lynch. 2007. *Math for All: Differentiating Instruction, Grades 3–5.* Sausalito, CA: Math Solutions.

Daniels, Harvey, and Steven Zemelman. 2004. *Subjects Matter: Every Teacher's Guide to Content-Area Reading.* Portsmouth, NH: Heinemann.

Daniels, Harvey, Steve Zemelman, and Nancy Steineke. 2007. *Content-Area Writing: Every Teacher's Guide.* Portsmouth, NH: Heinemann.

De Francisco, Carrie, and Marilyn Burns. 2002. *Teaching Arithmetic: Lessons for Decimals and Percents, Grades 5–6.* Sausalito, CA: Math Solutions.

Duckworth, Eleanor. 1987. *The Having of Wonderful Ideas and Other Essays on Teaching and Learning.* New York: Teachers College Press.

Everyday Learning Corporation. 1995. *Everyday Mathematics: Teacher's Reference Manual.* Chicago, IL: Everyday Learning Corporation.

———. 2002a. *Everyday Mathematics: The University of Chicago School Mathematics Project, Grade 5.* Chicago, IL: Everyday Learning.

———. 2002b. *Operations Handbook: Grades 3–6.* Chicago, IL: Everyday Learning.

Fosnot, Catherine Twomey, and Maarten Dolk. 2001. *Young Mathematicians at Work: Constructing Multiplication and Division.* Portsmouth, NH: Heinemann.

———. 2002. *Young Mathematicians at Work: Constructing Fractions, Decimals, and Percents*. Portsmouth, NH: Heinemann.

Gavin, M. Katherine, Suzanne H. Chapin, Judith Dailey, and Linda Jensen Sheffield. 2007. Project M3: Mentoring Mathematical Minds. Dubuque, IA: Kendall Hunt, 2006–2008. (Series of 12 books for promising students in grades 3–5.)

Glass, Julie. 1998. *The Fly on the Ceiling: A Math Myth*. New York: Random House.

Goodman, Ken. 1986. *What's Whole in Whole Language?* Portsmouth, NH: Heinemann.

Greenes, Carole, and Carol Findell. 2006. *Groundworks: Algebraic Thinking, Grade 5*. Chicago, IL: Creative Publications.

Greenes, Carole, Carole Findell, Barbara Irvin, and Rika Spungin. 2005. *Groundworks: Reasoning with Numbers, Grade 5*. Chicago, IL: Creative Publications.

Guskey, Thomas R., and Jane M. Bailey. 2001. *Developing Grading and Reporting Systems for Student Learning*. Thousand Oaks, CA: Corwin Press.

Harvey, Stephanie, and Anne Goudvis. 2000. *Strategies That Work: Teaching Comprehension to Enhance Understanding*. Portland, ME: Stenhouse.

Hiebert, James, et al. 1997. *Making Sense: Teaching and Learning Mathematics with Understanding*. Portsmouth, NH: Heinemann.

Hyde, Arthur. 2006. *Comprehending Math: Adapting Reading Strategies to Teach Mathematics, K–6*. Portsmouth, NH: Heinemann.

Hyde, Arthur, Susan Friedlander, Cheryl Heck, and Lynn Pittner. 2009. *Understanding Middle School Math: Cool Problems to Get Students Thinking and Connecting*. Portsmouth, NH: Heinemann.

Keene, Ellin Oliver, and Susan Zimmerman. 2007. *Mosaic of Thought: The Power of Comprehension Strategy Instruction*. 2d ed. Portsmouth, NH: Heinemann.

Kenney, Joan M. 2005. *Literacy Strategies for Improving Mathematics Instruction*. Alexandria, VA: Association for Supervision and Curriculum Development.

Kindlon, Dan, and Michael Thompson. 1999. *Raising Cain: Protecting the Emotional Life of Boys*. New York: Ballantine Books.

Krpan, Cathy Marks. 2001. *The Write Math: Writing in the Math Class*. Parsippany, NJ: Dale Seymour Publications.

Lappan, Glenda, James Fey, William Fitzgerald, Susan Friel, and Elizabeth Difanis Phillips. 1998. *Bits and Pieces I: Understanding Fractions, Decimals, and Percents (Connected Mathematics 2)*. Menlo Park, CA: Dale Seymour Publications.

———. 2006a. *Data About Us (Connected Mathematics 2)*. Boston: Pearson Prentice Hall.

———. 2006b. *Prime Time: Factors and Multiples (Connected Mathematics 2)*. Boston: Pearson Prentice Hall.

———. 2009. *Stretching and Shrinking (Connected Mathematics 2)*. Boston: Pearson Prentice Hall.

Lilburn, Pat, and Alex Ciurak. 2010. *Investigations, Tasks, and Rubrics to Teach and Assess Math, Grades 1–6*. Sausalito, CA: Math Solutions.

Litton, Nancy. 1998. *Getting Your Math Message Out to Parents*. Sausalito, CA: Math Solutions.

Litton, Nancy, and MaryAnn Wickett. 2009. *This Is Only a Test: Teaching for Mathematical Understanding in an Age of Standardized Testing*. Sausalito, CA: Math Solutions.

Martinie, Sherri. 2004. "What Does It Mean to 'Do Math' in Today's Classroom?" *Mathematics Teaching in the Middle School*. Reston, VA: National Council of Teachers of Mathematics.

———. 2005. "Families Ask: Rules or Understanding." *Mathematics Teaching in the Middle School*. November 2005: 188–89.

Massachusetts Department of Education. 2000. *Massachusetts Mathematics Curriculum Framework*. www.doe.mass.edu/frameworks/math/2000/toc.html.

———. 2009. The Massachusetts Comprehensive Assessment System (MCAS) Released Spring Items. Grade 5. www.doe.mass.edu/mcas.

McNamara, Julie, and Meghan M. Shaughnessy. 2010. *Beyond Pizzas and Pies: 10 Essential Strategies for Supporting Fraction Sense, Grades 3–5*. Sausalito, CA: Math Solutions.

Mokros, Jan, Susan Jo Russell, and Karen Economopoulos. 1995. *Beyond Arithmetic: Changing Mathematics in the Elementary Classroom*. Parsippany, NJ: Dale Seymour Publications.

Moon, Jean. 1997. *Developing Judgement: Assessing Children's Work in Mathematics*. Portsmouth, NH: Heinemann.

Moon, Jean, and Linda Schulman. 1995. *Finding the Connections: Linking Assessment, Instruction, and Curriculum in Elementary Mathematics*. Portsmouth, NH: Heinemann.

National Council of Teachers of Mathematics (NCTM). 1989. *Historical Topics for the Mathematics Classroom*. Reston, VA: National Council of Teachers of Mathematics.

———. 2000. *Principles and Standards for School Mathematics*. Reston, VA: National Council of Teachers of Mathematics.

———. 2006. *Curriculum Focal Points for Prekindergarten Through Grade 8 Mathematics: A Quest for Coherence*. Reston, VA: National Council of Teachers of Mathematics.

———. 2009. *Focus in Grade 5: Teaching with Curriculum Focal Points*. Reston, VA: National Council of Teachers of Mathematics. Reston, VA: National Council of Teachers of Mathematics.

———. *Mathematics Teaching in the Middle School*. (Journal). Reston, VA: National Council of Teachers of Mathematics.

———. *Teaching Children Mathematics*. (Journal). Reston, VA: National Council of Teachers of Mathematics.

National Governors Association Center for Best Practices and Council of Chief State School Officers. 2010 Common Core State Standards Initiative. www.corestandards.org/the-standards/mathematics.

O'Connell, Susan. 2003. *Writing About Mathematics: An Essential Skill in Developing Math Proficiency, Grades 3–8.* Online course. Accessed at: http://www.ber.org/onsite/course.cfm?CR=MWO

———. 2007. *Introduction to Communication.* Portsmouth, NH: Heinemann.

Parrish, Sherry. 2010. *Number Talks: Helping Children Build Mental Math and Computation Strategies, Grades K–5. A Multimedia Professional Learning Resource.* Sausalito, CA: Math Solutions.

Randolph, Tamela D., and Helene J. Sherman. 2001. "Alternative Algorithms: Increasing Options, Reducing Errors." *Teaching Children Mathematics.* April: 480–84.

Raphel, Annette. 2000. *Math Homework That Counts.* Sausalito, CA: Math Solutions.

Rectanus, Cheryl. 1997. *Math by All Means: Area and Perimeter, Grades 5–6.* Sausalito, CA: Math Solutions.

Reys, Barbara. 1999. "Estimating Fraction Benchmarks." *Mathematics Teaching in the Middle School.* May: 530–32.

Russell, Susan Jo. 2000. "Developing Computational Fluency with Whole Numbers." *Teaching Children Mathematics.* November: 154–158.

Russell, Susan Jo, Karen Economopoulos, et al. 2008. *Number Puzzles and Multiple Towers: Multiplication and Division 1.* Glenview, IL: Pearson Education.

Saphier, Jon, and Mary Ann Haley. 1993. *Summarizers: Activity Structures to Support Integration and Retention of New Learning.* Acton, MA: Research for Better Teaching.

Schultz-Ferrell, Karren, Brenda Hammond, and Josepha Robles. 2007. *Introduction to Reasoning and Proof, Grades 3–5.* Portsmouth, NH: Heinemann.

Schuster, Lainie. 2008. *A Month-to-Month Guide: Fourth-Grade Math.* Sausalito, CA: Math Solutions.

Schuster, Lainie, and Nancy Canavan Anderson. 2005. *Good Questions for Math Teaching: Why Ask Them and What to Ask.* Sausalito, CA: Math Solutions.

Schwartz, David M. 1999. *On Beyond a Million: An Amazing Math Journey.* New York: Random House.

Stenmark, J. K. 1989. *Assessment Alternatives in Mathematics: An Overview of Assessment Techniques That Promote Learning.* Berkeley: EQUALS, University of California.

Stoessiger, Rex, and Joy Edmunds. 1993. "The Role of Challenges." In *Language in Mathematics,* ed. Jennie Bickmore-Brand. Portsmouth, NH: Heinemann.

Tank, Bonnie, and Lynne Zolli. 2001. *Teaching Arithmetic: Lessons for Addition and Subtraction, Grades 2–3.* Sausalito, CA: Math Solutions.

Thompson, Denisse, R., Gladis Kersaint, Janet C. Richards, Patricia D. Hunsader, and Rheta N. Rubenstein. 2008. *Mathematical Literacy: Helping Students Make Meaning in the Middle Grades.* Portsmouth, NH: Heinemann.

Van de Walle, John A. 2004. *Elementary and Middle School Mathematics: Teaching Developmentally.* Boston: Pearson.

Wadsworth, Barry J. 1971. *Piaget's Theory of Cognitive Development.* New York: David McCay Company.

Wickett, Maryann, and Marilyn Burns. 2001. *Teaching Arithmetic: Lessons for Extending Multiplication, Grades 4–5.* Sausalito, CA: Math Solutions.

———. 2003. *Teaching Arithmetic: Lessons for Extending Division, Grades 4–5.* Sausalito, CA: Math Solutions.

Wickett, Maryann, Katherine Kharas, and Marilyn Burns. 2002. *Lessons for Algebraic Thinking, Grades 3–5.* Sausalito, CA: Math Solutions.

Wiggins, Grant, and Jay McTighe. 2005. *Understanding by Design.* 2d ed. Alexandria, VA: Association for Supervision and Curriculum Development.

Wilson, Jeni, and Lesley Wing Jan. 1993. *Thinking for Themselves: Developing Strategies for Reflective Learning.* Armadale, Australia: Eleanor Curtain Publishing.

Wood, Chip. 1997. *Yardsticks: Children in the Classroom Ages 4–14: A Resource for Parents and Teachers.* Turner Falls, MA: Northeast Foundation for Children.

Wormeli, Rick. 2006. *Fair Isn't Always Equal: Assessing and Grading in the Differentiated Classroom.* Portland, ME: Stenhouse.

Literary Resources

Birch, David. 1988. *The King's Chessboard.* New York: Puffin Books.

Carroll, Lewis. 1986. *Through the Looking-Glass and What Alice Found There.* New York: Ariel Books/Alfred A. Knopf.

Christelow, Eileen. 1993. *Five Dog Night.* New York: Clarion Books.

Dahl, Roald. *Esio Trot.* 1990. New York: Puffin Books.

Dodds, Dayle Ann. 2004. *Minnie's Diner: A Multiplying Menu.* Cambridge, MA: Candlewick Press.

Enzensberger, Hans Magnus. 1997. *The Number Devil: A Mathematical Adventure.* New York: Henry Holt and Company.

Fleischman, Paul. 1997. *Seedfolks.* New York: HarperCollins Children's Books.

Haddon, Mark. 2003. *the curious incident of the dog in the night-time.* New York: Vintage Books.

Henkes, Kevin. 1991. *Chrysanthemum.* New York: Greenwillow Books.

Hest, Amy. 2008. *The Dog Who Belonged to No One.* New York: Abrams Books for Young Readers.

Juster, Norton. 1961. *The Phantom Tollbooth.* New York: Random House.

Lee, Harper. 1960. *To Kill a Mockingbird.* Philadelphia: J. B. Lippincott Company.

Meddaugh, Susan. 1996. *Martha Blah-Blah.* New York: Houghton Mifflin.

Rowling, J. K. 1997. *Harry Potter and the Sorcerer's Stone*. New York: Arthur A. Levine Books.

———. 1999. *Harry Potter and the Chamber of Secrets*. New York: Arthur A. Levine Books.

———. 1999. *Harry Potter and the Prisoner of Azkaban*. New York: Arthur A. Levine Books.

———. 2000. *Harry Potter and the Goblet of Fire*. New York: Arthur A. Levine Books.

———. 2003. *Harry Potter and the Order of the Phoenix*. New York: Arthur A. Levine Books.

———. 2005. *Harry Potter and the Half-Blood Prince*. New York: Arthur A. Levine Books.

———. 2007. *Harry Potter and the Deathly Hallows*. New York: Arthur A. Levine Books.

Twain, Mark. 1994. *The Adventures of Huckleberry Finn*. New York: HarperCollins.

Activities and Games: Index

Index

Continued from page ii.

Filling Boxes investigation (Nets for Boxes, How Many Cubes?, More Boxes to Fill, and the Painted Cube Problem): Adapted from *Containers and Cubes: 3–D Geometry: Volume, Grade 5* by Michael T. Battista and Mary Berle-Carman (Dale Seymour Publications 1998).

Esio Trot: Adapted from *Math and Literature, Grades 4–6, Second Edition*, by Rusty Bresser (Math Solutions 2004).

How Much Is Blue? and Put in Order: Adapted from *Teaching Arithmetic: Lessons for Introducing Fractions, Grades 4–5*, by Marilyn Burns (Math Solutions 2001).

The Comparing Game: Adapted from *Teaching Arithmetic: Lessons for Extending Fractions, Grade 5*, by Marilyn Burns (Math Solutions 2003).

Remainders Race game and game board and Multiplication Tic-Tac-Toe game: Adapted from *Nimble with Numbers, Grades 4–5*, by Leigh Childs and Laura Choate (Dale Seymour Publications 1998).

Dog Yards investigation and Put in Order activity: Adapted from *Sizing Up Measurement: Activities for Grades 3–5 Classrooms* by Chris Confer (Math Solutions 2007).

Percent Designs: Adapted from *Teaching Arithmetic: Lessons for Decimals and Percents, Grades 5–6*, by Carrie De Francisco and Marilyn Burns (Math Solutions 2002).

Division Dash game and score sheet: Adapted from *Everyday Mathematics: The University of Chicago School Mathematics Project, Grade 5, Third Edition*, by Everyday Learning Corporation (Everyday Learning, 2002).

Custom worksheets: Adapted from *Groundworks: Reasoning with Numbers, Grade 5* by Carole Greenes, Carole Findell, Barbara Irvin, and Rika Spungin (Creative Publications 2005).

KWC Chart for Problem Solving: Adapted from *Comprehending Math: Adapting Reading Strategies to Teach Mathematics, K–6* by Arthur Hyde (Heinemann 2006).

Decimal Garden Problem: Adapted from *Bits and Pieces I: Understanding Fractions, Decimals, and Percents (Connected Mathematics 2)* by Glenda Lappan, James Fey, William Fitzgerald, Susan Friel, and Elizabeth D. Phillips (Dale Seymour Publications 1998).

What Do You Mean?: Adapted from *Data About Us (Connected Mathematics 2)* by Glenda Lappan, James Fey, William Fitzgerald, Susan Friel, and Elizabeth D. Phillips. (Pearson Prentice Hall 2006).

What Makes a Rep-Tile?: Adapted from *Stretching and Shrinking (Connected Mathematics 2)* by Glenda Lappan, James Fey, William Fitzgerald, Susan Friel, and Elizabeth D. Phillips. (Pearson Prentice Hall 2009).

Chart of Double-Meaning Words: Adapted from *Writing About Mathematics: An Essential Skill in Developing Math Proficiency, Grades 3–8*, by Susan O'Connell (Washington Bureau of Education and Research 2002).

Area and Perimeter activities (Area Stays the Same; Perimeter Stays the Same): Adapted from *Math By All Means: Area and Perimeter, Grades 5–6*, by Cheryl Rectanus (Math Solutions 1997).

Good Questioning Techniques for Parents: Adapted from *Good Questions for Math Teaching: Why Ask Them and What to Ask, Grades 5–8*, by Lainie Schuster and Nancy Canavan Anderson (Math Solutions 2005).

Checking for Multiplication Understanding and Silent Multiplication: Adapted from *Teaching Arithmetic: Lessons for Extending Multiplication, Grades 4–5*, by Maryann Wickett and Marilyn Burns (Math Solutions 2001).

Leftovers: Adapted from *Teaching Arithmetic: Lessons for Extending Division, Grades 4–5*, by Maryann Wickett and Marilyn Burns (Math Solutions 2003).